The Making of Italy
1796-1866

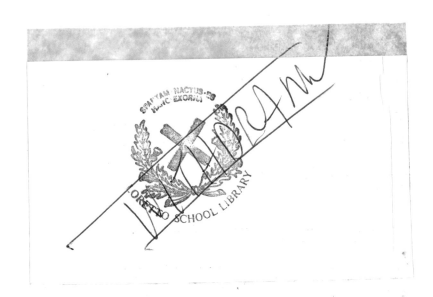

THE MAKING OF ITALY
1796–1866

DENIS MACK SMITH

Senior Research Fellow
All Souls College, Oxford

MACMILLAN

First edition (Macmillan; Walker; Harper & Row) 1968
Reissued with a new preface (Macmillan; Holmes & Meier) 1988
Reprinted 1992

Published by
THE MACMILLAN PRESS LTD
Houndmills, Basingstoke, Hampshire RG21 2XS
and London
Companies and representatives
throughout the world

ISBN 0–333–43807–8 hardcover
ISBN 0–333–43808–6 paperback

A catalogue record for this book is available
from the British Library.

Printed in Hong Kong

Contents

Maps

facing page 1

Preface to the 1988 Reissue

Anyone interested in the history of Europe during the nineteenth century must sooner or later be drawn to the study of contemporary documents. For some people this may be an acquired taste, but few will fail to discover in the end that there is nothing to equal the drama and the authenticity when events are studied at first hand rather than through the eyes of some later historian. The main difficulty is to thread one's way through the overwhelming amount of material, much of it very hard to find; and this is especially true for the study of foreign countries, because published books are not easily available and unpublished sources are inaccessible.

The process of nation-building took place more quickly in Italy than elsewhere, and in few other countries has the history of the patriotic movement been more spectacular as well as controversial. That is why the risorgimento has always aroused such widespread interest in the outside world. In Italy itself this collection of documents has gone through a number of editions in translation and has been adopted as a textbook in schools, partly because much of the material is unfamiliar, but mainly because it deals with one of the most fascinating periods in the whole of Italian history.

Documents are of course only the raw material that goes to make up history. Taken one by one they tell only part of the truth and sometimes may be a distortion of reality. Even the most ample collection of documents, however objective the choice, cannot entirely explain the course of events, but is bound to be partial, subjective, and allusive rather than conclusive. All one can do is try to make the selection as comprehensive as possible within the space available.

Where the documents selected for this volume are in English, or where an already existing translation has been available, a few very minor changes have occasionally been made in punctuation and spelling, purely in the interests of clarity and uniformity. Far the greater number of these documents are here translated for the first time. Each one is an excerpt and hence removed from its detailed context, but an attempt has been made to minimize the distortions and establish the essential background. Where passages have been omitted in the course of one of these excerpts, the fact is indicated: such breaks have been made only to reduce repetition, digression, and overcomplication. Brackets have been used for occasional explanations. The source of every document is cited. Commentaries have been provided not only to give the general context of each document, but also as link passages which may enable this volume to be used as an outline history of the making of Italy.

Acknowledgments

I am grateful to many publishing houses and editors who made documents available for this volume. In particular I would like to thank *Zanichelli* of Bologna for permission to use their fine series of Cavour's letters:—the *Carteggio Cavour-Nigra dal 1858 al 1861, Cavour e l'Inghilterra, La Questione Romana negli anni 1860–1861,* the *Carteggio Cavour-Salmour, La liberazione del mezzogiorno e la formazione del regno d'Italia.* This edition has by now become the most important of all available sources for the political history of the central years of the risorgimento. The individual editors of these volumes hide modestly behind the *Commissione per la pubblicazione dei carteggi di Camillo Cavour,* but Maria Avetta, Alessandro Luzio, and Gian Carlo Buraggi should in particular be mentioned.

Another fundamental source for the life of Cavour is the diary of Giuseppe Massari. An incomplete and extremely inaccurate edition of this diary was published in 1931, but Professor Emilia Morelli with immense pains has now produced a correct version, published by *Cappelli* of Bologna with the title of *Diario dalle cento voci, 1858–1860.* I am grateful to *Cappelli* and to Professor Morelli for permission to quote from this edition, and to *Cappelli* also for a letter from their *Edizione nazionale degli scritti di Giuseppe Garibaldi. Paolo Galeati* of Imola allowed publication of several documents from the national edition of Mazzini's writings by Professor Menghini—*Scritti editi ed inediti di Giuseppe Mazzini.* Five documents come from the French archives and are published by courtesy of the *Ministère des Affaires Etrangères;* four come from Crown Copyright material in the Public Record Office, quoted by permission of *Her Majesty's Stationery Office;* and two have been taken from the *Clarendon Papers* in the Bodleian Library with permission of Lord Clarendon.

Acknowledgment is also made to Noel Blakiston and *Chapman and Hall* for Odo Russell's interview with Pope Pius IX taken from *The Roman Question;* to the *Oxford University Press* and Professor E. R. Vincent for the latter's translation of Azeglio's *Things*

I Remember (I miei ricordi), and Abba's *The Diary of One of Garibaldi's Thousand (Da Quarto al Volturno)*; to the Director of the *Museo del Risorgimento* at Milan for a letter from the Cattaneo archives; to Professor Engel Janosi at Vienna for the minutes of a meeting of the Austrian cabinet in April 1859; to *La Nuova Italia* of Florence for excerpts from Cavour's speeches in the *Discorsi parlamentari* edited by Luigi Russo and Armando Saitta; to Howard M. Smyth and the *Journal of Modern History* for Radetzky's report on the armistice of Vignale in 1848; to the *Archivio Segreto Vaticano* for quotations from Father Pirri's edition of the letters between King Victor Emmanuel and Pius IX in the *Miscellanea Historiae Pontificiae;* to *Le Monnier* of Florence for the edition by Antonio Panella of the *Diario di Marco Tabarrini;* to the *Rivista Storica Italiana* for one of Cavour's letters and for Professor Guichonnet's edition of a note by Archbishop Charvaz; to the *Istituto per la storia del risorgimento* at Rome for a letter from the *Carteggi di Vincenzo Gioberti* (ed. V. Cian); to the *Ministero degli Affari Esteri* for permission to use the *Documenti Diplomatici Italiani* (ed. W. Maturi); and the *Ministero dell'Interno* for a cabinet minute of 1864 quoted by Emilio Re in the *Notizie degli Archivi di Stato;* to the *Deputazione di Storia Patria per la Lombardia* and to Franco Arese for the account of an interview between Metternich and Capitani; to *Aldo Garzanti* and Professor Ernestina Monti for a letter of Luigi Torelli edited by Antonio Monti; to *Rizzoli* for a passage from Ennio di Nolfo's edition of Giuseppe Bandi's *I mille;* to Zanichelli for a quotation from Luigi Rava's edition of the *Epistolario di Luigi Carlo Farini;* and to Professor Camerani and the *Istituto storico Italiano per l'età moderna e contemporanea* for use of their edition of Ricasoli's letters. *La Nuova Italia* also allowed use of their edition (by Marcus de Rubris) of Azeglio's writings. The dating of the Manzoni fragment was by Dr. Barbara Reynolds.

For help with some of the translations I am very grateful to Bernard Wall, Violet M. Macdonald, and Catharine Mack Smith.

D. M. S.

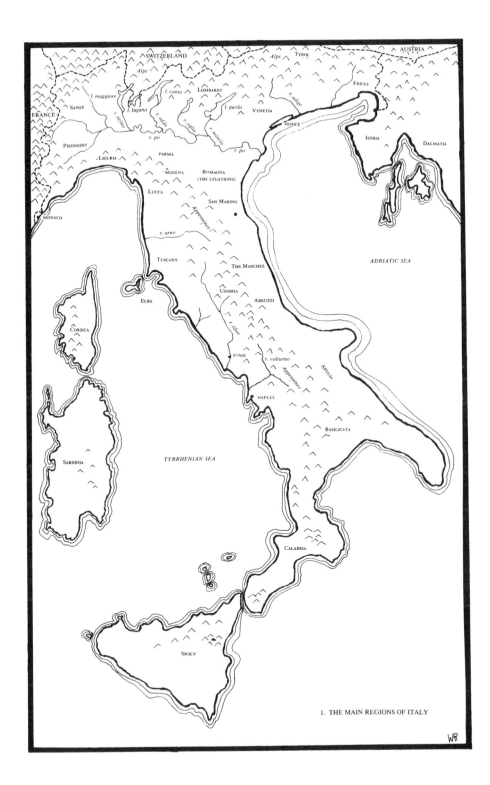

1. THE MAIN REGIONS OF ITALY

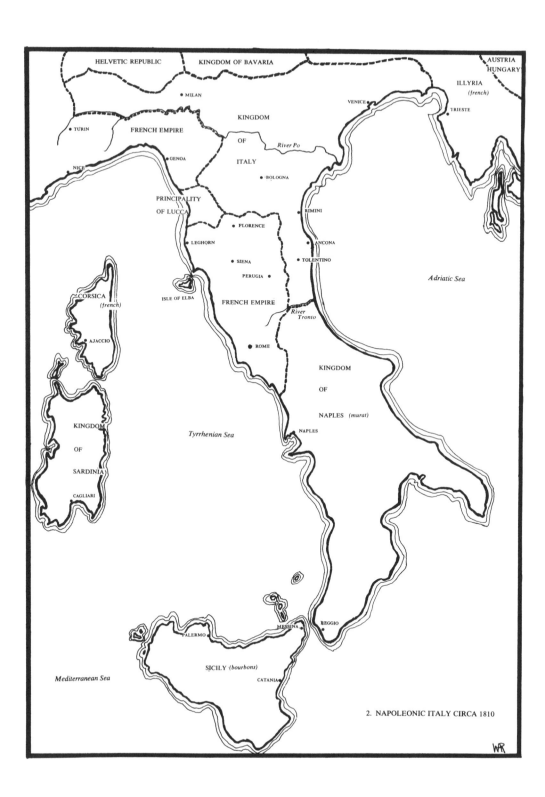

HELVETIC REPUBLIC   KINGDOM OF BAVARIA

AUSTRIA
HUNGARY

ILLYRIA
(french)

• MILAN

VENICE •

• TRIESTE

• TURIN

FRENCH EMPIRE

KINGDOM

OF

ITALY

River Po

• GENOA

NICE

• BOLOGNA

PRINCIPALITY

OF LUCCA

RIMINI

• FLORENCE

LEGHORN

ANCONA

• SIENA

TOLENTINO

PERUGIA

Adriatic Sea

ISLE OF ELBA

CORSICA

(french)

FRENCH EMPIRE

River
Tronto

AJACCIO

• ROME

KINGDOM

OF

NAPLES (murat)

KINGDOM

OF

SARDINIA

Tyrrhenian Sea

NAPLES

CAGLIARI

REGGIO

MESSINA

PALERMO

SICILY (bourbons)

Mediterranean Sea

CATANIA

2. NAPOLEONIC ITALY CIRCA 1810

WR

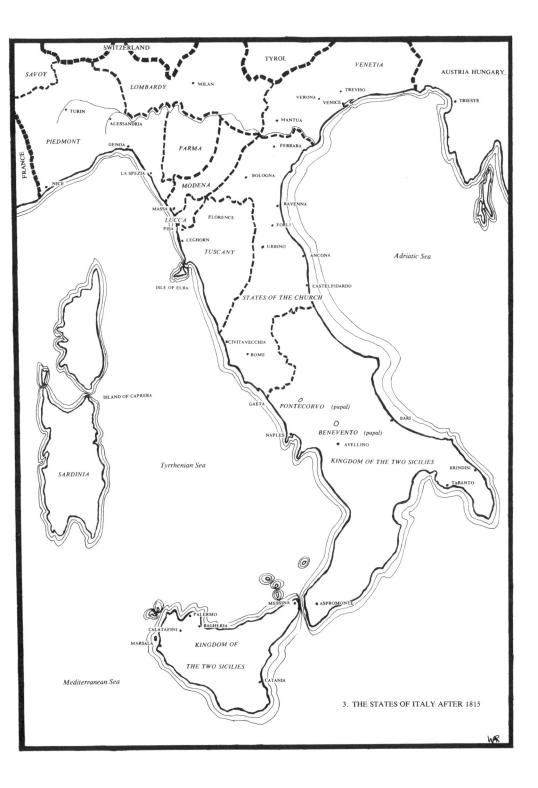

SWITZERLAND

SAVOY

TYROL

VENETIA

AUSTRIA HUNGARY.

LOMBARDY

• MILAN

• TREVISO

VERONA

VENICE

• TRIESTE

• TURIN

PIEDMONT

ALESSANDRIA

• MANTUA

FRANCE

GENOA

PARMA

• FERRARA

LA SPEZIA

MODENA

• BOLOGNA

NICE

MASSA

• RAVENNA

LUCCA

FLORENCE

• FORLI

PISA

• LEGHORN

• URBINO

• ANCONA

Adriatic Sea

TUSCANY

• CASTELFIDARDO

ISLE OF ELBA

STATES OF THE CHURCH

• CIVITAVECCHIA

• ROME

ISLAND OF CAPRERA

GAETA

PONTECORVO (papal)

BARI

BENEVENTO (papal)

NAPLES

• AVELLINO

SARDINIA

Tyrrhenian Sea

KINGDOM OF THE TWO SICILIES

BRINDISI

• TARANTO

MESSINA

• ASPROMONTE

PALERMO

CALATAFINI

BAGHERIA

MARSALA

KINGDOM OF

THE TWO SICILIES

CATANIA

Mediterranean Sea

3. THE STATES OF ITALY AFTER 1815

WR

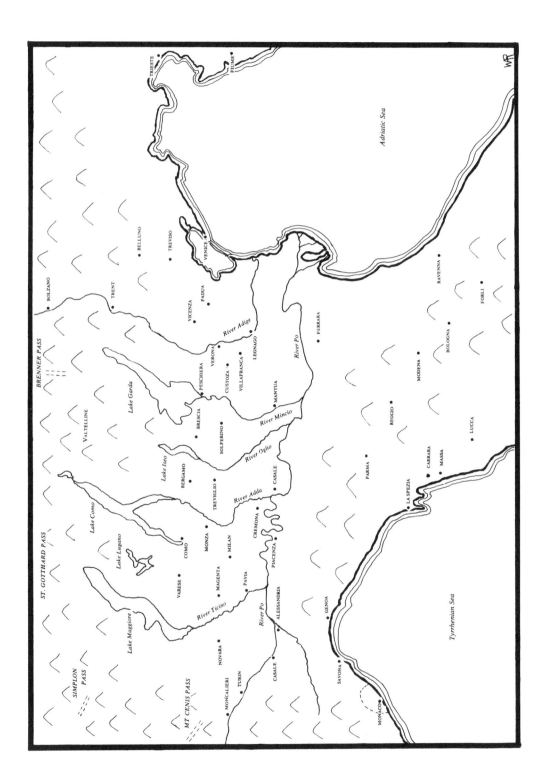

Introduction

How THE Italian peninsula was transformed into a united nation has become the subject of a vast literature, and an impressive quantity of documents is by now available in print. Dozens of the leading participants wrote diaries or memoirs. Innumerable collections of letters have been printed, and of Mazzini's writings alone there is now an edition which runs to well over a hundred volumes. Half a dozen different regions had parliamentary assemblies of which the debates have been published, and in each of the provincial capitals a legion of devoted local historians has illuminated every stage of the patriotic movement. State papers, newspapers, the reports of foreign ambassadors and press correspondents, all these can be used to check and to amplify the knowledge which is already familiar through contemporary books and pamphlets.

One of the old controversies which is still alive on this subject is a debate over what limits in time should be attached to the theme of the making of Italy. Sometimes the risorgimento is said to have reached its fulfillment in March 1861 with the formal establishment of a united kingdom. An alternative date is October 1870 when a plebiscite among the inhabitants of Rome seemed to put a more final seal on the process of national unification. The more extreme nationalists sometimes went further and treated as part of the same unified period of history the years until 1919 when the territorial settlement after the First World War rounded off Italy's Alpine frontier in the north. Still more extreme, the fascists thought of Mussolini as the logical sequel to Mazzini, Garibaldi, and Cavour.

Even more difficult to say is when the risorgimento began. On one argument it was only after 1843 that national feeling became at all widespread among the population of the various Italian regions. Alternatively historians could choose the convenient moment of the treaty settlement in 1815 after the Napoleonic wars; or else the arrival in the 1790's of French troops carrying the new and challenging message of the French Revolution; or they could start still earlier with the reformers of the eighteenth-century Enlightenment. One interpretation takes the story back as far as the early Middle Ages when Goths and Byzantines fought each other in order to create a large Italian state.

Although nearly all the documents in this present volume come from the period between 1800 and 1870, it should be borne in mind that Italy had been an idea in some people's minds for a long time before the nineteenth century. No doubt it was only a vague idea, and one without practical significance except to a select few; but national consciousness was not created out of nothing after 1800. Dante and Petrarch in the fourteenth century had a poetic ideal of what Italy might be, and Machiavelli in *The Prince* had hoped that a liberator would appear to deliver Italians from foreign domination. Machiavelli, however, like Petrarch and Dante, was a citizen not of Italy but of Florence. Even though he had in mind more than just his own state of Florence, the reality of his world was one in which Italy was divided into independent principalities, republics, and city states. Each city had been able to command strong and practical loyalties at a time when the larger idea of Italy was little more than a dream. Even the Italian language was known only by a few, and the spoken vernacular of one region was unintelligible in the next. Not only was Italian used far less than these dialects, it was also less important than Latin at Rome, French at Turin, and Spanish in Naples, Sicily, and Sardinia.

The Italians of these different regions had for centuries fought against each other in the interests of local rivalries. Regularly they had instigated the invasion of one foreign ruler after another to help them against neighboring Italian states. No foreign conqueror in Italy failed to find active support among the local population: this was true of the French in the 1490's, as of the Spanish in the 1280's, the Germans in the twelfth century, and the Arabs in the ninth. It was also true of Napoleon's invasions in 1796 and 1800.

Foreign rule, perhaps just because it was remote and relatively free from involvement in local antagonisms, found a positive welcome among many people. This point is important for an understanding of the risorgimento, because the main obstruction in the way of the patriotic movement was not foreign governments; an even greater obstacle was the slowness of the great bulk of Italians to accept or even to comprehend the idea of Italy. A "Patriotic Society" was formed at Milan in 1776, but its concern was Lombard and not Italian patriotism; and when it permitted itself some "foreign" members, these included Venetians and Piedmontese as well as English and Germans. Even among intellectuals, the very concept of "Italy" often continued to be distant and indefinite.

Books could be entitled *History of Italy* and yet leave out Lombardy altogether, as others omitted Venice and others Sicily. The individual regions of the peninsula kept their own distinct character, just as they kept their own separate foreign policy; and no one region could aspire to a pre-eminent political position without the others reacting vehemently and almost automatically against it.

For example, the papal kingdom, with its capital at Rome, had a strong inducement to thwart Italian patriotism, and its government was quick to invoke foreign help against any threat from Naples, Florence, Milan, or Venice. The Pope's position as spiritual overlord of Christianity gave him a special position which made the Papal States much more than something merely Italian. As well as the Popes themselves, nearly all the ecclesiastical hierarchy were Italians, and this fact gave many of the educated *élite* throughout Italy an international allegiance which helped to delay the development of any Italian loyalty. The Papal States stretched across the peninsula from the Adriatic to the Tyrrhenian Sea. This was an apparently insuperable obstacle to any political union of north and south Italy, especially as maintenance of the Pope's temporal power was occasionally made into what became almost a dogma of religion.

South of the papal kingdom were Naples and Sicily, sometimes known as the Two Sicilies. For a very long time before 1700, these two large areas were ruled by Spanish viceroys as part of the Spanish Empire; and a large proportion of the governing aristocracy in both countries was Spanish by origin. From the 1730's onward, Naples and Sicily were jointly ruled by a cadet branch of the Spanish Bourbons. To the far north of the Papal States was Lombardy, which had Milan as its most important city. Lombardy in the eighteenth century was part of the Habsburg Empire and was administered from Vienna. Venice, too, after a thousand years as an independent republic, was taken over by the Austrian Habsburgs at the end of the eighteenth century. Another branch of the same family inherited Tuscany. In the Middle Ages, Tuscany had been made up of independent city states, the most notable of which were Florence, Siena, Pisa, and Lucca; and each of these towns had possessed a real life and culture of its own. Lucca alone of the smaller towns kept some degree of freedom. The others were swallowed up by Florence and became part of the Grand Duchy of Tuscany.

In the northwest region of Italy, Genoa remained an independent republic until nearly the end of the eighteenth century. Genoa, like Venice, had once possessed a far-flung empire of its own, with settlements all over the Levant and in the Black Sea. That empire fell in course of time to the Turks. In 1768, Genoa ceded Corsica to France, just in time for Napoleon in 1769 to be born a Frenchman and not a Genoese subject. Genoa remained master of just the Ligurian coast. Inland, further north, was Turin, the capital city of a principality which comprised Piedmont and Savoy on each side of the Alps. Here, too, a process of aggregation was gradually making a single state out of regions which had considerable dissimilarities of character and history. In 1720 the Duke of Savoy acquired the island of Sardinia and was allowed by the other European powers to take with it the title of king. One ruler of Piedmont-Sardinia was said to have remarked that he would accumulate other Italian provinces successively, peeling them off like the leaves of an artichoke; and the "artichoke" policy of this ambitious dynasty was to be one ingredient in the making of Italy.

Another ingredient was a great change which began to come over the various Italian states under the influence of enlightened reformers in the eighteenth century who challenged some of the underlying principles of the *ancien régime*. Pietro Giannone, the great historian of Naples, questioned what he called the excessive influence of the Church in politics and identified the Pope as a main obstacle in the path of change. Naples was also the home of Antonio Genovesi, who as professor of political economy helped to educate a school of economists and humanitarian reformers in southern Italy. Genovesi recognized that the fractionalization of the various Italian states was a bar to their economic progress. In northern Italy, Francesco Vasco was another who envisaged some of the benefits which might follow from making trade freer between one region and its neighbor. A fairly strong reformist tradition also grew up at Florence and Milan under the Habsburg rulers. Beccaria's views against torture and capital punishment were widely discussed and even began to be applied; land reforms were introduced; taxation was made fairer; the privileges of feudatories and ecclesiastics were curtailed by governors who thought themselves not so much rulers by divine right as under obligation to serve society and improve the lives of their subjects.

This shows that the pace of change in Italy was quickening before the French Revolution after 1789 speeded up the process and gave it new direction. Some of these pre-revolutionary intellectuals, especially among the economists, occasionally speculated about the possibility of a closer political union between various Italian states. Nevertheless, this illuminist movement did not have deep roots. Giannone, too enlightened for his age, died in 1748, a prisoner of the Piedmontese king. Vasco, too, spent twenty years in a Piedmontese jail and died still a prisoner in 1794. The Marquis Caracciolo, who as Viceroy of Sicily staged a very serious campaign against feudal abuses in the 1780's, had to acknowledge that the past was too strong to be radically altered. What is even more to the point, the more influential of these reformers were effective only insofar as they were loyal servants of absolutist government. They were never more than a tiny minority, even though a significant one. They believed in theories rather than practice. Nor did they have any serious idea of liberating Italy from foreign rule. Some denunciations could be heard against tyranny, as one can see from the tragedies of Count Vittorio Alfieri, but none against enlightened despotism, and not as much more than a literary or theoretical exercise. These reformers may have been proud to be Italians as well as Neapolitans and Milanese, but they did not believe in unifying the peninsula as a program of practical politics.

What shattered the old regime in Italy was not this kind of reformist movement from within, but rather the revolutionary conquests of Napoleon after 1796. It was Napoleon's invasions which destroyed the existing state system; just as the ideas of the French Revolution, which arrived with the invaders, completely upset old categories of thought and behavior. Existing kings were deposed; the centuries-old republics of Venice and Genoa were destroyed; and even the Pope was turned out of Rome so that the Papal States could become a department of France. Of all the regions of Italy, only the two islands of Sardinia and Sicily, protected by the British navy, retained their independence under the kings of Piedmont and Naples. The rest of Italy could never be the same again.

Napoleon's victories were possible with only a small army, because the existing governments of Italy were divided and thoroughly enfeebled. Napoleon could also rely on considerable support from many Italians who looked on his invasion as a deliverance, and the initial acceptance of his conquest seems to show that not a national government but simply good government was what politically con-

scious citizens wanted. Even after his ministers had become less benevolent, tens of thousands of Italians went on joining his forces
and serving the administration which he imposed on the various
Italian regions. Many others became rich under his regime and were
encouraged to join or even displace the old-established aristocracies
as the ruling class in the peninsula. It was from families who gained
power or wealth under Napoleon that the leaders of the nineteenth-
century risorgimento emerged.

In other ways, too, the Napoleonic occupation of Italy had important effects on the growth of nationalism. Not only did the
French bring something positive to Italy, but the high taxes which
they imposed, and which Napoleon's wars made necessary, in time
generated a strong opposition which took its place in the development of national consciousness. Whereas the reformers of the
eighteenth century had worked happily in a context of enlightened
despotism, this generation and the next were open to much more
radical aspirations after political liberty; and a causal chain was to
lead from ideas of popular sovereignty to those of Italian patriotism.
Filippo Buonarroti, a Tuscan radical who in the 1790's became a
Frenchman by adoption, belonged to those who talked this new
language of popular sovereignty: he and the more progressive
among Italian Jacobins were able to glimpse some possibility of a
more unified peninsula, and the detached position of exile sometimes enabled them to see more clearly the relation between their
own home provinces and the Italian nation at large.

Many parts of Europe were to experience the search for national
identity in the years after 1800 as various peoples tried to discover
their common heritage and develop the use of their national languages. Italy shared in this process. The movement was very small
at first, for growth of national feeling had to wait on education, on
a greater facility in communications between one part of the country
and another, and on the development of a literature which people
from different regions could recognize as their own. It was thus an
important fact that, even in remote Palermo, by 1810 there was a
small but enthusiastic audience for Alfieri's tragedies. Alfieri had
left his native Piedmont and gone to live in Florence and Paris, for
he felt the need to become less provincial in his language and general outlook: he died at Florence in 1803. There he and other voluntary or forced exiles had encountered refugees from every other
Italian region. In another direction, refugees from southern Italy

emigrated to serve Napoleon's regime at Milan, and there they learned more of a common Italian identity as well as being enabled to recognize the comparative backwardness of their own home states. In the years after 1814, the poetry of Ugo Foscolo became a common bond for such *émigré* Italians from every part of the country. Nevertheless the idea of Italy remained literary above all, and not very much more. "Occasionally we hear the word *Italy*," wrote one contemporary writer, Pietro Giordani, in 1816, "but it finds no echo in people's hearts."

Just because local forces were so weak, foreign help and example were needed to bring Italians together in a single nation. The influence of Byron was thus important as a liberating influence on Foscolo's generation, just as that of Walter Scott was on the next, and Voltaire had been on that of their predecessors. Scott's historical novels found a select and eager audience everywhere, and the model was taken up by Manzoni, Guerrazzi, and Massimo d'Azeglio, who together brought a new class of reader to the historical awareness which was an indispensable preliminary of patriotic feeling and action.

Only when one or more outside European powers developed a serious interest in creating a strong Italy would a political risorgimento become feasible in practice. Before 1800, other countries had rather felt it in their interest to keep Italy weak, if for no other reason than that they could then fight out their quarrels on Italian soil and not on their own. Napoleon had been quite unusual in his eagerness to attract Italian support; but even he, after he became emperor and had no more to gain from it, was less friendly and helpful. In 1813–15, it was rather the Austrians and British who needed to play for Italian support as part of their campaign against Bonaparte; but they too, once they had succeeded in defeating him, lost interest.

The settlement of 1815 left Austria so much in command all over Italy that, for the moment, none of the local rulers had any leverage against her. On the contrary, most of them felt that without Austrian support they might well lose their thrones. Only much later, when France had had time to recover from her catastrophic defeat, would something of a balance of power be restored in southern Europe, and then the indigenous sovereigns of Italy would once again have a chance to become a makeweight in the scales. In the meantime, foreign initiative of various kinds remained an indispensable element in Italian politics; events in Spain touched off a revolt in Naples in 1820, as a revolution in France started another in central Italy ten years later, and an insurrection at Vienna made possible the "Five days of Milan" in 1848. Subsequently the rivalries between Austria and France, between England and Russia, and between France and Prussia, all these were successively to create situations which a growing number of patriots in Italy were able to turn to advantage.

The varied contribution made by other countries is an example of the different kinds of motive and process which went toward the formation of Italy. Inside the country, too, there were many separate currents of opinion and action which were to lead toward this one goal, some of which in retrospect seem almost contradictory. The growth of national consciousness played its part, but so did something which was almost a denial of national consciousness, namely the quarrels and rivalries between different groups of Italians. For example, there was a strong dislike of Neapolitan rule among a great number of Sicilians. This was in part simply a dislike of taxes and governmental interference, but it was also a feeling shared by every class in Sicily that Neapolitans with their strange, unintelligible language were an alien people; and this resentment against Naples was a vital element in the Sicilian insurrections of 1848 and 1860 which had a decisive influence on the success of the risorgimento. At a still lower level, local inter-city rivalries helped to reduce the regional cohesion which was such a formidable barrier in the way of forming a larger Italian state: some of the documents in this volume will show how the traditional animosity of Pisa against Florence, of Treviso against Venice, of Savona against Genoa, or the sometimes extremely belligerent feeling of Messina for Palermo, all these relics of old historical controversies had their part to play in creating the nation.

Other factors in the national movement must be sought in social and economic history. In some places, very slowly, there was developing a commercial and industrial capitalism which sooner or later was bound to discover a material interest in creating a closer union between neighboring regions. Merchants and industrialists— and of course any farmers who produced an export crop such as wine or citrus fruit—were increasingly inclined toward lowering or abolishing tariffs at state frontiers so as to create something of a common market in the peninsula. They would need road and railway systems to be conjoined, instead of each state legislating and building for itself alone. Milanese exporters would have liked the freedom to choose Genoa as well as Venice or Trieste for a possible outlet to the southern sea. They saw the advantage of being able to mobilize capital on a large enough scale to build communications over or through the Alps—something which would benefit the whole of northern Italy and which arguably should be paid for collectively. The diversity of weights, measures, and coinage systems made commerce extremely difficult, and this diversity was another complaint by every economic reformer. In the Kingdom of Naples alone, there were a thousand different terms for measures of various kinds, and some of these had dozens of different meanings in various places or circumstances: naturally this discouraged foreign trade, while the resultant confusion and litigation were expensive and stultifying.

Meanwhile social developments generated pressures which helped to push the governments of post-1815 Italy in the direction of change. Some districts had until latterly possessed almost no middle class at all; now one was emerging, and, though the middle elements in society did not as a body take the lead in proposing political reform, they did provide an important strand of public opinion which was ready to accept such reform once it became a serious possibility. Many people who under Napoleon had been clerks, junior army officers, tradesmen, and local-government officials, found after 1815 that they were without jobs, or at least that their standard of living was much lower than before. The re-establishment of state and tariff barriers after 1815, the abolition of Napoleon's legal code and the French metric system, the restoration in some cases of feudal and clerical privileges, all this was oppressive to those who relied on talent and personal initiative for a career. In many towns there also came into existence a combustible element of students and ex-students who, in protest against their elders and against the difficulties of finding employment, became excellent material for secret revolutionary societies.

Another devastating revolutionary force lay in the peasants; for a growing population was pressing on the available food supplies, and standards of life, though they had often been precarious enough already, fell sharply after 1815 with the collapse of the wartime boom. The end of feudalism put farm laborers at the mercy of new landlords who, partly because they showed less sense of social responsibility than their feudal predecessors, partly because land-owners now faced economic difficulties of their own, could be exacting to the point of cruelty. New problems also faced agri-culture when farmers were forced, often for the first time, to confront the vagaries of a market economy. Again and again the revolts of the risorgimento proved *au fond* to be largely social insurrections which seemed to have little immediate con-nection with politics. Sometimes the decisive fact in their out-break was simply that excessive rain or drought caused two harvest failures in succession, for this could place many peo-ple in a position where armed force and robbery offered the only chance of keeping their families alive. As a rule, the poli-tical revolutionaries saw all too clearly the improbability of these revolts succeeding, and an explosion occurred only because slum dwellers and landless laborers were confronted with starva-tion. Initially therefore, the patriots would generally discourage or even oppose this kind of social and economic revolution; but they might be forced to accept it once it proved a success; and in sheer self-defense they would then try to impose on it a political pro-gram which the original instigators of rebellion neither welcomed nor even understood.

These many various elements in the risorgimento will help to make the point that there was little in it of any preconceived plan. It was one of those complex movements which developed along lines that were sometimes far removed from the intentions of any participant. After all was over, of course, some people could easily look back and explain the whole sequence of events as having possessed much greater coherence than there can possibly have been at the time. That is why any illustrative document which is recol-lection, instead of contemporaneous with the events described, must be used circumspectly. Many individuals quite innocently con-trived in later recollection to make their own conduct seem finer and more meaningful than we know it to have been. Others, out of straightforward patriotism, overstressed the compulsive effect of national consciousness. They made the history of unification too much into a simple story of deliverance from the Austrian oppres-sor, ignoring that most of its wars were civil wars, and never men-tioning that many Italians continued to fight and fight well in the Austrian army. There was an understandable temptation in retro-spect to exaggerate the heroism and the sacrifice. Partly this was to

compensate for the fact that the expenditure of national energy
had been less than many would have liked. By official reckoning,
indeed, Italian casualties in all the wars of the central twenty-five
years of the risorgimento were fewer than were lost in one single
day of the Franco-Prussian War in 1870.

Any selection of documents on this subject must give due place
to both the thinkers and the active politicians; it must cover those
who prepared the ground by propaganda and isolated example, and
also those who, especially in the dramatic years 1848–9 and 1858–
61, brought about the union of Italy by fighting and diplomacy.
Something must also be shown of the defeated parties in these civil
wars; for the defeated are too often forgotten or left as mere stereo-
types, and for this reason the Austrians and the Neapolitan Bourbons have not always been given their due. It is important not to
forget the individualists who stood apart from the mainstream,
people such as Cattaneo, Montanelli, Tommaseo, and Ferrari; because, even if many of their views were discarded or generally
ignored by the victorious party, they themselves contributed to the
final solution, and, insofar as they were critics of the result, their
criticism is authentic and at first hand. Some room should preferably be provided for military as well as diplomatic history, for
economic and social affairs as well as for the world of parliaments,
journalism, and literature. Each region, too, ought to be represented
if the variety which went into this unity is to be properly estimated.
Inevitably Mazzini and Cavour will remain in the forefront of
events. Giuseppe Mazzini was the chief propagandist of the national
revolution. Indeed he was the best-known theorist of nationalism
anywhere in contemporary Europe. He imagined that, if only the
various nations of the world could be given the frontiers which God
intended for them, this would almost automatically ensure international peace and good will. Mazzini lived at a time when such
questions seemed a good deal simpler than they do now. He
thought that Germany and Holland should compose a single nation;
that Hungary should be joined with Rumania, and Greece with
Bulgaria. Likewise Scandinavia should be a single united nation,
whereas Ireland was apparently not a nation at all. Mazzini was
no simpleton, yet it was these oversimplifications at the very core
of his doctrine that allowed him to be so uncritically sure of himself in other matters. His own life he dedicated almost entirely to

the making of Italy. The sheer certainty of his vision, and the singlemindedness of his life as an agitator and pamphleteer, made him enormously successful despite the obvious faults in some of his facts and theories.

Nevertheless, Mazzini thought that he had failed, just because Cavour took over the whole movement and changed the rules of the game. Camille de Cavour had little patience with theories. He was much more of a professional politician. He was a diplomat who had, as he himself said, a fairly elastic conscience and thus could do many things which were outside both Mazzini's competence and his code of morality. Many people will find Cavour the most interesting and most important person in this story. His ability as financier, parliamentarian, and party manager was almost as striking as that intuitive awareness of the European diplomatic scene which enabled him to use the strength of foreign countries in order to make his own nation. Cavour successfully employed the force of Italian patriotism which Mazzini had done so much to create. By also harnessing the aggressive urges of Piedmont and its sovereign, he was then able to exploit the balance of power in Europe and to create a Kingdom of Italy just a few months before he died.

1. The Napoleonic Period, 1796-1815

In 1796, after Napoleon's successful invasion of Piedmont and Lombardy, the French-dominated administration at Milan offered a prize for an essay on what type of government would best suit Italy. Essays could be in Italian, French, or Latin, and foreigners could also compete. About sixty entries of various kinds and sizes were received. Most were academic, typical competition pieces. The circumstances of the competition dictated that their general tone would be solidly pro-French and anti-Austrian, pro-republican and anti-monarchic. Some contributors interpreted "Italy" as meaning just what they called "the Lombard nation"; others, even when they included the whole peninsula, left Sicily out; and at least one thought that Italy should include Malta, Corsica, and part of Switzerland. Others tried to please the judges by advocating complete union of Italy with France. Entries ranged in optimism from one which thought that "there never had been a time when Italians were not superior to the men of all other nations in things of the mind," to another which assumed that it would be a century before southern Italians would want to join the north. Nevertheless there was a clear assumption that some kind of Italian nation existed, or ought to exist. Beyond this they differed enormously, so showing how little there was of a common system of beliefs to build on. The prize, a gold medal, was won by Melchiorre Gioia with his advocacy of a unitary republic.

The Italian problem in 1796, as seen by Melchiorre Gioia

Both REFLECTION and history will convince us that an Italy divided into small isolated and independent republics can hardly survive. For while these were fighting to dominate each other, their foreign enemies would be watching. As hatreds grew within the nation, these enemies would seize any opportunity that advanced their aims. The House of Austria which, alike in peace and war, thinks only of its own expansion; which has requisitioned so many of our archives to prepare its claims to more territory; whose ambition never loses sight of any country that has once belonged to it; which, however other nations change their principles and conduct, retains a uniform policy—the House of Austria would find people in Italy blind enough to be duped, weak enough to accept its favors, and so embittered with each other as to throw themselves into its arms. It would foment discord so as to soften Italian determination;

it would offer a hand to the oppressed so as to gain their friendship, and pretend to be an ally and benefactor of the people. Having prepared public opinion and won allies, with strength enough to overthrow its enemies yet careful to avert suspicion, it would gradually advance, and once in a position of power would remove the mask and say to Italians: these are the laws I impose on you. And we would be obliged to obey.

One possible reply to this and in favor of a divided Italy can be heard coming from intellectuals and dilettanti who never notice the blood spattered on the ground nor suffer in their own persons the hostility of governments. These people are strangers to current events but live only in the past; they are those who single out in history a poem or a philosopher's dream and never look at politics in the round; they are obsessed by the glorious centuries of Greek and Italian history when talent could be found in a multitude of independent states, when human reason was uplifted to a degree from which political revolutions have since dethroned it, possibly for ever. These men, I say, preach that a multiplicity of states fosters competition, and that it is there that genius takes wing. To answer this objection shortly, opposing erudition with erudition, I maintain that if the mutual jealousy of tiny states operates against inertia and discourages indolence, if the divisions of Greece and Italy brought glorious talents into existence and gave renewed life and splendor to the arts, they also spilt rivers of blood and dealt mortal wounds to mankind . . .

Let us examine the possibility of federalism. Anyone who has analyzed political communities and knows how avid they are for esteem, how sensitive to contempt, how ready to take alarm, how difficult to reconcile, how fertile in ruses, obstinate in their scheming yet limited in aims, will readily conclude that a confederation of various political bodies with separate existences, laws of their own and local interests, is inevitably slow when it comes to planning, slower still when it comes to carrying plans out, and only too ready for disagreement. Each member of the confederation will consult its own interests only, will put aside thoughts for the future, will exalt its own contribution regardless of that of the others, will shut its eyes to the general good, and hence will inevitably oppose decisions lacking in immediate advantage to itself . . .

If Italy were divided into a number of federal republics, the seaboard cities would have already fallen to an invader before the general Italian congress had decided what to do. And when the congress eventually ordered its armies to move, the enemy would have already withdrawn or be about to resume the attack with re-doubled force. Supposing the fires of war break out in the Alpine foothills; repeated appeals will not bring help speedily from Calabria. Supposing a Xerxes from the mountains of Tyrol de-scended on the Lombard Republic, it might well be that other republics, with their jealous local patriotism, would be ready to fight only if led by Eurybiades, and perhaps a Themistocles would not be forthcoming to save Italy as Greece was saved at Salamis. The ease with which Italy can be invaded, the difficulty of bringing about general collaboration in her defense, the jealousy natural to confederated republics, the slowness inherent in confederation—all these are reasons why I dismiss the prospect of a federal system ...

There is something to be said for those federalists who warn us that the more extensive the state the wider the powers it must possess if laws are to be applied throughout the republic, and that such immense powers can easily become an instrument of oppres-sion; for it is not the number of soldiers relative to the population but their absolute number that can ruin the state. A hundred men do not subjugate ten thousand citizens, but ten thousand soldiers can make millions tremble. To this I reply that our historical records show that Italy has almost always been the patrimony of foreigners who, under the pretext of protecting us, have consistently violated our rights, and, while giving us flags and fine-sounding names, have made themselves masters of our estate. France, Germany and Spain have held lordship over us in turn. For countless centuries our soil has been the theater over which foreigners have disputed their claims. As Italy is easily accessible from almost all sides to foreign enemies, it is therefore best to provide her with the sort of govern-ment capable of opposing the maximum of resistance to invasion. That government is beyond question a unitary republic: *vis unita fortior*.

> [Melchiorre Gioia: *Quale dei governi liberi meglio convenga all'Italia*, ed. C. Sforza (Rome, 1944), pp. 68–76]

Napoleon's successive invasions were the biggest physical shock that Italy had received for three centuries, and the existing arrangement of states was shattered irreparably. Yet Napoleon found enthusiastic support among the cleverer and more forward-looking Italians. What he represented in their eyes was a new age of equality, freer government, and a general subversion of old ways and attitudes. Many of the common people saw him as a liberator against feudalism. Some men of property, on the other hand, welcomed his support in raising agricultural prices and seizing Church lands. The middle class at last found that careers were open to mere talent; and that efficient government, the metric system, and vastly better communications made possible new ways of money-making. The Napoleonic code of law, the abolition of entails, primogeniture, and mortmain, as well as new techniques of modern administration all worked in favor of social and economic change.

Of course Napoleon was also a conqueror, an exploiter, and a dictator. He imposed very heavy taxes and squandered Italian men and money for his imperial wars. Yet this aroused less opposition than one might have expected. Italians were repeatedly summoned to Paris to hear of new territorial arrangements and constitutional experiments he was imposing on them: the Cisalpine Republic, the Cispadane Republic, the Parthenopean Republic, the Kingdom of Etruria, the abolition of the Pope's temporal power, these were some of his experiments. The republics of Venice and Genoa, which in splendor had survived countless wars and invasions, were abolished at his command. Piedmont, Liguria, Parma, Tuscany, Umbria, even Rome itself, he simply annexed to France, so that the leading figures of the Italian risorgimento were in fact born Frenchmen. But he also created a *Kingdom of Italy*, which included Lombardy, Venice, and central Italy down to Ancona. This kingdom of nearly seven million inhabitants was the largest state in Italy. Though ruled by a French king and a French viceroy, and though heavily taxed for the benefit of France, its administration was almost entirely given over to Italians. Its capital, Milan, was the most important political center in the peninsula.

Napoleon, at Paris, establishes a Kingdom of Italy, March 17, 1805

Article 1:—Napoleon I, Emperor of the French, is King of Italy.

Article 2:—The crown of Italy is hereditary in his direct male descendants, whether natural or adoptive. Women and their descendants can never succeed, and adoption must be confined to citizens of the French Empire or the Kingdom of Italy.

Article 3:—As soon as foreign armies have left Naples, the Ionian Islands and Malta, the Emperor will hand over the crown of Italy to one of his legitimate male children, natural or adoptive.

Article 4:—Thenceforward the crown of Italy will never be united with that of France, and the successors of Napoleon I in Italy must permanently reside in the state.

Article 5:—During the current year the Emperor Napoleon, advised by the Council of State and deputations of the electoral colleges, will give the Italian monarchy a constitution founded on the same bases as those of the French Empire, and on the same principles as the laws he has already given to Italy.

[J.-E. Driault: *Napoléon en Italie, 1800–1812* (Paris 1906), p. 315]

Tens of thousands of Italians were killed in Napoleon's service all over Europe and in Russia; and even when his power declined in 1814, the army of the Kingdom of Italy supported him loyally. In Italy, unlike Spain, there was no significant popular rising to drive the French out of the peninsula. Of course the old deposed rulers, in particular the Pope and the kings of Naples and Piedmont, were glad to be restored to their thrones by Austrian arms, and at the last moment some of the Milanese nobility also appealed for Austrian help.

In 1808, Marshal Murat had been appointed by Napoleon as ruler of a semi-independent Naples with the title of King Joachim-Napoleon. Hoping to survive Napoleon's defeat, Murat negotiated in 1814 with both Britain and Austria, though neither trusted him. In March 1814 a British force under General Bentinck landed at Leghorn and called on Italians to rise and free themselves from the French. Not to be outdone, Murat desperately issued a fine if somewhat fanciful appeal for patriotic support. It is significant that the Neapolitans in Murat's entourage thought such patriotism strong enough to be worth appealing to, and this suggestion of an Italy liberated by Murat fascinated the Lombard poet Manzoni. But the practical effect of the proclamation was nil, a fact which could be variously interpreted: perhaps political independence had little attraction; or perhaps Italians were not anxious to accept a lead from Neapolitans; or else, coming from a foreigner himself, and from an ambitious, somewhat disreputable foreigner, this appeal fooled nobody. Murat concluded that "Italians were not ready for liberty," and a few days later the Austrians defeated his hopes at the battle of Tolentino.

Proclamation to the Italians by Marshal Murat, from Rimini, March 30, 1815

PROVIDENCE IS at last calling you to be an independent nation. From the Alps to the Straits of Sicily can be heard a single cry:

"Italian independence!" By what title do foreigners deny you this primary right of every people? By what right do they lord it over your beautiful country, taking your wealth elsewhere, conscripting your children to fight and die far from the tombs of their ancestors? Was it in vain that nature created the Alps as your defense and gave you that even greater barrier provided by differences of language, customs and character? No! Away with foreign domination! You were once masters of the world, and have expiated your glory in twenty centuries of slaughter and oppression. But today you can recover that glory by breaking free from your masters.

Every people should keep to the limits assigned to them by nature, and your limits are the sea and the mountains. Do not ask for more than that, but at least drive out the foreigner who violates your territory. Eighty thousand soldiers from Naples led by their King [i.e., Murat himself] have sworn not to rest until they have liberated Italy. We call on Italians from every province to help this great design. Take up arms again and let your young men learn how to fight. Let every free man who has courage and intelligence learn to speak for Italy to every true Italian. If national energies can be fully released, that will decide if Italy will be free or else humiliated and enslaved for further centuries.

> [M.-H. Weil: *Joachim Murat Roi de Naples, la dernière année de règne* (Paris, 1909), vol. III, pp. 504–5]

2. The Restoration, 1815-1820

The Congress of Vienna found Austria well established throughout Italy by right of conquest. No other major power had much interest or much opportunity to challenge her position there, nor could Italians do so, especially as they had contributed so little to overthrowing the various Napoleonic regimes. A few Italians had learned the desirability of political independence, and a very few were even speaking of the need for a wider Italian union; but far more noticeable than any common aspiration toward independence was the conflict between different classes and different areas in Italy which made foreign domination easy and even welcome.

The Austrians were therefore greeted as friends when they arrived in 1814–15 to take over an enlarged Kingdom of Lombardy and Venice. Austrian troops under General Bubna restored the ex-King Victor Emmanuel I of Piedmont-Sardinia to his throne. Bentinck liberated Genoa, but instead of reviving the old Genoese republic as one Genoese aristocrat at Vienna requested, the Ligurian coast was given to the Piedmontese, and the latter also regained Savoy and Nice. The Pope was restored to his domain; so was the Bourbon sovereign of the Two Sicilies at Naples. One Austrian archduke took Tuscany, and another Modena. Parma kept a nominal independence. So did Lucca, though after a life interest this would revert to Tuscany. San Marino and Monaco were left as tiny, insignificant states. When settling these new frontiers, legitimism was held more important than any natural boundaries such as rivers, mountains, or existing trade routes. Benevento and Pontecorvo were left as islands of papal sovereignty inside Naples; some Tuscan territory remained isolated inside the Duchy of Lucca, and Lucca possessed villages inside Modena. Pavia went to the Austrians, but part of its natural hinterland to the Piedmontese.

Piedmont, ruled by the House of Savoy, was later to find a role as the Prussia of Italy and to show a greater ambition and sense of purpose than other Italian states. Her potential rivalry with Austria appears from a memorandum presented to the Czar Alexander in 1818. Its author, Count Cotti di Brusasco, in 1817 had succeeded the political philosopher De Maistre as Piedmontese ambassador at St. Petersburg, and, like De Maistre, he saw that Piedmont possibly might one day win Lombardy if she could drive a wedge between the Holy Alliance of Russia and Austria. His politics were strongly conservative in all other respects.

The condition of Italy before and after 1815, as seen by a Piedmontese

As EVERYBODY knows, after the barbarian invasions, Italy became the cradle of science, letters and art. But it may not be so generally known that all the modern political doctrines were discussed in our small Italian states before they were heard of in the rest of Europe, and that every system of government has been suggested, tried out and debated there. In the midst of many errors, great truths found expression; and if Italy had been left alone, what with the progress of enlightenment and the help of experience, a system of wise freedom might perhaps have been established. But this chance of happiness was lost owing to foreign interference. In the sixteenth century the rule of Spain, established by Charles V and strengthened by Philip II, deprived Italy of any form of political independence. At that time, too, the taste for religious reform having spread through many countries, the Court of Rome, in concert with that of Spain, thought it necessary to isolate Italy from the rest of Europe by setting up a rigorous censorship, under which literary communication of any kind was forbidden or at least controlled, and all liberty of speech and writing destroyed. While one half of Italy was being governed by Spanish viceroys, the small States, paralyzed by the power of Spain, saw no hope of ever using their military forces for the purpose of resistance, and abandoned the use of arms altogether. Unable thenceforth to seek distinction in either a political or a military career, the Italians lost their national spirit and their warlike habits.

Spanish domination came to an end at the beginning of the eighteenth century, but neither the War of Spanish Succession nor the Treaty of Utrecht [1713] brought any essential change in the political situation. It is true that Piedmont, the only country whose position could have enabled it to maintain a military establishment, acquired henceforth a little more strength and stability. But the rest of Italy merely changed masters. Instead of being solely dependent on Spain, it was now more or less partitioned between the Houses of Bourbon and Austria, which waged war on each other more than once for possession of its tattered remains and the domains of the Farnese and the Medici.

Spectators of such quarrels, and victims of wars waged for such ends as these, how could Italians preserve any national spirit? Prolonged humiliation leads to indifference, and they finally lost not only all hope, but all idea of independence, and grew inured to seeing their estates ravaged by foreigners every fifteen or twenty years as a means of determining which of these foreigners they were to submit to.

This was the moral situation in which Italy found herself when, soon after the middle of last century, foreign books, especially French works on political and philosophical subjects, began to find their way into the country and were read with avidity. When soon afterwards some of the governments relaxed their censorship, a number of writers made their appearance: Genovesi, Galiani and Filangieri in Naples, Beccaria, Carli and Verri in Milan. Throwing light, as they did, on matters of finance and legislation, and setting themselves to correct certain abuses, they succeeded in turning people's minds toward political ideas. After them, and along a different road, came Alfieri, who by the power of his thought and the energy of his poetry, sought to fill the souls of his compatriots with noble feelings and the desire for independence. Kept as they had been up to now under the severest restraint, as it were in a state of nonexistence, and seeing the light again after three centuries, it was not surprising that people in Italy should have adopted these new ideas with too much enthusiasm and some exaggeration. Moreover, as their awakening had been brought about by French philosophy, Italians were more or less bound to absorb some of the errors which that philosophy had mingled with important truths.

The ground was thus prepared when the French Revolution broke out in 1789. Many writers have asserted that this revolution had a number of partisans in Italy, and there is no doubt that in 1796, during the French invasion and for some time afterwards, many errors, excesses and acts of folly were committed. But so far as I know, no political writer of our time has pointed out that the Italians were perhaps the first people of Europe to realize the falsity of the revolutionary doctrines and repudiate them, while trying to derive some benefit from the great upheaval. There were many men in Italy, cultured, judicious and high-minded, who had desired change only in the hope of liberating their country and saving it from being eternally the theater of war between other nations. These men were soon disgusted by the excesses of the revolutionaries; relinquishing their democratic dreams and false ideas of exaggerated liberty, they decided to make use of prevailing conditions to wipe out old divisions and awaken a sense of patriotism. Unable to succeed at once, they set about preparing the country by degrees, and so submitted to the power of Bonaparte while trying to make it serve their own purposes.

Although the new ideas had taken root all through the peninsula, they flourished most in those provinces that composed a single state under the name of the Kingdom of Italy. For the enormous difference between this Kingdom of Italy and the Italian provinces which were incorporated into France must always be borne in mind. It has never been sufficiently recognized. By one of those despotic caprices with which he appeared to delight in affronting accepted notions and doing violence to nature, Bonaparte had decided to make several millions of Italians into Frenchmen. First the Piedmontese, then the Genoese, then the Tuscans and finally the Romans. An artificial line now separated populations who were intended by their topographical position, by their language and common origin, by nature itself, to form a single nation. Bonaparte imagined he could level the Alps, or rather transport them to his arbitrary line of demarcation by simple decree. This led to an entirely novel phenomenon. Beside the same river, in the same country, the national language was encouraged on one bank and proscribed on the other. To speak of the independence of Italy was a crime in Parma, a virtue in Modena. The whole of French Italy was peopled with French employees, from the prefect to the lowliest tax collector. Italian conscripts were used to fill up the ranks of French regiments, and the humblest petition could be rejected simply on the score of its being written in the language of the country.

The Kingdom of Italy, meanwhile, was governed in an entirely different way. Bonaparte preserved its language, created a national army and a military spirit, appointed people of the country to all official posts, and indeed left no foreigner there except the Viceroy. Men of great ability found themselves at the head of affairs, and this lent great impetus to the national spirit; they directed education and guided the growing generation; young men learned the use of arms; the arts were encouraged; monuments worthy of the ancient Romans were erected; and the national language and literature were cultivated with enthusiasm.

The inhabitants of these different provinces, separated hitherto not by distance but by their customs, by the old cleavage between themselves and the government, began to know one another, to visit, to look upon one another as members of one same nation. From year to year, from day to day, this union became more intimate; these feelings grew in strength, these hopes became more general. Forced to obey the ruling power, which at that time seemed irresistible, they preferred to submit to the French ruler rather than to the French nation. Forced to fight for a foreign cause, they consoled themselves with the thought that they were practicing for the day when they would be fighting for their own. This future condition of independence was felt to be not so far off: it seemed inevitable that with the death of Napoleon, or his fall, the Kingdom of Italy, already constituted, with an established government, an army and political ideas, would become self-supporting, make itself independent of France, and help French Italy to escape from bondage.

These were the ideas prevailing in Italy when in 1812 Bonaparte's star began to pale. The Russian campaign had been generally condemned by the Italians; in any case, seeing an army corps composed of the *élite* of their warriors, the flower of the Italian nobility, entirely destroyed in an alien cause, they could not but detest the author of such a catastrophe. When the Czar Alexander, having delivered his own territory, advanced in 1813 to the relief of the German nation which was looking to him as its deliverer, the Italians applauded the German effort and Alexander's generosity. The tyranny and pride of Bonaparte had provoked a general scandal; they longed to see him humiliated; during the whole of 1812 and part of 1813, feelings in Italy were in complete accord with those of the rest of Europe. As everywhere else, the Allies' success was secretly prayed for. So why in this final crisis did the Italians play no part in aiding the cause of Europe? This is the accusation leveled at Italy by her enemies. They have repeated it triumphantly because nobody has ever replied. I shall now attempt to do so.

To begin with, Italy had been under French rule for fourteen years; very little was known there of the events occurring in the rest of Europe; all communication with other countries was either strictly forbidden or closely supervised, and the power of the government was not relaxed until the last moment. Holland and Germany may be cited as examples of resistance, but Holland was very lightly garrisoned by the French, and what troops were stationed there were mostly Dutch. Prussia, Bavaria and the other provinces of Germany had a government of their own, whereas the Italian departments had only French prefects, and Italian conscripts were scattered among the French army in every corner of Europe. Throughout French Italy, therefore, no possibility existed of a rising.

As for the Kingdom of Italy, with a French viceroy at its head, and half its army composed of French divisions, there was little chance of taking any decisive step. And anyhow, was it the business of an army to take such a step, to decide the political fate of the nation? Was it for the armed forces to come to a decision? What would have been said if they had deserted their flag? And which *was* the flag for them to follow? Which side should they have declared for? It was neither a Russian nor an English army that was now drawn up before the walls of Mantua; it was an Austrian army, the army of those Austrians who in four different wars had formerly sought to subjugate Italy. Their intentions were known; they made no attempt to conceal that their object was the establishment of their own rule over the country.

By destroying the Kingdom, Austrians reduced most of it to the status of a dependency, and revived old divisions inside the re mainder; they extinguished the hopes of all good Italians by forcing them to take a backward step, and plunged Italy afresh into the state of weakness, dependence and nullity from which she had been trying to emerge. Once these facts are seen in their true aspect, every man of sense must agree that, far from being to blame, the Italians followed the only line of conduct consonant with their character and suited to the position in which they found themselves.

The capture of Paris brought the war to an end at last, and the bravery of the Russians led to the triumph of Austria. An armistice was concluded, the French troops retired, and the north of Italy was occupied by the Austrian army. The peoples of French Italy recovered their independence and had the joy of seeing their fetters broken; but inhabitants of the Italian Kingdom remained in a state of uncertainty and fear. Disaffection ran high, but was kept under control. Their fortunes were about to be decided, and at this fateful moment they found themselves powerless in the hands of their enemies, without support or protection.

For as ill luck would have it, Italy at that time had no govern- ment, no Italian prince who could have been the mouthpiece of the nation and enforce its demands. King Ferdinand, confined in Sicily, aimed only at the recovery of his Kingdom of Naples; Murat thought only of retaining this same Kingdom, and his tainted voice and revolutionary conduct brought discredit rather than approval to the cause of Italy. There remained the King of Piedmont, the only scion of an Italian race, and actually sovereign of the most war-hardened province of Italy. The Lombards begged him to assume the Iron Crown [of Lombardy]; a numerous party in Milan wanted to see all Upper Italy united under his scepter. But the Prince, having received his crown from the hands of the Great Powers and having recovered his states by force of their arms, was obliged to rely entirely on the decision of his allies. As Italy had therefore no representative either in Paris or Vienna, and as the powerful enemies of her independence had encountered no opposi- tion, it is not surprising that the latter should have won their case in the peace settlement . . .

It remains to describe the situation in the country today. Sicily and the Kingdom of Naples have gained by becoming subject once more to a single [Bourbon] sovereign; their former relations and their commercial interests demanded this union. Piedmont has recovered its old dynasty; it has a government of its own again and an army. Its annexation of Genoa, necessitated by recent political events, had long been required by nature, for Liguria had trade but no territory, whereas Piedmont had agricultural produce and no market for it. Their reunion should henceforth be the source of greater prosperity for both countries, and greater security. But strong as this state is on the side which faces France, it is exposed where it confronts the Austrian possessions. Moreover, occupying as it does such a limited area, with only a small population and military forces greatly disproportional to those of its neighbors, it cannot but live in continual anxiety.

Austria, possessing the richest and most fertile regions of the peninsula, besides nearly a quarter of the total Italian population, and also holding sway over Tuscany, Parma and Modena through princes of her ruling House, cuts Italy in half and is its actual mistress. On the other hand, by the re-establishment of the entire temporal domain of the Pope, two and a half millions of Italians have been plunged afresh into a state of absolute nullity, and the King of Naples, relegated to the end of the peninsula, has no longer any means of contributing to the defense of Italy; while on the other hand Austria threatens the King of Piedmont on his flank, pressing upon him with all her weight, and by merely calling up her garrisons in Lombardy could sweep down upon him, reach his capital in a couple of marches and destroy his resources.

Hemmed in at the foot of the Alps, the King of Piedmont-Sardinia is continually exposed to the attempts of his neighbors and enjoys only a very precarious independence. His anxiety is all the better founded in that Austria's designs have often been plainly discernible, as in her assumption of the right to garrison the two important positions of Ferrara and Piacenza; in her attempt to rob the King of Piedmont of Upper Novara; in her plan for an Italian Confederation under her auspices (on the precise pattern of the Confederation of the Rhine), and in declaring Alessandria a federal fortress. It may even be said that not only the Piedmontese King but the whole of Italy is more powerless now than before the revolution, owing to the destruction of the Venetian Republic which was the only rampart against the ambition of Austria.

These fears are common to all the states not directly dependent on Austria; but in the provinces directly subject to her rule the situation is far worse.

The government of Austrian Lombardy before 1796 was a sort of national government under the suzerainty of Austria; the laws and customs of the country were respected, and the whole business of governing was in the hands of Italians. This regime was in no sense re-established in 1815. The present government of the Lombardo-Venetian Kingdom has not even any connection with that of the former Kingdom of Italy; it is rather like that of what used to be French Italy. The Lombardo-Venetian Kingdom is an empty name; it merely represents a couple of provinces added to the Austrian Empire, with Venice and Milan as their capitals. The Ministries, Institutions and Establishments of all kinds that helped to give Milan the appearance of a real capital are not suppressed, but this has not benefited any of the other cities. Year after year, in Venice, a number of houses built at great expense on land reclaimed from the sea are pulled down, and in time her beautiful palaces will have been turned into orchards. While the free port of Trieste attracts the merchant shipping of all nations, the port of Venice is entirely deserted. All attempts at restoration have failed. It looks as if Austria herself feels that only Trieste really belongs to her, and that she has merely the usufruct of Venice. Trade communications with the other states of Italy are artificially hampered, while the entry of Austrian products and manufactures is highly promoted, so that Italian products and trade are entirely sacrificed to those of the Hereditary Provinces north of the Alps.

The whole administration, legislation and judicature have been completely altered. Under the new organization a number of native employees have been dismissed in favor of foreigners. The Italians have been given a legal system codified by the Austrians, as though the same laws could easily be applied to different peoples. Any description of the defects of this legislation, both civil and criminal, and the endless difficulties they engender, would exceed the scope of the present account. These innovations are all the more burdensome, in that none of them offers any advantage, or represents any progress or improvement. Among all these alterations only one department of the administration has been kept more or less on the same lines, that of finance. In a condition of profound peace, as much is exacted from the provinces as a conqueror would exact in a state of war—the only difference being that the number and pay of employees have been enormously reduced; there is no longer an army or a navy; public works have all been halted. In fact it is obvious that the Kingdom is looked upon merely as a mine to be exploited, the products of which are to be used to pay the debts and increase the wealth of the provinces so aptly named Hereditary.

But to prevent the mine from being exhausted too soon, all energy, all military spirit must be extinguished; Italy must be thrown back into her old state of apathy, indolence and political nullity. The Austrian cabinet has given striking proof that it realizes this by destroying the Italian army. This army, formerly so numerous and so seasoned, has now been reduced to less than four thousand men, not one of whom has been retained in Italy. The Austrians have done all they could to annoy the officers by subjecting them to frustration of every description, especially by posting them far from their native country, in bad garrisons, and by constantly promoting Austrian officers over their heads. As a result, the majority have resigned their commissions, and the only ones remaining are those whose lack of means leaves them no other resource . . .

Leaving aside any idea of rights or of generosity, and considering only the interests of the other peoples of Europe, is the present state of Italy favorable or not to their peace and prosperity? In all fairness it must be said that, at the Congress of Vienna, considerations of general interest may perhaps have led the Allied Sovereigns to consent to the present partition. The pressing need at that time was the promotion of immediate peace; all other considerations had to yield; and if the subjection of Italy was necessary to the tranquility of Europe, I as an Italian would have consented to seal it at that price.

But will the present political state of Italy help in future to maintain the tranquility of Europe? This is quite a different question. A glance at history will show that Italy has been the object of innumerable wars, and that distant peoples with no natural enmity butchered one another incessantly to gain possession of it. Leaving aside the wars of the Middle Ages, the expeditions of the Frankish

Emperors and the Emperors of Germany, leaving aside the rivalry between the Houses of Anjou and Aragon, and considering only the last three centuries, we see Charles VIII [in 1494] opening the scene with his expedition to Naples, the Italian Princes driving him out, his successor Louis XII returning to the fray and forming an alliance with Ferdinand the Catholic to rob the King of Naples. Having dethroned Ferdinand, they fought each other over the spoils. They joined forces again at Cambrai [in 1508] to destroy the Venetian Republic, and hardly won a measure of success before quarrelling again and covering Italy with blood and tears. Soon afterwards the rivalry between Charles V and Francis I, lasting nearly half a century, brought the whole of Europe under arms and turned Italy into a huge field of carnage. Princes were dethroned, republics destroyed, cities plundered, the countryside devastated.

Italy has never recovered from the sufferings she underwent at that period. But she was not the only one to suffer: Flanders, Lorraine, Provence, Navarre and Germany too, had become so many battlefields on which the claim of Francis I to the Duchy of Milan were disputed. Religious quarrels weakened France for a time, but on recovering strength under the ministry of Richelieu she again began fighting the House of Austria for the control of Italy. There followed the wars of succession to Montferrat, the war of the Valtelline, further wars during the minority of the Duke of Savoy, and the expedition of the Duc de Guise to Naples. Louis XIV's greatest captains, Catinat and Vendôme, exerted all their skill in efforts to make France the ruling power in Italy. The long-drawn-out unrest having subsided, an interval of peace had hardly begun when in 1718 Spain attempted to recover the Two Sicilies. War came again in 1733 to establish a Bourbon in Naples and an Austrian in Tuscany. Another war began in 1745 to establish a Bourbon ruler in Parma. And what of the events we ourselves have witnessed? After all this fighting and bloodshed we are just where we were before, and yet the triumph of Austria will still allow France no peace.

These examples ranging over several centuries prove that there will always be blood to shed until Italy is left alone, with all foreigners alike excluded. Neither France nor Austria will ever consent to yield to the other. Neither of them will feel safe while the other has a foot in Italy. And so, half through fear, half through cupidity, they will continue to disturb the tranquility of Europe. Even if they agreed to share Italy between them, they would still be in a constant state of suspicion, each of them thinking out a way of increasing her share or driving out her rival altogether. It is obvious, therefore, that so long as this rivalry subsists, Europe can hope for no real peace. The only means of extinguishing it would seem to be the establishment in the north of Italy of a state strong enough to defend the Alps and bar the gates of Italy to all foreigners. The frontiers of such a state are defined by nature: the Alps and the Apennines naturally enclose the basin of the Po, that lovely valley which starts at the foot of Mont Cenis and ends under the mountains of Carniola. Language separates the Italian Tyrol from the German Tyrol, and the various Venetian states from the Illyrian. And not only mountains and languages, but customs, habits and affinities play their part, for Piedmont has nothing in common with the Dauphiné, nor Venetia with Austria; whereas each part of northern Italy is at exactly the same stage of civilization; there is a general consensus of opinion and a community of interests; in fact, in many ways the inhabitants resemble one another far more than they do those of Tuscany, Rome or Naples.

Northern Italy, excluding the Duchies of Parma and Modena, would have a population of seven or eight millions. A state of that size could not give rise to jealousy. Situated between two Great Powers, each of which has more than three times its population, it would hardly be able to maintain its independence without the help of Russia. Two hundred years ago Henry IV himself perceived this truth, and suggested placing the House of Savoy on the throne of the Lombard Kings. The natural course of things and the wishes of Italy now demand this solution. The House of Savoy is the only truly Italian dynasty which still survives, and it may well be of importance to the peace and stability of Europe that the Iron Crown [of Lombardy] should be assumed by princes who are neither Habsburgs nor Bourbons.

Let it not be thought, from the ideas I have formulated on the state of my country, that I desire any further upheavals. I share the wishes of the friends of peace. But it is precisely for the sake of peace that I think it useful to stress the factual truth: desire by outsiders for the possession of Italy having been the source of so many wars, nothing short of her liberation will place the stability of Europe on a firm foundation and ensure its tranquility, in so far as such things are possible in human affairs.

> [Memorandum by the Piedmontese ambassador, Count Cotti di Brusasco, to the Czar Alexander, March 1818: *Storia documentata della diplomazia europea in Italia dall' anno 1814 all' anno 1861*, ed. N. Bianchi (Turin, 1865), vol. I, pp. 443–55]

In Lombardy and Venice after 1815, some Austrian administrators (including Prince Metternich) at first favored ruling with a light hand and introducing quite considerable reforms. Much of the Napoleonic legislation was retained, and in some respects was improved on. Unlike Piedmont and other Italian states, ecclesiastical privileges here were restricted and the clergy were not exempt from the ordinary laws. Economic policies were relatively enlightened. The civil service was on the whole more able than elsewhere, better trained, more experienced, and less obsequious to the privileged classes.

Metternich's reformism, however, was frustrated by the centralizing spirit of the emperor. Decisions were referred to Vienna on even quite miniscule points, and this made the administration seem inordinately slow and remote. Taxes remained high. Customs barriers were restored for a time even between Venice and Lombardy. No longer was there a local Lombard army as there had been under Napoleon, but conscription was used to obtain recruits for the Austrian forces. Any political concessions were unthinkable, and this was bound to cause trouble in a country which was the richest and best-educated part of Italy. Economically these Italian provinces were regarded as an important part of the Austrian Empire. Politically, too, they had to be kept submissive, for any example of unpunished rebellion might have triggered off other movements in Hungary and among the southern Slavs.

Metternich to the Emperor Francis, November 3, 1817

OF ALL the Italian governments the Piedmontese is indisputably the one which calls for the most anxious attention. This country unites in itself all the different elements of discontent, and from this point of view I find Manzi's representation correct. [Count Tito Manzi was an Italian who was in the Austrian service and had been employed formerly by Napoleon's Kingdom of Italy.]

His remarks on the anxiety which the arming of this power must create are not so just. The King of Piedmont-Sardinia constantly occupies himself since his restoration with the formation of his army, and chiefly with the preparation of the means of bringing it quickly to a strength out of all proportion to the population and finances of his states. However, the results have not so far corresponded with his efforts or his expectations.

I observe, too, that notwithstanding the widespread and well-founded grounds for dissatisfaction in the Sardinian states, and even in Genoa, which bears the yoke of Piedmont with great impatience and does not conceal its annoyance, a revolutionary movement is not to be feared in this country. Consequently, it is the intrigues of the Turin cabinet alone which require our careful observation . . .

I have for some time been certain of the existence in Italy of several secret fraternities, which, under different names, foster a spirit of excitement, discontent, and opposition. The designs and resources of these, their leaders and relations to each other and to foreign nations, are all points needful for us to discover in order to form an estimate of the dangers which may grow out of them for the peace of Italy. Two years of active and unbroken observation convinced me that the actual existence of these different sects cannot be denied, and if their tendency is mischievous and in opposition to the principles of the government, on the other hand they fail to enlist leaders of name and character, and lack central guidance and all other necessary means of organizing revolutionary action. In design and principle divided among themselves, these sects change every day and on the morrow may be ready to fight against one another. Manzi is here, I believe, quite right when he observes that the surest method of preventing any of them from becoming too powerful is to leave these sects to themselves.

If these explanations are for the moment less disquieting, yet we must not look with indifference on such a mass of individuals, who, more or less adversaries of the existing order of things, may easily be led to disturb the public peace, especially if they are ever united by the alluring pretext of Italian independence.

England has for the moment relinquished these chimeras, and since she gave her consent to the union of Genoa with Piedmont and the withdrawal of the Bentinck constitution in Sicily, she has almost entirely lost the confidence of the Independents.

> [*Memoirs of Prince Metternich 1815–1829*, trans.
> Mrs. Napier (London, 1881), vol. III, pp.
> 97–9]

*Memorandum by Count Strassoldo, the Governor of Lombardy,
to Prince Metternich, July 29, 1820*

THERE ARE enough troops in Lombardy to maintain public peace
and calm, for the Lombards will never revolt unless success is
pretty certain. Hence, whatever the outcome of the present unrest
in Naples, even if we were faced by an effective constitutional
government managing to restore law and order, our garrisons in
Lombardy would still be adequate to hold down the liberals; and
this is true despite the considerable numbers of liberals, and despite the unfortunate example of Naples. The liberals will restrict
themselves to attempts to corrupt public opinion, by meeting and
corresponding secretly, and mere café talk.

There would be no real danger even if the fires of revolution
extend to the Papal States (a danger only too likely, even though
the actual moment may be remote). The example would have
harmful results here in Lombardy and protests would increase, but
even then I could always guarantee law and order save perhaps for
minor incidents, at all events so long as our troops remain at their
present strength.

But if the political plague infects Piedmont—and, as I need not
enlarge to Your Highness, the Piedmontese army is the only one
that could by itself cause a revolution—then the threat would be
too close, and our present garrisons would be unable to give Lombardy complete protection.

If, as I hope with all my heart, our august master should agree
to send substantial forces into Italy and assure quiet throughout
the whole peninsula, then there would be less reason to fear insurrection in Lombardy than anywhere else. If—and Your Highness
will be so kind as to forgive such suppositions made by a provincial
governor inexperienced in high politics—one army corps were sent
to Naples and another perhaps to uphold legitimacy in Piedmont,
all we would need here would be some relatively weak garrisons
under the command of a man such as Count Bubna, whose very
name is a term of praise—so long, at least, as other troops were not
far off and our main military operations were victorious, as cannot
be doubted. But we must not blind ourselves to the fact that, in
taking the necessary measures, we would have to combat that force
of inertia which the nationalists use against us whenever they can
do so without risk. Disaffection and continual alarm would make

administration very thorny and difficult. But it is unthinkable that Austrian soldiers should fail in expeditions of this kind, so there is no point in enlarging on the grievous consequences of failure.

As things now stand, I cannot see any immediate peril, and I hesitate to presuppose its existence where the Papal States and Piedmont are concerned; yet danger there is for all that, because (and this is a very painful truth) our Italian possessions at this moment are guaranteed by physical force alone; moral force we lack entirely.

Let me assure Your Highness that this is no wild talk (and what civil servant would dare mention such things without good reason?). The old nobility and that class which is attached to what is here called the old regime (that is to say the pre-Napoleonic administrative system of 1796) failed in 1815 to secure the restoration of that regime; they have witnessed instead the virtual consecration by present laws of the abolition of all aristocratic privileges, as well as the confirmation of most French innovations. As a result, they have lost all the friendly feelings toward us that they carefully retained during the revolutionary period. The unenlightened clergy, that is to say the majority, are more upset by us than even by Bonaparte. For instance our anti-papal laws, especially our marriage law which they are forced to apply, to say nothing of our schoolbooks which have been put on the Roman *Index*, these are worse than anything imposed by Bonaparte even when he held the Pope captive at Savona. So this class of clergy uses its vast influence over the people to the government's detriment. The Third Estate is generally too constitutionalist and liberal to like a government that is upright and paternalist but which does not adopt the demagogic slogans of the age. The shopkeepers have been seriously damaged by restrictive practices that have dried up the springs of the country's prosperity —and, as for a long time they used to provide nearly all Italy with foreign products, they are bound in some degree to join the chorus of discontent. Finally those who are in the civil service (and I feel particularly obliged to say this) carry out their duties with ability and uprightness on all occasions, but are far from inspired by that active and passionate zeal which we need so badly at this time—a zeal which now finds an outlet only in party politics. *A truly zealous party is just what we lack in Lombardy.* However much I look at Milan and the Lombard provinces (except the Valtelline), all I find are either people who would obey any government whatever, or else adherents of an *ancien régime* which it would be impossible for us to re-establish, or else a large number of more or less incorrigible liberals: the last are the only active people, and unfortunately they are in opposition to us. This makes it easy to diagnose the real state of things: it points to the conclusion that in the last analysis we are reduced to using force, and only on force should we base our calculations for the future.

However unfavorable the picture I have drawn, it is far from exaggerated; it is an accurate account of what no one responsible for public quiet in Lombardy can or should pass over in silence.

All that now remains for me to do is to describe to Your Highness one of the principal causes for the total absence of any political party on our side.

Always, and in Italy just as all over the Empire, the government of our adorable Monarch is paternal, just, gentle and generous. The peoples of Lombardy and Venetia enjoy (as even our enemies admit) all the advantages for which constitutional governments are extolled. There is equality before the law, equality in taxation, a wide toleration, and no arbitrary governmental behavior. Splendid public works have been undertaken and completed. General education has been raised to a level far higher than under the Italian government. Nothing, or very little, is lacking in comparison with the very best governments in Europe.

But in the eyes of His Majesty's Italian subjects, all these advantages have not been sufficient to compensate for one simple fact that has irritated their national self-esteem in such a way as to make them lose sight of the many advantages that they really enjoy.

The Lombards have been and always will be unable to get used to the Germanic forms imprinted on the government of their country; they loathe them, and they detest the system of uniformity by which they have been put on a par with Germans, Bohemians and Galicians.

Now this uniformity, which so prejudices the attachment of the different peoples of the Austrian Empire to their august monarch, persists in all its strength, and this despite the fact that His Majesty has on a number of occasions and in no mean terms expressed his will that his Italian peoples should not be completely subjected to laws and forms designed to meet quite other needs, characteristics and customs.

[*Zeitschrift für Social- und Wirthschaftsgeschichte* (Weimar, 1895), vol. IV, pp. 127–31]

Austrian police measures gradually became harsher, especially after the spread of secret societies. A distinguished Milanese literary magazine, the *Conciliatore*, was closed down in October 1819 after one year of life. One of its sponsors, Count Confalonieri, became involved with the secret societies, and this led to his imprisonment in distant Moravia. His colleague, Porro, who in 1814 had actively supported the Austrian invasion, fled the country just in time. Gioia, Romagnosi, and Silvio Pellico were among other famous Lombard intellectuals who suffered a greater or lesser degree of police persecution. The province of Venetia was more easily controlled. Venice and Trieste were the only two seaports in the immense Austrian Empire and they therefore required special attention.

Secret orders to the Austrian police in Venice, c. 1820

ALL THAT might immediately concern the sovereign interest of His Imperial and Royal Majesty, and of the administration and integrity of the state, are the special concern of the Director-General of Police and the secret service. Their duties include:—

1. Seeking out and unmasking conspiracies, plots, plans, undertakings and enterprises which tend to endanger the safety of the sacred person of His Majesty, of the august imperial house, of the constitution of the state; and in general all influences that might be detrimental to the internal and external public safety of the monarchy.

2. *Unmasking unions, associations, corporations, secret societies and sects,* whether they be ostensibly religious or not; the respective relationships between national or foreign members and partisans of such societies; promoters and propagators of sects, etc., etc.

3. *Watching and directing public feeling in all classes of inhabitants, and their views on political events;* surveillance over anyone who exercises a major influence on public feeling and over anyone who invents or propagates false, faked or alarming news; keeping a watch on remarks, judgments, complaints or desires made about public dispositions and measures, such as those regarding the employees and the administration of the state in general; also on the effect produced upon public opinion by theatrical representations, etc.

4. *Keeping a watch over the influence* on public opinion *of gazettes, newspapers, pamphlets, books or pictures* of any sort, but especially *if they are of a political nature* (whether they be of national or foreign origin, passed by the censorship, with or without

restriction, or prohibited); the strictest vigilance over the devices by which booksellers or sellers of printed matter or pictures may attempt to market prohibited writings or other material, or by which such writings may be clandestinely introduced and disseminated by some other individual; and the strictest control on the way in which offices for revising and censoring books, etc., fulfill their particular functions regarding manuscripts, and especially foreign literary productions which arrive in the realm already printed.

5. *The most scrupulous control in the widest sense over all branches of public administration, and vigilance over the official and domestic behavior of individual employees, servants, and guards generally*, and of all those persons who are employed by any public treasury, institute of education, in administration, or any other branch of public service; the surveillance *of the conduct, doctrine and any statements made by the clergy abroad;* the watching over *the bearing and spirit of the military of every arm and of the various branches of security guards.*

6. *General control over the implementation of sovereign orders and prescripts, of regulations of the higher offices, and of laws in general.*

7. *Surveillance and control of foreign consuls, of diplomatic personnel and other agents of foreign powers*, whether accredited or secret, *of emissaries, adventurers, travelers*, etc., especially of their machinations and contacts—not only those they cultivate in the city of Venice and in the Venetian provinces, but those they may have in the rest of the realm, and abroad.

8. *Gathering and obtaining information on the conduct of public affairs and on public opinion in foreign states bordering on Italy,* but also in the different *states of Italy*, and having in view particularly the Ionian Isles, Malta, Greece and the rest of the Levant; and wherever possible collecting information regarding states and countries still further away insofar as such information may reach the various agents operating in Venice by means of shipping, merchants' letters, couriers, or other travelers.

9. The despatch of agents and men of trust, in the case of *events of vital importance for foreign states*, especially with a view to warlike activities and in actual time of war, and in general all the dispositions necessary to *form and maintain* secret espionage over

and Royal Majesty that suitable means should be employed to make foreign subjects or employees betray their respective duties toward their own governments, or vacillate in fulfilling them.

10. *The secret service* should be ready to use salaried or voluntary *confidants* as well as *surveillance over private correspondence*. For this delicate service use can be made of other channels or means, to seek out and unmask revolutionary or other plots and associations of a criminal character.

> [*Carte segrete e atti ufficiali della polizia Austriaca
> in Italia, dal 4 giugno 1814 al 22 marzo 1848*
> (Capolago, 1851), vol. II, pp. 267-9]

3. The Revolutionaries, 1820-1832

The carboneria was one of many loosely organized secret movements. It was especially strong in Naples, but had affiliations throughout Italy and further afield. Although its political program was thoroughly indeterminate, it represented a number of minor grievances and had some importance as a generalized movement of protest. Some of its followers wanted constitutional government; some simply wanted more personal freedom and lower taxes, or were being nostalgic for Napoleon's "career open to talents." Until Mazzini arrived with a more positive patriotic doctrine, carbonarism was a focus of discontents which undermined loyalty to the restored monarchies after 1815.

The secret societies were particularly strong in the Neapolitan army; and when, early in 1820, the Spanish king was forced by his army to adopt a constitution, the example led to a small rising in a military unit near Naples. The government of the Neapolitan Bourbons, though in some ways reasonably enlightened, was spineless, and with little pressure King Ferdinand was persuaded to yield. Just because the Spanish constitution was available, this was the type of government now proclaimed at Naples. There seems to have been no widespread popular support for the army, and there was little sign anywhere of much "Italian" feeling. Nor were the parliamentary leaders who now emerged consistently liberal. When Sicilians took the chance to rebel and ask for a constitution of their own, the parliamentarians at Naples refused to recognize what they called an illegal government born of violence, and an army was sent which soon brought Sicily to heel. By this time Ferdinand had prepared the way for a counterrevolution, and with the help of Austrian troops he restored absolutist rule early in 1821.

Meanwhile, at Turin, another military rising had taken place. Piedmont had shown herself one of the most reactionary of all the Italian states. King Victor Emmanuel I had returned in 1814 wearing his powdered peruque and pigtail as a sign that the clock was being put back to before 1789. He pursued no individual vendettas, but French appointees lost their jobs, Roman law came back to replace the *Code Napoléon*, feudal customs were restored, and the aristocracy got back their privileged position in the army (and their monopoly of boxes at the opera). Jews and Protestants lost the equality of treatment they had enjoyed from the French. There was even talk of destroying the fine "jacobin" bridge which Napoleon had built at Turin over the Po, and of stopping traffic on his new-fangled road over the Mont Cenis. Half a dozen internal customs barriers were also restored to cut off different parts of the kingdom from each other.

Dissatisfaction with this took many forms. In Genoa and Savoy, regional movements of protest began to take shape against the unenlightened police rule of Piedmont. Some democratic and carbonarist elements were present in the army. Other secret societies, notably the *federati* and *adelfi*, were fashionable among some elements of the Piedmontese aristocracy: these were generally hostile to anything so democratic as the Spanish constitution, but they were anxious to obtain liberal reforms, and some of them hoped to persuade the king to defy Austria and annex Lombardy. News of the constitutional movements in Spain and Naples reinforced the wish for change. At one point the students took over the university and had to be dispersed by a saber charge.

Santorre di Santarosa, an officer in the guards, was the leader of a small group who were ready to use force. He tried, but failed, to persuade Cesare Balbo and his other aristocratic friends to make a common front with more democratic elements and so use the prevalent discontent to obtain positive reforms. From Charles Albert, a cousin of the King, some encouragement was received for a revolutionary plot. In March 1821, army units took over Alessandria and marched on Turin. The king abdicated, appointing Charles Albert as temporary regent, and the latter then formally introduced the Spanish constitution. But many of the *federati* strongly disliked this, and the division proved fatal. Ordinary citizens seemed indifferent, and the army commanders quickly turned against Santarosa when the soldiers claimed to elect their officers and voted themselves more pay and rations. Charles Albert saw what was happening and decided to betray his friends. The new king, Charles Felix, then followed Ferdinand's example and asked for Austrian soldiers to enter Piedmont and suppress the revolution. Santarosa fought courageously, but in a skirmish at Novara the royalists and Austrians were easily victorious.

Santarosa's conclusions about his conspiracy at Turin in 1821

I HAVE now finished my painful task as honestly and usefully as I could. My first object in writing was to show that the revolution took place because Piedmont was subjected to an utterly arbitrary government, under which property and persons were unprotected. I had to show that our object was the aggrandizement of the House of Savoy, the consolidation of its power, but also the emancipation of Italy. So our most sacred duty and our dearest affections were alike involved.

I also wanted to demonstrate that our enterprise, however audacious, had good chances of success. But Charles Albert, in whom the nation trusted, confounded our plans by his inaction while in office as Regent, and then by his unworthy flight. Our courage might have restored the hopes he had deceived if the Neapolitan people had not also been unexpectedly betrayed. Men who fluctuate between two different policies can be fatal to their country. A liberal prince whose actions belie his opinions must expect the reproaches of posterity. He will be despised by those against whom he has not dared to fight and whose victory he yet prepared by his feebleness and irresolution.

My intention has also been to show that true patriots will sacrifice their particular political allegiance whenever the larger interest of their country requires it. Once the Neapolitan parliament had adopted the Spanish type of constitution, Piedmontese liberals could not have accepted any other without bringing discord to Italy. By its justice and moderation, our constitutional government then won popular affection and esteem. The result was that the cause of liberty, in spite of misfortune, could be vanquished only by foreign help. But I also had to show how circumstances enfeebled unfortunate Piedmont and rendered our defeat at Novara irreparable . . .

But this is not sufficient, and it is not the sole purpose of my treatise. Italians must examine their country's situation and the weaknesses exposed by the revolt. Ours was the first revolution for centuries which was attempted in Italy without foreign help; it was the first in which two Italian peoples worked together at the two extremities of our peninsula. Its result, I know too well, has been to subject Italy entirely to Austria; but let the Austrians beware; Italy is conquered, but not subdued. Besides, what was

Italy before July 1820? Had it not already been enslaved to the Austrian Emperor by the courts of Naples and Turin when they promised him to refuse to their people any beneficial political institutions? Our late misfortunes have only rendered our position clearer, our servitude more direct, our chains more obvious.

Oh Italians! Even if we must bear these chains, let us not wear them too openly; let us at least keep our hearts free. Young men of my unfortunate country, the future is yours. When full of youthful ardor you leave college and your parents' homes, you will everywhere meet foreigners who humiliate you. No honor or glory awaits you. You cannot be sure you will be allowed even to enjoy your own property, nor is there any pleasure which will not be poisoned by the insults and scorn of your masters and their yet more odious henchmen. They despise you, young men of Italy. They hope that a soft and lazy life will have unnerved you. They think that your courage is of words not deeds. These tyrants smile as they despise you. And if you doubt this, cross the Alps and you will see what the foes of liberty think of you and what her friends have the right to expect from you.

The emancipation of Italy will occur in this present century; the signal has already been given. Our enemies may prepare at leisure their proscription lists, and docile Italian princes may continue to serve Austria, for they would sooner reign by her strength than by law. The Austrians may leave them to do so and thus begin to reap the fruits of their blindness. But all are deceived, because our passion for national independence feeds on the sacrifices which it imposes on us. Austria may retard the moment, but that will serve only to make the explosion more terrible. Our ancestors have given us great examples which will not be wasted; and when another European war shall arrive, when Austria then demands our children and money to support her cause, Italians will perhaps know better how to employ their resources.

Arbitrary royal rule is now confusing the great issue which confronts Europe. Italy is more involved in this than other nations. We have to conquer our national identity and win internal liberties, both at the same time.

> [Santorre di Santarosa: *De la révolution piémontaise* (Paris, 1822, third and enlarged edition), pp. 171–80. An English translation of the first edition appeared in *The Pamphleteer* (London, 1821)].

The secret societies were obviously an ineffective answer for anyone who wanted reforms. They lacked any common belief, their methods were clumsy, and often they disliked each other more than they hated their nominal enemies. Santarosa went to join the equally disillusioned poet Ugo Foscolo in England; like Porro and other exiles from various regions, he lived there by teaching Italian, and he later died fighting for Greek independence. Dozens of other Neapolitans and Piedmontese became professional soldiers in Spain and Portugal.

Giuseppe Mazzini was another man who spent most of his life a refugee in England. When Mazzini wrote of uniting Italy, this was not, as it had been with Gioia, a literary exercise; it was not, as with Bentinck and Murat, a wartime expedient; but it was a sincere and even obsessive conviction to which he was ready to devote his life. All subsequent leaders of the risorgimento, whether or not they knew it and were prepared to acknowledge the fact, learned many lessons from this lonely exile. With astonishing persistence and courage he pounded away at his conviction that patriotism was a religion, and so doing he gradually convinced enough people that it was not only practical politics but in the long run irresistible.

Mazzini did not know Italy well. Born in a middle-class family of Genoa, he had traveled no further than Tuscany when at the age of twenty-six he fled abroad. His many enemies never tired of giving this as the reason why he remained so confident about the possibilities of an Italian revolution. Mazzini, indeed, always remained something of the mystic who was remote from merely material calculations. As well as a united Italy he also envisaged a United States of Europe toward which his Italian nation might lead the way. Somewhat naively he thought that international peace and national independence not only went together but could not help doing so. Believing that political liberties and patriotism were aspects of the same thing, he also advocated abolishing all privilege and building a world where the common people were sovereign.

As is common with prophets, Mazzini's vision often paid scant respect to practical realities. His occasionally totalitarian methods and his uncompromising, religious sense of patriotism are sometimes daunting. But his historical importance is not in doubt. "One cannot execute ideas," was his reply when Metternich, Charles Albert, and Ferdinand of Bourbon killed many of his agents; "but ideas ripen quickly when they are nourished by the blood of martyrs." Unalterably convinced that the common people were always ready to rise—and that moderate liberals, even if they cravenly helped kings and aristocracies to stop revolution, would follow once he had proved successful—he spent his life organizing one insurrection after another, only to find that others in the end captured and perverted the revolution which he had done so much to make a success.

Long afterwards, in the years after 1861 when he had both won and lost, Mazzini looked back to his youth: to April 1821 when he had a vision which changed his life, to 1827 when he became a carbonaro, and to 1831 when he founded "Young Italy" as a school of patriotic republicanism.

Mazzini's recollection of how he became an Italian patriot

ONE SUNDAY in April 1821, while I was yet a boy, I was walking in the Strada Nuova of Genoa with my mother and an old friend of our family named Andrea Gambini. The Piedmontese insurrection had just been crushed; partly by Austria, partly through treachery, and partly through the weakness of its leaders.

The revolutionists, seeking safety by sea, had flocked to Genoa, and, finding themselves distressed for means, they went about seeking help to enable them to cross into Spain where the revolution was yet triumphant. The greater number of them were crowded in San Pier d'Arena, awaiting a chance to embark; but not a few had contrived to enter the city one by one, and I used to search them out from amongst our own people, detecting them earlier by their general appearance, by some peculiarity of dress, by their warlike air, or by the signs of a deep and silent sorrow on their faces.

The population were singularly moved. Some of the boldest had proposed to the leaders of the insurrection—Santarosa and Ansaldi, I think—to concentrate themselves in and take possession of the city, and organize a new resistance; but Genoa was found to be deprived of all means of successful defense; the fortresses were without artillery, and the leaders had rejected the proposition, telling them *to preserve themselves for a better fate.*

Presently we were stopped and addressed by a tall black-bearded man with a severe and energetic countenance and a fiery glance that I have never since forgotten. He held out a white handkerchief toward us, merely saying, *For the refugees of Italy.* My mother and friend dropped some money into the handkerchief, and he turned from us to put the same request to others. I afterwards learned his name. He was one Rini, a captain in the National Guard which had been instituted at the commencement of the movement. He accompanied those for whom he had thus constituted himself collector, and, I believe, died—as so many of ours have perished—for the cause of liberty in Spain.

That day was the first in which a confused idea presented itself to my mind—I will not say of country or of liberty—but an idea that we Italians *could* and therefore *ought* to struggle for the liberty of our country. I had already been unconsciously educated in the worship of equality by the democratic principles of my parents, whose bearing toward high or low was ever the same. Whatever the position of the individual, they simply regarded the *man*, and sought only the honest man. And my own natural aspirations toward liberty were fostered by constantly hearing my father and the friend already mentioned speak of the recent republican era in France; by the study of the works of Livy and Tacitus, which my Latin master had given me to translate; and by certain old French newspapers which I discovered half hidden behind my father's medical books. Amongst these last were some numbers of the *Chronique du Mois*, a Girondist publication belonging to the first period of the French Revolution.

But the idea of an existing wrong in my country, against which it was a duty to struggle, and the thought that I too must bear my part in that struggle, flashed before my mind on that day for the first time, never again to leave me. The remembrance of those refugees, many of whom became my friends in after life, pursued me wherever I went by day, and mingled with my dreams by night. I would have given I know not what to follow them. I began collecting names and facts, and studied as best I might the records of that heroic struggle, seeking to fathom the causes of its failure.

They had been betrayed and abandoned by those who had sworn to concentrate every effort in the movement; the new King [Charles Felix] had invoked the aid of Austria; part of the Piedmontese troops had even preceded the Austrians at Novara; and the leaders had allowed themselves to be overwhelmed at the first encounter without making an effort to resist. All the details I succeeded in collecting led me to think that they *might* have conquered if all of them had done their duty. Then why not renew the attempt?

This idea ever took stronger possession of my soul, and my spirit was crushed by the impossibility I then felt of even conceiving by what means to reduce it to action. Upon the benches of the university (in those days there existed a course of *Belles Lettres*, preparatory to the courses of law and medicine, to which even the very young were admitted), in the midst of the noisy tumultuous life of the students around me, I was somber and absorbed, and appeared like one suddenly grown old. I childishly determined to dress always in black, fancying myself in mourning for my country. *Jacopo Ortis* [the romantic novel written in 1798 by Ugo

Foscolo] happened to fall into my hands at this time, and the reading of it became a passion with me. I learned it by heart. Matters went so far that my poor mother became terrified lest I should commit suicide.

By degrees a calmer state of mind succeeded this first tempest of feeling. The friendship I formed with the young Ruffinis—a friendship which, both toward them and their sacred mother, better deserves the name of love—tended to reconcile me with life, and afforded a relief to the inward passion that consumed me. Conversing with them of literature, of the intellectual resurrection of Italy, and upon philosophico-religious questions, and the formation of small associations (which proved a prelude to the great) for the purpose of smuggling books prohibited by the police, I perceived an opening—even though on a small scale—toward action, and that brought peace to my mind. A little circle of chosen friends, aspiring toward a better state of things, began to gather round me. Of all who formed that nucleus—the memory of which yet lives in my heart like the record of a promise unfulfilled—none save Federico Campanella (now member of the Provisional Committee for Rome and Venice in Palermo) still remain to combat for the old program. Some are dead, some have deserted; and others, though still faithful to the idea, have sunk into inertia. They were to me at that time a group of Pleiads and a salvation to my tormented spirit. I was no longer alone . . .

Whispers were rife amongst us of a revival of carbonarism. I watched, questioned, and searched on every side, until at last a friend of mine—a certain Torre—confessed to me that he was a member of the sect, or, as it was called in those days, the Order, and offered me initiation. I accepted.

While studying the events of 1820 and 1821, I had learned much of carbonarism, and I did not much admire the complex symbolism, the hierarchical mysteries, nor the political faith—or rather the absence of all political faith—I discovered in that institution. But I was at that time unable to attempt to form any association of my own; and in the carbonari I found a body of men in whom—however inferior they were to the idea they represented—thought and action, faith and works, were identical. Here were men who, defying alike excommunication and capital punishment, had the persistent energy ever to persevere, and to weave a fresh web each time the old one was broken. And this was enough to induce me to join my name and my labors to theirs.

And now that my hair is gray, I still believe that next to the capacity of rightly leading, the greatest merit consists in knowing how and when to follow. I speak, of course, of following those who lead toward good. Those young men—too numerous in Italy, as elsewhere—who hold themselves aloof from all collective association or organized party, out of respect for their own *individuality*, are generally the first to succumb, and that in the most servile manner, to any strongly organized governing power. Reverence for righteous and true authority, freely recognized and accepted, is the best safeguard against authority false or usurped. I therefore agreed to join the carbonari.

I was conducted one evening to a house near St. Giorgio, where, after ascending to the topmost story, I found the person by whom I was to be initiated. This person was—as I afterwards learned—a certain Raimondo Doria, half Corsican half Spaniard, a man already advanced in years, and of a forbidding countenance.

He informed me, with much solemnity, that the persecutions of the government, and the caution and prudence required in order to reach the aim, rendered numerous assemblies impossible; and that I should therefore be spared certain ordeals, ceremonies, and symbolical rites. He questioned me as to my readiness to *act*, and to obey the instructions which would be transmitted to me from time to time, and to sacrifice myself, if necessary, *for the good of the Order*. Then, after desiring me to kneel, he unsheathed a dagger, and recited the formula of oath administered to the initiated of the first or lowest rank; causing me to repeat it after him. He then communicated to me two or three signs by which to recognize the brethren, and dismissed me. I was a carbonaro . . .

[After the French insurrection of July 1830, this carbonaro group began to bestir itself, though with little enough of any definite purpose. The Marquis Doria was, however, a spy in the service of the Piedmontese police, and at his instance his *confrère*, Mazzini, was imprisoned in the fortress of Savona.]

During the first month I had no books, but afterwards, through the courtesy of the new governor, Cavalier Fontana—who, fortunately for me, replaced De Mari—I obtained a Bible, a Tacitus, and a Byron. My prison companion was a greenfinch, a little bird very capable of attachment and full of pretty ways, of which I was excessively fond.

The only human beings I saw were the sergeant Antonietti, my kindly jailer; the officer or guard of the day, who appeared at the door for an instant in order to note his prisoner; Caterina, the Piedmontese woman who brought me my dinner; and Cavalier Fontana. Antonietti invariably asked me every evening, with imperturbable gravity, *if I had any orders to give;* to which I as invariably replied, "Yes, a carriage for Genoa."

Fontana, an old soldier, was not without Italian feeling; but he was profoundly convinced that the aim of the carbonari was plunder, the abolition of all religion, the guillotine erected in the public squares, etc.; and feeling compassion for such errors in a youth like me, he endeavored to recall me into the right path by kindness, even going to the point of transgressing his instructions so far as to invite me to drink coffee in the evening with him and his wife, a graceful little woman related—I forget in what degree—to Alessandro Manzoni.

Meanwhile, through the medium of my friends in Genoa, I continued to exhaust every effort to strike a spark of true life from carbonism. Every ten days I received a letter from my mother, unsealed, of course, and previously examined by the agents of the government. This letter I was permitted to answer, on condition of my writing the answer in the presence of Antonietti, and handing it to him unsealed. But these precautions in no way prevented the execution of the plan of correspondence I had previously agreed upon with my friends—*viz.,* to construct the sentences in such a manner that the first letters of every alternate word should form the only words of real interest to them; and these, for better pre-caution, were in Latin.

My friends therefore dictated to my mother the first seven or eight lines of her letter; and I, for my part, had no lack of time to compose and learn by heart the phrases containing my answer.

In this way I contrived to tell my friends to seek interviews with many carbonari of my acquaintance, all of whom, however, proved to be terror-struck and repulsed both my friends and their proposals. Thus also I learned the news of the Polish insurrection, which, with youthful imprudence, I allowed myself the pleasure of announcing to Fontana, who but a few hours before had assured me that all was tranquil in Europe. He must surely have been confirmed in his belief that we had dealings with the devil.

However, the silly terror shown by the carbonari in that impor-tant moment, my own long meditations on the logical consequences of the absence of all fixed belief or faith in that association, and even a ridiculous scene I had with Passano, whom I met in the corridor while our cells were being cleaned, and who answered my whispered communication: *"I have means of correspondence, give me some names,"* by instantly *investing me with the powers of the highest rank*, and then tapping me on the head in order to confer upon me I know not what *indispensable* masonic dignity—all confirmed me in the conviction I had acquired some months before, that carbonarism was in fact dead, and that, instead of wasting time and energy in the endeavor to galvanize a corpse, it would be better to address myself to the living, and seek to found a new edifice upon a new basis.

It was during these months of imprisonment that I conceived the plan of the association of Young Italy (*La Giovane Italia*). I meditated deeply upon the principles upon which to base the organization of the party, the aim and purpose of its labors—which I intended should be publicly declared—the method of its formation, the individuals to be selected to aid me in its creation, and the possibility of linking its operations with those of the existing revolutionary elements of Europe.

We were few in number, young in years, and of limited means and influence; but I believed the whole problem to consist in appealing to the true instincts and tendencies of the Italian heart, mute at that time, but revealed to us both by history and our own previsions of the future. Our strength must lie in our right appreciation of what those instincts and tendencies really were.

All great national enterprises have ever been originated by men of the people, whose sole strength lay in that power of *faith* and of *will*, which neither counts obstacles nor measures time. Men of means and influence follow after, either to support and carry on the movement created by the first, or, as too often happens, to divert it from its original aim.

It is unnecessary here to relate the process of thought by which, after deep study both of the history and the intimate social constitution of our country, I was led to prefix Unity and the Republic, as the aim of the proposed association. Many of the writings reproduced in this edition are upon that subject.

I may, however, state that I was not influenced by any mere political conception, nor idea of elevating the condition of the single people whom I saw thus dismembered, degraded, and oppressed; the parent thought of my every design was a presentiment that regenerated Italy was destined to arise the *initiatrix* of a new life, and a new and powerful Unity to all the nations of Europe. Even at that time, in spite of the fascination exercised over my mind by the fervid words in which France at that day asserted her right of leadership amid the general silence, the idea was dimly stirring within me to which I gave expression six years later—the sense of a void, a want in Europe.

I felt that authority—true righteous and holy authority—the search after which, whether conscious or not, is in fact the secret of our human life, and which is only irrationally denied by those who confound it with its false semblance or shadow (and imagine they have abolished God himself, when they have but abolished an idol). I felt that authority had vanished, and become extinct in Europe; and that for this reason no power of *initiative* existed in any of the peoples of Europe.

The labors, studies, and sorrows of my life have not only justified and confirmed this idea, but have transformed it into a *faith*. And if ever—though I may not think it—I should live to see Italy One, and to pass one year of solitude in some corner of my own land, or of this land [England] where I now write, and which affection has rendered a second country to me, I shall endeavor to develop and reduce the consequences which flow from this idea, and are of far greater importance than most men believe.

At that time even the immature conception inspired me with a mighty hope that flashed before my spirit like a star. I saw regenerate Italy becoming at one bound the missionary of a religion of progress and fraternity, far grander and vaster than that she gave to humanity in the past.

The worship of Rome was a part of my being. The great Unity, the One Life of the world, had twice been elaborated within her walls. Other peoples—their brief mission fulfilled—disappeared for ever. To none save to her had it been given twice to guide and direct the world. There, life was eternal, death unknown. There, upon the vestiges of an epoch of civilization anterior to the Grecian, which had had its seat in Italy, and which the historical science of the future will show to have had a far wider external influence than the learned of our own day imagine—the Rome of the Republic, concluded by the Caesars, had arisen to consign the former world to oblivion, and borne her eagles over the known world, carrying with them the idea of right [*recte*, "law"], the source of liberty.

In later days, while men were mourning over her as the sepulcher of the living, she had again arisen, greater than before, and at once constituted herself, through her Popes—as venerable once as abject now—the accepted center of a new Unity, elevating the law from earth to heaven, and substituting to the idea of right an idea of duty—a duty common to all men, and therefore source of their equality.

Why should not a new Rome, the Rome of the Italian people—portents of whose coming I deemed I saw—arise to create a third and still vaster Unity; to link together and harmonize earth and heaven, right [law] and duty; and utter, not to individuals but to peoples, the great word Association—to make known to free men and equal their mission here below?

Such were my thoughts in my little cell at Savona in the intervals that elapsed between the nightly question of Antonietti and the attempts made to convert me by Cavalier Fontana; and I think the same thoughts still, on broader grounds and with maturer logic, in the little room, no larger than that cell, wherein I write these lines. And during life they have brought upon me the title of Utopian and madman, together with such frequent disenchantments and outrage as have often caused me—while yet some hopes of *individual* life yearned within me—to look back with longing and regret to my cell at Savona between sea and sky, and far from the contact of men.

The future will declare whether my thoughts were visionary or prophetic. At present [in the 1860's] the revival of Italy, directed as it is by immoral materialists, appears to condemn my belief. But that which is death to other nations is only sleep to ours. Meanwhile, the immediate result of these ideas was to convince me that the labor to be undertaken was not merely a political, but above all a moral work; not negative, but religious; not founded upon any theory of self-interest or well-being, but upon principles and upon duty. During the first months of my university life my mind had been somewhat tainted by the doctrines of the foreign materialist school; but the study of history and the intuition of conscience—the only tests of truth—soon led me back to the spiritualism [idealism] of our Italian fathers.

The duty of judging me had been handed over to a committee of senators at Turin; their names, with the exception of one (Gromo), I forget. The promise given to Cottin reduced the evidence against me to that of the carabineer who had seen me in his room with a drawn sword in my hand; while, on the other side, my own assertions counterbalanced his. It was clear, therefore, that I should be acquitted, and henceforth have a fair field opened before me wherein to begin my undertaking.

I was, in fact, acquitted.

> [*Life and Writings of Joseph Mazzini* (London, 1864), vol. I, pp. 1–40; this English translation was presumably by Mazzini himself]

The need for Mazzini's new message could not have been better exemplified than by several minor and uncoordinated civic insurrections which took place in 1831. In the Papal States, which stretched across central Italy from sea to sea, Bologna was, after Rome, the second largest town. The Romagna—or the area taken up by the four northern Legations, Bologna, Ferrara, Ravenna, and Forlì—had formed part of Napoleon's Kingdom of Italy and did not take kindly to being returned after 1815 to rule by Cardinal Legates and the clergy. Here, in the least unprosperous part of the Papal States, there remained a strong feeling of separatism against Rome on the other side of the Apennines. Whereas Napoleon had suppressed the Inquisition and opened the ghettos, the strongly anti-Semitic Leo XII antagonized many people by going to the other extreme. There were many complaints that ecclesiastics obtained all the best jobs, owned the best land, and possessed tax immunities, while laymen suffered considerable legal disabilities in the multitude of different codes and courts which were now restored. Latin was still the language of administration and of the law. The State accounts were secret. Napoleon's attempt to standardize weights and measures had been discarded along with street lighting and vaccination as works of the devil—the same attitude which was shortly to obtain toward railways.

In 1831 there was a short three-week revolt in the Legations. It was essentially a social revolution with very slight patriotic overtones. Just as the movements of 1820–1 had been sparked by events in Spain, that of 1831 was in part the result of the French revolution which brought Louis Philippe to the throne. The first outbreak occurred in the Duchy of Modena. Parma and Piacenza showed little interest, but in the Papal States a provisional government was set up at Bologna. One volunteer fighter here was the young Louis Napoleon Bonaparte who later had a decisive part to play in Italian history. Representatives from various papal towns just had time to devise a constitution for a short-lived *United Provinces of Italy*. But they showed little revolutionary drive, and they refused to make common cause with Modena, which they referred to as a "foreign" city. In response to a desperate papal appeal, an Austrian army once again crossed the Po to keep Italy divided and safe for conservatism.

Proclamation by the provisional government of Bologna, February 8, 1831

CONSIDERING THAT public opinion, as can be seen in a thousand ways, demands an immediate ending of our subjection to the Roman Pontiff:

Considering that, in the absence of other more legal authority, we are empowered by the urgency of the moment and the consent of our fellow citizens to be their only representatives, and hence we must proclaim the manifest wishes of the people:

Considering, moreover, that an expression of the general will is needful in order to create a more legitimate government:

WE THEREFORE DECLARE—

Article 1:—The TEMPORAL power of the Roman Pontiff over this city and province is legally at an end for ever.

Article 2:—A general assembly of the people is summoned to choose deputies who will form a new government.

Article 3:—This will soon be explained in more detail when other nearby cities have joined us and we know how many deputies are to be elected. A legal national representation will then come into existence.

[A. Vesi: *Rivoluzione di Romagna del 1831* (Florence, 1851), p. 15]

Charles Albert, when he became king of Piedmont in 1831, was anything but a liberal or an Italian patriot. He did not reprieve the Piedmontese liberals whom he had betrayed in 1821, for by now he was a thoroughgoing legitimist. He had fought against the liberals in Spain and would have liked to fight to restore the Bourbons against Louis Philippe. Devoutly Catholic, fiercely anti-revolutionary, he at once on his accession signed a military alliance with Habsburg Austria and had to be restrained by Metternich from declaring war on the "immoral" regime in France. Not that he was particularly well disposed toward the Austrians, but he needed their support in defending throne and altar against the revolution. Like Victor Emmanuel I, he married a Habsburg archduchess; his son, the future Victor Emmanuel II, was married at Charles Albert's wish to another; and his sister married an Austrian archduke.

Against this man and all he stood for, Mazzini from Marseilles and Switzerland planned another revolution based on Genoa, a town which had many grievances under Piedmontese rule. The plot was betrayed and put down in 1833 with extreme severity, for the King was frightened to find that elements in his army had been corrupted by the impious doctrines of Young Italy. Mazzini was condemned to death *in absentia*. So was Giuseppe Garibaldi, whose task had been to help start a mutiny in the navy. The abbé Gioberti, another future hero of the patriotic movement, was imprisoned for several months and then exiled.

Garibaldi had been born at Nice in 1807. He was a sailor by profession, but in long years of exile he was to become a specialist in guerrilla fighting and make himself the most distinguished Italian general of modern times. Jessie White Mario, an Englishwoman who was a close companion of both Garibaldi and Mazzini, describes them when they were both fugitives from Charles Albert's police.

Garibaldi's first encounter with Mazzini

EVEN THE Emperor of Austria had not yet executed fourteen youths in cold blood! Charles Albert did yet more; he conferred the grand cross and the grand cordon on all the savage executors of his barbarous commands. Naturally, as soon as the first arrest commenced, all who feared a similar fate escaped across the frontier, some reaching France, some Switzerland, others wherever the vessels they could get on board landed them. One of these, G. B. Cuneo, of Savona, a youth of considerable talent, and a devoted member of the association of Young Italy, chanced to be set on shore at Taganrog [northeast of the Crimea], where Garibaldi, as he tells us, had landed from one of his voyages.

Patriots and exiles had now but one idea—to avenge their murdered brethren by carrying out the object for which the young martyrs had been sacrificed. Cuneo was telling the history of their fate, and the plans for freeing and uniting all Italy, to a number of sailors assembled at a little inn in Taganrog. Garibaldi, who had -been much excited by his visit to Rome, who, on his return voyages to Nice, must have heard from time to time the terrible stories of Central Italy, Lombardy, and now of Piedmont, was already worked up to that state of mind in which a desire to redress the wrongs of his countrymen, to set slaves free and send tyrants to their doom, was only restrained by his utter want of knowledge of how to set about it. He entered the room as Cuneo was holding forth, listened attentively to all his arguments and entreaties; then with one bound reached him and clasped him speechless to his heart. From that day he became the intimate friend of the "believer," as he called the man who initiated him in the doctrines of Young Italy, and from that hour devoted his whole life to the redemption of his country; went purposely to Marseilles to find out Mazzini, and in one single interview they settled their plans.

Partisan biographers, who would fain erase the Young Italy's membership from their hero's life history, represent Garibaldi at the time of that interview as a daring, artless youth led blindfold by the arch-conspirator to his doom. Now, Garibaldi was never led by anyone against his will, and knew far more of the world and its ways at six and twenty than did Mazzini at the age of twenty-nine. Reared with the tenderest care by his idolizing mother, Mazzini's boyhood and youth had been passed in the studious seclusion of a home where only a few chosen friends were admitted. With the exception of his one journey to Tuscany, he had seen little of life and men till he was suddenly cast out an exile among exiles, and brought face to face with the first results of his ideas and efforts to ensure the triumph of right over might—to set the few armed with principles against the many armed with musket and cannon. The catastrophe, while it wrung his heart with agony, steeled his soul for sterner deeds. His views of humanity were to the last broad, high, and hopeful. His influence over all with whom he came in contact was extraordinary; men became better by contact with his own nobility and his confidence in theirs; the very intensity of his faith in the destinies of Italy veiled the immensity of the mountains that must be removed before the goal could be reached. A merciful gift of nature, this power of beholding the unseen, to a man destined for a lifelong struggle after a "utopia," an "unattainable chimera," as the whole world called his dream of "Italy united, free, and independent," until it stood forth a realized and accomplished fact! It was precisely the clearness of his vision, the utter, absolute certainty of its reality, that won the tens, the hundreds, the thousands to live and die for its attainment. The martyrs sacrificed by Charles Albert or self-slain had gone up to join the band of waiting witnesses of Italy's wrongs and rights, to prove the willingness of her sons to die, so that she, their mother, might live. What could be the duty of the survivors but to avenge their death and complete their work but just begun?

Clearly the indication of this supreme duty, enjoined with the vehemence of passionate conviction, was calculated to intensify Garibaldi's enthusiasm and strengthen his purpose to devote himself to his country's cause; but we may be also very sure that the immediate plans of action were fully discussed and approved of before he consented to take a responsible part in their execution. Garibaldi had lived in constant contact with facts from his childhood, and for the last ten years his experience at sea and on shore had brought him into the closest acquaintance with them; with facts hard as rocks, relentless as the ocean—facts which might be dealt with successfully by sheer courage and force of will, or be circumvented by strategy and skill, but which could not be ignored or left out of account with impunity. Used to buffet with the waves, to scud with bare masts, close his portholes, and screw his hatches tightly down when a cloud not bigger than a man's hand was discerned by his eagle eye, now he would watch for a fair wind or wait for the turn of the tide; or, if needs must be, trim his vessel to an inch, veer her far out of her course for safety, then dash along before the wind and make for his predestined harbor by a longer route. Prudence and daring were his distinctive and equally balanced qualities, and he brought both of them to bear on his self-sought, consciously accepted task. Drawing upon his own experience of the qualities of men and the best means for securing those needful to his purpose, he would have put the quantity and quality of heroes at a much lower figure than the man whom for the time being he called "master." He, with heroic daring in his heart, had seen much of the unheroic side of life—had dealt with cunning and haggling traders, sordid, heartless, greedy shipowners, who cared nought for the crews and captain if their vessel and cargoes were insured; and he had done battle with ferocious pirates, who would mutilate and murder for sheer spite because others of their craft had been before them with the spoil. Even among sailors, his superiors, then comrades, finally subordinates, he had found more of them ready to throw a cargo overboard than to caulk a gaping seam or pump their arms weary out of duty to their owners; and had often seen a rope's-ending and groglimiting discipline secure obedience where kindness, persuasion, and example had failed. Italy's young knight could count upon his own prowess; with regard to the courage and constancy of the masses he probably had his doubts. The chief of Young Italy, and the scores of fugitives who, halting for refuge at Marseilles, painted Italy as a volcano on the eve of eruption, the Genoese and Piedmontese as thirsting for revenge; the Savoyards themselves ablaze with wrath at the absolute power given to Jesuits and

Catholic priests, to the detriment of religious liberty and peaceful living generally; fully believed that every Italian felt as they felt: even in those days we suspect Garibaldi of putting all this enthusiasm into quarantine.

Still, one likes to dwell on that meeting, fraught with such momentous consequences for Italy's future, between those two men, so unlike in character, in training, in feature, and even in dress, yet so absolutely one in hopes and aims, in singleness of purpose, in capacities of self-sacrifice, of devotion, of constancy, both endowed with the qualities that made them leaders of men, both born dictators for the discomfiture of despots. One can see the muscular, broad-chested sailor, well-knit and stalwart as a forest oak, his long chestnut-golden hair flowing back from the fair and ample forehead, his brows slightly knit, his keen eyes gleaming from under their long lashes, as he entered the little inner room where the chief of Young Italy, condemned already to ignominious death by the King of Sardinia, and sought for by the minions of Louis Philippe, found a precarious asylum in the house of a French citizen. One sees the Chief himself lift up that broad, high, wondrous brow overhung with black masses of softest, finest hair; raise his frail, slender, yet upright form; then, on learning who was his guest, spring forward with outstretched hands and eyes luminous with the fire of genius and the light of holiest passion, to welcome this bronzed, lion-featured, tawny-bearded captain, who had come so far to volunteer his services to Italy in her hour of defeat.

What a contrast, yet what counterparts!

Suffice it, they had met, clasped hands, exchanged their pledge and pronounced their vow. What if, in the future, their notions as to the bést and shortest path to the fixed unalterable goal should differ, their wills and their opinions clash? What if in life they were destined to walk each on his separate, lonely road? Those roads were convergent, and along them both, following in their leaders' wake, martyrs and consecrated victims, pioneers and heroes, marched through blood and torture, through failure and defeat, onward to death and victory. Would that victory have been won, would Italy today be living her third life "of the people," honored among the peoples, a nation peerless among her peers, had Joseph Mazzini and Joseph Garibaldi never met that autumn in Marseilles,

and parted with the "now and for ever" as their watchword from
that moment to their death-hour?

[*Autobiography of Giuseppe Garibaldi* (London,
1889), vol. III, *Supplement by Jessie White
Mario*, pp. 30–6]

4. *Various Views Among the Moderates, 1831-1843*

The Grand Duchy of Tuscany possessed a more tolerant and easy-
going government than others in Italy, with the result that even radical
opinion in Tuscany rarely become immoderate. The Leopoldine legal
code was in some ways better than the Napoleonic; censorship was
fairly liberal, tariffs were lower than elsewhere, and there were some
attempts at land reform. Browning, Landor, Hawthorne, and Trollope
were among the many foreigners who liked living in Florence, and at
Pisa sometimes half the students were from other countries inside and
outside Italy. Here was a favorite refuge for exiles. Vieusseux, who
came from a Swiss family, made his home in Tuscany, and his journal,
the *Antologia*, was the one Italian periodical known if not read in
northern Europe. The fact that some of the Piedmontese aristocracy
regularly sent their children to boarding school at Siena had an important deprovincializing effect on them.

Tuscany took the lead in starting up annual scientific congresses each
autumn which were open to all Italians "from the various Italian states,"
and the inaugural speech at Pisa in 1839 openly called the delegates to
"increase the glory of the Italian nation." This first congress was attended by 421 scientists. Altogether at the first five (Turin 1840, Florence 1841, Padua 1842, Lucca 1843), 685 delegates came from Tuscany, 565 from Piedmont, 460 from Lombardy and Venice, 140 from
the small Duchy of Lucca, 45 from the Papal States, 25 from the very
large area of Naples and Sicily, 25 each from Modena and Parma.

Giuseppe Montanelli took his degree at Pisa University. Thereafter
he was a professor, journalist, soldier, and politician by turns. Strongly
influenced by Mazzini and then by the French socialists, he became a
liberal Catholic and a strong individualist who fitted into no easy
category.

Reform and revolution in Tuscany

AFTER THE revolution in France of 1830, Gino Capponi, Cosimo
Ridolfi and the Marchese Rinuccini (the civic administrator of

Florence) prepared a popular holiday to greet the Grand Duke Leopold on his return from Germany. Their hope was to encourage him to make liberal concessions. Leopold refused their proffered celebrations and, far from making any concessions, became harsher than before. He went so far as to expel Poerio, Giordani and other illustrious refugees who for some years had enjoyed the hospitality of Tuscany undisturbed. Thereupon the three promoters of the festivities took offense and resigned their office as honorary chamberlains at the palace.

It was a lawyer named Ciantelli who, as head of the Tuscan police, had counseled such an outrageous divergence from custom, as he planned to substitute horrific police rule for merely soporific police rule; but when this change provoked a threatening demonstration in Florence, Leopold pensioned Ciantelli and inaugurated a less harsh policy with the *motu proprio* of September 11, 1832. This somewhat restricted the powers of the police minister and allowed some right of appeal against judicial sentences in financial matters.

Then the Grand Duke set his hand to some notable administrative reforms. He modernized the mortgage system; he simplified the execution of justice; he gave women some legal rights; and, yielding to the suggestions of Aurelio Puccini, a councillor who had always pressed for the restoration of judicial methods formerly practiced under the French occupation, he restored magistrates' courts, as well as the old high court and court of appeal. He also allowed publicity for judgments in criminal cases, and various other practices of the French regime which had been abolished in 1814. He handed over the work of the existing police agents to a properly constituted body of *carabinieri*.

But it was the establishment of scientific congresses and a broader system of higher education that did most to increase Leopold II's fame as a liberal prince. When Prince Canino wanted to have scientific congresses as in other countries, he allowed this, though they were prohibited from discussing the moral and political sciences. The first of these meetings was held at Pisa late in 1839, and another, with extraordinary pomp, at Florence in 1841. The chairman of the Florentine congress was Cosimo Ridolfi who, after returning his chamberlain's key and retiring to a villa he owned at Meleto, had there founded an agrarian institute which won high praise throughout Italy. Ridolfi now made his peace with the Grand

Duke and thereafter joined the court as tutor to the heir apparent. This won the approval of certain liberals who were happy to see this man given charge of the future ruler, a youth whom most held in low esteem.

Flattered by the praises of the scientific world, and rewarded in England with an honorary doctorate at Oxford, Leopold II then aimed at drawing Italy's illustrious men of learning to Tuscany, regardless of their political opinions. He appointed Bufalini professor at the Santa Maria Nuova hospital in Florence; he invited Regnoli, Matteucci and Puccinotti—exiles from the Papal States— to the University of Pisa; he gave the chair of astronomy at Pisa to the great Mossotti, an exile from Piedmont. He also enlarged the universities of Pisa and Siena, and gave permission for political economy and the philosophy of law to be taught.

These reforms, however admirable in themselves, provided no real remedy for Tuscany's ills, and police rule still remained intact. Legal reforms gave some help against arbitrary judges, but power over economic cases still lay with the minister-president. The defense of order was handed over to a properly constituted Public Prosecutor, but the investigations preceding trials were left in the hands of police officials, as was also the control of prisons. Though a Supreme Court had been established to maintain a uniform interpretation of the law, the old legislative confusion was not removed. The *carabinieri* took the place of the old police agents, but then the latter reappeared in charge of the *carabinieri* in every police station. University chairs in law were established, but no comment on legislation was tolerated in the press, and when I exercised my patriotic rights by trying to discover why this was so, I was more than once reprimanded by the ministry which notified me of the Duke's intention that university professors should educate good lawyers, not lawmakers . . .

Besides literature, besides university education and some administrative reforms made by Leopold's government, another contribution to the political education of Tuscany came from the secret brotherhoods.

As is well known, the *carbonari* were a political sect born in Calabria as a protest first against the French invasion and subsequently against the Austrians. In 1820–1 they started movements to obtain a political constitution in Naples and Piedmont. They also spread in Tuscany, though without causing any open disturbance. Their Tuscan gatherings, or lodges as they were called, would not be worth mentioning if Fossombroni's attempt to frustrate them had not caused the suicide of Francesco Benedetti, a young man of robust sentiments and author, at the age of twenty-eight, of a volume of good tragedies.

This happened when the correspondence between the Tuscan *carbonari* and the Neapolitan *carbonari* was intercepted. The Florentine police chief asked the ministry's permission to proceed with all rigor, to which Fossombroni, with his usual smirk, answered that Florentine *carbonarism* was just a boyish prank and should be treated by sending the letters to their respective addresses with a police visa attached. Benedetti was one of those warned in this way. He took refuge with a friend who betrayed him out of cowardice; this personal treachery, coming on top of political despair, led him to commit suicide.

After the 1830 revolution in France there was some exchange between liberals in various central Italian cities. Indeed a revolution, just like the one at Modena and Bologna in February 1831, was planned to break out on the last Thursday of Carnival in the Pergola Theater in Florence. Its aim was to demand constitutional government from the Grand Duke. Among those involved were some ex-Bonapartists; their leader was thought to be Guglielmo Libri, who had come back from the three days' revolution at Paris with reassuring views about Louis Philippe's liberalism. The movement failed and was followed by the usual recriminations between the leaders and their followers. It was a year later that some Tuscan liberals organized themselves into a new brotherhood known as *Young Italy*.

The origins of this association may be traced back to the ideas propagated by the *Indicatore Livornese*. Both Guerrazzi and Mazzini, despite notable disagreements, had worked together in the compilation of that little paper. After the suppression of the *Indicatore*, Mazzini had taken to writing articles in the *Antologia* under the signature of "An Italian." In 1830 he visited Tuscany and, together with Carlo Bini, went to see Guerrazzi; the latter had been confined to Montepulciano because of a funeral oration read to the Leghorn academy on behalf of Colonel Del Fante, a local man who had served valiantly in Napoleon's army. The founders of the defunct *Indicatore* then agreed on a bold plan of action.

The central committee of *Young Italy* made its headquarters at

Marseilles whither Mazzini moved when he too was forced into exile. Its first sign of life was a letter to Charles Albert in which Mazzini called on the Piedmontese King to obliterate the memory of his faithlessness in 1821 and take over the task of forming a united and independent Italy. On finding the royal ear deaf to this invitation, they raised the standard of republicanism.

Young Italy set itself two goals: to carry on its apostolate by publicizing its principles in a paper, *Giovane Italia*, which was printed in Marseilles and circulated clandestinely in Italy; and to create a material force sufficient to overthrow the oppressive governments of the peninsula. Its associates were organized in squads of tens and hundreds, each man having to provide himself with a gun and cartridges. Rankers were set under decurions, who were under centurions, and they under committees; finally there was a central committee at Marseilles which, when the means and the moment for taking action were judged correct, would give the signal for battle and establish a provisional revolutionary government.

Neither of these two aims was realized by the new brotherhood, and any idea that the associates of *Young Italy* were in agreement with the principles professed by Mazzini, or that the clandestine legions really represented the material force as it appeared on paper, would be very mistaken.

Mazzini proclaimed as articles of the faith for *Young Italy*: the alliance of politics with religion; a new religious *synthesis* based on belief in *God and the people*; and Italian unity as the initial step toward the European unity yet to come. It was only among a restricted number of associates that this *credo* went at all deep. In Leghorn it appealed to Pietro Bastogi and Enrico Mayer. The first was a rich tradesman who went to Pisa almost every Sunday during the *Young Italy* agitation and intoxicated his student guests at patriotic banquets held under Mazzini's inspiration. The other was a distinguished educationalist, who at the birth of the *Young Italy* movement had thrown himself headlong into the conspiracy and made a swift, dangerous swoop to disseminate committees in central Italy. Guerrazzi, generally viewed as the most hardheaded man of the party, laughed at Mazzini's *credo*. When I first met him and propounded to him the politico-mystical theories to which my enthusiastic temperament, my youth, and my philosophic studies inclined me, he said that we all seemed to him like Arcadian shepherds, that he was going on a different path, but that these different paths might one day reach the same goal. Carlo Bini protested that he could not understand a word of such theoretical matters and spoke of Mazzini as a "dear good boy" who confused reality with the gilded phantoms of his imagination; but one thing he could not forgive was Mazzini's attempt to direct the Italian movement from outside Italy, because, as Bini put it, a ship cannot be steered from the shore. *Young Italy* was in fact quite unlike what the Marseilles paper suggested; it was far from being a society of strict believers in the same political and religious faith. Like other earlier political societies, it was a coalition of potential revolutionaries to whom the negative idea of overthrowing governments served as a social link, while they did not bother about their different opinions on politics or religion.

Under the banner of God and the people, atheists held out their hand to deists, and the vague formula of national unity banded together partisans of a French type of centralization with partisans of federal unity. Guerrazzi was a federalist; but Mazzinianism, in other words the theological-political doctrine of Giuseppe Mazzini, envisaged a very close organization right down to its tiniest sections.

Just as contradictory opinions did not matter, so no one bothered overmuch about the military capacity of those recruited to fight. The decurions and centurions were chosen from among those held in highest esteem for their position in civil life: counts, marquises, rich landowners, doctors and lawyers—most of them complete strangers to the arts of war. Nor was a man's physical strength, courage or initiative taken into consideration when enrolling him. I myself have seen a frightened dwarf taking the oath to this militant society. And this was their way of preparing for the day when the clandestine army was to rise in arms and everyone would have to fight or command in real earnest!

Meanwhile Mazzini was telling Europe of the existence of thousands of *armed apostles* straining for battle; and many of the local leaders, when they contrasted such boasts with the wretchedness of the personnel they themselves had at their disposal, consoled themselves with the thought that their own circumstances were exceptional and that things were better elsewhere. It is always like this in conspiratorial enterprises; there is always the same story of thousands of imaginary combatants, and calculations for one area

are based on hearsay concerning another. Conspiracies directed
by exiles have a further disadvantage, that the leaders find it especially hard to learn from experience. Exiles who wrongly take it
into their heads to run the national movement dream up an imaginary world and give way to incorrigible illusions and obstinacies
that are brought by power; they regard every city or province
where they have two or three correspondents as a key position in
their command; they brag of imaginary forces, and their short-
sighted boasts bring persecution down on the heads of their friends
within the country; they make pedestals for themselves of the
victims of their ill-considered views, and from a safe position in
other countries they advocate profitable martyrdom for their
brothers in danger. The *carbonari* had in one sense been better than
this, for leaders and subordinates had at least been united in common danger; nor were they guilty of such an absurd mixture of
publicity and secrecy.

Nevertheless, though Mazzini bears the heaviest responsibility
for the mistaken guidance given to the Italian political brotherhoods of the *Giovane Italia*, he deserves praise for some good that
he did—not as an exile directing powerless plots involving sacrifice,
but as a writer who expounded spiritual ideals. The Catholic spirit-
uality of Manzoni, Tommaseo and Rosmini had no impact on the
youth of our universities, because, to liberal opinion, Catholicism
sounded like the Inquisition. Post-1830 French neo-religious systems fared better: and in 1832 a small Saint-Simonian clique was
formed amongst the scholars of Pisa. Mazzini's mystical and exalted
message gave impetus to this new movement of ideas. Nor was this
a small service, for, just as it is a supreme misfortune for a nation to
lose faith in ideal truths, every system however imperfect that brings
it nearer to recuperating such ideals must be counted amongst the
most potent aids in that nation's resurrection . . .

The butcheries by the government of Piedmont [in 1833], and
the unhappy outcome of Mazzini's attempted expedition into Savoy
in February 1834, brought to an end·all hopes of the kind of imminent political redemption which the various politico-military
brotherhoods had been preaching.

For some years the exiles refrained from mounting further ill-
considered revolts, but put their sad independence to better use.
Those who were soldiers by vocation went to places where freedom
was being fought for: Borso di Carminati, Nicola Fabrizi and the

brothers Durando joined the constitutional army in Spain, while Garibaldi went to Montevideo where he recruited the Italian Legion that was to become famous for its heroism. Mamiani philosophized in Paris and Gioberti in Brussels. General Guglielmo Pepe wrote his memoirs and a useful book of military instruction. Tommaseo, forced to leave Tuscany for Paris after the suppression [in 1833] of his journal, the *Antologia*, composed notable works in verse and prose, including *Scritti inediti del Padre Savonarola*, which was a masterpiece of political satire, philosophy and style. Mazzini wrote articles on literature and politics in French and English periodicals. He also took charge of a welfare institute for the instruction of Italian workers in London, and ran a small Italian periodical there, *L'Apostolato*. Meanwhile an Italian review, *L'Italiano*, to which the most distinguished *émigrés* contributed, appeared for a short time in Paris.

And in Tuscany, as soon as these merely artificial bonds had been broken and the movement became local once again, the secret brotherhoods ceased to be so authoritarian. Instead they formed spontaneous links in each city, based on those men whose intelligence and valor inspired the greatest trust—and thus became in a sense so many independent centers of revolution. There was no longer any thought of calling the people to arms for ideas that they did not yet understand; rather they were to be made aware of their interests and rights; the Italian was to feel an Italian, the man a man; and the independent brotherhoods did some incredibly hard work in this preparatory apostolate. Every city had a group of liberals who carefully read various illicit publications and maintained relationships with other groups elsewhere. They not only looked after the persecuted, but also those in transit who were recommended— as they put it—by friends. By means of writings, discussions and gatherings they ingeniously inculcated ideas of liberalism into the minds of the common people. Of all the Tuscans, it was among the common people of Leghorn that the religion of the motherland counted its most ardent devotees; and in the Venezia quarter, a substantial number of ordinary workingmen held meetings every Sunday to read some piece of the liberal gospel.

[Giuseppe Montanelli: *Memorie sull'Italia e specialmente sulla Toscana dal 1814 al 1850* (Turin, 1853), vol. I, pp. 32–47]

Many of the moderates had no doubt but that their chief hope for reform without revolution was by promoting foreign intervention in Italy. From the events of 1831 they could learn that much greater co-hesion—on a provincial if not a national level—was needed if they were to obtain reforms in government, and hence they would have to appeal to more conservative, middle-of-the-road elements in the population. But yet more obvious was that only the presence of Austrian soldiers enabled the Pope and the other despots of Italy to continue with their absolutist rule. If this dominant Austrian position was to be challenged, other foreign help would be required.

It was the more promising that Louis Philippe, in the interests of the balance of power, began to challenge the Austrian presence in Italy. At his instance a conference met at Rome, and the major powers (including Austria) then advised the Pope to liberalize his government so that another revolution would become less likely. One of their sug-gestions was to revive some of the old provincial liberties which used to exist in the Papal States. But the papacy did not seem grateful for the advice, and, as soon as the Austrian troops had withdrawn, the papal irregular army of *sanfedisti* was unleashed to commit the most fearful atrocities. Bologna was glad to welcome back the protection of the Austrian troops, and this time the French insisted on themselves gar-risoning Ancona as a kind of makeweight. This dual occupation, which lasted until 1838, showed that the Italian problem was again thrusting itself on the rest of Europe. The inability of the Pope to act as an effec-tive temporal governor was giving a formidable weapon to those who wanted change.

Prince Metternich was the first to bewail that the inefficiency and corruption of the papal government ("both detested and detestable") was a threat to the peace of Italy and of Europe. But his recommenda-tions to Rome for leniency and reform went unregarded, and any move to appoint laymen to high office met the indignant opposition of Cardinal Bernetti and his colleagues. To Palmerston in London the harsh conduct of the Cardinal Legate at Bologna seemed "abominable." Fearful of losing his temporal power, the Pope was being driven into a more and more open condemnation of liberal and national feelings.

Memorandum to Pope Gregory XVI, by Austria, Britain, France, Prussia and Russia, May 21, 1831

It is the opinion of the representatives of the five Powers, that, for the general advantage of Europe, two fundamental principles ought to be established in the states of the Church:—

1. That the government of these states should be placed upon a

solid basis, by means of timely ameliorations, as His Holiness himself intended and announced at the outset of his reign.

2. That such ameliorations, which, according to the expression of the edict of Cardinal Bernetti, will found a new era for the subjects of His Holiness, should, by means of internal guarantees, be placed beyond reach of the variations inherent in the nature of an elective government.

In order to obtain this salutary end, which is of great consequence to Europe on account both of the geographical position, and of the social condition of the Pontifical States, it appears indispensable that the organic declaration of His Holiness should set out from two fundamental principles:—

1. That the improvements should take effect, not only in those provinces where the revolution burst out [in 1831], but also in those which remained faithful, and in the capital.

2. That the laity should be generally admitted to administrative and judicial functions . . .

As regards the municipal administration, it appears that the following should be viewed as the necessary basis of every practical improvement:— the general re-establishment and appointment of municipalities elected by the people; and the institution of municipal privileges, which shall govern the action of the bodies corporate, according to the local interests of the communities . . .

The high importance of good order in the finances, and of such a management of the public debt as may give the security so desirable for financial credit, and may effectually contribute to augment its resources and secure its stability, appear to render indispensable a central establishment in the capital, namely, a supreme Board, charged with the audit of the public accounts for the service of each year, in each branch of the administration, both civil and military, and likewise charged with the care of the public debt, and having powers proportionate to its great and salutary purposes. The more independent such an institution shall be in its nature, and the more it shall present the marks of an intimate union between the government and the people, the more it will conform to the beneficent intention of the Sovereign, and to the general anticipations. On this account we think that it ought to include persons chosen by the municipal councils, who in union with the advisers of the Sovereign should form an administrative *giunta* or *consulta*. This body might or might not form a part of a Council of State, to be chosen by the Sovereign from among the persons most distinguished in birth, property, or talent.

[L. C. Farini: *The Roman State from 1815 to 1850,*
trans. W. E. Gladstone (London, 1851), vol. I,
pp. 58–66]

In the course of the 1830's, even quite moderate opinion in Italy came more and more to think of Austria as the chief obstacle to change, and many private quarrels were forgotten in concentrating on this common enemy. In Lombardy and Venice many Italians continued loyally to serve Austria as soldiers, civil servants, and policemen, but the fact of a common Italian nationality became harder to deny. Three times, in 1821, 1831, and 1832, Austrian troops had been sent to support anti-liberal legitimism in Piedmont, Naples, Sicily, Modena, and the Papal States. The famous Quadrilateral of fortresses, Mantua, Peschiera, Verona, and Legnago, dominated the route down from the Brenner Pass through Trent into the Adige Valley, and from here Austria was conveniently poised for both defense and attack. No other Italian state had a good army. Many Italian soldiers were (like the future army commanders Cialdini and Fanti) away fighting on one or other side of the incessant Spanish civil wars, or like Garibaldi they were serving North African and South American states, or else they were in the Austrian army itself

Until 1848 at least, Milan remained the most lively town in Italy. This was the city of Manzoni and Verdi, of liberal industrialists such as Porro and Confalonieri, of distinguished economists in the school of Romagnosi and Cattaneo. Life in Milan was highly praised by Stendhal. This town became the adoptive home of a Piedmontese author and painter who was to make himself the leading politician in Italy, Massimo d'Azeglio. Lombardy was before other regions in having steam power applied to industry. It had the most newspapers, and was ahead with savings banks and health legislation. Nowhere else was elementary education compulsory and free, and this was perhaps the most remarkable fact of all.

But Lombardy and Venice were also the scene of police harassments and political trials. In the *piombi,* which were the lead-covered prisons of the Doge's palace at Venice, or in the dreaded Spielberg north of Vienna, many new martyrs to Italian nationalism were being gratuitously created. Apart from Confalonieri and Pallavicino, the best known of these was Silvio Pellico who, after ten years in close confinement for a fairly trivial offense, published a book in 1832 about his experiences. *Le mie prigioni* had an enormous vogue all over Europe in dozens of translations, and possibly no other person except Mazzini had such an effect in arousing national indignation. Metternich at once tried to protest that the book contained not a word of truth. He even asked Charles Albert to punish the censor who had allowed its publication, and he tried (but failed) to make the Pope put it on the Index of prohibited books.

Austria was hardly any fiercer with her political prisoners than Naples, Modena, or Turin, and her prisons were no worse than theirs. A certain irony also existed in the fact that Pellico had not intended to write an incendiary manifesto: his idea was to compose a book of Catholic resignation, designed not to stir up resentments against Austria, but rather to demonstrate to believers that God did not abandon those who remained true in adversity. His repentant letters to the chief prosecutor, Salvotti, suggest that he accepted his sentence as not unjust. Yet the conscience of Europe reacted strongly the other way, and the Italian patriotic cause was thus linked with that of humanity and the moral law. An excessively severe punishment, which had been intended as a harsh lesson to conspirators, thus rebounded and became a major defeat for Metternich and his system.

An interview in 1832 between Metternich and Paolo de Capitani, a Lombard in the Austrian service

HIS EXCELLENCY Prince Metternich said to me: "When you judge a country you must first look at its geographical position, then at its history, then at its moral inclinations. The present situation of Italy is such that its northern regions can only be an appendage and possession either of the Austrian Empire or of France."

I answered: "It should belong to the dominant Power in Europe, just as it once belonged to Napoleon; and since his downfall no power other than Austria should or could take it over."

Prince Metternich: "But in Italy there are two tendencies of opinion. One looks to the spirit of revolution and would like an all-Italian kingdom. The other is the old Italian spirit of local sovereignty, of divided princedoms and partial independence. This latter feeling derives from the old Italian republics, and is mainly a matter of municipal sentiment, almost one of family rivalries. Above all you are dominated by family relationships."

Paolo de Capitani: "Historically that is correct. But now things have changed. The spirit of revolution is so strong in the fantasy of a few fools that they dream of Italian nationality and the creation of an all-Italian kingdom. Even Napoleon never went so far. That giant has now fallen, and no political contingency can ever make such a dream come true. As for our predilection for small states, I can assure Your Highness that the leading families of the old republics have died out, and with the extinction of their wealth and power even the memory of them has faded. The Lombard nobility is now connected with the nobility of Germany and France; there is hardly anything of the ancient Italian aristocracy left; now we have marquises appointed by the French, and Grafs and Barons deriving from the German Empire. Moreover there is a clear distinction between the Italians south of the Po and those beyond it."

Prince Metternich: "I quite agree. Northern Italy is divided by the line of the Po. The inhabitants on each side differ in spirit and in their views. As regards the interests of the Austrian Empire, there is also another notable division, that separating Venetia from Lombardy. The Venetian territory belongs to us absolutely. It is part of our states by necessity and this cannot be changed. Lombardy's position is different. In 1814, when the question of taking it over was raised, His Majesty was not very enthusiastic about accepting it. Possibly our strength would have been greater had we stood on the line of the Adige River instead of extending our positions further west. We obtained Lombardy as a result of mere political transactions. It is just a military bulwark. The Venetians are therefore more naturally Austrian subjects than the Lombards. Besides, your character contains a special susceptibility which makes it almost impossible to direct Lombard public opinion."

Paolo de Capitani: "But, my dear Prince, the whole nobility, the whole clergy, and all the rich middle classes, recognize that the basis of their peace of mind, their comforts in life, the safety of the state, the preservation of their prerogatives, of their property, all depends on the power of the Austrian Empire. No one could want any other domination. The French and the Piedmontese are not liked in Milan. We have a real horror of republicanism. Most Lombards are Austrian, first out of interest, secondly because past political vicissitudes have caused widespread disillusionment with any kind of change, and lastly because Italians know their own capabilities pretty well."

Prince Metternich: "But there can be no doubt about what I call your susceptibility. The Lombards were never more Austrian than when they were part of Napoleon's Kingdom of Italy, and yet never more hostile to Austria than under Austrian government."

Paolo de Capitani: "Both go back to the same cause. Public opinion was shocked by the French regime, just as national self-esteem is shocked today. Why, for instance, is it necessary for every notable fortress to be garrisoned by Tyrolese or people from other Austrian provinces? Why give us judges who know nothing of jurisprudence, who can have no knowledge of the laws of our country, and who are continually handing down contradictory judgments? The result is that there is no confidence in the bench. Perhaps judges from outside Lombardy are needed for cases of high treason, but it does not follow that most judges should be outsiders, or that talent, probity, knowledge and even devotion should actually be obstacles to promotion. This is something that happens every day. Good qualities are deliberately penalized in the interests of an exclusive circle of intriguers. The usual principle of conquerors is to refrain from removing the local magistrates from conquered countries. This is right, the more so when there are few other candidates with both the requisite knowledge and impartiality. Yet you also defy this principle with administrative jobs. At the least some Italians ought to be posted in Germany."

Prince Metternich: "His Majesty would like nothing better, but your young men do not want to leave Italy."

Paolo de Capitani: "I beg Your Highness's pardon. In Vienna there is not a single post of any standing held by an Italian. Four and a half million subjects have not a single magistrate in the capital of the empire. At least one secretaryship in the imperial chancellery should have been conferred on an Italian. Marquis Barbò applied for one, but the appointment went to someone who knew nothing about Italian administration, for his experience had been in Venice where different procedures are used."

Prince Metternich: "Your young men are soaked in Italianism."

Paolo de Capitani: "As to that I should say that, since our young men are discouraged and since an official career is closed to them, it sometimes does happen that they are seduced by malcontents. It was another great mistake to dismiss from the Governor's court a number of ladies who had formerly been admitted there. The facilities provided by the Verona Decree partly corrected this, but few people took advantage of them. Many said, 'I won't go back to a house from which I was driven away.' As these ladies were the youngest, the young gentlemen followed suit. No new court uniform for the nobility has been granted yet, which is another reason for their not appearing. Young people are not keen on dressing up in clothes which look as though they have come out of a French farce."

[In *Archivio Storico Lombardo*, (Milan, 1950), vol. LXXVII, ed. Franco Arese, pp. 6–9]

Silvio Pellico to Karl Voigt, February 5, 1835

I HEAR from Manfredo de Sambuy the happy news that my book *Le mie prigioni* resulted in your joining the Catholic Church. This gives me the very greatest pleasure, and I must sincerely congratulate you on what must be the finest event in your life. My book has no merit, but I thank providence it gave you some small help; and I rejoice for both our sakes, since for me too it is truly a benediction.

When I published those memoirs, my only intention was to give witness to the excellence of the Catholic religion and to inspire my readers with elevated thoughts. People with non-Christian passions made out that the book had other more subtle aims, but I understood neither their praise nor their criticism. Only simple souls who took it at its face value could truly understand what I wrote, and I am delighted that you are one such.

[*Il Risorgimento Italiano, rivista storica* (Turin, 1909), vol. II, pp. 135–6]

Very important in delaying Italy's national movement was the absence of a generally agreed national language. Strong regional sentiments had kept many dialects alive which were unintelligible to strangers from other provinces, and these were the normal speech of nearly all Italians. Goldoni preferred to write plays in Venetian, and Meli his poems in Sicilian. Alfieri, like most Piedmontese, could never escape from being basically French by culture. Apart from this, the geographical boundaries which some people were beginning to think of as Italy's natural frontiers contained considerable German, French, Greek, and Slav minorities. Garibaldi's language, as a Niçois, was not Italian but a Franco-Provençal dialect. When Cavour spoke Italian, according to Brofferio, "in fact he spoke a mutilated kind of French, and his mistakes were such that even an Italian dictionary was not much help." Rome itself in the center of Italy had one of the least intelligible of all dialects, and the second language there was not Italian but Latin. The clergy everywhere—and that also meant universities—used Latin as a *lingua franca*, and Piedmont did not abolish Latin as the medium of university instruction until 1852.

A written Italian did of course exist, but it was known only by a small minority and spoken by even fewer, and creative writers such as Foscolo and Leopardi found this a serious handicap. Manzoni's *I promessi sposi* was published in 1827 and became the most popular novel of the century, but its language seemed stilted and awkward even to its author. Then he visited Tuscany and was captivated by the local speech, especially that found at Florence itself. He at once began to study this and, with local advice, to eliminate from his book the Milanese expressions and the dead rhetorical frills which he had used. In the 1830's he made notes for a treatise on the Italian language, though it was never completed. Then in 1840 he brought out a rewritten edition of his novel. Even though not everyone agreed with what he had done, in the end it had a decisive effect in preparing a canon of accepted diction. For a long time yet, however, Italians from different provinces would have to speak to each other in what many of them felt to be a dead language.

The difficulty of creating a national language: notes by Alessandro Manzoni, c. 1833–6

UNDOUBTEDLY THERE exists a written language which the whole of Italy has in common: but how does it emerge from the primary, essential test of every language that it should be written the same way everywhere? Do you find in other countries that certain writers are admired by some as masters and exemplars (I am not talking just of style) while others scorn them? Do you find that some books are laughed at for their strange vocabulary, while elsewhere they are held up as a model? Or that a book can in one place be called uncouth or barbarous at the same time as elsewhere its choice of words may seem not very strange or even positively good?

Perhaps this variety, or indeed opposition, of views about what constitutes Italian arises because of our incorrigible desire to argue about anything or nothing? No, the obvious reason unfortunately is that the same sentiments can be expressed in more than one way. Show me in Italian literature that uniformity of language can go along with variety of style, and I will then agree that Italy is like other countries where this kind of problem does not exist. If you could show me such a uniformity, we could forgo what would then be the superfluous task of trying to create a common tongue.

Granted, too, that over all Italy there is a common spoken language of a kind. But suppose you have a group of Milanese, not just ordinary people, but well-to-do and well educated; and suppose they are talking in the local dialect, as would be the normal custom throughout Italy: then introduce into the circle a Piedmontese, a Bolognese, a Venetian, or a Neapolitan, and watch them give up dialect and try their hand at our common Italian language. Tell me if their conversation goes as before; tell me if those Milanese can touch various subjects with the same richness and sureness of vocabulary. Will they not have to use a generic or imprecise term when before they had a precise one? Will they not use some circumlocution to describe something when before they had identified it exactly, or sometimes guess where before they were certain? Or in desperation perhaps they will use a word they know is not Italian, trying to dress it up to look as plausible as they can. Tell me if those Milanese (and especially the better educated ones) will not suspect themselves of committing some unintentional solecism. Or perhaps they will use some Italian suffix and otherwise try to Italianize a Milanese word or phrase, the very thing they would find ridiculous if others did it. The non-Milanese stranger, too, will he not find just the same, that he lacks the full, ready and sure command of speech that he would have at home? And is this really to possess a language in common?

As I say, it is a general custom in Italy, among all classes and even among scholars, to speak local idioms which are recognized to be such by those who use them. Some people think that this is done out of culpable whimsicality. But it would be a strange whim to use idioms in speech which one would not use in a letter, or in drawing up a legal document, or in taking notes; especially if we recognize those idioms to be somewhat shaming to use in front of strangers, or not very beautiful. Unfortunately there is a good reason for using them. It is, as I have already said, that people in general are unwilling, except when compelled, to use an unfamiliar instrument when they already possess one they know very well. If we Milanese, or all those other Italians who speak a regional dialect, were to throw away our local idiom and use what language we all have in common, we would find ourselves without a large number of lovely, subtle and appropriate expressions. We would lack many terms employed for some of the most frequent and essential actions of ordinary living—for things we see every day, that we have in the house or on our person, or which serve the most basic uses of life.

Existing habits will not change except insofar as we can find a common language which could serve the same purpose, a language which would alter our manner of speech but not lessen our powers of expression. This language will have to be acquired by those who are ignorant of it; but first of all it will have to be identified, and we must secure general agreement on what it is.

> [A. Manzoni: *Opere inedite o rare*, ed. R. Bonghi
> (Milan, 1891), vol. IV, pp. 40–3]

The language problem in Piedmont

"EVEN IN Piedmont [said the Marchioness Arconati], difference of language is our great difficulty: our three native languages are French, Piedmontese, and Genoese. Of these, French alone is generally intelligible. A speech in Genoese or Piedmontese would be unintelligible to two-thirds of the Assembly. Except the Savoyards, who sometimes use French, the deputies all speak in Italian; but this is to them a dead language, in which they have never been accustomed even to converse. They scarcely ever, therefore, can use it with spirit or even with fluency. Cavour is naturally a good speaker, but in Italian he is embarrassed. You see that he is translating; so is Azeglio; so are they all, except a few lawyers who have been accustomed to address the tribunals in Italian." "Why, then," I said, "do not they speak in French? That is a language in which they must be able to think." "Without doubt," she answered, "they would speak better in French: but we should not like to hear French, except from a Savoyard. It would be doubly unpopular—first as not being Italian, next as being French; for, next to the Germans, we dread and dislike the French."

> [Nassau William Senior: *Journals Kept in France
> and Italy from 1848 to 1852* (London, 1871),
> vol. I, pp. 291–2. Entry dated Turin, Novem-
> ber 6, 1850]

A considerable fact in 1843 was the publication (at Brussels, where he was still in exile) of Vincenzo Gioberti's *On the Moral and Civil Primacy of the Italians*. This book hammered home to Italians that they were still a great people despite their superficial divisions and apparent political weakness. It also aimed to provide an alternative program to the dangerously democratic and revolutionary doctrines of Mazzini; because Gioberti and the moderates, far from believing that patriotism necessarily meant revolution, hoped that they might be able to preserve the existing rulers inside a federal union.

Gioberti pinned his particular expectations on the papacy. The neo-guelphs, as his followers were called, rejected the plausible theory of Machiavelli that the Popes, just because they ruled over Rome and central Italy, must always stand firmly against Italian patriotism. It was only unfortunate that the existing Pope was Gregory XVI, who had refused to introduce the mild reforms which even Metternich had recommended, and who recently, in his Encyclical *Mirari vos*, had given an outright condemnation of *detestabilis libertas* and freedom of thought.

It is not easy to be sure of knowing Gioberti's essential thoughts, for he believed different things at different times. Moreover, as a deliberate *ruse de guerre*, he carefully chose his words so that the various Italian censorships would allow his book to circulate and win converts among the lukewarm and the orthodox. There was no criticism of Austria in the *Primato*, for that would have cut off his intended audience. There was no advocacy of constitutional government, but he rather advised Italians to revere and obey their princes. There was no sign in this book of Gioberti's animosity against the Jesuits, and no word about reform of the Papal States. It is even possible that he did not entirely believe what he said about the providential primacy of the virile Italian race and their capacity to imitate the dynamic Prussians. On other occasions he accused his fellow countrymen of a lethargy and moral corruption which hindered their attaining greatness. In private he even showed certain reservations about the papacy as a potential leader of the nation.

Gioberti was a man of erudition and considerable intellect—even if, as Cavour said, he lacked common sense and soon proved to be a thoroughly ineffective politician. Perhaps he had been away from Italy too long. He was pompous and egocentric, and wrote in a long-winded style that some have found unattractive and tedious. Yet the book was very important. For a brief moment many people, including the clergy who were a class with enormous influence, were able to think of the Pope as leading a crusade for the resurrection of Italy. Many who otherwise would never have bothered their heads about politics now found Italy for the first time a legitimate topic of conversation. In particular, Gioberti's condemnation of Mazzini's dream of a completely united Italy led to a federal state being discussed as a possible alternative.

Gioberti wants a federal union under the Pope, 1843

ONCE MY thesis is accepted that the chief cause of Italy's political decline was the barbarian invasions, we must then look for a remedy, and incidentally see if my claims for the primacy of Italy are justified.

I propose to prove that *Italy contains within herself, above all through religion, all the conditions required for her national and political resurrection or risorgimento, and that to bring this about she has no need of revolutions within and still less of foreign invasions or foreign exemplars.* And to begin with I say that Italy must first and foremost regain her life as a nation; and that her life as a nation cannot come into being without some degree of union between her various members. This union can be interpreted and established in various ways, but, however it is achieved, it is a necessity, and if it fails our nation will be weakened and enfeebled beyond repair.

Now given that Italy in order to be happy needs in some fashion to be drawn together, it remains to discover the principle best suited to bring union to birth. I believe that the principle of Italian association should be sought in what is concrete, living and deeply rooted, not in what is abstract and in the air, for states are not governed by chimeras or abstractions. The principle of union must be of an effective, pre-existing kind that becomes national and political as it develops, and that contains within itself an impulse toward this development. Many see such unity already existing in the Italian people, though in my view it is a mere desire and not a fact, a presupposition not a reality, and I do not even know whether its name is yet found in our dictionary. Of course there certainly exists an Italy and an Italian breed, conjoined in blood, in religion and in an illustrious written language, even though divided in governments, laws, institutions, popular folklore, customs, sentiment and habits. The conjunction of this Italian race makes a people in potentiality; but division prevents them from being a people in fact. Were Italians effectively a people it would be pointless and absurd to create a political unity which they would already possess. For unity is the cause, and being a people the effect, not vice versa; whence for example the French, the Spanish and the English are genuine peoples because each has been living in political union for many centuries. This communal way of living is lacking with the Germans who are approximately in the same position as the Italians, though they are nearer union in the matter of a spoken language.

So if we are looking for an Italian union, we must not assume that it is already in process—as do those who wish to procure it simply by means of the people of the peninsula, and who talk of Italians in the same way as they talk of the French, British or Spanish people. Our goal should be that of bringing our potential to a state of effectiveness, but this will not become practical politics unless by means of a principle that is distinct from it, rejecting the idea that cause and effect are one and the same.

Whenever those who rely on an Italian people that does not exist try to be more practical, they have to say that they put their hope in the inhabitants of the various provinces of Italy, that is to say in a number of different peoples and not in the single population of the peninsula; which peoples could perhaps reach an understanding between themselves to abolish their respective governments, thereby making a single state. But this needs too much imagination, because such a convergence among Italians is morally impossible, and anyway it could never bring about the end proposed, that of procuring the desired union of our common motherland. I say it is impossible, because the only possibilities on which the wise man should count in politics must be probabilities. A change that would gravely harm most of those who bring it about is not to be hoped for, however much it might benefit others who came later; because men normally think of themselves and of the present, leaving the care of the future to posterity. Union might also involve an element of risk if it were sought merely to avoid a certain and imminent evil; or if one part of this universality dominates the rest and is motivated to act only by a fury born of extraordinary circumstances. But this is not the case with the Italy of our time, where that tyranny is lacking that can arouse the anger of a whole people and drive it to extremes—lacking, either because of the mild nature of Italian rulers, or because of custom which mitigates even absolute power and saves it from too many gross abuses. Moreover oppression would have to flare up simultaneously in the various states of the peninsula; a thing even more unlikely, and too inhuman to be either expected or desired.

Extraordinary circumstances are thus excluded from our presupposition, just as I also exclude those which as the effect of a revolution cannot also be its cause. Thus the power of the Committee of Public Safety and the National Assembly that kindled the fire in France toward the end of the last century was born of the radical changes already introduced through the Constituent Assembly—which last, incidentally, was able to come peacefully into being because the state had for long been politically united. Now there is no applicable parallel in our country; moreover the political lethargy of Italians has gone so far that it would be vain to count

on any heroic virtue, for magnanimous impulses are rare enough
even in strong peoples. As for an uprising operated by a handful of
malcontents, it is mere folly to think it could succeed against public
force, internal or foreign; since any Power which possesses an
Italian state will always do everything possible to prevent a basic
revolution, while any Power which does not will never raise a
finger to help the revolution but only delude it with pious promises
and then slip into the place of our former masters. It would not be
to my purpose to inveigh against the simplicity of those who believe or hope the contrary, for their attitude provides a wonderful
corroboration of my judgment.

Supposing we succeeded in putting an end to the present division
in Italy by revolutionary means? Far from achieving the union we
desire, we would be opening the door to fresh disorders. For
political union cannot bring happiness to a people if it is confused
and vacillating instead of tranquil and stable. The principle of
public peace and security must be sought in the sovereign power,
whatever form it may take; because without sovereignty there is
no order, and without order there is neither peace nor security nor
free living nor any other civil good. The sovereign power is based
partly on moral force, that is to say on law, and partly on material
force, that is to say on the army; and although, given human wickedness, arms are needed to protect public opinion, they cannot replace it, for it is impossible to restrain a few malcontents unless
there is a general consensus among many men of good will. Only
moral authority can justify a sovereign power, it being inconsistent
that others should be expected to obey a system of rule that they
think it morally legitimate to offend or annihilate.

Now there are two kinds of revolution: one kind changes the
state without essentially violating its sovereignty; the other turns
it upside down and aims at founding a new state on the ruins. The
first kind can occur when the sovereign power is divided, and when
one part of it, being unjustly attacked by the other, rises up by
right of self-defense; this kind is lawful, but is not applicable to
states where the whole sovereignty is gathered together in the
person of one ruler. The second kind of revolution is illegitimate
for it seeks to uproot law and open the door to anarchy, that worst
of all evils which inevitably develops as soon as force has become
capricious and arbitrary. Thus it is that, when such changes take
place, law and order do not return unless the former rule is sub-

stantially restored purged of the abuses that brought about its ruin.

We can see this in the French Revolution of 1789 when every lawful power had been suppressed and the state was given over to the fury of the people, the tyranny of the demogogues and the arbitrary will of a soldier; order was restored only when the heirs of the former princes were recalled, and that part of sovereignty was re-established that was theirs by law, before royal ambition had turned a moderate monarchy into despotism. The latest revolution in France, that of 1830, provides an example of both kinds of political change, the tumultuous and the regular, the violent and the lawful, the illegitimate and the legitimate, according to whether we are considering the action of people or parliament. To the extent to which it was born of the sovereign power and preserved the substance of the old, it produced a stable government; but insofar as it was accompanied by popular revolt, the new government could not get rid of disturbances and conspiracies, and even today is not cured of the vices of its origin.

Really violent revolutions benefit no one except insofar as they purge society of the bad humors that afflict it. On the contrary, they strike down people and princes with unspeakable ills that are terrible to recall. Only when disorder has reached its peak is the ancient order gradually reborn; but owing to the destruction of its component parts and the bad habits acquired in the interval, much time and hard work are needed to re-establish it. Now this would be the nature of the revolution, or rather revolutions, in Italy if certain people had their way; for the customary and time-honored mode of life would be replaced by a merely theoretical state, a weak nonexistent government with no roots in the past, with no strength in the present or trust in the future, and incapable of holding down the political factions, provincial rivalries and municipal hatreds which would quickly turn the country upside down and open the road to a worse version of what had gone before. Anyone with doubts about this should take a look at Italian history over the last half century, and he will see in those fifty years of shame and pain a picture of what would happen if Italy returned to the path of revolutions after having several times tried it with grievous results.

There remain those who want political unity and yet would like it brought to us by foreigners: as to which foreigners, most favor the French, others the Germans. This is undeniably a bold hope, but against it stands the immutable nature of things and the experience of twenty-five centuries. If such a belief contained any aspect of harmlessness and plausibility I would not have the heart to argue against anyone who cherished it. In fact, however, the idea must be ruled out as absurd; because it is thoroughly contradictory to want a nation to depend on outsiders for its independence and receive from the outside something that can only be achieved when native and spontaneous. I would go further and say that it is cowardly and blameworthy to deny Italy's autonomy or to despair of the intrinsic courage of twenty million people, whatever their misfortunes may have been. Now what are we to say of those generous men who in the last century wanted to redeem their Italian motherland not just by using French arms to liberate her, but by turning her into an actual province of France? Men who dreamed of a new cisalpine Gaul that would extend from the Mont Cenis to Etna? What name could we give to those magnanimous men whose doctrines are still alive today? Cowards! Italians unworthy of the name! Artificers of ruin and shame for the motherland! I cannot think with whom to compare them except those Roman legions which under Vespasian swore loyalty to Gaul and by their felony heralded the dominion of the barbarians and the downfall of the Latin name.

The methods of such people who aim at a united Italy are intrinsically vicious because they do not start out from a patriotic idea, nor correspond with the special conditions of Italy; they simply build castles in the air and use doctrines and examples drawn from abroad. If there is anything certain in politics it is that political changes have no duration or vitality if they are not a spontaneous contribution of the people and a natural outcome of a practical situation. The attempted or badly carried-out revolutions of these last fifty years—in Italy, Spain, Germany and elsewhere—were simply misguided imitations of the French Revolution, and they owed their birth to, and were governed by, French opinions and successes. This is why those attempts either turned out to be vain or took only weak root—like rich, thriving plants that become consumptive when transposed to a foreign and artificial soil under a sky alien to their native genius.

Statesmen, like poets and artists, must avoid illusions; nothing is great in the world of nature and art unless it is spontaneous; nothing flourishes or proves itself except in conditions which truly suit its character; servile imitations are no more successful or felicitous in politics than in letters and the fine arts. Every people has been made by God, and from its birth it bears enclosed within its breast its own future destiny, different from that of all other peoples; because nature, as rich and varied as the supreme being, never copies itself exactly. Any nation that seeks to contravene this law is punished, like the individual who goes against his natural vocation; it becomes barren; or only enjoys an apparent and transitory fertility, like those closely related animal species which, if perversely mated, cannot propagate their kind.

Notwithstanding its horrible excesses, the French Revolution was the natural offspring of its time and had many splendid aspects. It brought about lasting results and produced great numbers of outstanding statesmen and generals. True, the first and the last chronologically, that is to say Mirabeau (whose family name was Arrighetti) and Bonaparte, were not true Frenchmen: two gifted men of Italian stock, transplanted onto Gallic soil, had their characters vitiated by such an unhappy adoption. On the other hand Italy itself, which gave France these two supreme leaders and which still abounds in talent of every kind, seems politically sterile in her revolts; not that some great men were not produced by her upheavals, but, standing alone in the midst of servile copiers and imitators, they were not understood; they lived abandoned or even calumniated and persecuted, and died without achievement. And (a thing even more painful) some of them were dragged along by the crowd, unable to dominate it, obeying it, and—at least outwardly—conniving in its faults and misdeeds. So rare is it for even great and select spirits not to give in to the influence of the masses.

What happened to Italian politics during the past century was the same as occurred with its literature, which was insipid, impoverished and abject because it was imitative. From amid that literary poltroonery there arose a few gifted men who threw off the yoke; but political life was not so lucky, and had no Alfieri to call it back to its origins, to temper it once more in the true fire of Italian genius. And this in spite of the fact that even Alfieri, who saw the salvation of Italy in political and literary independence from the French, let himself be carried away by the torrent; indeed he wrote certain pages which he regretted bitterly in later and more mature years. Had he lived ten years longer his remorse would doubtless have been all the greater, for he would have seen that the only man capable of maintaining Italian dignity, and of triumphing even from prison over his powerful and popular adversary, was the same *Pope and King* about whom he had once written so unappreciatively. Nor was this example new, for the freest and most independent men in the Middle Ages, those most kindly to the weak and most formidable to the powerful, those who deserved best of Italy, of Europe and the whole human race, were the Popes; whose heroic intentions were handicapped by the fact that they were not political leaders of the Italian nation but only princes of Rome and religious leaders of the world.

There, I say, we have the real principle of Italian unity, and the mention of Alfieri's error brings me back to my argument. This principle, the Papacy, is supremely ours and our nation's because it created the nation and has been rooted here for eighteen centuries; it is concrete, living, real—not an abstraction or a chimera, but an institution, an oracle and a person. It is also ideal, because it expresses the greatest concept that can be found in the world. It is supremely efficient because it is enshrined in worship, corroborated by conscience, sanctified by religion, venerated by princes, adored by the people, and is like a tree that has its roots in heaven and spreads its branches over the whole earth. It is as everlasting as our own family and earthly reign of the true, because it is the divine guardian of the true and, so to speak, the patriarchate of the human race. It is essentially peaceful and civil because it is unarmed, and supremely powerful by the mere authority of its counsel and utterance. In fine, it is perfectly organized in itself and in the mode of its procedure, because it is a power organized by God himself and constitutes the center of the most wonderful society that could be found or imagined in mankind.

Hence the error of those who want to make of the Pope an instigator and artificer of brawls, tumults and violent revolutions; as if such a disordered use of power were possible or desirable in the supreme head of the priesthood. This last is a foreign idea born in the confused brain of a French priest [Lamennais] whose recent condemnation [in *Mirari vos*] proved that Gallic whims do not prevail over the common sense of Rome. The political activity of the Pope is not inconsistent with his spiritual and peaceful character as supreme pastor of the Church; the inconsistency would arise only should the common father of Christians stir up peoples against princes. Even when the barbarities of the age, the unbridled customs and the incoherent and disorderly ways of those in power forced him to use a tighter rein and more pragmatic expedients, the Pope was never a violator of national sovereignties, nor did he exercise any empire over rulers other than what they agreed to. Hence, even when he deposed princes according to the *jus gentium* then prevailing in Europe, he observed so far as possible the rights of princedoms and of families enjoying their possessions. Indeed he acted much like the French parliament which, when obliged in 1830 to remove authority from a King who broke his word and a dynasty which both disseminated strife and defied national feelings, nonetheless maintained the Bourbons in their privileged position by choosing a close branch of the same family. We see the same wisdom in the medieval Popes. So it is not by arousing subjects against their sovereigns that the pontiff can save Italy, but rather by bringing the princes and peoples of the peninsula to lasting peace and concord, and rendering their ties indissoluble, by means of a league of the various states of Italian origin over which providence has destined him to be the leader and moderator.

That the Pope is naturally, and should be effectively, the civil head of Italy is a truth forecast in the nature of things, confirmed by many centuries of history, recognized on past occasions by the peoples and princes of our land, and only thrown into doubt by those commentators who drank at foreign springs and diverted their poison to the motherland. Nor, to achieve this confederation, is there any need for the Pope to receive or take over any new power, but only to revive an ancient and inalienable right that has merely been interrupted. This selfsame right has been exercised in many ways, but always directed to one end, namely that of bringing the Italian states together in union. Thus, if Leo III provided for Italy's salvation by reviving the Empire and crowning Charlemagne (in which we should admire the intention rather than the outcome), at a later date Alexander III championed freedom by opposing that Emperor's degenerate successors. Alexander precisely obtained his intention by forming the Lombard cities into a League of which he was supreme head and military chief; and if this League was transitory and embraced only a part of Italy, the fault was certainly not that of the Pope.

The benefits Italy would gain from a political confederation under the moderating authority of the pontiff are beyond enumeration. For such a cooperative association would increase the strength of the various princes without damaging their independence, and

would put the strength of each at the disposal of all: it would remove the causes of disruptive wars and revolutions at home, and
make foreign invasions impossible; inasmuch as Italy, dominated by
the Alps and girt by the sea, can resist the onslaughts of half Europe
only if we are united; it would give us anew an honor we had in
bygone times by placing Italy again in the first rank of the Powers;
and whereas today Italian princes are not even consulted in matters
concerning the common interests of Europe, they would once more
regain their rightful part in the organization of the continent. By
pooling the wealth and forces of our various states, they would be
able to build a common navy to defend our ports and safeguard
the freedom of the Mediterranean; for which no Italian state, taken
alone, suffices.

Among other benefits would be that of providing opportunities
to resume expeditions and the establishment of colonies in various
parts of the globe; for the practice of colonialism is supremely right
and Christian, not only useful but essential, and the only peaceful
way of spreading civilization and smoothing the way for the spiritual conquests of faith and the ultimate union of the human race. By
means of colonies Europe can extend its sovereignty over the other
parts of the globe, communicate its enlightenment and culture to
them and receive many advantages in return, of which not the least
is scientific: for example, geography, ethnography, philology,
archaeology, natural history, anthropology, the philosophy of
human history and other like disciplines, all of which are needed
for redressing the ills of the world. Now Italy, whose sons were
once such wanderers, does not want to lack a single acre of land
outside her borders, for not only England, Russia, France and Spain,
but even Portugal, Holland, Denmark, Sweden and Belgium all
have their colonies!

Finally the Italian League would eliminate, or at least reduce, the
difference in weights, measures, currencies, customs duties, speech,
and systems of commercial and civil administration which so
wretchedly and meanly divide the various provinces and in a
thousand ways impede the traffic of ideas and commodities between
the various members of the nation; it would bring the best Italian
speech to the people, it would give more scope to the national
genius, and it would gradually do away with municipal divisions
and rivalries. Reciprocal agreements would also ensure that, on the
extinction of the line of any Italian prince, his dominions would be

transmitted without any need for further invasions by barbarian overlords and disastrous wars of succession.

I know that my federal idea will not please many people who will think it at once useless for Italy, unseemly for the Pope, and unacceptable to our sovereigns as well as to foreigners. But, granted it will not do all we want, it would improve our lot considerably, especially if done without bloodshed, tumults or revolutions. The aims of the strict unitarists may be good in theory, but they would suit us only if effective in practice. In politics, the attainable is best, and half a loaf is better than nothing. It is madness to think that Italy, which has been divided for centuries, can be peacefully united in a single unitary state; and to want this brought about by force is a crime, something which could be desired only by immoral people who are a disgrace to the name of Italy. A united state would be almost impossible to create even at enormous cost, let alone keep in being. I would go even further and say that a centralized Italy is against the sheer facts of history and the character of our people; at least all the available facts go to show this.

> [Vincenzo Gioberti: *Del primato morale e civile degli Italiani*, ed. U. Redano (Milan, 1938), vol. I, pp. 70–9]

5. Observations on Society and the Economy, 1844-1846

Cesare Balbo's *On the hopes of Italy* was dedicated to Gioberti, and the book agreed with Gioberti that Mazzini's idea of Italian unity was "a puerile notion, held at the most by pettifogging students of rhetoric, common rhymsters and café politicians." Balbo, as a historian, was conscious that Italy had never been a state or a nation, and he thought Italians would never agree to sacrifice their provincial capitals for a national capital. Unlike Gioberti, however, he was convinced that the papacy, far from wanting a large Italian state to exist, was more likely to be its enemy. Before talking of Italian primacy, he said, "better moderate our customary ambition" and wait until we can bring ourselves to the level of parity.

Balbo was a Piedmontese aristocrat, as proud of his class as of his home province. He was a strong monarchist, and in 1821 had advised

Charles Albert not to compromise himself with the constitutional party. As someone who always feared popular agitation, he was bound to detest Mazzini; while, as a conservative, even somewhat of an authoritarian, he was ready to postpone questions of individual liberty. His main concern was to make Italy independent of foreign occupation and interference. In his youth he had been a loyal civil servant in the French Empire, but he now hoped for an extension of Piedmontese power in north Italy, and the best chance of doing this without a revolution was if the break-up of the Ottoman Empire would allow Austria to exchange her Italian provinces for acquisitions in eastern Europe.

Balbo was not an economist, but his remarks on an Italian customs union gave the widest publicity to what a small group of intellectuals and politicians had been urgently discussing. The economic barriers established after 1815 by every Italian state against each other had obviously done enormous harm, and already in 1819 Gioia had pointed out that their removal would do as much as anything to increase prosperity and make Italians feel a common identity. There were seven such barriers along the 37-mile route which separated Mantua from Parma, and along the Po River there were as many as eighty places where boats could be stopped for searching. Both Charles Albert and the Austrians did something to free trade, but still in 1839 it could take forty or fifty days for goods to travel two hundred miles from Florence to Milan. Any improvement in this situation would recover some of the advantages which Napoleon had once brought to Italy.

Balbo recommends free trade and a customs union

THE NEED for a customs union in Italy will be obvious to everyone, especially if it can be both broadly based and promptly brought into being. It is, for example, universally accepted that, when many neighboring nations are advancing economically, any country that stands still will fall back relatively and even perhaps absolutely. At the beginning of the sixteenth century, Italian trade still led the world; but once Portugal and Spain, followed by England, Holland and France, had opened up new trade routes and markets, Italy could no longer compete and hence declined. This was true of her shipping and almost all her industries; if her agriculture did not decline, it at least remained stationary.

In our own time many European countries have more and faster-growing commerce than Italy. England has established new markets in China and the East, and has opened a new route through the Mediterranean and Egypt which will bring new markets as well as increase old ones. France has speedily profited from this same route. Holland still has flourishing eastern colonies which she, too, can now reach through the Mediterranean. Germany is gaining from her customs union and her policy of commercial liberalism. Perhaps soon Spain as well, if she can shake off her bad political habits, will use this new route with profit, and she seems to be already moving into a period of commercial development. All these states are obviously progressing, or at least are on the verge of progress. If we do not do the same we shall yet again experience a deterioration in our relative position, and hence in all likelihood an absolute decline, so that even our existing activities will be partially or wholly curtailed.

So how can we progress? Certainly not by conquering large colonies in our turn, for we lack the strength; nor by opening out new markets in the East where we would be not only late arrivals but total outsiders; nor yet by hoping to compete through industrial production, for here we are too far behind; and even our agricultural produce is relatively too scarce and too dear. Our only hope of commercial advancement is through our marvelous position in the center of the Mediterranean, to which sea—through no effort or merit of our own—the main path of world trade has returned. All those who are once again bringing European-Asiatic trade (the greatest in the world) to our sea are working in our interest; their ships pass within sight of our country or even touch at our ports.

But we must have no illusions; we must see the advantages of our new situation as they are and neither exaggerate nor minimize them. Our one advantage is a geographic position which could make our products more easily exchangeable with those of the East simply because we are near to it. Our maritime towns could also become landing stages or depositories for other traders as ports of call. But, of these advantages, only one will help Italy so long as she continues to consist of small separated states. Our exports, in fact, should increase anyway, but our imports and harborage facilities cannot be fully exploited unless encouraged by a larger domestic market and easy disembarkation, neither of which can be attained save by big countries or else small ones leagued together. We have not a single port that offers a sufficient market or the necessary docking facilities for foreigners; what conveniences we possess cannot in fact be developed without wider markets and easier means of access to them. Even for our own nationals this is true. As long as Otranto and Naples serve only the Kingdom of the Two Sicilies, as long as Ancona and Civitavecchia serve only the Papal States, and Leghorn only Tuscany, and Genoa only Piedmont, no large despatch of goods will ever take place through them. But if each of these could be a market, a depository, a transit point, for all or much of Italy, then the attraction would be multiplied for both foreign and national shipping; and hence not only would the industries and trade peculiar to transit traffic be increased, but so inevitably would all our national industry and agriculture. It would be mere pedantry to press this point further, since it is familiar even to those who know only a little economics.

And for those who are well informed, they can have no doubt that an Italian league should be established on the widest commercial principles. Everyone knows that Germany gained less from her customs union itself than from the broad principles on which it was based. Not only in Germany, but in England, France, Italy and everywhere else, scientific theory is unanimous and dogmatic about the need for such breadth and liberality. In practice, however, the theory is sometimes disregarded, for a dogma can be true at the same time as its feasibility or applicability can in practice be challenged. Not that it would be difficult to show the invalidity of almost all the exceptions which are usually made to this rule; but let us restrict our field of view and see whether opening up our ports and abolishing protective taxes would harm or favor our shipping, industries and agriculture.

1. Against freedom of navigation it is customary to quote the English navigation act which, by excluding or discriminating against foreigners, is said to have promoted home shipping. But this example seems to me to involve piling one error on another. No one can prove that it was this restrictive act which caused home shipping to increase; for commerce would have developed anyway, owing to England's geographical situation at the center of many new trade routes opened up in the sixteenth century—the same situation as Italy today finds herself in. Next, our shipping is in a very different state from English shipping at that time; it is in decline or at least standing still; the question is not one of teaching us to build and man ships, but rather to emulate our rivals, and in this field rivalry would be beneficial and privileges detrimental. Above all, England has now abandoned her old restrictions and thus teaches us to abandon them too—for we ought to follow not the practices she is giving up but those she is adopting. When shall we cease copying fashions that have become outdated elsewhere? . . . There can hardly be one great Italian port where some foreign boats do not

enjoy more privileges than Italian. This is a disgrace as well as extremely harmful. But disgrace recently went further still; for the government of Rome proposed to set the shipping of all other Italian states on the same footing as its own if they were prepared to provide reciprocal privileges; and yet not one Italian state has responded to this generous proposal!

2. As for industries, are there truly any that need protection either by complete or partial restrictions? The cotton industry, iron, hemp, linen—which of these? At the time of writing (1843) there is not a single Italian industry that outdoes its competitors elsewhere whether in European or extra-European markets. Even the once-famous silk works of Genoa, Florence and Turin now count for nothing abroad; and as for other industries, one could almost say they do not exist. Neither trade fairs, nor medals and prizes, nor even comparative figures of annual increases in output, serve any purpose here. The reader need only compare our statistics with English, German and even French; he can then draw his own conclusions without being obliged to find nonexistent details to flatter this ruler or that people. Then he will see the fine industrial future that Italy is preparing for herself! Such a sorry future might even suggest doing the very opposite of everything we have done up till now; for things could not be worse and might possibly be better. Since restrictions have reduced us to this level, it could be argued that we should remove them just to see what would happen.

Considerable amelioration, on the other hand, would follow if the present Italian rulers, who are mostly men of education (this will not be taken as flattery), applied that great principle of *laissez faire* and *laissez passer* for which perhaps no nation is so well adapted as Italy. Since existing industries are scarce, allowing competition could do only a limited amount of harm. Moreover, as I have had frequent opportunity of observing, the Italian genius shows at its very best where flexibility and adaptation are needed. It will adapt itself even to this. The less powerful and less "natural" industries will decline; but those naturally more healthy will develop. If politicians go on making detailed calculations about the optimum quotas of imports or exports to be fixed for Italian industries, they will probably be wasting our people's talents and energy, as they have done so often in the past. If, on the other hand, they put their trust in the traditional skills and newly awakened activity of the Italians, there is a 90 per cent chance that this activity, frustrated now on so many sides, would leap to the new outlet and perform miracles. Is it possible that we, who produce so much silk, could fail to manufacture it as well as the French and Germans? Is it possible that we, in using the Egyptian cotton that lies so near to us, cannot compete with those whose factories are in the very heart of the European continent? Hence it is mistaken to say that nature deprived us of equal facilities when she denied us coal deposits and therefore steam engines! Have all Italy's water supplies been tapped? Do not let us be misunderstood. Water is not the same as steam where railways are concerned; but for ordinary factories, the rain that still falls so providently where it has always fallen is worth far more than steam; and as long as there remains a river or a stream in Italy whose current has not been exploited, we have no excuse for blaming providence or affecting a resignation which in the last analysis is mere laziness.

It is not coal that we lack but the will to work and competition—competition which will doubtless harm the lazy, but will benefit the hard-working upon whom the nation depends. All Italians, but above all their rulers, must understand this: the enemies of their glory, of their profit and power are the lazy, the ne'er-do-wells, all that rabble who insist on doing nothing, who envy and impede everyone who works. If such people were to lose because others work hard, little harm would be done. We must not penalize the industrious and protect the idle.

3. Finally, there are some who say that Italian industry always will be a mere nothing compared with agriculture. I personally do not believe this; but let us suppose that it is so, and that Italian material hopes must be based solely on agriculture. In such a case these hopes would increase immensely with a broadly based customs union. Cereals, rice, hemp, linen, oil, wine, dairy products and silk are our chief agricultural products. But all these (except dairy products) are also found in all other Mediterranean countries. In one or another country it may be that a particular branch of agriculture does very well and ends up much cheaper and more efficient than in Italy. No new methods, no agricultural associations, no governmental incentives can prevent this sort of thing happening. All such artificial remedies would be useless.

There could in fact be no major remedy here save either an absolute tariff wall that reserves our domestic market exclusively to our own products, or else an absolute free trade that puts them on the same footing as foreign merchandise. Free trade, as well as causing unprofitable forms of production to stop, would incidentally make other forms of production flourish. An absolute tariff wall, however, as everyone knows, would be difficult or impossible to apply in a country so varied as Italy, a country situated on the world's most important trade route and where smuggling is so easy; moreover while it would give us an advantage in our own domestic market, it would increasingly harm our products in foreign markets. Thus the second remedy—that of opening out, putting all our products on the same footing as foreign ones and so fostering our most natural industries—is in the last analysis the only profitable or desirable course. It is not our methods of cultivation that should be changed but the things cultivated; our methods of manufacture have been satisfactory over the centuries and still are, but the type of product needs to be modified in accordance with new conditions, and this is where we have hitherto failed.

For example, I expressly except our dairy products and meat from the list of things in Italy that have cause to fear competition. And in fact if we looked for similar conditions in the whole Mediterranean we would hardly find a region comparable to northern Italy and much of the south. So we can assume that other Mediterranean regions will perhaps never, and certainly not for a very long time, be able to compete with us in cattle and dairy produce; and meanwhile the reduction in our cereal acreage resulting from competition will be offset by the compensation that we shall gain from this other kind of agriculture. As the standard of living of the other Mediterranean coastal regions increases, their demand from us for these products will grow, all the more so as these are commodities which by their very nature cannot be brought from afar. We can be sure that Italy is destined to increase this side of her production enormously by turning over all possible land to pasture, exploiting the irrigation complex which she has built up over generations, and even extending it. This is a future unique to her and which should be highly fruitful in hard work and riches of every kind.

Here, beyond question, lies our main agricultural hope. And yet it is not the only one. Up till now our rice has been unrivaled in the regions round the Mediterranean; our oil has held out against all competition, or very nearly so; and if our wines cannot stand up to competition, perhaps this is one field where incentives would lead to real improvements. All these products are likely to increase by reason of our proximity to immense regions which are in process of development. Growth elsewhere will stimulate our own. The only limit will be our own laziness by which we might let others get ahead of us in satisfying what will be an ever increasing demand. If we obstinately go on trying to produce grain as efficiently as they can do in south Russia or north Africa and Egypt; if we confuse (as so many agriculturalists, administrators and economists do) agriculture in general with grain growing; if we still, in an age of unlimited communications, want to produce everything, and to this end omit to specialize in more efficient forms of production that would provide us with either money to buy grain or at least arms and ships to procure it, then Italy will miss her chance and suffer a further decline in both trade and agriculture. But behind this material loss will come an even graver consequence, namely laziness, unemployment and the vices that always accompany them. In recent centuries this idleness has affected only the so-called upper classes and possibly the class of artisans. Agriculture, which flourished throughout Italy's great centuries and survived through the lean ones, ensured that a great part of the nation remained industrious. It would be a disaster if this changed and the rest of our nation likewise gave way to inactivity at a time when foreigners are working even harder. Then our cup of woe would be filled. Only extreme remedies would then serve, remedies which, even though strictly permissible, should always if possible be avoided.

For this reason we must act very quickly indeed. In these years around the middle of the nineteenth century, and perhaps even in the remaining years of its fourth decade, our commercial, industrial, and agricultural future will be decided for centuries to come. These will be climacteric years in economics for every European country, but especially for Italy. Are we going to let them slip by? If so, world commerce will adopt other habits; and, as everyone knows, commercial habits are subsequently hard to change. Or are we going out to meet this new, great and possibly final opportunity that providence offers us? Shall we exploit our magnificent situation in the center of the Mediterranean where we find ourselves the best-placed European country on the reopened trade route to the East? And, not to mince matters, shall we be able to profit from this more than the other countries around the Mediterranean? Shall we be able to land and load goods more efficiently than other countries?

If so, the more distant nations that lack ports of call in the Mediterranean, such as Holland, Germany, Sweden and America, will use our ports to the full, and even the nations that do possess docking facilities, for instance England, France and Spain, will come here likewise if our facilities are good enough. Once such habits have been adopted, they will continue even if England, France and Spain follow along the path where we shall have preceded them. But let us get one point very clear in our heads: the race has begun; it is a matter of getting in first, and we must make use of any possible advantage. Other nations have other advantages, more ships, more industries, more markets; we cannot take these from them; what we can have, and what they have not so far been able to achieve, is free trade.

[C. Balbo: *Delle speranze d'Italia* (Capolago, 1844), pp. 437–52]

Where Balbo subordinated internal liberties to the independence of Italy from foreigners, Carlo Cattaneo wanted individual liberty first. Other patriotic leaders could not understand Cattaneo's suspicion that nationalism might possibly become illiberal. Though he felt himself an Italian just as they did, he did not see why patriotism should require a strong, centralized state. Small societies were in his view more educative and liberating because they associated the people with government. In the long run, like Mazzini and Garibaldi, Cattaneo hoped for a United States of Europe; but in the short run he was not sure that Italians were materially or psychologically ready for a war of independence, and he feared what such a war might bring. The immediate task should rather be to create a freer and more progressive and prosperous society, leaving nationalism and internationalism to develop pragmatically and in their own good time. In his view, as in that of Giuseppe Ferrari, another Lombard federalist, Mazzini's idea of Italian unity was too dogmatic and too closely tied to sentiment and emotions, while Mazzini's method of secret conspiracies was corrupting as well as ineffective. Moral education was more important than national unity, reforms than revolutions. Until 1848, it seems that Cattaneo would in fact have been quite content for Lombardy to be an autonomous state inside a federal Austrian Empire. Nor by any means was he alone in this. Though Cattaneo opposed Metternich's despotic and centralizing policy, he even more distrusted Piedmont as an aristocratic, authoritarian, priest-ridden state which lagged behind Lombardy in culture, tolerance, and economic growth.

Cattaneo was not strictly a politician but a polymath whose interests stretched into politics as into almost every human activity. A pupil of

Romagnosi, he could perhaps best be described as a scientific journalist campaigning for practical improvements in education, industry, agriculture, and communications. His own journal, the *Politecnico,* was exceptional in finding as many as seven hundred subscribers, and it must have been read by a sizeable proportion of the intellectual *élite* of Italy. His essentially pragmatic approach was something much needed to balance the rhetoric of such as Gioberti, and so was his and Ferrari's view that the risorgimento must be placed in a practical European context. As early as 1834, for example, Cattaneo was praising the German Zollverein in the *Annali di Statistica* and recommending that Venice and Lombardy should try to join that northern customs union. Neither Mazzini and the radicals, nor Balbo and the moderates, could sympathize with this degree of detachment from nationalistic considerations.

Cattaneo wrote his general notes on Lombardy for delegates to the congress of Italian scientists which met at Milan in 1844. After five successive meetings, these congresses had come to represent one of the best possible applications of his positivistic view of social problems. Already they were electing committees of members representing various Italian states to study such common problems as elementary education, the search for coal deposits, the silk industry, the reintroduction of a uniform metric system, steam power, and certain prevalent deficiency diseases. Apart from their immediate practical value, these scientific meetings were perhaps nearly as helpful as Mazzini's doctrinaire sermons in developing a common sense of *italianità*. In describing his own home province to the visiting scientists, Cattaneo was at his best.

Cattaneo on the economy of Lombardy

ALREADY IN the early eighteenth century Lombardy was a land of promise in spite of its poverty. With its open-minded, sensitive, warm-hearted population, Lombardy seemed to any well-disposed observer like a fertile field in which a good farmer could try out some new crop. The plain truth is not generally known, but while France was vainly intoxicating herself with new modes of thought, and announcing to Europe a new era which she succeeded in introducing only through bloody revolution, lowly Milan was setting out on a new phase of progress, led by a new school of thinkers trained in the law. Pompeo Neri, Rinaldo Carli, Cesare Beccaria and Pietro Verri may not be names known throughout Europe, but all are venerated here by their fellow citizens. Philosophy had inspired lawmaking among the old Roman jurists; but it was something new for intellectuals to administer finance, the supply of food, or local government, and they rose worthily to the occasion. All those public-welfare reforms that Turgot envisaged— and which he tried vainly to apply in France despite the ignorance of the common people and the wiles of the privileged—are to be found inscribed in our laws and reflected in the prosperity of our province and its inhabitants.

A census of property was thus undertaken on a principle that few nations have accepted even today. Calculations were based on a notional coinage called the ducat which served as a measure of comparative value. If hard work by landowners improved a property, the improvements were not taxed, for the taxable value was already determined; and so a family that doubled its output could thereby lighten its tax burden by half in comparison with an idle family which paid the same tax though netting less profit. The concession of this reward for hard work had the effect of stimulating families to make continual improvements. To double the productivity of one field with toil and saving was more profitable than to possess two fields and cultivate them half-heartedly. By thus increasing the value of property, with time and care the smallholding rivaled the large estate in output, until gradually the land in general became capable of providing for two families in a space that elsewhere provided only for one. The wisdom and profit of this principle compare well with the practice of other civilized nations; because where taxes are rather on produce or on rent, this means a levy on the landowners' capacity for hard work!

The census also eliminated all those immunities by which, in the former period of Spanish rule, a third of all property was exempt from tax in that it was possessed by the clergy, which made the burden unendurably heavy for everyone else. The census became a basic fact in local government, for our cities were so many tiny states which, under central guidance, decreed public works and levied taxes on themselves. No more was heard of those crippling forms of taxation on work done, on cattle, on produce, all of which had been the terror of the peasants and an instrument of oppression and corruption. Contracts were devised for road development which encouraged a builder to make his work as solid and yet as simple as possible. But this is not the place to discourse on all the reforms introduced by our reformers—for instance the redistribution of land, the redemption of regalian rights, the abolition of tax farmers, the supervision of ecclesiastical property, and reform of the currency . . .

We can show foreigners the plain of Lombardy cultivated throughout, as though re-created by our own hands—so much so that botanists deplore an agriculture that has changed every vestige of the primitive vegetation. We have taken waters from deep riv-erbeds and marshy valleys and spread them over the parched flat-lands. Half our plain, more than four thousand square kilometers, is now irrigated; and through artificial canals there flows a volume of water estimated at over thirty million cubic meters a day. By an art exclusively our own, part of the plain bears fruit even in winter when all around is snow and ice. The most marshy parts of the land have been turned into ricefields; so that, at the same latitude as the Vendée, or as Switzerland and the Crimea, we have established an almost Indian type of cultivation.

Subterranean waters, brought by the hand of man up to the light of day, transported over the low-lying plains, then gathered once more and spread over even lower fields, flow at different levels with a calculated speed. They meet, pass over one another by canal bridges, pass under one another by means of a syphon system, and interweave in ways beyond enumeration. In a space of only two hundred yards, the road from Bergamo to Cremona near Genivolta encounters thirteen aqueducts and bestrides them with what is known as the *Thirteen Bridges*. These water conduits are governed by a legal principle peculiar to our country, whereby properties are obliged to grant each other a right of way for water supplies with-out any need for intervention by government or any decree of ex-propriation. This is not a bond that infringes the sacred rights of property, but a useful addition to law so as to increase the fertility of every piece of land.

The final outlets of these channels have locks to take off the overflow of the swollen rivers. A canal crosses the center of the whole Cremona province from the Oglio to the Po; all the aque-ducts that make its lower part fertile cross this canal on stone bridges which allow an overflow for any waters that by chance exceed the pre-established measure; and should the daily rainfall make irrigation superfluous, the aqueducts are closed with sluices and their waters pouring into the lower beds are diverted into the Oglio and the Po. The whole province of Mantua has been re-claimed from the marshes; its drainage canals cover three quarters of a million square meters; and even the water that surrounds the city of Mantua, where there was once a swamp, has been trans-formed into a navigable lake.

Our internal lines of navigation, part of which are viable by steamer, amount to 1,200 kilometers, or 56 meters to every square kilometer of land; whereas Belgium has only a proportion of 48, and France 27—not all in use the whole year round. Our land, wholly Mediterranean though it is, in this respect resembles Holland. Our canals for navigation and irrigation are constructed on a special principle: they are not a series of trunklines like the northern canals which serve merely for navigation, but genuine rivers, first steeply inclined, then progressively moderated so as to collect from the trunklines the water which irrigation thereafter drains off.

Once this system had been begun, it survived every kind of political change. Each year meant greater prosperity; each year the network of roads was extended; each year more mulberry trees were planted. These mulberries were at first restricted to the hills, but they became positive forests over the Oglio and Adda plains, and used to grow at a height of 1,000 meters up in the Alpine valleys. Their annual crop has been valued at a hundred million francs in an area corresponding to a twenty-sixth part of France. Each year irrigation becomes more widespread, but more accurately planned and hence less unhealthy. The peasants' hovels have been changed into good houses; there are schools in every rural hamlet; crêches tame the wild roughness of the children of the poor; letters and the arts are taught even to the gentle sex; and, finally, exhibitions have fostered a love of the fine arts among the people, together with a real elegance in craftsmanship.

All the inhabited areas of our plain are linked to each other by good roads; there is roughly one kilometer of roadway to every square kilometer of surface. This network now includes all the hills up to an altitude of 800 meters; it tunnels through the rocks that interrupt the shores of our lakes; it winds up Alpine valleys as far as the highest passes; and yet the highest coach-passes on earth are also provided with defenses against avalanches. The Simplon road, model for all the rest, is the work of our engineers, and they were also in charge of the Splügen and Stelvio passes. Engineers who came from that part of our land which now belongs to Switzerland mapped out the Saint Gotthard and the Little Saint Bernard roads. Our building contractors are scattered through the Grisons, the Tyrol, Dalmatia, Bohemia and Galicia, teaching other peoples how to extend the links of civilization through their mountains. Our road-making bears all the marks of Roman magnificence; the bridge that links the two banks of the Ticino at Buffalora has eleven granite arches spanning over 300 meters. Railways are not unknown to us; one line [Milan to Monza] was completed four years ago; two have been begun [Milan to Como and Bergamo]; and others [to Genoa and Venice] are being mooted and planned.

It is no easy matter to give a succinct idea of the sheer variety of our agriculture in the different provinces. While in one place rice is floating in water, elsewhere cattle must slake their thirst with stale rainwater or water drawn from wells a hundred meters deep; while one district is continuous meadowland, green even in winter and rich in dairy produce, another can scrape together only a little goat's milk but is successful with small gardens of olives and lemons, the most elegant kind of agriculture. Hemp is grown in the mountains where flax is almost unknown, whereas round Crema and Cremona flax is the prime product and hemp is neglected. The plain of Pavia stretches out in abundant ricefields, and mulberries are hardly to be seen, whereas the Cremona plain has dense and thriving plantations of mulberry trees. Wine is the agriculturist's hope in both the Alpine Valtelline and the southern plains of Canneto, at Casalmaggiore and south of the Po. Around Brescia, oxen plow deep into the heavy soil; around Lodi, horses plow shallowly so as not to stir up the poor shingle over which an artificial layer of soil has been spread by the work of time.

The circumstances of nature that demand such variety in crops also call for variety in methods of ownership. In the unwatered plain a farmholding could not be cultivated with profit unless it were large enough, because it needs complicated rotations, multiple crops, difficult water distribution, and an intelligent family for managing the complicated business side of affairs. The owner is already too well-off to like a solitary rural life without amenities; therefore he lives in a city; he spends his holidays on the sunny hills or on the lakes, and often scarcely knows the name of the large estate that maintains his family in such comfort. The work of cultivation passes into the hands of a lessee who himself needs to be a capitalist to provide proper management. Some of these are richer than the proprietors, and may well own other properties which they entrust to other cultivators. They live in the midst of domestic plenty, with large families and many horses, and form what is almost a feudal order among a population of day laborers who know no other masters. Here we can see the development of a quite peculiar social order. A district of some twenty villages and

measuring about a hundred square kilometers has in each village
four or five such families who often live in isolated homesteads like
the ancient Celts. Scattered among them are a few parish priests,
the odd doctor, an occasional pharmacist, the local government administrator, and the magistrate who enforces justice. This is the
intelligentsia of the district; everyone else is merely a number, or a
hand. Each cultivator sells grain and buys cattle. He keeps smiths
and woodcutters employed, but commerce and industry extend no
further; there is just the occasional shop selling the peasant's rustic
apparatus. One gets the impression that this is the ancient model
on which British agriculture was based. These were the men who,
beneath the walls of Pavia and below the castle of Binasco, stood
without arms to confront Bonaparte after his victories at Monte-
notte and Lodi.

If we leave the plain and go up into the mountains we find a
totally different social order. Here the steep slopes—laboriously
arranged in tiers and supported by stone walls, up which the farmer
sometimes carts on his back the small amount of earth needed to
hold firm the roots of a vine—hardly yield a marginal compensation
for his toil. And were the farmer to share his meager produce with
a landowner, he could scarcely survive. The earth has hardly any
value except as a space on which a man's work takes place, as
what might be called the farmer's workshop. Here he is almost
always the master of his plot, or at least a perpetual leaseholder;
with any other arrangement the vines and olives would revert to
brushwood and rocks. While part of the family labors with the
sweat of their brow and bring up their poor offspring to love the
land, other members go down to the plain to find employment; or
they set off beyond the mountains to engage in trade and bring back
their savings to the family, thereby giving it the strength to carry
on the struggle against nature and poverty. A region of this kind
contains as many thousand proprietors as there are families; but
the wealth does not come from the soil; what is invested in agriculture comes from some skill or trade. Hence we find a curious mixture of rustic ways and worldly experience, a love of gain yet
warm hospitality, a facility for living in foreign lands but also an
undying affection for the region, and this sooner or later arouses
thoughts of return. In some mountain areas private property is still
an exception, and the village owns large areas of pasture and wood-
land . . .

As a result of all this the Lombard plain is the most densely populated region in Europe. It counts 176 persons to the square kilometer, whereas the Belgian plain has only 143. And even if we
include the Alpine region in our calculations, we still have 119
inhabitants to the square kilometer, whereas France has only 64
and, in its southern portion which is even further south than Lombardy, only 50. The population density in the British Isles and Holland is only two thirds of ours; in Portugal and Denmark, one
third; in Spain a quarter; in Greece an eighth and in Russia a tenth.
Thus our people, as a result of principles of administration all their
own—such as those of the perpetual copyhold lease, the communal
supertaxes, and the right to take water across other people's property—have made their land so fertile that, over an area which in
France would provide for one family, it provides approximately
for two, though all the while paying the same amount of taxation
in proportion to its surface. Our rural communes have a larger
number of schools; and trade and industry are more closely woven
in with all orders of agriculture—so that we have no crowds of
rootless industrial workers. Iron, silk, cotton, linen, skins and sugar
are objects of manufacture on a large scale. The iron industry between Como, Bergamo and Brescia, given the wide extent of the
region, has a large annual turnover of eight million francs. Milan
and Como have more than eight thousand silk looms and ninety
thousand cotton spindles. Olona alone has 424 steam-powered
engines.

The poor receive more generous assistance than elsewhere. In
1840 our infirmaries numbered seventy-two; within three years another six were added; another seven are now being built; and they
are open to all, without grace or favor, the one condition being
infirmity and need. Their total assets are about two hundred million. In the course of a year the Milan hospital alone takes in 24,000
sick; Paris, which has more than four times the population, takes in
only three times as many patients. London cares for the same number as Milan though it is ten times as large a city. The poor are also
attended in their houses by doctors and surgeons, and this not only
in the cities but in the remotest country places. About half our
doctors and three quarters of our midwives are paid a salary by the
villages to tend poor families. The number of doctors is equivalent
to one for every thirteen square kilometers of the country, while in
Belgium each doctor has to serve an area twice that size. This army

of doctors, surgeons, pharmacists, veterinarians and midwives adds up to nearly five thousand persons. The country is similarly provided with engineers, who in the city of Milan alone amount to around 450, whereas in France the whole body of hydraulic and road engineers is only 568. The large number of educated people whose job brings them into active contact with the common people exercises a beneficial influence; it helps to remove prejudice, and instills an upright sense of service.

We have 400,000 city dwellers in all, and there are many townships and boroughs of six, eight and ten thousand inhabitants, which, though not called cities, contain numerous well-to-do families. Ownership is widespread amongst all classes. Hence, all things considered, Lombardy may well have a larger number of educated families in relation to the uneducated population than any other country in Europe.

> [C. Cattaneo: *Notizie naturali e civili su la Lombardia* (Milan, 1844), vol. I, pp. xciv–cx]

Cattaneo had been one of the first railway enthusiasts in Italy and one of the first to conceive of linking the Black Sea with the Atlantic via Lombardy. In 1836, when the Austrian government began to plan a railroad between Milan and Venice, he became secretary of the planning commission at Milan. The Austrians, like the Venetians, naturally had strong reasons for attaching this route to Austrian Trieste rather than to Piedmontese Genoa, a fact which did not altogether suit Milan. A more serious problem was that Bergamo and other Lombard towns delayed construction by fighting each other over which precise route should be taken. Another delaying factor was the unwillingness of Milanese and Venetian capitalists to put up the necessary money, with the result that in Lombardy as in Piedmont the idea began to prevail that the government should become responsible for most railroads.

In 1845, Carlo Petitti published a study of a possible national railway system which would minimize municipal and regional rivalries. Like Gioberti and Balbo, Petitti came from Piedmont, yet his book like theirs had to be printed abroad, for the government of Charles Albert at Turin was not notorious for encouraging independent thought. A famous review of this book was published at Paris by another Piedmontese, Count Cavour. Few people in Italy knew more about the subject than Cavour, for he had personally been involved with planning and financing railroad construction. Few people, moreover, were better equipped by education and outlook to see the implications for the development of national consciousness—and, for that matter, of European consciousness too. The fulsome flattery directed at Charles Albert in this essay was a deliberate attempt to penetrate the stuffy world of the court which Cavour so despised. Along with some penetrating social commentary, his review was also intended to set out the arguments for gradualism and moderation in politics.

Cavour on railways and national independence

THE RAILROAD from Turin to Chambéry, crossing the highest mountains in Europe, is going to be the masterpiece of modern industry and the finest triumph of steam. After having tamed the swiftest rivers and the tempestuous ocean, the steam engine will then have conquered the eternal snows and glaciers which now seem an insuperable barrier separating one people from another. This railway will be one of the wonders of the world; it will immortalize the name of King Charles Albert if he has the courage and energy to build it. Incalculable benefits will follow, which will make eternal the memory of his reign, already marked by so many glorious achievements. Not only his own subjects but all Italians will recognize this.

Some may say that we exaggerate the importance of this route: but if we reflect that it is destined, so to speak, to remove the distances which separate those centers of enlightenment, London and Paris, from Venice, Milan, Genoa, Turin and the main Italian cities, it will be agreed that, far from valuing too highly the effects of the Alpine raiway, we have if anything underestimated its influence on the industrial and political future of Italy.

This line will make Turin a European city. Situated at the foot of the Alps, at the extreme end of the Italian plain, Turin will be the junction point between north and south, the place where the German and Latin races will come to exchange products and ideas, an exchange which above all will profit the Piedmontese nation which already combines the qualities of these two races. This admirable and magnificent destiny, Turin will owe to the enlightened policy of its Kings . . .

Lombardo-Venetia was the first area of Italy where railways became a serious proposition. In 1838, a private company undertook at its own risk the short line from Milan to Monza, open to the public six years ago. Another society obtained a concession from the Austrian government for the Milan-Venice line. This fine project encountered immediate difficulties which hindered its progress. Municipal and provincial rivalries, that inveterate sore and prime cause of all our troubles in Italy, delayed agreement for years on which route to follow, and nearly ruined the company. After surmounting these first obstacles one would have expected work to begin vigorously. Far from it—the deplorable, almost culpable, apathy of Milanese capitalists and the distrust of foreign shareholders retarded the enterprise, and only the generous intervention of the Austrian government saved it from inevitable failure. On this occasion the Viennese cabinet showed itself enlightened and benevolent toward its Italian subjects. We are indebted to Austria if energetic action replaced hesitation and delay. Already, thanks to the greater enterprise of Venetian shareholders, the huge bridge over the Venice lagoon is finished and a railroad runs from there to Vienna. Work has been vigorous over the past year just outside Milan, and within a few months work will begin at every point on the intervening route. So long as no unforeseen obstacle arises, the ardent wish of the population will soon be satisfied, and in a few years the wealthy capital of fertile Lombardy and the ancient queen of the Adriatic will be only a few hours apart.

The Lombardy-Venice network will never be complete until it is joined to the Piedmontese route to form a single artery along the Po Valley. This gap I have already mentioned, but it will soon be filled. Circumstances will easily triumph over a few petty political and commercial jealousies. Milan has a greater interest in this line than either Genoa or Turin; for it is through these latter cities that the cheese and silks of Lombardy must pass to arrive at the consumers' market on the Mediterranean coast, or beyond the Alps in France and England . . .

If the future holds a happy fortune for Italy, if this fair country, so one may hope, is destined to regain her nationality, it can only be the consequence of a remodeling of Europe, or as a result of one of those great providential explosions in which the mere ability to move troops quickly by rail will be unimportant. The time of conspiracies has passed; the emancipation of peoples cannot result from mere plots or from a surprise attack. It has become the necessary consequence of the progress of Christian civilization and the spread of enlightenment. Once the hour of deliverance sounds, the material forces which governments possess will be powerless to keep conquered nations in bondage. Moral forces are growing daily which sooner or later, with the aid of providence, must cause a political upheaval in Europe; and governments will then have to yield. From such an upheaval, Poland and Italy will benefit more than any other country. A railway connection bringing Vienna and Milan within a few hours of each other cannot impede such a great event.

That being so, a line from Vienna to Trieste is another whose construction is most to be desired; for it will immediately help Italian agriculture by opening many new outlets. In the future, moreover, when relations established by conquest have given way to relations of equality and friendship, it will render immense service by facilitating intellectual and moral contacts. More than anyone else, we wish to see such contacts established between grave and profound Germany and intelligent Italy . . .

So manifold are the attractions of our country that it is difficult to guess the number of foreigners who will one day seek here a purer and cleaner air for their impaired health, quite apart from historical interest or even simple distraction from the boredom fostered by the fogs of the north. The profits which Italy will draw from its sun, its cloudless sky, its artistic riches, its historical associations, will certainly increase enormously. That will be one undeniable gain from the railways. However we think it the least important benefit of all, despite its appeal to the general imagination. The presence of a great mass of foreigners in our midst is undoubtedly a source of profit, but it has its own inconveniences. Relations between Italians on the one hand, and rich and leisured foreigners on the other, whom the local population will exploit in order to live—this will hardly favor the development of industrious, moral habits; it may engender a spirit of guile and servility which will damage the national character. As a sense of its own dignity is of prime importance to a nation, we must not care for profits at the price of insolence and arrogance. Without wishing to stop the growing movement which urges foreigners toward Italy, we do not think it will really help us until our industrialization improves to the point where we do not depend on foreigners and so can treat them as equals.

Once the network of railways is complete, Italy will begin to enjoy a considerable transit trade. The lines which connect Genoa, Leghorn and Naples with Trieste, Venice, Ancona and the east coast of the Kingdom of Naples, will conduct a great wave of merchandise and travelers across Italy from the Mediterranean to the Adriatic. And if the Alps are penetrated, as we hope—between

Turin and Chambéry, between Lake Maggiore and Lake Constance, as also between Trieste and Vienna—the ports of Italy will share with those of the Atlantic and North Sea in supplying central Europe with commodities from far-distant lands.

Indeed if the Neapolitan lines stretch to the far end of the kingdom, Italy will be called to a new and lofty commercial destiny. Its position in the center of the Mediterranean, where like an immense promontory it seems destined to join Europe to Africa, will then render it the shortest and easiest route from East to West. Once people can embark at Taranto or Brindisi, the distance by sea from England, France or Germany to Africa and Asia will be halved. Undoubtedly, therefore, the great Italian lines will then transport most of the travelers and some of the most precious merchandise on these routes. Equally, Italy will lie on the fastest route from England to India and China, which will be yet another abundant source of new profit. Thus railways will open a magnificent economic future for Italy and should provide her with the means to regain the brilliant commercial position that she held throughout the Middle Ages.

Nevertheless, however great the material benefits to Italy from railways, they are much less important than the inevitable moral effects. A few brief considerations will suffice to justify this assertion to any who truly know our country.

Italy's troubles are of ancient origin. This is not the place to discuss them, and it would moreover be beyond our powers. But we are certain that the prime cause is the political influence which foreigners have exercised on us for centuries, and that the principal obstacles opposed to our throwing off this baleful influence are, first and foremost, the internal divisions, the rivalries, I might almost say, the antipathy that different parts of our great Italian family hold for each other; and, following that, the reciprocal distrust which divides our rulers from the most energetic section of those they rule. This latter group have an often exaggerated desire for progress, a keen sense of nationality and love for their country, which makes them the indispensable support, if not the principal instrument, of all attempts at emancipation.

If the action of the railways diminishes these obstacles and perhaps even abolishes them, it will give the greatest encouragement to the spirit of Italian nationality. Communications, which help the incessant movement of people in every direction, and which will force people into contact with those they do not know, should be a powerful help in destroying petty municipal passions born of ignorance and prejudice. These passions have already been undermined by men of intellect. The contribution of railways to this process will be denied by no one.

This first moral consequence seems so great that it alone would justify the enthusiasm felt for railways by all true friends of Italy; but there is a second moral effect, less easy to grasp, but still more important.

The settlement imposed on Italy by the Congress of Vienna was as arbitrary as it was defective. It was based on no principle, not even that of legitimacy—as may be seen in the treatment given to Genoa and Venice. Certainly it was not based on national interests or popular will. Disregarding not only geographical circumstances, but general interest and private interests created by twenty years of revolution, that august Congress acted solely by justifying the rights of the strongest, and hence raised a political structure devoid of any moral basis. Such an act could bear only bitter fruit. Also, in spite of the paternal behavior of several of our national rulers, dissatisfaction increased rapidly during the years following the restoration, and a storm did not take long to break. The fomentors of change, the more ardent spirits, exploiting the warlike passions encouraged by Napoleon, thus found support in the generous sentiments frustrated by the decrees of Vienna. Hence the unfortunate risings of 1820 and 1821.

These attempts at revolution were easily suppressed, because the upper classes were divided and the masses took only a feeble part; nonetheless they had deplorable consequences for Italy. The governments of the country, without becoming tyrannical, were thereby aroused to an extreme distrust of any idea of nationality. This fact stopped the development of progressive tendencies which had already begun to show themselves. Italy, enfeebled, discouraged, deeply split, for a long time could make no further effort to improve its lot.

Time was beginning to efface the fatal traces of 1821, when the revolution of July 1830 in France shook the European social structure to its foundations. The repercussions of this great popular movement were widespread in Italy. The French had won a victory against a blameworthy but legal government, and this excited democratic passions to the highest degree—if not among the masses, at least among those enterprising spirits who aspired to sway the masses. The possibility of a war of principle enveloping all Europe awoke the hopes of those who were dreaming of the complete emancipation of the peninsula by means of social revolution.

The movements organized after 1830, with one exception where peculiar administrative conditions applied, were easily suppressed even before they had broken out. Inevitably so; for these movements, relying solely on republican ideas and demagogic passions, were sterile. A democratic revolution has no chance of success in Italy, as can be seen if you analyze the elements which favor political innovation. For innovators find no great sympathy among the masses, because the common people, except for some occasional urban groups, are for the most part deeply attached to the old institutions of the country. Active power resides almost exclusively in the middle class and part of the upper class, both of which groups have ultra-conservative interests to defend. In Italy the ownership of property is not, thank heaven, the exclusive privilege of an upper class. Even where a feudal nobility still manages to exist, it shares landed property with the third estate.

The subversive doctrines of Young Italy are therefore taking little hold among those who have an interest in maintaining social order. Excepting the young, whose experience has not yet modified the doctrines imbibed in the exciting atmosphere of the schools, only a tiny number of Italians exist who are seriously disposed to apply the exalted principles of that unfortunate and embittered sect. If the social order were truly threatened, if the great principles on which society is based were really at risk, many of the most determined *frondeurs* and republicans would at once join the ranks of the conservative party.

The revolutionary agitations following the events of 1830 had consequences as baleful as the military insurrections of 1820 and 1821. The governments, passionately attacked, sought only how to defend themselves; putting aside all notions of Italian progress and emancipation, they concentrated on averting the dangers which menaced them and which were perfidiously magnified by the reactionary party. Without wishing to justify all the repressive measures they employed, we believe that they could not be justly reproached for their attitude. Because, for governments as well as individuals, there exists a supreme right of self-defense, and the most rigorous moralist cannot determine its limits without the risk of falling into gross contradictions or absurdity.

Thank heaven, the stormy passions aroused by the July revolution have now calmed down and their traces are almost effaced. Things in Italy have returned to their natural course, so that the shaken confidence of our national rulers has gradually been re-established. Ordinary people are already feeling the salutary effect of this happy change, and everything now points toward a better future.

This future, which we desire with all our prayers, will be the triumph of national independence. Here is a supreme good which Italy can obtain only by the combined effort of all her children. Without independence, Italy cannot hope for any durable political improvement or be confident of any real progress. What we are here saying is the same as was eloquently said by our friend Signor Balbo; it is not an idle dream, or the result of unexamined thought or exalted imagination; it is a truth which seems to us capable of a rigorous test.

All history proves that no people can attain a high degree of intelligence and morality unless the feeling of its nationality is strongly developed. This remarkable fact is a necessary consequence of the laws which govern human nature. The intellectual life of the masses moves within a very limited range of ideas. Among the ideas which they are capable of acquiring, the noblest and most elevated are first those of religion, then those of country and nationality. If political circumstances prevent such ideas from manifesting themselves, or if guided in a wrong direction, the masses will remain plunged in a state of deplorable inferiority. But this is not all; among a people who cannot be proud of their nationality, a sense of personal dignity will be possible only for a few privileged individuals. The numerous classes who occupy the humblest positions in the social sphere have a need to feel themselves important from a national point of view, otherwise they may not acquire consciousness of their own personal dignity. Now, this awareness, we do not hesitate to say it even at the risk of shocking the straight-laced, constitutes for peoples as well as for individuals an essential element in morality.

So then, if we desire so ardently the emancipation of Italy, if we declare that, faced with this great question, all other matters which could divide us must give way and all private interests be silent, it is not only to see our country glorious and powerful, but above all so that it can raise itself up the ladder of intelligence and moral development to the level of the most civilized nations.

Unless there is a European upheaval whose disastrous consequences are such as to make the hardiest recoil—and thank heaven this becomes less probable every day—it seems likely that the precious triumph of our nationality cannot be realized except by the combined action of all the live forces in the country, that is to say, of the national rulers openly supported by every party. The history of the last thirty years, as well as an analysis of the various elements in Italian society, will prove that military or democratic revolutions can have little success in Italy. All true friends of the country must therefore reject such means as useless. They must recognize that they cannot truly help their fatherland except by gathering in support of legitimate monarchs who have their roots deep in the national soil. It must be their aim to promote without impatience the progressive inclinations manifested by existing Italian governments. Such behavior, conforming to the wise counsel of a man whose patriotism and enlightenment are beyond doubt —Signor Balbo in his remarkable book *On the Hopes of Italy*—will restore the union which we must, of necessity, see established between different branches of the Italian family. This will enable the country to profit from such favorable political circumstances as the future must bring, and so free itself from foreign domination.

This union which we preach so ardently is not as difficult to secure as appearances might suggest. Despite the unhappy memory of our own divisions, the sense of common nationality has become general; it is growing daily, and is already strong enough to hold together all the parties in Italy in spite of their differences. It is no longer the exclusive possession of a sect or of men professing advanced doctrines. Thus we are persuaded that the eloquent appeal that Signor Balbo has lately addressed to all Italians will have thrilled more than one highly decorated breast among our leading statesmen, and that it will have awoken more than a single echo among those who, faithful to the traditions of their ancestors, make legitimacy the touchstone of their political beliefs.

Every class of society can, to some measure, cooperate in this important work. Everyone with some education and some influence in Italy has a limited mission to fulfill toward this goal, following the distinguished writers who, like Signor Balbo and Count Petitti, devote their efforts to the instruction and enlightenment of their fellow citizens. Even humble individuals, in the narrow circle where they move, can help to raise the level of intelligence and moral character of those who surround them.

All these individual efforts, it is true, would remain fruitless without the assistance of the various governments of our nation. But we shall not lack this help. The distrust aroused by the movements of 1830, long kept alive by a party weak in numbers but strong in intrigue, has been almost totally dissipated. Our sovereigns are now reassured. They are following their natural inclinations and each day give new proof of their paternal and progressive disposition.

It will suffice to cite in this regard what is happening in Piedmont. The development of elementary education, the endowment of several university chairs in the moral and political sciences, the encouragement accorded to the spirit of association whether in the arts or in industry, and many other measures, not to speak of railway building, all these are proof that the illustrious monarch who reigns so brilliantly in this kingdom is determined to maintain that glorious policy which in the past made his family the leading Italian dynasty. It will therefore have an even higher destiny in time to come.

But more than by any other administrative reform, as much perhaps as by liberal political concessions, the building of the railways will help to consolidate the mutual confidence between governments and people, and this is the basis of our hopes for the future. These governments have the destiny of their peoples in trust, and railway building is therefore a powerful instrument of progress which testifies to the benevolent intentions of each government and the security they feel. On their side the people will be grateful for this and will come to hold their sovereigns in complete trust; docile, but full of enthusiasm, they will let themselves be guided by their rulers in the acquisition of national independence.

If these arguments have any foundation, no one will contest that the moral effects of the railways in Italy are more important than their material effects, and their introduction among us presages a better future. This is why, borrowing the vigorous language of Signor Balbo, we like to call them one of the principal hopes of our fatherland.

> [C. Cavour: *"Des chemins de fer en Italie, par le
> comte Petitti,"* in *Revue Nouvelle* (May 1,
> 1846); reprinted in D. Zanichelli: *Gli scritti
> del Conte di Cavour* (Bologna, 1892), vol. II,
> pp. 10–50]

6. *Agitation and Subversion, 1845-1848*

During most of his reign (1831–49), Charles Albert remained a king on the old pattern. Not only was the island of Sardinia the last place in Italy (and almost the last in Europe) where the personal services and the baronial courts of feudalism continued to enjoy legal sanction, but even in Piedmont and Liguria Charles Albert restored the ecclesiastical courts and reinforced the Jesuits in their control over university education. A religious as well as a civil censorship continued to exist at Turin, with the result that Gioia, Romagnosi, and even Machiavelli were banned, while the list of unprintable words continued to include *nation, revolution, liberty*, and even *Italy*.

But if there was little sign in Charles Albert of much affection toward liberty or Italy, he soon came to resent Austrian patronage. He had a considerable opinion of his own ability as a soldier, and, like previous members of his dynasty, was on the lookout for any possible aggrandizement of his hereditary possessions, whether against France, Austria, or Switzerland. When Gioberti and Balbo after 1843 demonstrated the existence of a national party, this must have encouraged the king to turn against Austria. His minister, Solaro della Margarita, who passed as a pro-Austrian, still took care to warn him that the Austrian Empire was showing signs of internal weakness which one day might make Metternich withdraw from Italy.

More than any other Italian state, the Kingdom of Piedmont-Sardinia had an aristocracy with a tradition of loyalty and public service. The Marquis d'Azeglio was a Piedmontese aristocrat, a first cousin of Count Balbo. He had lived much of his life in Rome, Milan, and Florence where he was well known as a successful novelist and painter. More than most of his kind he had a vision of Piedmont leading the peninsula in a war of liberation. Like others of the moderates he was sure that Mazzini must be fought and that conspiracies and insurrections would succeed only in undermining social order, but a famous pamphlet in which he advocated this policy failed to pass the Piedmontese censor-ship and had to be printed at Florence. Azeglio, like Count Cavour, thought of Piedmont and Turin as intellectually stifling; nevertheless, as he recounted in his memoirs, he returned there in October 1845 to ask for an audience with the king in order to assess the possibilities of a "conservative revolution."

Massimo d'Azeglio reports to King Charles Albert on his visit to central Italy, c. October 12, 1845

As was Charles Albert's practice, the audience took place at six o'clock in the morning. At the time fixed I entered the palace, all lit up and functioning, while the city still slept. My heart was beating. After a short wait in an antechamber, the equerry on duty opened the door for me and there I found myself in an audience chamber in the presence of the King. Carlo Alberto was standing up straight near a window; he replied to my bow with a cour-teous inclination of his head, and indicated that I should sit down on a chair in the embrasure of the great window. He sat opposite me.

At that time the King was a mystery; and although his later con-duct has been plainly intelligible, he will perhaps remain partly a mystery, even for history. At that time, the principal events of his life, those of 1821 and 1833, were certainly not in his favor: no one could reconcile his grand ideas for Italian independence with the Austrian marriages, his and his sister's; his inclination to aggrandize the House of Savoy with his courting of the Jesuits, or keeping round him such men as L'Escarena, Solaro della Mar-garita, etc.; his display of piety and his old-womanish penances with the loftiness of thought and firmness of character demanded by bold enterprises.

No one, therefore, trusted Carlo Alberto. A great evil for a ruler in his circumstances. Trying to keep the support of the two par-ties by guile, you end by losing that of both. His very looks pre-sented something inexplicable. He was very tall and slender, with a long, pale, habitually severe face. When he spoke, however, he had a sweet expression; his voice was charming, and his words were familiar and friendly. He exercised a real fascination on those to whom he spoke. I recall that when he began to talk to me about myself, whom he had not seen for some time, with a typical courtesy all his own, I had to struggle all the time not to be conquered by his winning ways and words, and I kept on repeating inwardly: "Massimo, don't trust him." Poor gentleman! He had much that was good and noble in him; why would he believe in the use of guile?

In speaking politely of myself, he chanced to say: "And where have you come from now?", which was a remark on which I could hang what I had to say. I did not let it slip, and I spoke as follows. If I do not repeat the actual words, I certainly give their sense.

"Your Majesty, I have been traveling through a great part of Italy, city by city; and the reason for my having asked to be admitted to your presence is precisely because, should Your Majesty deign to permit it, I should like to give you an account of what I have found the present state of Italy to be, of what I have seen, and what I have said everywhere to men of all conditions with regard to political conditions."

C.A.: "Oh certainly! I shall be pleased to hear what you have to say."

I: "Your Majesty is not ignorant of all the unrest, plots, and little revolutions which have occurred since 1814. You are well aware of the influences which stimulate them; the discontent which promotes them; the foolishness of the leaders; the sad consequences resulting. The uselessness, indeed the harm, of such activities, which only serve to denude the country of its best men and exacerbate the foreign influence, has now struck the more intelligent people in Italy, and they want to discover a new path to take.

"Some months ago I was in Rome, where I have considered and discussed with others possible remedies for this sad state of affairs. Pope Gregory is old and failing; at his death, if not previously, something big will happen. The Romagna will go up in flames and the inevitable result will follow: another Austrian intervention, another series of executions and banishments, a worsening of all the evils which oppress us. It is therefore a matter of urgency to find a way out."

Here I told him at length of the disgust of all honest, sensible men at the Mazzinian foolishness and wickedness; of the suggestion made that I should start to do something or other to try to give a new and better direction to the people's activities; of the excellent disposition I had found, with few exceptions, wherever I went. I continued as follows:

"Your Majesty, I have never belonged to any secret society; I have had nothing to do with intrigues and plots; but as I have spent my childhood and youth in various parts of Italy so that all are acquainted with me, they know I am no spy and therefore no one distrusts me; I have, therefore, known about their secret affairs just as though I had been one of them. They still tell me everything, and I think I can assure you, without fear of deceiving myself, that the majority of them recognize the absurdity of what has hitherto happened and want to change their policy. All are persuaded that without force nothing can be done; that the only force in Italy is that of Piedmont; but that they cannot count even on this as long as Europe is peaceful and organized as at present. These ideas are sensible and give proof of a real advance in political understanding. Your Majesty will ask: 'How long will they last?' I myself confess that there is no certainty about this. I think I can say that I have a good deal of influence on the men who count in those regions at the moment. I have succeeded in convincing the majority; but the revolt at Rimini, which broke out a fortnight after I left Romagna, is a proof that I did not persuade all. Or, even if the leaders were persuaded, those immediately under them were not. In such a hierarchy, where the discipline is not obligatory and only relies on trust, obedience is always fortuitous. Sometimes passions and inter-ests of all sorts determine actions not generally approved. Finally one must bear in mind the sad conditions which oppress the people. Where arbitrary actions, violence, corruption, deceit, suspicion, etc., are seen in those above, it is only natural that those below rely on the same methods. Where the general material and moral condi-tions are so bad, without a hope of improvement, one cannot foresee up to what point or for how long prudence and reason will be able to restrain desperation and rage. Those who suffer are the only ones who can decide the great question as to how long they can endure. Men are made like that: a wise, far-seeing policy must be based on things as they are, and accept the situation, if it doesn't wish to take the wrong road.

"This is why I have tried to restrain a new outbreak of despera-tion with a new idea, and for this purpose I have gone about to spread it, as I have reported. I think, despite the case of Rimini, my efforts have borne some fruit. Perhaps Your Majesty will tell me if he approves, or not, of what I have done and what I have now said."

I stopped and awaited the reply, which, to judge by the King's expression, did not seem likely to be hostile. But I guessed that, in regard to the essential, it was likely to be sibylline, and that it would not leave one any the wiser. Instead, he said quietly but firmly, without any hesitation or turning his glance away, but looking me straight in the eyes: "Let those gentlemen know that they should remain quiet and take no steps now, as nothing can be done at present; but they can rest assured that when the opportunity arises, *my life, my children's lives, my arms, my treasure, my army, all shall be given in the cause of Italy.*"

Expecting something quite different, I remained for a moment speechless. I almost thought I had not heard aright. I pulled myself together at once, but perhaps the King noticed my surprise. The intentions he had so resolutely revealed to me, especially the phrase "Let those gentlemen know," had so surprised me that they did not yet seem real. It was essential for me to understand them right. Then, as always, I thought that all the cards should be on the table and that any equivocation and—above all—miscalculation could only do harm.

Thanking him and showing how moved I was (as indeed I really was), captivated by his frankness, I was careful to repeat his own phrase in which I said: *farò dunque sapere a quei signori*, etc. He nodded to show I had understood him, and then dismissed me. We both got up; he placed his hands on my shoulders, and offered me his cheek, first on one side, then on the other. However, this embrace seemed somewhat studied, cold, almost funereal, so that I felt chilled. An inner voice repeated that terrible phrase: "Don't trust him." It is a tremendous punishment for those who are professedly astute, to be suspected, even when telling the truth.

He had really spoken the truth, poor gentleman: events proved it. Who would have said then, as we sat at that window on two gilded chairs covered with green and white flowered silk (and every time I see them again they make me shudder); who would have said that when, through me, he offered his arms, treasure, and life to the Italians, I was unjust in not being immediately fully convinced? Who would have said that the great moment, so far beyond any expectation in 1845, and which both of us must have despaired of ever seeing, had been ordained by God to come three years afterwards? And that in that war, an impossible war as it then seemed to us, he was to lose his crown, his country, and then his life: and to me, as his son's Prime Minister, was reserved the sad duty of burying him among the royal tombs of the Superga, officially attesting the act in person?

Poor humans, who imagine they control events!

As may well be believed, I left the palace with my mind in a whirl. A great and splendid hope flew before me with beating wings. I returned to my little room on the top floor of the Trombetta Hotel, and sat down at the desk to write at once to my correspondents, who had to pass on the reply to all the others. Before parting from them I had invented a code, quite different from all the usual ones. It was absolutely secure and, in my opinion, proof against breaking, but very tedious to use. I therefore could not write the letter quickly. It gave the exact purport of Carlo Alberto's reply; but to be scrupulously exact and in order not to give as certain what was really my own impression, I ended my letter thus: "These are his words: God alone knows his inner thoughts."

> [M. d'Azeglio: *Things I Remember (I miei ricordi)*, trans. E. R. Vincent (London, 1966), pp. 338–42]

Azeglio's new message of hope was not received well by all the liberal patriots in central Italy. They were too suspicious of Charles Albert's anti-liberal past and of Piedmont's desire to dominate. More important was the fact that, in June 1846, a new Pope was elected and began his pontificate by freeing most of the political prisoners who had been cluttering up the papal prisons. An amnesty was customary on such an occasion, and it was accompanied by conditions and even threats; yet this innocent document had unintended results which made it a decisive fact in the building of Italy.

Pius IX was one of those Popes of real goodness and personal fascination, the kind of man about whom myths appear which acquire a life all of their own. The almost hysterical enthusiasm which greeted his proclamation of amnesty touched a weak point in his character, and soon he was so eager for popularity and applause that he let the initiative slip out of the hands of the Curia cardinals. He thus allowed consultative committees of laymen to be established, and even a civic militia. Decisions were taken to improve popular education, to lift press censorship, to introduce telegraph lines and build a railway system.

Pius's political program went little further toward laicization of the state than the memorandum of 1831 which Austria and other powers had presented to Pope Gregory, but the fact that these changes were being seen in Rome itself—the center of Italy and what under Gregory had seemed the center of European anti-liberalism—gave a great impetus to the concession of moderately liberal reforms all through the peninsula. The papal government even tried to persuade a reluctant Piedmontese government into joining an Italian customs league. Charles Albert was disturbed at this liberal trend at Rome, but feeling ran so high that he too had to dismiss his old ministers and allow a moderate freedom of the press. Metternich, though he had recommended the amnesty, realized that liberal and even national views were suddenly being made almost respectable by this unexpected papal patronage.

Amnesty granted by Pius IX, July 16, 1846

DURING THE days when the public rejoicing on our exaltation to the Pontificate touched Us to the depth of our heart, We could not restrain an emotion of grief, while reflecting that not a few families among our subjects were kept back from sharing in the general joy, because, in the loss of their domestic consolations, they were made to bear a great portion of the punishment, which only some one member of the family had deserved, by offenses against the order of society, or the lawful rights of the sovereign. We furthermore turned a pitying eye upon the numbers of inexperienced youths, who, although drawn by alluring flatteries into the vortex of political disorders, yet appeared to us less as seducers than seduced. On which account, from that time forward, We have been considering whether to stretch out our hand, and to tender peace of mind, to those of our erring children who might be disposed to give evidence of their sincere repentance. The affection that our good subjects have shown toward Us, and the incessant tokens of veneration that the Holy See has, in our Person, received from them, have now persuaded Us, that We may pardon them without danger to the public at large. We accordingly determine and command, that the opening of our Pontificate be signalized by the following acts of sovereign clemency:—

I. To all our subjects now actually in a place of punishment for political offenses, We remit the remainder of their sentences, provided they make in writing a solemn declaration that they will never, in any manner, abuse this favor, but that they desire faithfully to fulfill all the duties of good subjects.

II. Upon the same condition, all our subjects who have quitted our dominions for political reasons may return to them, provided that they shall make known in a proper manner, within one year from the publication of the present decree, and through the

Apostolic Nuncios, their desire to avail themselves of this act of our clemency . . .

But should our hopes in any degree be frustrated, We shall then, with whatever bitterness or pain to ourselves, constantly recollect, that if mercy be the most pleasurable attribute of sovereignty, justice is its first duty.

> [Farini: *The Roman State from 1815 to 1850*, trans. Gladstone, vol. I, pp. 179–81. Farini's book was dedicated to Balbo]

Until 1848, Sicily and Naples participated less than north Italian regions in the liberal and patriotic movement. The Bourbon regime was corrupt, intolerant, and inefficient, even though it had been a little more enlightened and well-meaning than later patriotic propaganda made out. The first steamship in Italy had been launched in 1818 at Naples; the first iron suspension bridge was that over the Garigliano in 1828–32; the first Italian railway was built not in Piedmont or Lombardy, but in Naples. If Ferdinand failed to make the Sicilian landowners surrender all their feudal practices, it was not for want of well-meaning legislation; but the result of his attack on feudalism was that many important (and not noticeably liberal) people acquired an interest in denigrating his reputation.

A variegated opposition was coming into existence at Naples and Palermo, both of those who opposed Ferdinand's authoritarianism and those who thought him not authoritarian enough. Nowhere in Italy was Gioberti's book more enthusiastically received than in Naples, especially among the poorer clergy who were almost the only educated people in the country villages. Inconsistent and even absurd Gioberti's ideas might be, but they had a great rhetorical appeal; he had made the word *Italy* legitimate, so that it was used with pride even by Santangelo the Bourbon minister. Perhaps, after all, a federal Italy could be created without revolutions and without tears.

In 1847 an anonymous pamphlet appeared at Naples which criticized Santangelo and the king in the harshest terms. Its author, Luigi Settembrini, was a teacher and minor literary critic who had spent years in the prisons which Gladstone's protest to Lord Aberdeen was soon to make notorious. King Ferdinand II was not so evil or so stupid as he was depicted in this pamphlet, and future history would show that some of the things he was blamed for were as bad or even became worse under the liberal government of united Italy after 1860; but this strong anti-government feeling helps to explain why southern Italy, now as later, remained so hard to control and became such an ideal field for revolutions of every kind.

Neapolitan misgovernment, 1847

NAPLES SAW the birth of economic science and still boasts distinguished economists, yet its administration is in the hands of knaves and fools. The Ministry of the Interior is scandalously corrupt. The Minister, together with a few grain merchants, maintains a ruinous hold on the economy, and he personally shares some of the filthy profits of the public-works contractors, choosing those who offer him the highest bribe. Scholarly thief that he is, he has filched from Pompeii and Herculaneum the finest and most precious relics of antiquity to make a magnificent museum—an all-time marvel to those who do not expect to see knowledge hand in hand with robbery. His employees—bootlickers, clowns and hangers-on —do what he does, and he merely follows the Kings bad example.

Our agriculture, which needs government protection and the most assiduous care, comes under a subdepartment run by two or three idiotic clerks. Our land is as fertile as almost anywhere in Italy, but it is deserted, or else is cultivated by a handful of wretched, weary peasants. Immense territories in Sicily, in the Calabrias, in the Abruzzi, in the Principati and even in Apulia are abandoned and malarial. If there is any question of land reclamation, as for instance near the mouth of the Volturno, the Minister gives the job to some personal friend who spends and spends but does nothing. The Minister personally takes some of the land at a light rent and then leases it back to the peasants. If there is an outcry, a Commission is set up whose head is none other than the Minister himself. In such a fertile Kingdom, which could feed double its present population, there is often a bread shortage and people can be found dead of starvation. Often grain has to be brought from Odessa, or from Egypt and other so-called "barbarous" lands. If you ask the Ministers how much grain is grown, or how much the Kingdom needs, they do not know. Every father of a family does better than this, for he balances intake and output, he sells any surplus, and provides for extra needs in good time. If he is well stocked and then runs short, he knows he has been robbed. But the Ministers and the King cannot reach these heights. Their only statistics are every three years to take a census of the poor sheep who are their subjects. Otherwise all is left to God's providence and to the landowners. When they see that the people are hungry, they simply forbid the export of grain, remove the flour tax for a couple of months, and tell the friars to give out generous alms and pray for a good season.

Instead of being protected and helped, landowners are treated as sponges to be squeezed dry. They are oppressed by taxes, by Intendants, Under-Intendants and officials of every kind. Trade is restricted because the provinces lack roads, and the Minister and his ultra-rich friends have made road building a sordid monopoly. Growers therefore must sell their produce at a paltry price which barely covers outlay; hence they become poor and reduce their laborers' wages; and the result is that the latter take to robbery and brigandage. The condition of the peasants is appalling. They dig all day for fifteen or twenty *grani*, just enough to obtain bread and oil and make a soup of wild herbs, often without salt. In the winter, hunger forces them to ask the landlord for food; he gives it but only if they repay him twice as much or even more at harvest time, and only if they let him make love to their wives and daughters. Thus the government leaves the landlord no way of getting richer except by usury, while the peasant has to sell his honor for bread. Everyone is offended. The poor rage against their immediate oppressors, failing to see that these too are suffering and that the government is to blame.

We have had many proposals for agricultural credit schemes and a savings bank. And think of all the other useful proposals that would be made if this blind and bestial government understood its own advantage! It cannot even see that with an increased population the country would grow richer and taxes higher. Local chambers of commerce, like the provincial councils with their solemn meetings, never propose any serious changes because the government takes no notice of them. When a government is bad, even the best institutions decay into uselessness. We should praise the King (lest it be said that we speak ill of everything) because at least he has partially freed trade; he has signed commercial treaties, and ensured that the flag is respected. But when things are decaying within, external polish does not matter; when producers are oppressed, when industries are few and backward, and commerce at home is held up by a thousand obstacles, what is the use of treaties? We have such treasures in our soil that everyone could live well, yet people are reduced to destitution. The balance of trade goes against us, and craftsmen also suffer when agriculture, the mother of all, is dying.

Charitable institutions are fine and holy things, but here they are in greedy and pitiless hands. The Benevolent Society of the Province of Naples has eight hundred thousand ducats in annual income, and that of the Terra di Lavoro seven hundred thousand, yet apparently this million and a half ducats will barely pay for a few poor people, ill clad, ill nourished, and shut up in places worse than prisons. For many years now, the director of the Naples poorhouse has been Felice Santangelo, the Minister's brother; he filled it with penpushers who battened on the poor orphans like horseflies, and who were in league with the purveyors of clothes and food to steal what they could. One boy threw himself out of a window and was mortally injured; in his last moments of life they asked him why he had wanted to die, and he answered, because of hunger and despair. Some of these poor children, who after all are human beings, have died of hunger; others fled in terror from this place of pain, infamy and fear. The King, weary of hearing tales of Santangelo's thieving, dealt out justice in his fashion; he removed him from the post of director, but gave him another good job with a large salary, and then set up a commission of eight honest men to run the poorhouse.

The worst place of all, where you see cruelty at its most impious, is the Nunziata, or the foundling hospital. Each wet nurse has three or four babies—fleshless, pale and starving. Out of every hundred, eighty-nine die, and still more would die if the good simple womenfolk of Naples did not piously take these *children of the Madonna* into their own families. To seize bread from the mouths of beggars and innocent little creatures is a cruelty that could only happen under a government like ours. The Minister looks no further than at the accounts; then he carefully draws up or suggests proposals for building, for exterior decoration, or for improving the rooms where the governors meet—works on which one can spend little and rob much.

The sick and the insane have their butchers too. At a recent congress in Naples, a commission of doctors and surgeons was chosen to inspect the hospitals. They made their inspection, were overcome with pity and indignation, and wrote a long, heartfelt report; but nothing was mentioned in the published proceedings, for the report was suppressed by the chairman of the congress, the Minister Santangelo. In the *Annali Universali di Medicina*, printed in Milan by Calderini (in February or March of 1846), there is a reference to this and to the fact that *they did not want the voice of the pauper to reach the throne*. Ferdinand's ears are deaf to the loudest cries. He wanted to conceal the shame of it from foreigners: but the good Milanese did well to unveil this oppression suffered by their unfortunate brothers in the Two Sicilies.

The prisons are also in a terrible state. The government grants just over four *grani* a day for each prisoner, on which sum the "contractor" has to provide bread, soup, oil, and earthenware receptacles; he has to whitewash the prison every six months, give good tips, and still make his own profit. One single ladleful of fetid beans and a piece of rotten bread are all those wretched men are given to eat. They should have something fresh to wear twice a year, but in practice it is every eighteen months. Here you see not men but beasts, naked as when they were born, pale, starving, gnawing at the crusts and remains thrown away by some prisoner who has bought his own food; for a *grano* they submit to any oppression, undergo any shame. Two hundred thousand ducats were allocated to improving the prisoners' lot, and the Minister of the Interior, that brilliant conjuror, made the sum disappear: the King removed him from the administration of prisons in punishment, and entrusted this task to the Minister of Finance. There is justice and honesty for you!

Another affliction in our poverty-stricken country are the beggars who you see all over the Kingdom and who pour into Naples from the provinces. The government does nothing to employ this vast number of unemployed. It moves only when some foreign sovereign arrives here (for instance that ferocious beast of prey, Nicholas of Russia); then all sorts of people are arrested or sent back to the provinces to die of hunger. No other country in the world has so many beggars. Private people, out of kindness, help them, but the government does nothing to supplement the work of private institutions; it just uses them as a further excuse to oppress and to rob. Hence the beggars multiply daily, and some, with monstrous cunning, even may hire a cripple or a halfwit and take him out on show through the streets; or they hire babies and teach them to cry, pinching and hitting them to make them howl and so arouse the pity of passers-by. To prevent these heart-rending screams, with mixed feelings of pity and resentment you are forced to give them alms. Now who is to be blamed for these tragic crowds of starving people in a country made by nature to be as rich and happy as anywhere in the world? And this King and government call themselves Catholics!

They think they can provide a remedy by public works, on which the King and Santangelo—the one an expert architect and the other a well-equipped spender—are continually congratulating each other. The King's palace has been restored with money from the city of Naples; around half a million has been spent in a few years to refurbish the San Carlo Theater for the entertainment of the Court, of foreigners, and of high-class tarts; three hundred thousand ducats are going to repair the Posillipo road to provide a more comfortable way for carriages, and the poor fishermen are being driven from the area lest their poverty should disturb the beatitude of the carriage owners. All these works may satisfy a King's childish whim, but they do not benefit a nation. Private property is being ruined in the process, on the plea that public utility must come first. Two railways have been built, one from Naples to Nocera with a branch line to Castellammare, and the other from Naples to Capua. This last was made *to link up the two royal palaces* of Naples and Caserta, as is inscribed on the medals struck to perpetuate its memory; and a sleepy branch line extends it as far as Nola where the King can review his troops.

This is all done for Naples. Nothing is done for the provinces, nothing for luckless Sicily. When Sicilians go to market to exchange or sell the meager produce of their lands and wretched industries, they have to clamber over precipices, or risk plunging into crevasses and drowning themselves in swollen rivers. Railways are fine and desirable, but only when there are ordinary roads too: otherwise they are, I should say, almost a luxury. Incredible as it may seem, however, when a village wants to build a road at its own expense, the government withholds permission; or else the money is inadequate to feed the hungry clerks through whom permission has been obtained and the architect who has to be appointed by the government. The work therefore remains half finished, or not begun at all. There is only one road in Calabria, and that a bad one; Sicily has two, short and bad; the Abruzzi two; very few cities have connecting roads which link them to these main routes which the French government built [under Napoleon]. In the interior, the only method of transport is on foot, or with difficulty on horseback. Official policy on public works is therefore stupid, and has no serious or useful end; apart from which it is inefficiently carried out.

This reflects the character of a King who always acts by whim, who claims he does everything, and in fact does nothing.

> [L. Settembrini: *Protesta del popolo delle Due Sicilie* (Naples, 1847), pp. 35–42]

By the treaty of 1815, Austria could keep garrisons in Piacenza and Ferrara south of the Po River, and late in 1847 the ominous news from all over Italy made Metternich decide to push these rights further than he was legally entitled. This brought him up against the Pope, to whom Ferrara belonged. In December 1847, moreover, a secret treaty with Modena and Parma gave him a more threatening position on Piedmont's eastern frontier. Both these facts provided an excuse to the ultra-Catholic Charles Albert to move one stage further toward defending Italian and papal independence against the Austrians.

Meanwhile, at Milan, a novel and semi-revolutionary idea began to infect even those who feared Mazzini's advocacy of violence: tentatively they started a series of peaceful protests and demonstrations against Austrian rule. Occasionally the imperial army was provoked to use force to stop these demonstrations, but that only underlined the repressive nature of the existing regime. Short of armed repression, there was no way the government could meet this kind of passive resistance, unless it could drive a wedge between the conservatives and radicals among the liberal Milanese. Meanwhile the Austrians became more and more anxious.

Metternich defies Italian nationalism, 1847

THE WORD "Italy" is a geographical expression. Though it is a term that slides easily off the tongue, it has none of the political implications which the revolutionary ideologists are trying to attach to it—implications which would threaten the very existence of the individual states which constitute the Italian peninsula.

The Emperor is King of the Lombardo-Venetian Kingdom, which, though south of the Alps, forms part of the Austrian Empire. At the time of the great territorial systematizations in 1814, the late Emperor Francis wanted no reference at all to any *Kingdom of Italy*, for the very idea seemed a permanent threat to other rulers in the peninsula.

The difference between Austria and France, or indeed any other country, does not lie in the political fact of whether they are an Italian Power or a non-Italian Power; the difference rather lies in material conditions of geographical situation and practical, effective authority. All countries should be judged by this same standard. I have touched on this question only to show the French cabinet that we are very much concerned over the possible diffusion of these erroneous ideas of *nationality*. Such ideas are being dangerously exploited by elements of disorder who are pitting themselves against the hard reality of political fact.

> [Prince Metternich to Count Apponyi in Paris, April 12, 1847: *Aus Metternich's nachgelassenen Papieren*, ed. R. Metternich-Winneburg (Vienna, 1883), vol. VII, pp. 388–9]

Luigi Torelli describes the strong feelings in Lombardy, writing to Maurizio Farina in Piedmont, February 1848

EVENTS ARE being precipitated by the brutality of the police and the ferocity of Radetzky [the Austrian commander in Milan]. Four months ago I could never have believed that hatred could spread everywhere so fast. The police are desperate, and we are expecting them to confiscate arms. Two months ago the existing list of arms' permits in each province had to be sent to the Milan police. Gunsmiths are under continual surveillance and must declare the names of whoever buys arms or takes them to be cleaned.

The army of spies has been doubled. People live in continual fear of being arrested even on the slightest excuse. All hopes are concentrated on Piedmont. Charles Albert's name is now known even in country districts; and you can imagine how I praise him wherever I can, directly or indirectly.

In Milan people were repeating a doggerel phrase about: "Nothing in '48; a little in '49; in '50 the floodgates will open so that in '51 we can turn the Austrians out." As things are now, public opinion even expects to improve on this schedule. There is talk of next spring. Radetzky issues absurd threats, but he is bound to make some gross blunder. There is such solid confidence in the valor of your troops that everyone hopes for him to commit some idiocy and attack you, so that his army will be annihilated.

But enough of this. We rely on Piedmont to save us, and you will find that every village in Lombardy, however small, is on your side. Even the Italian Tyrol is burning to join the common cause. It would now be impossible to prevent a fight between Austrians and Italians, between slavery and the cause of national independence. We are at a terrifying crossroads, and it is your army and your King who must pull us out of this agonising situation—your King whom we hope shortly to hail as ours too, with all our heartfelt gratitude.

> [A. Monti, ed.: *La guerra santa d' Italia in un epistolario inedito di Luigi Torelli (1846–9)* (Milan, 1934), pp. 107-8]

7. The Revolution of 1848

The start of 1848 found Italy in a highly combustible state, with demonstrations in Milan, wild enthusiasm at Rome and Bologna over Pius IX's concessions, Charles Albert eager to show his prowess as a soldier, Mazzini in England weaving a tangled fabric of conspiracy, Neapolitan intellectuals indignant at police rule, and everywhere a threatening social revolution. Poor people were brought close to desperation by rising prices and the far from easy problem of how food supplies could be kept in pace with a growing population.

Revolution finally began in almost the poorest part of Italy, Palermo, on January 12, 1848. The Neapolitan Bourbons had some five thousand soldiers in this Sicilian town, and normally that would have sufficed to keep order. But a long tradition of brigandage and quasi-mafia activity had resulted in there being many arms in circulation among the people and considerable skill and experience in using them. This was a social environment where vendettas and family feuds were normal, where conspiratorial networks were constructed with loving artistry, and where many people were waiting for any momentary weakness in government so that they could enforce their own kind of rough justice outside the law. Grinding poverty made a mob easy to collect and ensured that acts of violence were never far from the surface of ordinary life. All classes in Sicilian society, moreover, had reason to resent that for a century they had been ruled by what they called an alien people in Naples. Patriotic feeling for Italy was not very strong here, but other revolutionary sentiments were enormously powerful, and so was insular Sicilian patriotism. Together they combined in January 1848 to touch off a dramatic year of revolt all over Italy.

Giuseppe La Farina, one of the leaders of this Sicilian revolution, later wrote its history; and a brief footnote in a private letter explained, what he had not liked to say in his history, the activities of Scordato, Miceli, and the gang leaders of the mafia, who were playing a double and treacherous game.

The Sicilian revolution, 1848

GREAT WAS the excitement and perturbation early in 1848.

At Messina, on January 5, the populace smashed the windows of the Royal Palace; the Bourbon coats of arms in the theater were torn down before the eyes of the police; and the latter, realizing the threat to themselves, tried to "place citizens between the bayonets of the soldiers and the knives of the assassins" by releasing notorious criminals from prison to terrify the timid and give a bad name to the movement. Robberies and disorders did in fact ensue, but were speedily repressed by the populace with such vigor and fury as to terrify these contemptible auxiliaries of the royal authority.

Other demonstrations followed in Catania, Trapani and the other chief towns of the island. The clandestine press became wonderfully busy, publishing daily news sheets, expounding Sicily's right to a constitutional government, voicing the ideas and hopes of the people, addressing words of affection and national brotherliness to the Neapolitans, and exhorting the militia to cease acting as the hired assassins of a brutal tyranny and become the soldiers of national independence. A booklet entitled *Letter from Malta* had as great a success in the island as Settembrini's famous *Protesta* had in Naples.

Finally a singular challenge was issued, now famous in history, declaring that "The day of mere requests is over: protests and peaceful demonstrations are useless." After further provocative phrases, it concluded: "On January 12, at daybreak, the glorious era of universal regeneration will dawn. Palermo will joyfully welcome every Sicilian who takes arms to defend the common cause. Our policy is to establish reforms and institutions suited to the present age and demanded by Europe, Italy and Pius IX. Union, order, subordination to the leaders! Robbery must be declared treason to the country and punished as such. Those that lack resources will be provided with them. If we have good principles, heaven will assist our righteous enterprise. Sicilians, to arms!" This was the work of a certain Bagnasco, a young man of Palermo. There were in fact no leaders, there were no resources, but there was that which mattered more: the common consent of the people.

During the night of January 9 the police, in the hope of hamstringing the conspiracy, imprisoned eleven of the most prominent supporters of these peaceful demonstrations, but this produced the very opposite effect and inflamed the spirit of the conspirators. Many a revolutionary lost control of himself, and some of the reformists their last hope.

On the night preceding the twelfth, the streets of Palermo were silent and deserted, but inside their houses the citizens were waiting, torn between fears and hopes. When the new day dawned, it was found that armed militiamen were standing by. A few battalions of infantry and some policemen and police spies occupied the Prefecture of Police and the Royal Palace, where General de Majo the Governor, General Vial the commandant of the fortress, and other royal officials were assembled in council. The guns of Castellamare fired a salute for the birthday of Ferdinand II. The streets were crowded with people, all waiting for the conspirators to appear, for the signal to be given, for the first shout to arise. A certain Buscemi, a bold youth who was truculent by nature and weary of delay, brandished a gun he had kept concealed, and shouted resolutely, "To arms. To arms!" Whereupon Pasquale Miloro came out, armed, into the via de' Centorinari. The Abbé Ragona, and Venuti, another priest, exhorted the people to rise in the name of God. Iacona the lawyer, Giuseppe Oddo, Prince Granmonte, Baron Bivona, Lo Cascio, Pasquale Bruno, Francesco Ciaccio, Giacinto Carini, Amodei, Enea and a few others ran up, all of them armed. Giuseppe La Masa tied a white handkerchief and a red one to the end of a stick with a green ribbon, and began waving the three Italian colors. Santa Astorina the glover went round distributing tricolors and cockades.

At the sight of weapons, and of the small number of those bearing them, the crowd thinned out and then entirely disappeared. Shops were closed. This handful of intrepid spirits found themselves almost deserted. Only a few of those without arms stayed to share the perils and the honor of the enterprise, among them Vincenzo Errante and Baron Casimiro Pisani, both noted for their nobility of spirit and spotless integrity. But no one lost heart. The bells of Sant'Orsola began ringing an alarm, those of the Convent of the Gangia replied: the revolution could not now be stopped. Little bands and squads of people began to form here and there; the more forceful took the lead and the rest followed their example, not their orders. There were no rules, ranks or plans. No one barricaded the streets or cordoned them off as might have happened elsewhere.

People did not even assemble in any one place. Troops of children ran ahead, dancing and singing. They ventured close to the military to observe their movements, and then returned, often bleeding from gunshot wounds, to report to the insurgents. One band put a patrol to flight in the via dell' Albergaria; some were as successful in the via Raffadale, others by the church of San Gaetano, near the Santo Antonio Gate, and in the via de' Calderari and elsewhere. So the whole day went by. Two of the insurgents, Amodei and another, were dead, and so were ten soldiers; the wounded were more numerous. The insurgents then returned to the Piazza della Fiera-vecchia, which ever since the morning had been the center of their activities and the headquarters of an organizing committee. Not more than fifty carried firearms. A single company of infantry would have been enough to disperse them; but the militiamen had not stirred from their posts; remembering the events of 1820, they would not venture into the densely populated parts of the city. Meanwhile every house was festively illuminated, balconies and windows crowded with people clapping their hands and shouting: "Long Live Italy, the Sicilian Constitution and Pius IX!" This was a spontaneous, unexpected and universal assent of the people, which put the authorities in a quandary and took the heart out of the soldiers.

That night support for the insurgents began to come in from the countryside and the neighboring villages, first sixty peasants from Villabate, then others from Misilmeri and elsewhere. By next day there were about three hundred men in the Fieravecchia, some armed with guns, others with sickles, billhooks, knives, spits and the various iron objects that popular fury converts into weapons. The fortress of Castellamare began bombing the city, and the Palace artillery fired grapeshot along the Cassero; but the insurgents attacked, overcame the divisional police, and captured the military hospital of St. Francesco Saverio. The soldiers taken prisoner were embraced as brothers and supplied with all their needs, but no pity was shown to policemen. After these first successes the numbers and courage of the combatants increased: peasants from the hill villages came down into Palermo, the timid turned bold, the lazy worked frenziedly. Next day those who had been directing operations invited the civic officials and other prominent townsmen—whether because of their love of liberty, their connections, or family name and wealth—to share in the honor and peril of the enterprise, and four committees were set up. The first was for victualling the city, presided over by Marchese Spedalotto, who held the office of Mayor; the second was for war, presided over by the Prince of Pantelleria, a name dear to the people ever since 1820; the third was for finance, presided over by Marchese Rudinì; the fourth was for propaganda and the collection of information, the president of which was Ruggero Settimo, who has already been mentioned in this History for his honorable conduct in 1816 and 1820. The committee of Fieravecchia was entrusted with the provision of urgent military supplies.

That day there were only a few slight skirmishes and clashes, because the Governor, who had informed Naples by telegraph of what had happened, was waiting for help and reinforcements before proceeding to more serious military operations. Next day the police headquarters was attacked and taken by storm after many policemen had been killed. On that day, too, a certain Giuseppe Scordato of Bagheria turned up in Palermo with a band of partisans and a good number of captured soldiers. A brother of his had been a famous and greatly feared brigand: he had been dead for some years, but the people insisted that he was still alive and in revolt against the government. Giuseppe was now mistaken for his brother, and his sudden appearance was a great encouragement to the people at a moment when they most needed it. For five steam frigates and four corvettes now arrived under the command of Conte d'Aquila, brother to the King, and soon we saw five thousand soldiers disembark before the walls of the city, with artillery to match, commanded by General de Sauget. Encouraged by which assistance, the royalists intensified the bombardment that had been devastating the city for three days.

On the following day the streets were almost deserted again: the sudden arrival of these fresh troops, while the insurgents were still without enough arms and munitions, produced consternation and confusion. Following the exhortations of La Masa, who had won great popularity, a new armed band was formed and after severe fighting repulsed a royalist force by the Porta Macqueda. Meanwhile the Consuls of Austria, France and Piedmont had gone to the committee, offering to intercede with the Conte d'Aquila, and exhorting its members to ask for pardon from the clemency of the King. Many members of the committee, despairing of victory, had fled; among those remaining was Mariano Stabile, who replied:

"Sicily wants to recover her ancient liberty. The real rebel is not the people but Ferdinand II who once swore to keep our constitution and then broke his word."

Loud cries were heard at that moment, bells were ringing, and the enemy artillery opened fire furiously aaginst the city. The royalists, having re-formed their ranks, had returned to the assault at the Porta Macqueda and the Porta Carini; but after three hours of sanguinary fighting they were routed and defeated, retreating in confused and disorderly flight. This day brought enormous fame to Giuseppe Scordato, a rough fellow, ignorant of the arts of war, but whose natural disposition fitted him superlatively for such a war as this.

Next day a man named Salvadore Miceli, whose standing in Monreale was like that of Scordato in Bagheria, made his appearance in Palermo at the head of a band of armed mountaineers; he too had a good many captive soldiers with him. Meanwhile the bombs thrown on the city had set fire to the pawnshop of Santa Rosalia, destroying everything deposited there, all of it belonging to the poor and valued at 3,750,000 lire. The soldiers, having entered the monastery of the White Benedictines near the Royal Palace, murdered Fathers Beaumont and Campisi, four lay friars and Baron Turrisi, and ten other citizens, all of whom had taken refuge there thinking they would be safe in such a holy place. They seriously wounded Abbot Carella and several other religious, and pillaged the monastery and the church. When the news of this slaughter spread through the town, the people rushed to the monastery and entered it by main force. Many of the royalists were unable to flee from the rebels, who killed a great number and captured others, wresting from them the sacred vessels and all the loot they had seized.

The authorities in the Palace were in a state of great anxiety and confusion, and the Governor asked for an interview with the Mayor, who gave him this report: "The city bombarded; a building in which the poor have such an interest burnt down; myself attacked by rifle fire when I was with the Austrian Consul and carrying a flag of truce; foreign consuls fired at on their way to the Royal Palace, even though preceded by two white flags; unarmed monks assassinated. The people treat captured soldiers with respect, feed them and regard them as brothers. This is the state of things in Palermo. A General Committee of Defense and Safety has been set up. If Your Excellency wishes, you may submit your proposals to it."

Pressed further by the Governor, the Mayor replied: "The committee can do no more than apprise you of feelings universally held. This people, having courageously revolted, will not lay down their arms or suspend hostilities until Sicily, in a general assembly of parliament, can revive and remodel its old constitution to which its Kings have sworn and which all the Powers recognize. Until this is done, no attempt at negotiation will be of any use."

This was the program of the Sicilian revolution. All honor and praise to the committee and the people for having remained absolutely firm in this affair and refused to come to any settlement. A revolution that makes overtures for peace is a moribund revolution.

The Governor replied: "I am glad to know at last what are the intentions of the Sicilian people, and I have the honor to inform you that I shall submit them to His Majesty for any decisions that in his wisdom he may see fit to pronounce."

Base and misplaced servility, old tricks to gain time! But they were of no use, because the people went on fighting. They stormed the Santa Zita barracks and took three hundred soldiers prisoner; they drove the cavalry encamped outside the walls into the plains between the Porta Sant'Antonio and the Porta Montalto, and kept it confined to quarters at Santa Teresa and the Borgognoni; and during the night they set fire to the forage stores and burnt them all down, to the great loss and alarm of the troops. Meanwhile the gunnery officers Longo and Orsini, having escaped from the royalist camps where they had been held prisoner, joined the insurgents, who thenceforth derived no little advantage from the military knowledge of these two expert soldiers.

On January 21 the Governor sent the Mayor four royal decrees dated the eighteenth. These increased the powers of the Council of State; they abolished some of the centralization on Naples which dated from 1837, promised a general amnesty, appointed Conte d'Aquila (who had once bombarded the undefended town of Reggio and had now fled from Palermo) to be Lieutenant of the King in Sicily. Other appointments were of the Prince of Campo Franco as chief Minister, together with the Duke of Montalbo, Buongiardino the Advocate General, and Councillor Cassisi.

The Mayor replied in the name of the committee, repeating that arms would not be laid down, nor hostilities suspended, until the Sicilian parliament could meet again and adapt her ancient constitution to modern times.

Arms were not laid down, and after two days of fighting the people opened a breach in the Noviziato barracks. The boldest rushed inside, but as the troops continued to resist, the building was set on fire, and some soldiers fled in disorder, while the others surrendered at discretion and suffered no harm. The royalists behaved less generously. At that very time they were plundering the houses round the points they were occupying, and massacring all who fell into their hands, armed or unarmed. When the Governor sent to dissociate himself from these brutal deeds, he obtained only this simple reply from the committee: "When we have brought this war to a glorious conclusion, history will judge the conduct of both sides."

On January 24, in order to give more unity to the revolutionary government, the four committees elected a President and a Secretary "of the General Committee." These were Ruggero Settimo and Mariano Stabile, who had won general esteem by their firmness and constancy and their moral courage. Next day an Order of the Day was read out to the squads, inviting them to attack the Royal Palace, which was still in the hands of the enemy. "An evil genius," said the committee, "is determined to defile this pleasant land with blood, and to set brother against brother. The fault is not ours. We have acted under provocation, and God will let fall the weight of this great disaster on the accursed head of the despot. Europe will declare, and our brothers throughout Italy will declare even more loudly, that this war is not waged against the Neapolitan soldiers who deny us the freedom bequeathed us by our fathers, but against him whom they obey. Though they are betraying their country they are unaware of what is done in their name."

The royalists had occupied the monastery of Santa Elisabetta, the Municipal Hospital, the Palazzo Reitano and the Archbishop's Palace, all large, very solid buildings which, with the San Giacomo barracks, surrounded the square in front of the Royal Palace, flanked at that time by ramparts furnished with cannon. The people began by attacking the monastery of Santa Elisabetta and the Hospital; having cleared these of the enemy, they occupied the Cathedral, the monastery of the Sette Angeli and the neighboring houses, from which they opened brisk musketry fire on the troops defending the

Archbishop's Palace and the San Giacomo barracks. The soldiers fought obstinately, the artillery thundered, Castellamare bombarded the city. All the bells rang out, encouraging the people and disheartening and confusing the enemy. The women applauded, cheering the combatants and waving them on; children threw themselves on the bombs almost as they fell, seizing the burning fuses and rolling the hot bullets along the sidewalk with shouts of joy and scorn. So the terrible battle went on, all that day and part of the night, till it was discovered that all the powder the rebels had amassed or manufactured during the last few days had been used up. But this deficiency, which at first caused so much dismay, was supplied soon after by a stroke of fortune, in the following way.

The Governor, de Majo, having summoned Generals Vial, Giudice and Pronio in council, told them that there were nine hundred persons in the Royal Palace, including women, children, wounded and sick. To withdraw with so many helpless people would be impossible, to abandon them would be cruel. Meanwhile the danger would increase, munitions would run out, the troops would lose courage, the rebels would be emboldened; they must come to some decision. The generals therefore decided to withdraw the militia to the Quattro Venti, where De Sauget was encamped with the troops just arrived from Naples. Those who could not fight were left behind, along with the field and even the mountain artillery. Fighting had ceased by two in the morning; the withdrawal, or rather the flight, began at three. The Royal Palace was abandoned with everything in it—munitions, cannon, baggage trains, a battalion of infantry, wounded and sick, soldiers' wives and children. The barracks of San Giacomo, Santa Teresa, and the Borgognoni, crammed with munitions, were left with all they contained. Generals and privates, cavalry and infantry fled in a general helter-skelter. Colors and ranks were ignored. The brave waited with the last of their comrades, the cowardly ran out with the first. The noise and confusion were such that the Municipal Guards were alerted and took arms. The bells rang out again. The boldest ran to pursue the fugitives in the plains of the Olivuzza. The terror and disorder of the royalists can be imagined: they suffered the injury of a defeat without the honor of a battle. Having reached the Quattro Venti, De Majo and Vial took ship for Naples, leaving De Sauget to bear the whole burden of the war.

The people swarmed into the Royal Palace; costly furniture,

tapestries and fittings, everything was broken, thrown about or carried off, according to the anger of many and the greed of a few, all except for the silverware, which was found hidden away in the stables and handed over to the committee. But the people's anger changed to pity when more than a thousand women, children and wounded were found there abandoned by their relations and friends. These were tended and comforted with the respect due to the weakness of their sex, their age and their misfortune.

Having occupied the Royal Palace, the people seized the barracks of the Fonderia and the Treasury. Outside the city, now completely evacuated by the troops, stood ten thousand men under the command of De Sauget. The spot where they were encamped was a good, safe one: at their back they had the steep Monte Pellegrino, on their left the fortresses of the Molo, Castellamare and the Garitta, converging on the city; on their right were the strong buildings of the new prison. Notwithstanding all this, whether because of dwindling victuals or for some other reason still unknown, De Sauget sent a message through the commanding officers of the English and French ships anchored in the port, asking the committee to suspend hostilities as he intended to withdraw. In reply, he was told to free the eleven political prisoners detained in Castellamare since the night of the ninth, and hand over the arsenal, the prisons and the fortresses, with the ordinance and munitions they contained. Negotiations were going on during the night of the twenty-seventh, when De Sauget, having evacuated the Castle of the Molo, the Arsenal and the prisons, leaving their doors open or easily forced, suddenly decided to strike camp and by-pass the city up in the hills to the south.

More than five thousand convicts and prisoners, almost naked or badly covered with filthy rags, emaciated and starving, then entered Palermo (where nothing was known of this move), crying: "Viva Santa Rosalia! Bread and arms!"—a spectacle to arouse both pity and disgust, made even more horrible by the darkness of the night. The committee gave them bread: some of them later expiated their guilty lives by a glorious death; nearly all seemed for a time to have become honest men again. But once the thunder of the guns had ceased, when the thrill of liberty, assuaging their wicked desires, had subsided, the majority returned to their old criminal habits and became one of the plagues with which revolutionary Sicily was afflicted.

The royalist army made for Bocca di Falco, destroying, ravaging and massacring as they went, with the city squads following and molesting them. When the troops reached cultivated land made impassable by the rains, they were bogged down in the vineyards and lost their way; ranks became confused, and discipline was soon at an end. They made their way down to the plain of Gamastra, thence to Porrazzi and Guadagna, leaving wagons, guns, rifles and a good many dead and wounded by the way. They took their revenge in Villabate, where they burnt down houses, butchered the unarmed inhabitants, and left with the heads of women and old men, and the corpses of children spitted on their bayonets. De Sauget, still pursued by the Palermitan squads, who inflicted not a few losses on his army and wounded him in person, proceeded to Solanto, thence to Favara, and reached Castel d'Accia on the twenty-ninth, halting there till the thirtieth. Next day the sun rose on an abandoned camp, in which more than three hundred horses lay dead, killed by the soldiers for lack of means or time to embark them. The ground was strewn with arms, knapsacks and military equipment. Far away on the horizon the royal ship could be seen that was to transport to Naples the remains of a defeated and dishonored army.

[G. La Farina: *Storia d'Italia dal 1815 al 1850*
(Milan, 1861), vol. II, pp. 114–26]

La Farina to Mazzini, in 1851 when the Bourbons had reconquered Sicily

No REVOLUTIONARY government can possess authority or force unless elected by the people. I agree that revolutions are started by minorities, but they will collapse unless accepted and organized by the majority. Saliceti's suggestion [that governments should be nominated by those who lead the initial insurrection] is not apt, at least by our experience at Palermo. Does he know who led the January 12 rising? It is something not to be set down in a history book, but we must not conceal the fact from you and other members of the National Committee. Those leaders were Santoro, later killed by the people as a traitor; Miloro, who was then arrested and tried in Sicily for misappropriation of public funds, and who recently was implicated in another robbery in Malta; Bivona, who now has a job as a Forest Guard under the Bourbon ruler of Sicily;

the Pagano brothers, who have now become policemen and are cousins of the famous Malvica who was given command of the police when the royalist counterrevolution triumphed in Palermo; Scordato, who is also a police chief in Bourbon Sicily; and Miceli, who has a job there as a customs officer.

[*Epistolario di Giuseppe La Farina*, ed. A. Franchi
(Milan, 1869), vol. I, pp. 422–3]

At the end of January 1848, this Sicilian revolt forced Ferdinand in despair to grant a constitution to Sicily and Naples. In February another revolution at Paris was the signal for further risings all over Europe. The ruler of Tuscany and even the Pope decided to grant constitutions in sheer self-defense. Charles Albert had at first condemned Ferdinand for surrendering to violence, and he assured his friends that he would never go so far himself, but he very quickly changed his mind when he discovered what a torrent of public feelings had been unleashed. Rather than appear to yield to force, he quickly granted a constitution at Turin, first asking the archbishop to absolve him from the oath by which he had sworn not to deviate from absolutism.

The *statuto* of March 1848 was conceded with reluctance and in an acute emergency. It had to be prepared in a great hurry from such other written constitutions as were available for consultation at Turin. The resultant document was to remain the basic law of Italy until 1946. One can discern in it a deliberate intention to retain as much royal power as was compatible with representative institutions, but some important concessions were made to the liberals, and these allowed room for subsequent development. Certain articles were kept purposely vague.

The Statuto: *the Constitution of Piedmont-Sardinia, March 4, 1848*

Article 1. The apostolic Roman Catholic religion is the only religion of the state. Other cults now existing are tolerated, in conformity with the law.

Art. 2. The state is governed by a representative monarchical government. The throne is hereditary according to the Salic law.

Art. 3. The legislative power shall be exercised collectively by the King and two houses, the Senate and the House of Deputies.

Art. 4. The person of the King is sacred and inviolable.

Art. 5. To the King alone belongs the executive power. He is the supreme head of the state; commands all land and naval forces; declares war; makes treaties of peace, alliance, commerce, and other treaties, communicating them to the houses as soon as the interest and security of the state permit, accompanying such notice with opportune explanations. Treaties involving financial obligations or alterations of the territory of the state shall not take effect until after they have received the approval of the houses.

Art. 6. The King appoints to all of the offices of the state, and makes the necessary decrees and regulations for the execution of the laws, without suspending their execution or granting exemptions from the law.

Art. 7. The King alone approves and promulgates the laws.

Art. 8. The King may grant pardons and commute sentences.

Art. 9. The King shall convene the two houses each year. He may prorogue their sessions and dissolve the House of Deputies, in which case he shall convene a new House within a period of four months.

Art. 10. The initiative in legislation shall belong both to the King and the two houses. All bills, however, imposing taxes or relating to the budget shall first be presented to the House of Deputies.

•   •   •

Art. 24. All inhabitants of the kingdom, whatever their rank or title, are equal before the law. All shall equally enjoy civil and political rights and shall be eligible to civil and military office, except as otherwise provided by law.

Art. 25. All shall contribute without distinction to the burdens of the state, in proportion to their possessions.

Art. 26. Individual liberty is guaranteed. None shall be arrested or brought to trial except in the cases provided for and according to the forms prescribed by law.

Art. 27. The domicile is inviolable. No search of a house shall take place except by virtue of law and in the manner prescribed by law.

Art. 28. The press shall be free, but the law may suppress abuses of this freedom. Nevertheless, Bibles, catechisms, liturgical and prayer books shall not be printed without the previous consent of the bishop.

Art. 29. Property of all kinds whatsoever is inviolable. In all cases, however, where the public welfare, legally ascertained, requires it, property may be taken and transferred in whole or in part, upon payment of a just indemnity in accordance with law.

Art. 30. No tax shall be levied or collected without the consent of the houses and the approval of the King.

Art. 31. The public debt is guaranteed. All obligations of the state to its creditors are inviolable.

Art 32. The right to assemble peaceably and without arms is recognized, subject, however, to the laws that may regulate the exercise of this privilege in the interest of the public welfare. This privilege is not applicable to meetings in public places or places open to the public, which shall remain entirely subject to police control.

Art. 33. The Senate shall be composed of members who have attained the age of forty years, appointed for life by the King without limit of numbers, and from the following categories of citizens:

1) Archbishops and bishops of the state.

2) The president of the House of Deputies.

3) Deputies after having served in three legislatures, or after six years of service.

4) Ministers of state [and 17 other categories].

•   •   •

Art. 39. The elective house shall be composed of deputies chosen by the electoral districts as provided by law.

•   •   •

Art. 47. The House of Deputies shall have power to impeach ministers of the crown and to bring them to trial before the High Court of Justice.

•   •   •

Art. 50. The office of senator or deputy shall not carry with it any compensation or remuneration.

Arti. 51. Senators and deputies shall not be called to account for opinions expressed or votes given in the houses.

Art. 52. The sessions of the houses shall be public. Upon the written request of ten members, secret sessions may be held.

Art. 53. No session or vote of either house shall be legal or valid unless an absolute majority of its members is present.

•   •   •

Art. 56. Any bill rejected by one of the three legislative powers shall not again be introduced during the same session.

•   •   •

Art. 62. Italian shall be the official language of the houses.

The use of French shall, however, be permitted to the members coming from districts where French is used, and in replying to them.

. . .

Art. 65. The King appoints and dismisses his ministers.

. . .

Art. 67. The ministers are responsible. Laws and governmental acts shall not take effect until they shall have received the signature of a minister.

Art. 68. Justice emanates from the King and shall be administered in his name by the judges whom he appoints.

> [*Modern Constitutions*, ed. W. F. Dodd (Chicago, 1909), pp. 5–14]

The momentum of revolution in Europe was such that on March 13, 1848, a rising at Vienna brought about Metternich's fall and the grant of a constitution in the very citadel of European conservatism. The news of this great event triggered the rioting at Venice and Milan which precipitated the first Italian "war of liberation." There was little connection between events at Venice and Milan. At Venice, although the courageous Bandiera brothers in 1844 had made a futile attempt to stir up a Mazzini-type revolution elsewhere in Italy, most liberals had been looking for no more than home rule for Venice under Austria; but the two leading Venetian liberals, Daniele Manin and Niccolò Tommaseo, had been imprisoned in January 1848 for agitating on behalf of quite moderate reforms, and there was already considerable tension when news from Vienna brought matters to the boil. A report from the British Consul described the immediate effect. Later, on March 22, the workers at the arsenal ran riot and killed a senior officer. This example of successful violence emboldened the civic guard to turn against the armed forces, while some Italians in the Austrian army took the chance to desert or else fraternized with the citizens. Manin was then able to proclaim the restoration of the Venetian Republic which Napoleon had superseded in 1797.

Consul Dawkins, from Venice, to Viscount Palmerston, March 19, 1848

I HAD the honor to inform your Lordship, on the 16th instant, that all was quiet here, and that news had just been received of disturbances at Vienna. On the morning of the 17th, intelligence was received and immediately published in the "Gazette," that the Emperor had decided upon granting the freedom of the press and the convocation of the Central Congregations of the Lombardo-Venetian Kingdom. No accurate information, however, was received of the exact state of affairs at Vienna. Great excitement prevailed in Venice; crowds assembled in the Square of St. Mark and demanded an interview with the Governor. A deputation was admitted, and required the immediate liberation of Messrs. Manin and Tommaseo, whose arrest I mentioned in my despatches of the 9th and 20th ultimo. After some demur this demand was complied with, and was soon followed by a further demand for the liberation of three other persons, of minor note, likewise imprisoned for political offenses, which was also granted. Bands of the populace paraded the streets, breaking windows, and crying "Viva l'Italia!" and wearing tricolored ribbons. Tricolored flags were hoisted on the three flagstaffs in the square, and the ropes being cut, it was impossible to remove them. Troops were called out, and the Italian grenadiers loudly cheered by the mob. On one occasion the mob was driven back at the point of the bayonet by a body of German troops, when two persons were slightly wounded, and one person trampled to death in the crowd. No other accident occurred; in the evening the theater was illuminated, and the night passed off quietly.

Yesterday the 18th, accounts from Vienna were still wanting. Great crowds again assembled, bands of men went about demanding money for the love of Italy; all the shops and banks were closed. Troops were drawn out in the square and posted on the principal bridges; the mob, as on the preceding day, cheering the Italians, hissing and hooting the Germans. Not content with this, they soon proceeded to pelt the German troops with stones, and the pavement of the Square of St. Mark's was torn up in several places to furnish materials for this purpose. The patience of these men being at length exhausted, a party of them fired, and four persons were killed and five or six wounded. Great excitement was produced: a want of all union and energy was apparent on the part of the authorities, who, it must be admitted, in the absence of all accurate information of what was passing at Vienna, were placed in a very difficult situation, and for a time it seemed too probable that serious disturbances would ensue. Shortly after this a proclamation was issued by the municipality, authorizing, with the consent of the Governor, the provisional formation of a civic guard, which seemed to calm the people. The troops were subsequently withdrawn from the square, and before sunset bodies of citizens, wearing white scarfs and armed in various ways appeared, and tranquility was restored. About nine in the evening a steamer arrived from Trieste with a despatch for the Governor, who shortly afterwards appeared on his balcony and addressed the assembled multitude, saying that the Emperor had determined to grant a free press, to sanction the formation of a national guard, and to convoke the Central Congregations as soon as possible. The Governor concluded by expressing his joy at being the first constitutional Governor of Venice, and by exhorting the people to maintain order. This speech was received with great applause; most of the houses on the square were illuminated immediately; bands of armed citizens continued to patrol, and no further disturbances took place.

[*British Parliamentary Papers* (London, 1849), no. LVIII, pp. 267–8]

What happened at Milan is here told in the words of Marshal Radetzky, who commanded the Austrian forces. Radetzky was now a very old man. He had fought in Italy against Napoleon some fifty years before. He had about 13,000 troops guarding Milan, a city of about 200,000 inhabitants. But his men were spread around the town in over fifty different units, and he failed to see in time how hard it would be to keep them supplied in the event of serious street fighting. The "Five days of Milan" are one of the great glories of the risorgimento. At first spontaneous and uncoordinated, the insurrection was soon given a general direction by Cattaneo and some of his radical friends who formed a military committee, and their success against a regular army was remarkable. The conservative Mayor, Casati, supported them, and was persuaded by them to turn down Radetzky's offer of an armistice.

Field Marshal Radetzky, from Milan, to the minister Graf von Ficquelmont, March 18–22, 1848

MARCH *18–19*. Some days ago I had various information that an attempt at insurrection would be made in Milan on March 18. On the evening of the seventeenth, news arrived by telegraph from Vienna of the generous concessions made by His Majesty, and today notices about it were up at every street corner. I hoped that this would have calmed Milan. The Vice-Governor, Count O'Donnell, begged me not to use armed force against the citizenry unless requested by the civil authorities.

Toward midday I was informed that people were gathering at

various points and that schoolchildren were being fetched home by their parents. The armed forces were in their barracks because an outbreak of revolt seemed so improbable. I was in my office when the storm broke out and had to flee to the citadel so as to escape being surrounded by the mob. Increasingly alarming news soon began to come in. When I heard of barricades being erected in all the main streets, I alerted the troops. I received no further news until the Commissioner of Police, de Betta, arrived to say that all the small guard at Government House had been either killed, seriously wounded or disarmed. The building was sacked, a part of the archives destroyed, and the acting Governor, Count O'Donnell, taken prisoner. General Wohlgemuth, who was in command of the troops in that area, stormed the barricades, using artillery, and reoccupied the building. Countess Spaur [wife of the Governor who was himself absent] had taken refuge in a small attic room.

By this time fighting had broken out at various places. There was shooting from windows, and all sorts of objects were thrown from the rooftops. Many a brave soldier lost his life in this way. When General Rath moved his troops into the center to occupy the Piazza del Duomo and the main government buildings, there was tough fighting in the streets, but the soldiers got through despite the barricades.

At this point I was handed proclamations from a Provisional Government set up in the town hall. Amongst other things, a National Guard had been established. The orders came from Count O'Donnell, who probably had been compelled to sign. The head of this Provisional Government was Belatti, who signed as Director General of Police.

When evening fell after six hours of firing in the streets, I decided at whatever cost to assault the town hall and destroy the Provisional Government at its center. This took us four hours and was bitterly contested. Finally, when most of the carpenters whom I was using to break down the main gateway had been wounded, we brought twelve cannon with difficulty through narrow streets and broke in to become masters of the building. Over 250 prisoners were captured, including many with distinguished names, together with an important deposit of arms. Prisoners and arms were taken to the citadel.

Meanwhile a state of siege was proclaimed. Count Pachta, of the gubernatorial staff, had had his house sacked and only just escaped with his life, but toward evening he managed to reach the citadel. I provisionally put him in charge of civil affairs. Our losses in dead and wounded I do not know, but they cannot be small. For the moment, all is calm, but possibly fighting will start again at dawn. I am determined to remain master of Milan whatever happens. If the fighting does not stop, I shall bombard the city.

March 20, 5 p.m. The prisoners taken yesterday at the town hall unfortunately did not include the mayor Casati, who is the chief rebel, and so the directing committee was quickly reorganized. Their headquarters seems to be in the Palazzo Borromeo which I hope to capture later. By seizing the leader I would paralyze their action, and would also be able to take hostages for the peace of the city from among the most prominent citizens of Milan.

From the provinces I have received little news. The National Guard was called out in Monza and Como, and lack of firmness by the military allowed revolution to break out.

Unfortunately police action is completely paralyzed, and the Chief of Police, despite repeated orders, has not come to the citadel to speak with me personally. There is no possibility of making my proclamations known to the people. The streets of Milan are as if dead. No shop and no gate has been open today, and to provide meat for my troops I had to use strong military detachments. Luckily I learned in time that the meat had been poisoned, otherwise there would have been the most dreadful disaster.

March 21, 10 a.m. I had no means of sending my despatch because all communications out of Milan are cut off, and substantial forces are needed for sending or receiving news. Yesterday the fighting continued with great intensity and there must have been many casualties on both sides. I am still unable to give an account of my losses for I lack all details. The streets have been pulled up to an extent you can hardly imagine. Barricades close them by the hundred, even by the thousand. The revolutionary party is moving with a caution and cleverness which make it obvious that they are being directed by military officers from abroad. The character of this people has been altered as if by magic, and fanaticism has taken hold of every age group, every class, and both sexes. Yesterday morning I withdrew all troops in the city to the citadel, leaving only those barracks occupied with which we can still keep touch.

Nevertheless I control all the gates of the city. Generals Wohlge-muth and Clam are still holding their positions, and communications thus remain open from here to the gates. It was not possible to hold the inner positions any longer, for provisions and relief units could not get through without losses. Details on the various phases of the fighting are only partly known to me, or would take too long to recount.

One thing, however, must be said. The troops are really wonder-ful. Through four days of dreadful weather, with no rest, they have done marvels and are in excellent heart. It breaks my heart that such courage cannot be utilized against an open and honorable enemy.

Yesterday I received a written message from the foreign consuls in Milan who implored me not to bombard the city. I answered that this could be stopped by the citizens alone and only if they ceased attacking my men. Whereupon in the evening I was asked by the consuls to grant them an audience. A meeting took place early this morning in the citadel. News then arrived that a part of the Pied-montese army had crossed the border yesterday with orders to march straight on Milan. I shall meet this new situation as circum-stances dictate. There was discussion with the consuls about reach-ing a three days' armistice. My troops need rest in view of their superhuman effort, and I would then be better placed to invest the town.

My information from the provinces, though slight, is very alarm-ing, for the whole country is in revolt and even the peasants are armed.

The armistice is not concluded and the fighting continues with unabated fury. I had taken the decision to gather all my detached garrisons around me and to make a concerted attack on Milan. The execution of this plan would have stifled the revolt, but all communications are interrupted, a number of messengers have been shot or taken prisoner, and my units meet strong resistance in the barricaded streets and villages. Reconnoitering is impossible, since all communications are broken. I have still a few day's supply of bread left, though the bakeries have to be constantly defended by arms. I cannot obtain anything more from the city because the streets to the citadel are closed; and though I repeatedly demolished the barricades, they were always re-erected . . .

At nine o'clock the news spread that the Piedmontese army had deployed along the Ticino and that groups of volunteers had already crossed the river. From the Swiss border, and specially it seems from the Valtelline, about 10,000 armed peasants are said to be pouring into the plain. At Monza one of my Geppert battalions was surprised (the other I had recalled here); it lost some hundreds of men, its funds and its baggage. The Warasdiner Kreutzer battalion and two companies of the Prohaska regiment at Como seem to have suffered the same fate, but I have no certain news.

March 22. It is the most frightful decision of my life, but I can no longer hold Milan. The whole country is in revolt. I am pressed in the rear by the Piedmontese. All the bridges behind me can easily be cut, and I have no timber for replacing them. Similarly I have very little transport. What is going on in my rear I just do not know. I shall withdraw toward Lodi to avoid the large towns and while the countryside is still open.

[*Archiv für österreichische Geschichte* (Vienna, 1906), vol. XCV, pp. 150–9]

8. The Wars of 1848 and 1849

In Piedmont, when confronted with these revolutions, there were several schools of thought: one followed Gioberti and believed in trying to merge purely Piedmontese interests in those of all Italy; another rather put the stress on dominating Italy in the interests of Piedmontese expansion. Charles Albert gave the strong impression of belonging to the latter. For his first Prime Minister, in March 1848, he chose the scholarly but somewhat feeble Balbo, but he at once rejected Balbo's advice and crossed Gioberti's name off the list of ministers—the one man whose enormous popularity in the rest of Italy might have allayed suspicions of Piedmontese ambition.

When Milan rose and urgently asked for Piedmontese help, the king did not at once agree but waited for four vital days until he was satisfied that the war was likely to succeed and to be in Piedmontese interests. Sincerely though he wanted to lead a movement for Italian independence, he first had to be sure that Milan would not go republican and that no help would be sought from the ungodly regime in republican France. Cavour's ringing call to arms on the morning of March 23 was followed in the afternoon by a cabinet meeting, at which war was decided upon; but by this time Milan had defeated Radetzky on her own.

Cavour warns the king to act

THE SUPREME hour of the Piedmontese monarchy has struck, the hour of stern decisions, the hour on which hangs the fate of empires, the destiny of nations.

Faced with the events in Lombardy and Vienna, hesitation, doubt and delay are no longer possible; they would prove the most fatal of all policies.

As cool-headed men, ready to follow the dictates of reason rather than those of the heart, and having carefully weighed our words, conscience forces us to declare that one road alone is now open to the nation, to the government and to the King. War! Immediate War! War without delay!

Retreat is impossible: the nation is at war with Austria already. The whole nation is rushing to the succor of the Lombards, the volunteers have crossed the frontiers, our fellow citizens are openly making munitions and sending them to the Milanese. The situation is plain: peace with Austria has been broken; the old treaties have been trampled on and violated by both sides.

It is not a question, therefore, of deciding whether or not hostilities are to be begun. The only question is whether we are to declare, honestly and boldly, for the cause of humanity and Italy, or whether we are to persist for a long while yet in following the tortuous ways of a policy of evasion and doubt.

Given this state of affairs, hesitation, we repeat, is not possible. Even to the least hot-headed, the most prudent of statesmen, the duty of the government is patent and palpable. We are in a position in which boldness is the truest prudence; in which temerity is wiser than caution.

There may still be some to say we are not ready, that in declaring war we are assuming a terrible responsibility, that Russia and England may, in consequence, decide to join Austria to the injury of Italy.

To these objections reason itself opposes unassailable replies. If Lombardy were quiet, it would be madness to hasten proceedings and commence hostilities before we had assembled an army and prepared defense measures proportional to the strength of our enemies. But Lombardy is on fire, Milan is besieged; we must at all costs hurry to her succor. If we have no more than five thousand men on the frontier, they must march upon Milan. They may be beaten—that is possible, though we do not think it probable. But this bold move would force the Austrians to abandon Milan; it would allow the city to provision itself with food and munitions, and would put it in a position to continue the heroic resistance which has been causing us such terrible anxiety for several days.

The moral effect of an opening of hostilities and the relief of Milan would be of more use to the Italian cause than the defeat of a body of five thousand men would injure it. Let the regiments stationed at Novara, Vercelli and Vigevano be mobilized without delay; let them rush to share the perils and the glory of this heroic city!

Woe to us if for the sake of increasing our preparations we do not arrive in time! Woe to us if when we are about to cross the Ticino we are confronted with the fall of the Queen of Lombardy!

> [C. Cavour, article in *Il Risorgimento* (Turin, March 23, 1848), reprinted in *Camillo Cavour: Scritti politici*, ed. G. Gentile (Rome, 1930), pp. 106-7]

P. Pinelli, from Turin, to V. Gioberti, March 23, 1848

THE DIE is cast today, and I enclose Charles Albert's proclamation (if you have not already seen it) which will prove that we are moving into Lombardy. "After the fighting is all over," some cynics will say! But the phrase would be unfair, because after the fighting will come diplomacy and the treaty-making, and here our strength will count. In any case it is a matter of life or death for us, and I think our action will give us good hopes of increasing Piedmontese territory.

The King was quite admirable, and it was his view that carried the cabinet. He said the state would be lost if we did not fight. Perhaps in declaring war he might be risking his throne, but he was ready for that.

> [*Carteggi di Vincenzo Gioberti*, ed. Vittorio Cian (Rome, 1935), vol. I, p. 159]

Charles Albert's proclamation to Lombardy and Venice,
Turin, March 23, 1848

THE DESTINIES of Italy are maturing, and a happier future is
opening up for those who bravely stand up for their rights against
the oppressor.

We, out of love for our common race, understanding as we do
what is now happening, and supported by public opinion, hasten
to associate ourselves with the unanimous admiration which Italy
bestows on you.

Peoples of Lombardy and Venetia, our arms, which were concentrating on your frontier when you forestalled events by liberating your glorious Milan, are now coming to offer you in the latter
phases of your fight the help which a brother expects from a
brother, and a friend from a friend.

We will support your just desires, confident as we are in the
help of that God who is manifestly on our side; of the God who
has given Pius IX to Italy; of God whose helpful hand has wonderfully enabled Italy to rely on her own strength [*fare da sè*].

In order to show more openly our feelings of Italian brotherhood,
we have ordered our troops as they move into Lombardy and
Venice to carry the Cross of Savoy imposed on the tricolor flag of
Italy.

[C. Casati: *Nuove rivelazioni su i fatti di Milano nel*
1847–1848 (Milan, 1885), vol. II, pp. 202–3]

The subsequent story that Charles Albert had been counting the days
until he could attack Austria does not square with the fact that this army
was entirely unprepared for such a war. It evidently had no plans nor
even any maps of Lombardy, and almost all its strength was rather posted
on the French frontier as a defense against the menace of republicanism.
It is easy to conclude long after the event that, if only some preparations had been made, this was the moment of all moments when Austria could have been defeated. There had been a revolution in Vienna.
Radetzky had been beaten by the citizens of Milan and was in full
retreat long before a single Piedmontese soldier had crossed the Ticino.
Venice and a dozen other cities had liberated themselves. Many thousands of Italian conscripts were deserting from the imperial forces, and
sailors of the Austrian navy (largely Italian) would have had a decisive
effect on the war if they could also have been persuaded to defect.
But four days were wasted at Turin in deciding whether or not to

fight. Then, with greatly superior forces, a slow, timid advance took
place which did nothing at all to harry Radetzky or seize the mountain
passes and cut off his supplies. Instead of marching at once on Brescia
or Verona, not until the second week in April did any serious fighting
commence, and by that time the Austrians were well protected inside
the Quadrilateral. Charles Albert positively insisted on acting as commander-in-chief even though his abilities in this field were negligible,
and unfortunately there was no single senior officer of talent who could
make up for such a deficiency. Garibaldi's offer of help was turned
down by the king on the grounds that to accept support from mere
volunteers and ex-outlaws would be dishonorable for the army.

This fundamental military weakness was made worse by political differences. Instead of playing for support from the popular elements who
had chiefly manned the barricades at Milan and other towns, Charles
Albert preferred the small aristocratic element in Lombardy who were
not particularly noted for their combativeness or their liberalism. Instead of concentrating on the war, he insisted on holding a plebiscite to
make quite sure of the political fusion of Lombardy and Venice with
Piedmont, even though this was bound to arouse suspicions of Piedmontese aggrandizement and discourage other elements in Naples, Tuscany, and Rome who wanted a new union of Italy. Politics at once
became bitter, and the republicans and federalists gradually broke away
from what looked to them like an essentially royalist and anti-revolutionary war.

*Count Di Castagnetto, of the royal household in Turin, to Count
Casati, Mayor of Milan, April 16, 1848*

I BEG you, because of our joint faith in Italian independence,
not to forget what a real crisis this is, and how the opportunity
we now have to create a strong state may never recur. Today the
King told me about the meeting with his generals: they are extremely annoyed with the state of opinion in Lombardy, and national feeling in Piedmont is becoming really alarmed.

Tell me my friend, frankly and in confidence, what do you think
Piedmont has to gain by fusing with Lombardy? She may be
losing her existing primacy and all its attendant advantages just to
become a secondary planet in a different universe. Only posterity
will do justice to the blindness of your Lombards. Past experience
teaches them nothing. The generous and disinterested Piedmontese
nation, with massive and almost unprecedented enthusiasm, is sacrificing her blood, her money, and almost her position of primacy to
support her brothers; and yet, just when we could make one single
family, here she is received like a predatory foe! This, my dear

Casati, is too much. The only talk at Milan apparently is of a republic; and they even want Genoa to go republican too. Bad faith comes into this, and so does foreign intrigue and foreign money. To you, who can be called the father of your country, to you my dear friend I say frankly: "Open your eyes while there is still time." But you have no need of my warning, for you are too perceptive not to see the sad truth. Save your country and mine! Save it a second time, for this danger is no less than that you overcame a month ago.

I enclose a note from a trustworthy correspondent at Paris, which will show if I am not right. Please send it back. If after so much heroic effort, if after proclaiming ourselves a nation to the whole of Europe, we then divide into as many tiny states and republics as there are cities and municipal rivalries, and if we then are swallowed up or beaten by the foreigner, we shall have left a fine page of history! I watched the King for several weeks going through one Lombard village after another unhonored, as though in a foreign land, and I had to ask myself if this really could be the same Italian prince who is defending that Italian independence which his victories allow us to speak of so loudly.

[*Carteggio Casati-Castagnetto, 19 marzo–14 ottobre
1848*, ed. V. Ferrari (Milan, 1909), pp. 56–7]

Charles Albert's insistence on "fusion" with Piedmont, and his refusal to discuss war aims with other Italian powers or to encourage their (and notably Pius IX's) interest in a loose Italian confederation, helped to bring about a general desertion of his cause. For a brief moment, along with Mazzini's republicans and Cattaneo's federalists, the regular armies of Tuscany, Naples, and the Papal States had joined his forces in fighting against Austria. A papal Allocution of April 29 then came as a bombshell. Pius's defection was followed by that of Ferdinand of Naples, who backed out of the war and suspended his recently granted constitution on May 15.

The Allocution brought the myth of neo-guelphism to an end. For all his reforms, Pius had never seriously intended the liberalization of the Papal States. He had just allowed the legend to develop by default that liberalism was now orthodox; and by an even greater miscalculation he had not understood that his constitution made sense only if he was prepared to renounce authoritarian power. He admitted that "men have a natural feeling of nationality, and I myself would be glad to see the rebirth of an independent Italy." Moreover, as a temporal sovereign he had an army and claimed the right to defend his territory against Austrian encroachment. But just as he had not appreciated the implications of ministerial responsibility, so he had not seen that self-defense might lead him into an actual war against another Catholic power in which religion was not at stake and where his motives might be suspect. The shock of recognition was so great that he veered round to an opposite extreme where the risorgimento was no longer befriended but excommunicated. Having done so much to set the national movement on its course, Pius was driven into an exaggerated anti-liberalism which was to burden the Church for another century.

Allocution of Pius IX, delivered in the secret consistory of April 29, 1848

WHEN, BY the inscrutable decree of God, We were put in his [Gregory XVI's] place, We at the outset, not stimulated by encouragements or advice, but prompted by our own singular affection toward the people placed under the temporal dominion of the Church, granted more large indulgence to those who had departed from their duty of allegiance to the pontifical government; and We subsequently made speed to adopt certain measures, which We had judged conducive in themselves to the prosperity of that people. And the whole of the acts which We have thus performed at the very commencement of our Pontificate are in thorough correspondence with those most anxious desires of the European sovereigns [in the Memorandum of 1831].

But when, by the help of God, our plans had been brought to practical effect, not only our own people but those of neighboring states manifested an exulting joy, and applauded Us with public congratulations and testimonials of respect, in such a mode as made it our duty to take care, even in this exalted City, to keep within due bounds popular outbursts acclamations, and assemblages, that broke forth with an excess of vehemence.

Furthermore, Venerable Brothers, the words of the Allocution which We addressed to you in the Consistory of the fourth of October in the past year, are known to all. By them We commended the benevolence, and the affectionate solicitude, of the princes toward their subjects, and exhorted the subjects to the faith and obedience due to their princes . . .

Seeing that some at present desire that We too, along with the other princes of Italy and their subjects, should engage in war against the Austrians, We have thought it convenient to proclaim clearly and openly, in this our solemn assembly, that such a measure is altogether alien from our counsels, inasmuch as We, albeit unworthy, are upon earth the vice-gerent of Him that is the Author of Peace and the Lover of Charity, and, conformably to the function of our supreme apostolate, We reach to and embrace all kindreds, peoples, and nations, with equal solicitude of paternal affection. But if, notwithstanding, there are not wanting among our subjects those who allow themselves to be carried away by the example of the rest of the Italians, in what manner could We possibly curb their ardor?

And in this place We cannot refrain from repudiating, before the face of all nations, the treacherous advice, published moreover in journals, and in various works, of those who would have the Roman Pontiff to be the head and to preside over the formation of some sort of novel republic of the whole Italian people. Rather, on this occasion, moved hereto by the love We bear them, We do urgently warn and exhort the said Italian people to abstain with all diligence from the like counsels, deceitful and ruinous to Italy herself, and to abide in close attachment to their respective sovereigns, of whose good will they have already had experience, so as never to let themselves be torn away from the obedience they owe them. For if they should do otherwise, they not only would fail in their own duty , but would also run a risk of rending Italy herself, every day more and more, with fresh discords and intestine factions.

[L. C. Farini: *The Roman State from 1815 to 1850*, trans. W. E. Gladstone (London, 1851), vol. II, pp. 106–11]

Venice in March had declared herself to be an independent republic. Here too, however, Charles Albert demanded that the Piedmontese monarchy should be accepted (and he went on saying so even after he had privately agreed to hand Venice back to Austria). Other towns of the Veneto—Treviso, Padua, Vicenza, and Belluno—which had a long tradition of rebelliousness against Venice, took the chance to break away and declare their union to Piedmont, only to be easily reconquered by Radetzky when no Piedmontese help was forthcoming. Manin, who led the Venetian resistance, was a republican by conviction, yet he proposed on July 4 that Venice too should acknowledge Charles Albert, and the Venetian Assembly duly agreed to give up their republic. The deputies were even unwilling to hear Tommaseo's speech in opposition. Tommaseo had been a neo-guelph, and was a federalist and republican of a non-Mazzinian persuasion. He thought, and Manin later agreed, that the Piedmontese insistence on political fusion was the main reason for the failure of this first war of independence.

*Speech composed (but never spoken) by Tommaseo for the Venice
Assembly, July 4, 1848*

Now, CITIZENS, we have to discuss whether Venice should form
a state of her own or join Piedmont; and I must admit that, put so
baldly, it seems to me more and more inopportune that we are
called upon to settle such a matter in time of war. An association
contracted now might look much less suitable in peacetime, and
might even open the way to discord and revolution. Association at
the wrong time might well harm Piedmont herself, by arousing
regional rivalries; some distressing signs of this are already visible.
In such an emergency as we now face, neither Venice nor Piedmont
can really know what is for the best.

Having said this, having said what my conscience dictates, I
repeat that the alternative now proposed to fusion—namely, that
Venice should form a state of her own—is an entirely false one.
Venice cannot and ought not to remain alone; but any big change
in public affairs inevitably must take time, and the isolation of
Venice may come to an end in a very different way than just by
association with Piedmont alone. Yet now the question is put to us
in such a manner—quite apart from the fact that the Assembly has
gone on record for an immediate decision—that what we call fusion
with Piedmont must necessarily follow. As I do not accept the
alternative, I shall perhaps abstain from voting; but I ought to try
nonetheless to make other peoples' vote helpful to Italy's future
destiny. I must therefore state the disadvantages to be feared from
association with Piedmont, so that other people can seek a remedy
before it is too late.

Up till now Piedmont has been little known to the rest of Italy;
indeed until lately she thought of herself as being not Italian. That
is one reason, if we wish to allay resentment and suspicion, that
institutions should be chosen which take into account the different
natures and traditions of the various Italian provinces. According
to some of her distinguished writers, Piedmont has been guelph in
tendency, in other words friendly to the papacy; but in her political
actions she is somewhat ghibelline, for on occasion she betrays an
ill-concealed jealousy of the civil authority of the Popes. She has
also given too large a role in public affairs to the patrician classes.
Moreover the north of Italy should bow to the south in certain
areas where the south excels, for example in the greater antiquity

of its civilization and the greater depth of its Italian spirit. Privileges of birth or title should now be treated as a yoke to be broken. If Piedmont should come into possession of Lombardy and Venetia, it is possible that she would pay too much heed to the greed and ambitions of a few hotheads, and treat these provinces as conquered territory. She may try little by little to get out of her pledged word; she will argue about where parliament and the capital of the kingdom should be, and about what commercial advantages could be won. She will thus suffer the disadvantages peculiar to both great states and small municipalities; for the larger she becomes, the smaller and more provincial may tend to be her policy.

What Italy truly needs, on the contrary, is that Piedmont should act generously; she must give much more so that she can then receive much more, indeed so that she does not lose what she already has. It behoves her not to dominate if she does not wish to be dominated, not to be distrustful if she does not wish to perish by the distrust of others; she needs not only to respect the real, living rights of other parts of Italy, but to bestow new rights so that no region is unfairly treated; to respect the inviolable legacy of past traditions so that she does not herself appear to be another foreign domination. She needs to leave each province to govern itself insofar as it can, inside a broad national unity; to see that facilities and advantages are distributed among all with equity. Now that Germany and even Austria are being forced to take a more liberal path, it is for Piedmont to see that she is not outdone by foreigners.

Venice should therefore define very clearly the conditions on which she will yield. She should insist that a constituent assembly must meet to decide a new constitution. In particular she should insist that every alternative parliament will be summoned to meet on her soil; that she should be allowed to elect her own magistrates and professors; that her fleet of merchant ships and warships should receive special encouragement; and that she should not be dependent on any other city save in what concerns the general welfare of the state. To be sure Venice and the Venetian lands have much to learn from Piedmont: habits of firm and regular administration, a more solid educational system, and a broad-based foundation for the army. And Piedmont in her turn can gain something from other parts of Italy, so long as she seeks not to absorb Italy into herself but to make herself more Italian. There are two main things that Venetia and Lombardy can and should demand from Piedmont, so that we may free all Italy as far as our furthest linguistic frontiers, in other words up to and including Friuli and what is called the Italian Tyrol [the region round Trento]. We should demand that Piedmont unite herself with the other regions of Italy in a confederation; and also that a national parliament be set up in Rome in which common rights and duties should be discussed. It will be a sign of Piedmont's desire for fraternity if generous and harmonious agreements between the south and the north of Italy can thus be brought about.

To conclude, if we want association and not subjection, let us set forth our conditions carefully; for our weakness, however grave it may be, does not destroy our rights and our children's rights, and does not take away the duties of others.

[N. Tommaseo: *All'assemblea di Venezia: discorsi due* (Venice, 1848), pp. 1–4]

The Piedmontese army got so far as to capture Peschiera, but tactical mistakes then led to defeat at Custoza in July 1848. This was a minor reverse in which they lost fewer than a hundred men, but indiscipline and demoralization among the senior officers made it into an irreversible collapse. Seventeen years as an absolute king had left Charles Albert unequipped to fight a revolutionary war. His generals had been appointed for any reason but merit, and they had little belief in the Italian cause, yet in their official reports they unwarrantably put the blame on the behavior under fire of the rank and file. They grumbled at the small help they had received from the Lombards, but they had done little to encourage such help or inspire confidence in their own ability to use it.

Against the advice of the generals, Charles Albert decided to fall back on Milan, his main motive being to prevent the proclamation of a republic there. The king was anxious to avoid being saved by the French troops whose help was now being sought by the Milanese, as he was also anxious to discourage the kind of popular war that Garibaldi was now beginning to fight on his own. There were fairly good chances of defending Milan if a real effort had been made, but the king seems to have done almost nothing to exploit them. When General Salasco was instructed to conclude an armistice, not only Garibaldi but the king's ministers at Turin accused Charles Albert and the generals of doing this so as to suffocate the revolution.

Carlo Pisacane criticized the war from the point of view of a professional soldier. He was a Neapolitan who had served in the Bourbon army. After he became a follower of Mazzini he fled to join the French Foreign Legion, subsequently fighting in Lombardy in 1848 and at Rome in 1849. He was a man of strongly independent character who was ready to criticize Garibaldi and Mazzini as well as Charles Albert. Pisacane was one of the early Italian socialists. Though he disagreed with Mazzini in accepting socialism, he probably reached his views through Mazzini's determination to stimulate an initiative from the common people. It was Pisacane's conclusion that, without social reform, without for example giving land to the peasants, most Italians might see nothing to fight for in Mazzini's straightforward idea of Italian patriotism. Some of the Lombard peasants had initially helped to drive Radetzky back into the Quadrilateral, but then they discovered that the supporters of Charles Albert and Casati stood with the landlords in opposing any social or land reform. Not for nothing was the cry of "Viva Radetzky!" now heard among the common people of Lombardy. As long as the risorgimento was identified so exclusively with the landowning classes, the *braccianti* of Lombardy, like the *trasteverini* in Rome and the *lazzaroni* in Naples, might think that they had less to hope for from the patriots than from the paternalistic governments of the old regime.

The war of 1848–9, as seen by a Neapolitan of the Left

EVEN THOUGH popular hatred was concentrating against Austria [after 1846], the King of Piedmont tried to stop any action; he was ready to fight to protect his throne, but meanwhile his agents spread through Italy to calm the excitement and persuade people to await an initiative by their rulers. Yet everywhere hopes grew and produced the first signs of a storm. Action spread from south to north as terrified governments made one concession after another. Austria grew merciless in her Italian dominions and prepared to use force in curbing agitation elsewhere in Italy. Time was running short. Turmoil in Vienna hastened insurrection in Milan, and this was echoed in all the other Lombard cities. The same happened in the Venetian provinces. The Austrian army, half destroyed, took refuge in the fortresses along the Adige River, and the tricolor flag flew from the Tyrol to the Isonzo River [above Trieste].

The concept of *nationality* sufficed to bring about the insurrection, but it was not enough to bring victory.

Ordinary citizens were convinced by the moneyed classes that there was one ruler with an army prepared to fight and win; and ordinary people, who wanted only to drive out the foreigner, accepted this soldier-King. Only in Venice was a republic proclaimed, and this was not because of any new current of republicanism, only because Venice had traditionally been a republic.

Charles Albert, encouraged by the high spirits of his army and people, and spurred on by the Lombard aristocracy who pointed out that Milan would otherwise go republican, declared war on Austria while assuring other countries that he was marching to suppress republicanism. He advanced across the Ticino at the moment when the enemy was retreating over the Adda, and slowly moved into the country which the Austrians had abandoned. Had the Lombardo-Venetian rising been under proper leadership, had the people been less ready to accept mere promises, or had the King of Piedmont embarked on the campaign with the readiness that might have been expected of a man who for long had declared himself bent on war, victory would have been instantaneous. But the population was trustful, the King hesitated, and Austria was saved.

While Charles Albert was operating on the Mincio, the other Italian rulers, under popular pressure, let themselves be drawn into the war. In all the pages of history one could never find a monarch more favored by fortune than King Charles Albert at the end of April 1848. His army was keen, in good trim, and numerous; twenty-six million people were proclaiming him hero and savior of the fatherland; in other words he had both strength and prestige. Whereas the enemy, lacking in means and spirit, was reduced to passive defense.

But the King was heedless of his good fortune; always surrounded by the dark forces of Jesuitism, and not endowed with a warrior's fiery spirit, he thought it would be safer to annex just Lombardy alone. He promised the diplomats that he would be satisfied with a new Campoformio [a treaty by which Austria had taken Venice in 1797], and he thus let the Austrians overrun Venetia unopposed. Meanwhile his henchmen were breaking the most solemn agreements and imposing obedience on his new subjects by fusing Lombardy with Piedmont. He hoped that the Lombards out of sheer exhaustion would submit to this, so that the possessions of the House of Savoy would be increased by these rich provinces and the other Duchies south of the Po.

When the other Italian rulers saw that the war was just designed to increase the power of this rival who might threaten their existence, they began deserting the cause. The Bourbon King of Naples first set the example; he intrigued, corrupted, disarmed the citizens of Naples by deceit, and recalled those of his troops who had gone to fight Austria. The Pope and the Grand Duke of Tuscany were capable only of secret, though systematic, opposition; but what they most feared in the world was the reappearance of a large kingdom in northern Italy.

Meanwhile the Austrian commander was concentrating just on victory. He had secret agents at work again in Turin; he opened up roads and assembled military supplies without any molestation from Piedmont; he regrouped powerful reinforcements and concentrated them at Verona, ready to strike a decisive blow as soon as the moment presented itself.

The King's plan at first seemed about to succeed. Not only Lombardy but even Venice and the Veneto placed themselves in his hands. Though his real aim was conquest only up to the Mincio [i.e. without Venice], he pretended to accept the Venetian offer. He tried to give the impression of pushing forward to the Isonzo, but in fact he had affected to accept Venice merely so as to consolidate his hold over Lombardy.

The outlook then changed. The Piedmontese army, worn out by living in the open, irked by a completely untrustworthy administration, demoralized by inaction and surrounded and undermined by the intrigues of the Piedmontese camarilla (which, as a result of political fusion, feared that Milan might gain supremacy over Turin), was no longer fired by its former vigor, and kept the field only by force of sheer discipline. The prestige of the soldier-King soon changed into contempt for a diplomat-King.

Faithful to his project of stopping on the Mincio, the King of Piedmont gathered his forces below Mantua. The Austrian Marshal then emerged from Verona and broke through the thin line that opposed his advance. Charles Albert attacked with part of his army and was defeated; then, instead of threatening the Austrians by consolidating behind the line of the Po, he rushed to occupy Milan [in August 1848]. After an insignificant skirmish he surrendered this city and retreated over the Ticino amid the curses and stupefaction of the populace.

The republican party at Milan could have taken up the struggle if only it had been still in existence. Individual republicans had done nothing to indoctrinate the people, partly because they despaired of success. They also found themselves deluded and entangled by their involvement with the National Party and Italian Association, which were ready to sacrifice other political freedoms on the altar of national independence and unity. The generals Griffini and

Durando, who had been imposed by the King on the volunteers, were concerned only with leading them back to Piedmont and stopping them continuing the war on their own.

When the driving force and the overriding principle failed, the people were left leaderless. Their first and only aim, that of expelling all foreigners, remained unchanged. But where a regular army had lost, how could the ordinary people expect to win? Material interest might have urged them to continue fighting without leaders, for only by experience could they have become convinced of their own strength. But what was their real interest? Whether ruled by a King, a President or a Triumvirate, the people's slavery does not cease unless the social system can be changed.

Meanwhile the disillusioned men who were attempting to form a republican party, not knowing what to do, said that [Garibaldi's] skirmishes at Luino and Morazzone were greater victories than Goito, Pastrengo and Volta [fought by the regular Piedmontese army], in the same exaggerated way as these latter actions were compared by the royalists with Napoleon's victories at Rivoli and Arcola. And just as the monarchists had proclaimed Charles Albert a great captain simply on the grounds that he had an army, so the republicans declared Garibaldi a great captain even though he did no fighting and had no army. Lacking a true principle of action, they clutched at individuals and strove to feed the cult of personality.

The Lombards and Venetians then moved from dismay to despair. Naples fell under Bourbon tyranny again. The Sicilians, who had first ignited the revolution, were about to be deceived just like the Lombards. Only central Italy remained in a tumult of of uncertainty, looking for an integrating principle. When Montanelli [at Florence] proclaimed an Italian Constituent Assembly, this idea succeeded in focusing popular forces, and two rulers [at Rome and Florence] ignobly fled. They were succeeded by two popular regimes whose authority came less from the form of government adopted than from the honesty of their leaders. These governments should have translated into action the idea that had brought the people together; but each interpreted its mission from a partial viewpoint, and the people were thus divided; they fought but were beaten; and so it always happens when the destinies of a nation are directed by individuals without there being any single idea or principle among the masses to indicate the road ahead.

Meanwhile Piedmont was rent by two parties: one, the war party, had little familiarity with peacetime politics; the other perfidiously corrupted the army, intrigued with foreign cabinets, and then decided to sacrifice Charles Albert as someone inconsistent with the grand promises made in 1848. General Bava was dismissed, and in his place an unknown foreigner [Crzanowski] was appointed to the high command. This man was imposed by the camarilla and by non-Italian politicians—possibly he was even in their pay. Piedmont defied Austria again, yet remained almost completely inactive. The army accepted battle without any plan of campaign and without even a base. It met predictable and irremediable defeat [in March 1849].

The peoples of Rome and Venice were then left to struggle on alone; but, like their governments, they were not informed by any great integrating idea. In Rome it was thought that one could save Italy by respecting old institutions, and people marched to war under the banner of privilege and Catholicism. Venice sought to take refuge from the shipwreck by isolating herself. All Rome and Venice could do was to save Italian honor.

After three battles, four sieges and sixty skirmishes, and after Messina, Brescia and Catania had been put to fire and sword, despotism raised its loathed flag of victory and again bound the whole of Italy in brutal fetters. But 170,000 foreign soldiers, including Austrians, French and Swiss, had recourse to deceit so as to win. Martial law, imprisonment, torture and massacres made Italy a desolation, though even this did not satisfy her butchers. Was it human incapacity and perfidy that rendered such generous efforts vain? An affirmative answer would be degrading to mankind, for it would amount to admitting that a few individuals were arbiters of our destiny. A deeper cause must be sought in what directs a people's collective power. It is not heroes and powerful individuals who change the destinies of nations; but it is rather national needs which beget heroes; and these always represent the personification of a principle in the name of which they seize power. Creative geniuses, on the other hand, are ahead of their time; their voice is extinguished under the heavy weight of collective opinion, and can find its echo only in future generations.

[Carlo Pisacane: *Guerra combattuta in Italia negli anni 1848–49* (written in 1850–1), ed. L. Maino (Rome, 1906), pp. 308–14]

For Charles Albert, the Salasco armistice was thus only a feint, and he was determined to play "double or quits" with fortune and renew the war to recover prestige for the monarchy. Whatever might result from this, it was fairly certain that Britain and France would guarantee Piedmont against territorial loss. After some of the existing senior officers had been dismissed, General Crzanowski from Poland was persuaded to come and take over nominal command under the king; but, apart from creating language problems, this still further depressed army morale. Crzanowski was not given the time he requested for preparation. Instead of worrying about rearmament, Charles Albert was confidently preoccupied with planning a swift strike at Milan so as to be able to impose Piedmontese institutions on Lombardy before the Milanese could make difficulties as they had done in 1848. By a strange inadvertence, his final denunciation of the armistice was given to Radetzky in March 1849 and published in the newspapers before his own chief of staff had heard of it.

This second war of liberation lasted only four days. Radetzky had had plenty of time to make thorough preparations, and by now he knew that he need pay little regard to his enemy's plan of attack. Just as in 1848, there was culpable disobedience among the Piedmontese senior officers (General Ramorino was later executed for this), and many of the troops deserted as soon as fighting began. After losing an engagement at Novara on March 23, 1849, the king abdicated and left his son Victor Emmanuel to make what terms he could.

One forceful reaction to this catastrophe was a spontaneous movement at Genoa in favor of continuing the war alongside Rome, Florence, and Venice. But a Piedmontese corps under General Lamarmora, backed by offers of help from Radetzky, bombarded Genoa into submission. To Lamarmora there was no conflict of loyalties here, and there could be no interest in any Italian movement not led by Piedmont. Genoa was simply a rebel city, and revolutionaries were in his view a greater enemy than the Austrians. Rome and Venice were republics and as such deserved no support. Far better keep one regular state and army intact for the day when a third war of liberation might be possible. Fortunately for Piedmont, moreover, this view was shared by the other towns of Liguria who resented Genoa's claim to local preponderance.

The Pope late in 1848 had fled to take refuge at Gaeta in the Kingdom of Naples, and Rome was ruled by a republican triumvirate, of whom Mazzini was one. At Florence, too, the Grand Duke fled to Gaeta, leaving Guerrazzi and Montanelli to form a provisional government. Mazzini and Montanelli wanted Tuscany to join the republic of Rome, but municipal feelings were too strong, and the conservatives and the mob at Florence then brought the Grand Duke back. Meanwhile in Sicily, where another Polish general, Mieroslawski, had been employed to defend the island against Ferdinand, the revolution received a further defeat. But some units of the Lombard army and some of the Genoese managed to reach Rome along with Garibaldi, Pisacane, Felice Orsini, and other revolutionary leaders from many parts of Italy.

The republican government held out for several months at Rome against the armies of Austria, Spain, France, and Naples; and its gallant defense, together with the presence of so many Italians from other provinces, made this a very important episode in the development of national feeling. A Roman Assembly was elected by universal suffrage in January 1849—and a quarter of a million people voted, despite a papal prohibition. The Inquisition was abolished, a free press introduced, and laymen replaced the clergy in politics and administration. Mazzini, who was to be consistently condemned by the moderate liberals as a doctrinaire and impractical ideologue, governed with effectiveness and tolerance.

Declaration by the Constituent Assembly at Rome, February 9, 1849

Article 1:—The temporal government of the papacy in Rome is now at an end, in fact and in law.

Article 2:—The Roman pontiff will have every guarantee needed for the independent exercise of his spiritual power.

Article 3:—The form of government at Rome shall be that of pure democracy, and it will take the glorious name of The Roman Republic.

Article 4:—The Roman Republic will enter into such relations with the rest of Italy as our common nationality demands.

[G. Spada: *Storia della rivoluzione di Roma* (Florence, 1870), vol. III, pp. 201-2]

In August 1848, Garibaldi had demonstrated in Lombardy that at least one Italian commander knew something of tactics and strategy. Defending Rome in May–June 1849, he was responsible for the most spirited military action of the whole risorgimento. When Louis Napoleon sent a French army to put down the republic and restore papal authority in Rome, Garibaldi led five thousand surviving soldiers out of the city and up into the Alban hills. This small column found little support in the countryside. Arezzo and other cities barred their gates. After many adventures, however, Garibaldi reached Piedmontese territory, only to be arrested and sent into exile at Tangiers as an undesirable.

Garibaldi's speech to his soldiers in St. Peter's Square, Rome,
July 2, 1849

Soldiers! You who have shared with me the labor and the dangers of fighting for our fatherland, you who have won a rich share of glory and honor, all you can expect if you now come with me into exile is heat and thirst by day, cold and hunger by night. No other wages await you save hard work and danger. You will live in the open, without rest, without food, and there will be long night watches, forced marches, and fighting at every step.

Let him who loves his country follow me.

> [E. Loevinson: *Giuseppe Garibaldi e la sua legione*
> *nello stato Romano 1848–9* (Rome, 1907),
> vol. III, p. 114]

By the end of 1849 the revolution was over. Venice finally surrendered when an Austrian blockade was made worse by malaria and cholera. Although the Pope returned to Rome, the temporal power was enabled to survive only because enforced by foreign troops. A French garrison therefore remained in Rome for his protection. Italy found herself once more an occupied country. The national cause had been advanced, but many weaknesses had been exposed in these two years. Divisions had been opened up between republicans and monarchists, between different regions and neighboring towns, between federalists and unitarists, radicals and conservatives, Catholics and anti-clericals. Personal differences too—for instance between Mazzini, Cattaneo, Garibaldi, and Pisacane—contributed to the general feeling of disillusionment.

The diary of an English economist in Florence

November 18, 1850. Louis Napoleon's message was discussed, and great indignation expressed at his self-gratulation on the Roman expedition. If, they said, the French had secured liberal institutions, or even improved institutions, to Romagna, the crime of their invasion might have been forgiven; but they have done no more for the Romans than the Austrians have done for the Tuscans. They say that if they had not gone to Rome the Austrians would have done so. It is very probable; but in what respect would the Romans have been worse off? In one respect, and an important one, all Italy would have been much better off under an Austrian occupation, for then France would not have been an accomplice in the restoration of misgovernment. She would have been able to remonstrate, perhaps to act.

November 22. The Austrians are striving to bring back the higher classes of Milanese to the capital, but find it difficult. Those who took part against them fly from a place full of painful associations, and those who are supposed to have been favorable to them are ill-treated by their own countrymen. "A relation of mine," said Giorgini, "the Duke of Melzi, could not avoid receiving in his house some of the Austrian officers. This, however, has made him so unpopular that even his friends have advised him to leave Milan."

Giorgini joined the Tuscan contingent in the Austrian war. As professor he commanded a company of the regiment of students. I asked whether such an employment of youths at that age was wise. "Whether wise or not," he answered, "it was unavoidable. When the news of the insurrection of Milan arrived, the students became absolutely unmanageable. There were meetings and speeches, and if we had not submitted to the movement we should have been carried away by it. They would have joined Charles Albert, whatever we had done, and it was better that they should join him with some degree of discipline and under some command than as a mere mob of volunteers."

The excuse for every Italian folly is the same—"We could not help it; the people would do it." A bad prospect for a popular government.

November 23. [Salvagnoli] talked of the difficulty of writing Italian. "It does not consist," he said, "merely in the prevalence of dialects, at least as far as we are concerned; for what was formerly called the Tuscan dialect is now recognized as the Italian language. But there are two Italian languages: the old, or written one, and the modern, or spoken one. In French or in English a man writes as he speaks. But if I were to speak the language of Machiavelli it would be ridiculous; if I were to write as I speak it would sound intolerably vulgar. Even to a Tuscan, therefore, written Italian is a dead language."

November 27. I had a long conversation with M. Buonarotti, the representative of the great artist, formerly a judge, and now Councillor of State. He spoke with great but, perhaps, not undue bitterness of the republican faction, which, by the assassination of Rossi, the Neapolitan revolt, the unjust attack on Austria, and the insurrections of Genoa, Leghorn, and Florence, has ruined the happiness of this generation, and thrown back Italy for a century. "This little Duchy," he said, "is a specimen of Italian unity. Florence, Lucca, Siena, and Pisa all hate one another, even more than they hate Austria." Among the mischiefs which he feared from republicanism was trial by jury.

November 28. A hopelessly wet day. It was nearly all taken up by a succession of visitors. First came the Duke Serra di Falco [a Sicilian refugee in Florence]. "I regret Sicily," he said, "but yet I amuse myself here. Though I am a rebel and an exile, that was not my vocation. My favorite life is to employ myself with administrative business for an hour or two, then with literary and antiquarian researches for an hour or two more, then to ride till dinner time, to pass the evening in the theater or in society, and to read *The Arabian Nights* for a quarter of an hour before I go to bed. Politics, on a great scale, were forced on me, and I don't think that I shall ever take them up again. Men, at least my countrymen, are not worth the sacrifices which the attempt to serve them costs, and the attempt scarcely ever succeeds. Those who know what is right are too timid or too indolent to act on their convictions, and almost all the bold and active are ignorant and perverse. When the whole united force of all Italy was not more than was wanted to drive out the Austrians, we wasted our strength in civil war, and never were more thoroughly disunited, never feared and hated one another more deeply, than when we were proclaiming Italy united."

December 5. This was our last morning in Florence. After breakfast Sir F. Adam and the Duke Serra di Falco paid us a long parting visit. I asked the Duke if he agreed in Prince Butera's opinion [i.e., another Sicilian refugee] that under no circumstances whatever, however liberal the Constitution, or however honest and intelligent the King, could Sicily and Naples live together comfortably under one sovereign. He answered, "Perfectly; it is lamentable, but it is true; and you will be convinced of it after you have been a week in Sicily. It is a mistake to suppose that it is only a party in Sicily that is opposed to the Neapolitan dynasty. Hatred of Naples is almost the only feeling that belongs to every class and to every degree of education and intelligence. It governs the prince and the beggar, the professor and the clown. Centuries of good government, supposing it to be possible to govern well a hostile people, would not eradicate it. The experiment indeed has never been attempted."

[N. William Senior: *Journals Kept in France and Italy from 1848 to 1852*, vol. I, pp. 330–51]

9. Victor Emmanuel, Azeglio, and Cavour, 1849-1852

After his father's abdication, King Victor Emmanuel signed another armistice at Vignale. About this armistice, a politically inspired legend was subsequently manufactured to describe how his firmness against Austrian bullying saved the Piedmontese constitution which Radetzky asked him to renounce. The truth was different, for, as Professor Smyth established from the Austrian documents, Victor Emmanuel obtained unexpectedly good terms from the Austrians by volunteering that he would crush the large left-wing majority in parliament. In support of this undertaking he negotiated peace on his own responsibility alone, and then dissolved parliament when he was accused of acting improperly. Victor Emmanuel here showed courage and a realistic determination to make the best of a bad job.

Field Marshal Radetzky to Prince Schwarzenberg, Novara, March 26, 1849

THE ARMISTICE conditions had already been given to the Piedmontese general when I was told of King Charles Albert's abdication during the night; and the fact was confirmed later by the general himself.

Because of the King's utter untrustworthiness, we had made

these conditions severe; yet since they had already been delivered, I decided not to call the general back but to await events. I thought that the new King Victor Emmanuel would want this severity mitigated, and was therefore quite prepared to grant some concessions in order to win his trust.

What I foresaw, happened. The King consented to the first four conditions, *viz:* the disbandment of the Lombard corps, occupation of a part of his territory, reduction of his army to a peace footing, and evacuation of all territories on the right bank of the Po which were not Piedmontese property before the war. But His Majesty wishes the town and citadel of Alessandria to be occupied in common and equally by our troops and his.

The debate on this part of the negotiations lasted until yesterday morning; the armistice itself, signed by His Majesty, was therefore not returned till yesterday evening. I now transmit to Your Highness the earlier draft together with the ratified convention actually agreed upon.

In the afternoon of the day before yesterday, the King also had a personal conversation with me at our advance posts. He frankly declared his firm intention of defeating the democratic Revolutionary Party, to which his father had latterly given such free rein that it became a real threat to himself and his throne. He said he only needed a little time for this, but it was especially important for him to avoid being discredited at the outset of his reign, because otherwise he would not be able to find any suitable ministers. This was the principal reason why he wanted the clause concerning the fort of Alessandria altered, because our occupation of the *whole* place—the only garrison town he possesses in Piedmont—would alienate the loyalty of the army, which he needs for the maintenance of his throne. Apart from this it would also alienate the people and parliament.

There is so much truth in this point that I could not dispute it. I therefore consented, and consider that I did right in the matter. If we fail to win the confidence of the new King and if we do not help him to maintain his dignity, conditions in Piedmont will afford us no guarantee whatsoever of peace in the future.

["The Armistice of Novara," ed. H. McGaw Smyth, in *The Journal of Modern History* (Chicago, 1935), vol. VII, pp. 177-8]

The treaty with Austria was signed on August 6, 1849. Though its terms were as good as could have been expected, the demagogues in the Turin parliament, seizing their chance to assert themselves against the king, accused the government of violating the constitution. The only alternative would have been to continue fighting, but the government could not afford to explain to the country the extent of demoralization in the army. Nevertheless, the elections in July had returned a majority which now repudiated the treaty. Azeglio, whom the king had appointed in April as the eighth Prime Minister in the first year of the new constitution, therefore lacked parliamentary support, yet he and the king were determined to ignore this fact.

The refusal of parliament to accept the inevitable led to another dissolution and more elections for which the king issued his *Proclamation of Moncalieri*. In this famous document he scolded the electors and virtually warned them that, unless they returned deputies more amenable to common sense and the king's policy, constitutional government might come to an end. At Vignale he had promised the Austrians that he would master the opposition, and in his opinion, as in that of many moderate liberals, such an appeal to the electorate seemed the only way of keeping his promise. The new elections in December were accompanied by a good deal of intimidation and corruption to ensure the return of official candidates. The 80,000 voters dutifully confirmed the king's bold action, and the result was that the peace was approved and the Piedmontese parliament remained in being —the only one in Italy.

The proclamation from Moncalieri, November 20, 1849, signed by King Victor Emmanuel, and countersigned by Prime Minister Azeglio

CONSIDERING THE gravity of present circumstances, the loyalty I think I have displayed up to now in word and deed should suffice to remove any uncertainty from your minds. Nevertheless I feel the need, or at least the desire, to address my peoples in words that may be fresh pledges of security and at the same time an expression of justice and truth.

The dissolution of the Chamber of Deputies does not endanger the freedoms of the country in any way. These are safeguarded by the revered memory of my father King Charles Albert; they are entrusted to the honor of the House of Savoy; they are protected by the sanctity of my solemn oaths. Who dare fear for them?

Before convoking parliament I spoke frankly to the nation, especially to the electors. In my proclamation of July 3, 1849, I admonished electors to behave in such a way as not to make the constitution impossible to work. But only a third of you, or not many more, went to the polls. The rest of you neglected this right, which is at the same time the strict duty of every elector in a free country. I had fulfilled my duty: why did you not fulfill yours?

In the Speech from the Throne I made known to you—though there was little need to—the deplorable condition of the state. I pointed to the need to call a truce to all party passions and find a prompt solution to vital questions endangering the common weal. My words were inspired by profound love of our country, and by spotless loyalty. What fruit have they borne?

The first actions of the Chamber were hostile to the Crown. The Chamber was exercising its right; but if I was ready to ignore some things [parliament's irresponsibility?], the Chamber had no right to forget others.

I will say nothing of the uncalled-for attack made by the opposition on the policy followed by my ministers, which was the only possible policy in the circumstances.

I will say nothing of the attacks made to the detriment of the prerogative granted me by law. But I have every right to call the Chamber severely to account for the latest of its actions, and I appeal confidently to the judgment of Italy and Europe.

I concluded a treaty with Austria that was honorable and not ruinous. The public weal demanded this. Both the honor of the country and the sancity of my solemn oath bound me to fulfill it without duplicity or quibbling. My ministers asked for the assent of the Chamber, which, by appending a condition to it, made its assent unacceptable, since it destroyed the mutual independence of the Three Powers and thus violated the Constitution of the Realm.

I have sworn to maintain justice, and the freedom within his rights of everyone in this kingdom. I have promised to save the nation from the tyranny of parties, whatever the name, purpose or rank of the men composing them.

I am fulfilling these promises and these oaths by dissolving a Chamber that has become impossible; I am fulfilling them by convoking another at once. But if the country, if the electors, deny me their cooperation, it is not upon me, henceforth, that responsibility for the future will fall; and in the disorders that may then result, they will not have to complain of me but of themselves.

If I consider it my duty to speak severely on this occasion, I feel sure that the good sense and justice of the public will convince them that I have a profound love of my peoples and concern for their true advantage. I firmly intend to maintain their freedom and defend it against both external and internal enemies.

The House of Savoy has never yet appealed in vain to the loyalty, good sense and love of its peoples. I have the right, therefore, to trust them on the present occasion, and to feel certain that united we can save the Constitution and the country from the perils that threaten them.

> [M. d'Azeglio: *Scritti e discorsi politici*, ed. M. de
> Rubris (Florence, 1936), vol. II, pp. 195–6]

It was difficult to write openly about the king in his lifetime, but certain things were written in private which suggest that the *Re galantuomo* was slightly less straightforward and trustworthy a character than the man whose heroic virtues had (for political reasons) to be stressed in the difficult years after 1849. In November 1849, Victor Emmanuel told the papal nuncio that he had no use for constitutional government and was only awaiting a convenient moment to overturn it; and this attitude was also noted by Butenval, the French ambassador. Nevertheless, though the king did not greatly like either Azeglio or Cavour, though he several times tried to dismiss them and treated both of them somewhat shabbily on occasion, still for eleven years he kept as his prime ministers the two men who towered over the other politicians of their generation. Sometimes, moreover, he was to show more common sense than either of them. In practice Victor Emmanuel did not dare to carry out some of the threats which he mouthed in private. As a result of Charles Albert's pretentious failures in 1848 and 1849, the monarchy had been partially discredited, and this was an important reason why monarchical authority developed less in Piedmont than in contemporary Prussia.

*Baron His de Butenval, French ambassador in Turin, to Drouyn
de Lhuys, French Foreign Minister, October 16, 1852*

KING VICTOR EMMANUEL is in no sense liberal: his tastes, his education and his whole habit of behavior all go the other way. He tells everyone that "my father bestowed institutions on the country which are quite unfitted to its needs and the temper of its inhabitants." To some people he will add, "but my father and myself have both given our word, and I will not break it." To others, however, he will say confidentially, "I am waiting only for the *right moment to change everything*. That moment will be the outbreak of war. Whenever it comes, I shall be ready." Any

French official who finds himself alone with the King will be asked if the time has yet arrived.

In the King's view, the French army is the rearguard of the Piedmontese forces; or, as he puts it, "you Frenchmen must look on the Piedmontese army as the vanguard of your own." His object is to take Lombardy and keep it—jointly with us if need be.

Victor Emmanuel, I repeat, does not like the existing constitution, nor does he like parliamentary liberties, nor a free press. He just accepts them temporarily as a kind of weapon of war. He keeps the tricolor flag instead of restoring that of Savoy; but he looks on it not as a revolutionary standard, only as a banner of conquest. Once the conquest is over, he will bring back the old flag; but at once on the outbreak of hostilities he would suspend the constitution indefinitely. One must therefore not be deceived by any talk about the chivalrous attitude of the King and his ministers to the constitution they have sworn to observe.

Another thing to remember is the state of opinion in this small and divided monarchy. Piedmont is harboring all the *émigrés* from other Italian states. They have seats in parliament; a good number are in the armed forces or on the main newspapers. They thus form a kind of nation within the nation, a group apart, and one which is particularly active and calculating. Piedmont on the whole loathes the *émigrés* and the disastrous memories [of 1848–9] which they recall, as well as the warlike sentiments which they still retain; but the nation at large keeps quiet, and does nothing about them.

The Piedmontese are honest, quiet, busy with their own concerns, and they want peace. In their view, salvation must come from *foreign help;* and they now look to France and her sovereign. If ever they think that they could no longer count on France, they would overcome the humiliation of recent memories, and unreservedly, even blindly, ask for Austrian help. The King himself, however, temporizes and plays with the *revolutionary* element just because it might help him toward *military victory.*

[Archives of French Foreign Office, *Sardinia,* 332/73]

The fact that Azeglio was much better known in and outside Italy than any other Italian politician except Gioberti—and was more trusted than anyone—did something to establish the reputation of Piedmont. He generously welcomed many thousands of *émigrés* from other

Italian states. Despite the wishes of Balbo and the conservatives, Azeglio made the constitution in some respects more liberal. Along with his Minister of Justice. Siccardi, he abolished the separate Church courts and the old exemptions of the clergy from existing laws; rights of asylum in churches were also ended by the Siccardi laws; and when the Archbishop of Turin told his priests to disobey, he was simply put in prison. Azeglio's intention here was to encourage the process which eventually made Piedmont the most obviously liberal state in the peninsula, a state which aimed not at dominating the rest of Italy so much as attracting by her example.

If for nothing else, Azeglio's appointment of Cavour as Finance Minister would have made this period notable. Camille de Cavour was primarily a financier, and he was brought into the cabinet in 1850 to complete the switch to a free trade policy which Charles Albert had tentatively begun. Removing tariffs eventually had a dramatic effect in increasing foreign trade. Cavour also hoped that, as well as fostering individual initiative, free trade would combat the spread of socialism and encourage foreign investment in Piedmont. His presentation of these matters to parliament was in a much more down-to-earth, unrhetorical style than was customary in that assembly.

Cavour and free trade: speech of April 8, 1852

GENTLEMEN, THE protective system has far more disastrous effects when applied to the products of the soil than when applied to industry. Industrial protection has only one prejudicial effect, namely to divert capital and labor from natural objects of industry, and to drive them into artificial occupations where resources would be less productively employed. This is a serious drawback, but it affects only those resources which protection would divert from their natural channel, and moreover it would be partially diminished by internal competition. After a certain time, competition will always ensure that capital and labor in privileged branches of industry are remunerated no better than in industries which are not privileged.

But protection when applied to agriculture has far more extensive and, I do not hesitate to say, more disastrous effects. In fact, gentlemen, when by means of a protective duty you raise the price of wines and cereals, what follows? In the first place, certain lands which were not sufficiently fertile to produce corn and wine under the former conditions of the market, will now be brought under cultivation, or the prospective profit will now bring a greater investment in capital and labor. This first effect of agricultural protection is thus the same as in industry: that is to say, resources will be employed less productively than if things had been left to their natural course.

This is a serious inconvenience. It would, however, not be of great moment if the rise in agricultural prices affected only the produce of lands recently put into cultivation, or of additional capital and labor devoted to the improvement of lands which had been long since cleared. But the artificial rise in prices will extend to crops on all kinds of land, those of old as well as of recent cultivation. Who profits by this rise? Any gains are shared between the proprietors and the farmers, especially if the latter hold long leases; and after a certain time the entire profit is concentrated in the hands of the proprietors.

Thus, then, agricultural protection forces capital and labor into a less productive channel; and, at the same time, it increases existing rents at the expense of consumers, which means that it taxes consumers for the benefit of landowners.

[C. Benso di Cavour: *Discorsi parlamentari*, ed. L. Russo (Florence, 1936), vol. V, pp. 445-7]

Before long, Cavour was the indispensable man in the cabinet. He was more industrious, more talented, and far more ruthless than his colleagues. Azeglio was more respected and knew much more of Italy than Cavour, but he was an invalid, an idler, and by comparison an amateur politician who knew very little of parties, parliamentary technique, finance, or economics.

As early as October 1850, the very month he first joined the cabinet, Cavour had seriously debated whether he should not supplant Azeglio rather than join him. At first he had sat well over to the Right in parliament. He had the reputation of being a conservative aristocrat who was skeptical about Italy and a champion of the narrow interests of Piedmont. But, after the Proclamation of Moncalieri and the elections of December 1849, he recognized that his dread of revolution was no longer justified. Louis Napoleon's coup in December 1851 only confirmed this impression. By that time, Cavour had already begun secret discussions on how to break up the existing party structure and make a new broad coalition of the Center including both liberals and conservatives. Naturally he could not tell his colleagues what he was doing, because he would have lost his job before his plans were ready.

In a speech of February 5, 1852, when he was proposing a minor restriction on the perhaps over-generous press laws, Cavour astonished parliament by suddenly announcing that the government had decided to renounce the support of Balbo, Menabrea, and the Right. The government had in fact decided no such thing, and his colleagues in the cabinet were as surprised as anyone. This was Cavour's personal marriage (or *connubio*) with Urbano Rattazzi who led the Center Left, and was one of the episodes that gave him a reputation for untrustworthiness. Probably he had reckoned on provoking Azeglio's resignation, but the maneuver was too blatant to be immediately successful. Cavour was more proud of the *connubio* than any other act of his political life, and it effectively prepared the way for his subsequent success.

G. F. Galvagno, then Cavour's cabinet colleague as Minister of Justice, recalls the months before the connubio

THE PARLIAMENTARY Right was becoming less compact, less ready to defend the government, and rather divided into two factions of Extreme Right and Center. Cavour saw how he might use this fact to acquire greater popularity, and how he could reinforce public faith in his liberalism. For until now, to be frank, his fellow citizens did not trust him.

With this in mind his parliamentary speeches became full of fine liberal sentiments. Outside the Chamber, moreover, he spent more time with members of the Center Left than with those of the Right. I also gathered from a trustworthy source that he often went to Rattazzi's house and spoke to him of his financial policy, so much so that the Center Left knew more of this than did his cabinet colleagues. He never used to tell the rest of the cabinet about his schemes, and never brought them up for discussion. Indeed no important political business was ever seriously discussed by ministers collectively. Count Cavour was in complete charge of the situation. The Prime Minister was nothing; or rather the cabinet itself was nothing. Cavour could do what he liked, as he was Minister of Finance as well as Minister of Shipping, Agriculture and Commerce; though he himself claimed to discuss, delay, or even prevent the projects of his colleagues.

Thus Cavour's presence in the cabinet was becoming an insupportable burden for the other ministers.

[*Lettere edite ed inedite di Camillo Cavour*, ed. L. Chiala (Turin, 1884), vol. I, pp. 577–8]

Massimo d'Azeglio, the Prime Minister, to Eugène Rendu, May 24, 1852

SINCE THAT famous parliamentary session of February 5 when the *connubio* was announced, I have been very cool with Cavour. Just imagine! My own cabinet colleague, without so much as declaring war, had arranged everything privately with Rattazzi. The speech in which he specifically committed the whole government was made without a word to me. It was one of those many days when my wound kept me in bed, and there was a cabinet meeting at my house. Cavour buttonholed one minister in the window embrasure at the foot of my bed and said something like: "I am fed up with Menabrea and sometimes think of renouncing his political support." That is all we knew about it. Three intermediaries had fixed the whole intrigue. Immediately they left my house came that explosion in the Chamber. It was a very delicate moment for us, and I did not want the general public to know of our internal divisions. So I behaved like the general who concealed a mutiny by putting himself at the head of the mutineers. But, you can understand, that could not last.

I had never had dealings with the Center Left. My view was that they should have moved toward us, not we toward them: that was the big difference between me and Cavour. So, when Rattazzi was subsequently elected President of the Chamber with the backing of the author of the *connubio*, I had had enough. Christian humility is not fashionable in politics. Apart from the personal question, the whole administration and its policy were going adrift.

The day Rattazzi was elected [May 11, as President or Speaker of the Lower House] I was again in bed (not the place for a Prime Minister, you will agree, though it is one extenuation that I earned my wound fighting for the country). Hearing of the election, I wrote to the King that my health prevented me from resisting this kind of intrigue, so I resigned. The King accepted our resignation; he charged me to form another government, which I did, excluding Cavour and Farini. By electing Rattazzi they had given me a slap in the face, so I showed them the door. It was a question not only of personal dignity but of holding to our political program. For that, I had to stay in office. But, good God, when can I get out of this mad game? I can't go on with it much longer. I am just not strong enough.

> [*L'Italie de 1847 à 1865. Correspondance politique de Massimo d'Azeglio*, ed. E. Rendu (Paris, 1867), pp. 73–5]

U. Rattazzi to M. Castelli, May 1, 1870

IT IS an excellent idea of yours to put together a political record of recent events. As regards the *connubio*, you were one of its main promoters, so no one is better placed to tell how it began and was completed. You will remember that the bases of the *connubio*— the fusion of the two Center groups in the Piedmontese parliament —were laid down at your house in October 1851 and January 1852. There was a meeting at which the others present besides yourself were the late-lamented Cavour (Minister of Agriculture and Commerce in the Azeglio cabinet), poor Buffa and myself.

At that meeting we agreed to lay the foundations in the Chamber for this fusion. Once this had been achieved, we would use the opportunity provided by some important parliamentary question to make it public. As a result, the *connubio* declared its existence during the debate on a change in our press laws. Before this, however, the whole plan had already been agreed by these four men. No one else knew anything of it.

Two main principles were to inspire the new party. In home affairs we would resist all reactionary tendencies that might threaten after the recent *coup d'état* in France. At the same time, in so far as circumstances permitted, we would promote a continuous and progressive development of the freedoms allowed by our constitution, alike in politics, economics and administration. As regards international affairs, we would prepare the way for Piedmont to liberate Italy from foreign rule.

Now that I recall those days, I remember that the credit for bringing about that meeting where the *connubio* was settled was largely yours and poor Buffa's. We should be grateful to you that a new party was formed which, without offending modesty too greatly, I feel was to render great services both to freedom and Italy. For at that time I had no close personal relations with Count Cavour. I must admit that I still felt somewhat distrustful as to the extent of his liberal and Italian sentiments. This distrust had been to a considerable degree dissipated by his attitude in parliament after the defeat of Novara [in 1849] but had not entirely disappeared. You, on the other hand, had intimate links with Cavour and were in a position to know and appreciate him better than I was. You were thus able to remove all uncertainty from my mind.

[*Il Conte di Cavour: ricordi di Michelango Castelli,*
ed. L. Chiala (Turin, 1886), pp. 46–8]

Cavour became Prime Minister in November 1852. As part of the pre-arranged cabinet program, Azeglio had introduced a bill to legalize civil marriage, and this was approved in the Lower House by 94 votes to 35; at which point the king suddenly announced, because of his conscience and certain private undertakings to the Pope, that the royal veto would be employed. Azeglio refused to countenance this irregularity, but Cavour proved more pliable and so got the job. Cavour felt sure that, once he had beaten Azeglio, he would find some way of keeping the king in his place.

Italy was fortunate to find such a man at such a time. Cavour had already demonstrated his skill as a financier. He was soon to show a mastery of parliamentary tactics and a skill in diplomacy which few had suspected. His in many ways attractive and outgoing personality went along with a remarkable combination of common sense, political tact, and sheer truculence. As his cousin De la Rive noted, "he was a bar of iron painted like a reed"; "an aristocrat by birth, taste and nature," who was perhaps too refined to understand the masses or be understood by them, but who could be harsh and peremptory where necessary, and could appeal either to the highest motives or to base passions with equal self-possession. Beneath his charm was an "inexorable stiffness of purpose."

Under Cavour's guidance, parliament was used and magnified as a check on royal authoritarianism. An older generation of aristocrats was eased out of sinecures and positions of responsibility (Cavour himself began to democratize his signature after 1853, and would sign simply "C. Cavour," instead of the more courtly "Camille de Cavour"; and more frequently he used the Italian form, "Camillo"). Bravely he built up a huge financial deficit as he tried to fit Piedmont for leadership in the next and decisive stage of the Italian movement.

Cavour's character, by Castelli, a close friend

AT THE beginning of Cavour's political life, the fact of his being an aristocrat counted against him, and anyone less self-confident would have found it an insuperable handicap. Later on, however, it proved an advantage. On his return from the Congress of Paris, when he was telling me the intimate story of how Italy gained such an unexpected advantage, I could not help saying that, for all his skill, if he had been a lawyer rather than a count he would have gained much less. He was struck by my remark, but merely answered: "My dear fellow, that's the way of the world."

His easy manners, his joviality, his genuine interest in new acquaintances, the affability with which he welcomed all who called on him, and his readiness to listen to serious men or any enterprising project, made him popular with all acquaintances as well as intimates. He was respected and loved by all his juniors and servants. They wept when he died as if for a father, and still venerate his memory.

Having set down his private and public qualities, I must recount what I saw in the daily intimacy of so many years. His perceptiveness, his benevolence, his instinctive understanding of our times made him a believer in political and civil equality. Yet deep down you could sometimes find traces in Count Cavour of a less progressive man.

From the outset I had set myself to study his real character and to clarify the distrust in which he was held. More than once I showed him apparent contradictions between what he said and what he did. He would be taken aback for a moment and usually ended up by turning the matter into a friendly joke, realizing that he was in the wrong; or else he would argue the point on a plane of political philosophy as if it were not a matter which touched him personally.

Cavour was certainly not emotional, but he was subject to first impressions; when struck by the story of some generous action or undeserved disaster, his eyes would grow moist and his whole countenance showed the depth of his sentiments. He would soon pick up, but this would not prevent his actions being governed by his initial feeling. Sometimes he suddenly became quite passionate about people, just as sometimes he would as suddenly take umbrage at certain questions, at acts that lacked the tact or delicacy which he prized as the very highest quality in an individual.

Cavour was slightly below average height, with a plump figure, a distinguished bearing, a somewhat red face, with fair hair, and blue-gray eyes twinkling behind his spectacles. He had a gay disposition. Both as guest and host he was almost always smiling, and he liked to begin a conversation with some joking phrase.

His activity was ceaseless; if he was not doing something, he was thinking; hence his occasionally abstracted manner, his odd forms of posture, his constant need to be at work. Whatever the season he was always at his desk at 5 a.m., receiving people and working through until ten. Then, after a light breakfast, he set out for the Ministry, or for Parliament, or wherever his business took him, though he almost always found time for a stroll under the arcades by the Po and the Fiera between midday and one o'clock.

He never went in for private revenges. He made it almost a duty to favor his political or personal enemies, so much so that I used to say to him: "To get what one wants from you, one must insult you or do you some real injury." Over and over again I noted this fact and the pleasure he took in it.

He usually saw the good rather than the evil side of things, and you could not apply to him what Foscolo said of some statesmen, that they are all brain and no heart. His affections were sudden and vivid, but they had little to do with his intellect. He had a chivalrous sense of honor and a belief in moral laws, both of which in his mind took precedence of any faith in absolute and unquestioned dogmas. He seldom referred to matters of religious practice; but he respected all convictions even when they verged on bigotry.

Once at an Alpine watering place we took long mountain walks together, and I recollect how the beauty and grandeur of nature turned his conversation toward religion, toward discussing the plurality of worlds and various resulting hypotheses. He talked about the metaphysical God, the origins of the world, about man and the teachings of ancient philosophy. But his essentially positive and practical mind could never reach firm conclusions save from bases of certainty, and finding none he would end with Montaigne's famous *"que sais-je?"*

His stable and serene intelligence had no room for any idea of asceticism, or for absolute dogmas, religious intolerance, or any disturbing fears about the immortality of the soul.

For the rest, who can plumb the depths of anyone else's mind? He was a man of deep religious feeling; and this inspired his political, civil and social principles; it was the driving force of many of his actions; and his words were never more eloquent and persuasive than when he proclaimed in parliament the principle of *a free Church in a free State.*

He did not put forward this great idea as a political strategem, nor was his phrase about *Rome must be the capital of Italy* a merely tactical step. He proclaimed both because an intuitive instinct, which is the greatest political gift, convinced him that they would effectively reconcile religion, the papacy and Italy.

Never in thirteen years of daily contact, during which we discussed every question which came up in that agitated period, never even in his most private conversation, did I ever hear Count Cavour utter a word of disrespect toward religious opinions, or toward the papacy as center of a religion professed by hundreds of millions.

It was as a politician, without hatred and without unjust bias, that he took action against the clericals when they banded themselves into a political party.

He set no time limit for his policy. It was his habit to proclaim a principle and hold to it, without creating difficulties by risking forecasts about time. Detailed policy was always governed by circumstances, though he kept his eye fixed incessantly on the final goal.

Count Cavour gave solemn proof in his parliamentary and political life of his profound knowledge of the British constitution, as of economic and social affairs in Britain and her political history. He was equally familiar with French history.

The same could not be said of his knowledge of Italian history and literature, or even that of Piedmont and the Savoy monarchy. This was a general defect of education rather than his own personal failing, for the whole Piedmontese upper class looked rather to monarchist France for their history, literature, language and customs.

Later, in the intervals allowed by successive political crises, he carefully studied the various histories of Italy. He admitted that he did not read the chapters on ancient history, only those which dealt with modern and contemporary events.

When Count Cavour came back from his early travels, he found an outlet for his great energy in farming, applying the latest discoveries he had found abroad.

It would be a mistake to attribute his later success in financial and political speculation to the speculative habits learned in this early period. At first he profited others more than himself, for in investment he was a better theorist than practician. He also took part in industrial enterprises which almost invariably ended with substantial losses. If by chance he alluded to these reverses, it would be with the greatest unconcern, nor would he ever admit himself defeated, or disavow his basic principles in economics or agronomy. He took sincere delight in other people's successes, and if anyone criticized the morality of some piece of "good business" in banking or industrial speculation, he did not hold it too much against the profiteers, but said that the b. . . . . . had only themselves to blame. He despised money as such. Though in his young days he had had a taste for gaming, all his friends relate that he lost or won enormous sums with the same equanimity.

He enjoyed a very large income. He liked the comforts of life but was totally indifferent to its luxuries.

He was deeply interested in agricultural progress, and I often heard him say: "When we have created Italy I shall retire to Leri and devote myself entirely to farming." I have no idea what he would have done had he lived, but I never saw him so happy as when he was setting out for Leri or in residence there . . .

Cavour was accused of having few scruples about his choice of friends or about the means he adopted to reach his ends. Some of his friends, for instance Massimo d'Azeglio, were occasionally angry over actions which to them seemed immoral.

[*Il Conte di Cavour: ricordi di Michelangelo Castelli*, ed. Chiala, pp. 8–20]

An independent view of Cavour by a backbencher, 1861

COUNT CAVOUR undeniably ranks as third among European statesmen after Lord Palmerston and the Emperor Napoleon. The loss of this man, in the prsent circumstances, would be an irreparable disaster for Italy. Count Cavour's strength does not lie in his principles; for he has none that are altogether inflexible. But he has a clear, precise aim, one whose greatness would—ten years ago— have made any other man reel: that of creating a unified and independent Italy. Men, means, circumstances were and still are matters of indifference to him. He walks straight ahead, always firm, often alone, sacrificing his friends, his sympathies, sometimes his heart, and often his conscience. Nothing is too difficult for him. He has a wonderful elasticity of spirit. He intuits everything and rarely makes a mistake—I mean a mistake about means rather than ends. Alongside a facility for solid calculation found more usually in the English temperament, he possesses the political genius of the Italian character, with all its lack of scruples, of idealism, even of generosity. Count Cavour is a cross between Sir Robert Peel and Machiavelli. There is something Byzantine about him: the cunning, the sharp logic, the effectiveness even when most paradoxical. Read his diplomatic notes. It is impossible to be simultaneously right and wrong with a more solid or compelling brilliance of argument. It takes you by the throat with its eloquence, and you are left impressed, dazzled, and often convinced.

Count Cavour, who unfortunately at times lacks the talent to assess men, always has the talent to assess a situation and the possibilities of exploiting it. And it is this wonderful faculty that has contributed to form the Italy of today. As minister of a fourth-rate power, he could not create situations like Napoleon III, nor has he possessed the support of a great nation like Palmerston.

Count Cavour had to seek out an opening in the complicated fabric of European politics; he had to wriggle his way in, conceal himself, lay a mine, and cause an explosion. And it was by these means that he defeated Austria and won the help of France and England. Where other statesmen would have drawn back, Cavour plunged in headlong—as soon as he had sounded the precipice and calculated the possible profit and loss. The Crimean expeditionary force, his behavior at the Congress of Paris, the cession of Nice, the invasion of the Papal States last autumn [i.e., in 1860], were all the outcome of his vigorous stamina of mind.

There in brief you have the man of foreign affairs. He is strong; he is a match for the situation, for the politicians of his time or indeed of any time.

The man of home affairs is less rounded, less finished. Count Cavour possesses overall knowledge of domestic politics; he has large ideas, at once very liberal and totally uncomplicated; but he lacks the practical skill for their implementation. Moreover he often has an unsure touch in his choice of subordinates. Witness the series of agents he despatched [in 1860–1] to South Italy, including Signor Nigra and the Prince of Carignano. Count Cavour feels himself to be above details, despite the fact that they are important in administration. This is the vulnerable side of his policy; whereas no one questions his superiority in foreign affairs.

Cavour's personality is one factor which sometimes jars in his conduct of affairs. He knows his own nature; he knows the men around him; he has a poor opinion of others, perhaps none at all, and he makes the mistake of letting them see it. And he has no toleration for equals, not being accustomed to meeting many. Whosoever he touches must bend to his will, must submit to being molded and kneaded by his powerful hand. The King himself experiences the magnetism of this man, as he also rails against him and is jealous; but the King's attempts at revolt are in vain. Anyone who refuses to let himself be swallowed up by Count Cavour is classified without much ado among his enemies, or rather adversaries; for though he can show ill temper and even bear malice for a while, he can never hate.

Add to this his brusque manners that show little concern for the susceptibilities of others; the sarcastic smile frozen on his face; his way of ordering people about. His whole upper-class bearing minimizes the effect of the courtesy toward, or should I say the flattery of, those he wants to sweeten or coax. Add to this his halting and embarrassed speech; his harsh metallic voice that puts people off the first time; his petulant, brusque and jerky movements; and you will then have a rounded view of your man—whose charms are few unless you are bound to him by other links.

In parliament Count Cavour behaves absolutely as if the Left did not exist, as if he were in his own sitting room among his intimates. Above all his attitude seems one of boredom there. He talks, laughs, turns his back petulantly on his colleagues, curls up, yawns, tortures the velvet on the table with his paperknife, makes epigrams. If he had American habits he would put his feet on the desk! All he can see in parliament is the majority, that is to say his faithful friends and confidants.

Count Cavour is an orator in the English, rather than in the French, sense. He has no easy flow of words because he does not want to say a single word too many, a single word that might convey the wrong impression. He does not address the Chamber, but Europe. His reasoning is close, firm and lucid; he reaches the heart of the question; and if he is not always right, he never falls into triviality or nonsense.

To sum up. As a diplomat he is a giant; as an administrator he is mediocre; as a man he seems contradictory. With him you never remain undecided: you either obey or rebel. He never lets himslf be led by his friends or depend on them. Abroad, he is

Italy's mind; at home, her heart. He is the real life of the cabinet, which completely identifies itself with him . . .

[*Postscript.*] Count Cavour left his work unfinished. Possibly the completion of that work has now been delayed by his death. But it is also possible that he died at the right time. He would now have had to make sacrifices which would have filled his heart with disgust even though counseled by expediency. The nature of his talent and the disposition of his mind were less suited to the period of persistence, obstinacy and *raideur* on which the Italian question has now embarked—less suited than to the previous period when the need was to struggle, provoke, intrigue, to startle Europe, cause alarm, create difficulties, and obtain advantages from a strength which Italy then lacked and which today is neglected . . .

He was our Pitt. And I would almost add greater than Pitt—for he had all this Englishman's constancy, tenacity, firmness of purpose, and implacable hatred for his country's enemy, and in addition had to struggle against the slenderness of the means that Italy could scrape together. Pitt took action and resisted with a lever called Great Britain; Cavour had only a tiny wedge called Piedmont. But, like Pitt, he made use of that independent dictatorship with which his King and his country had invested him—and the results he obtained from it were a hundred times more magnificent. Pitt overthrew a man; Cavour created a nation!

[F. Petruccelli della Gattina: *I moribondi del Palazzo Carignano* (Milan, 1862), pp. 58–65]

10. Constitutional Difficulties and the Crimean War

In November 1854, Cavour presented a bill to suppress all the "unnecessary" monasteries, or those whose main function was not charity or education. It was approved by the Lower House. Cavour hoped by secularizing monastic property to obtain the 900,000 lire a year which the government was still paying to the clergy as compensation for confiscations during the Napoleonic period. But this dissolution of the monasteries worried the king's conscience, and, just as Azeglio had been dismissed on the issue of civil marriage, the king thought that here would be a good occasion to get rid of the increasingly demanding and opinionated Cavour. He even wrote privately to ask the Pope to help him.

When the bill came before the senate—whose members were appointed by the Crown—the senior bishop, Calabiana of Casale, dramatically announced that the bishops would themselves raise the required 900,000 lire if the bill were dropped. Cavour was caught off guard, for Rattazzi and Cavour's new colleagues on the Left regarded dissolution of the monasteries as the touchstone of liberal sentiment. After first praising the generosity of the offer, the Prime Minister then saw that Calabiana's move must have been pre-arranged with the king. He therefore resigned. The king tried but failed to find a conservative who was ready to lead an alternative administration. When he had to reappoint Cavour, this was a triumphant victory for constitutionalism. The Pope launched a major excommunication against those responsible for the law, and this presumably included Victor Emmanuel himself who now had to sign it. A government's need of parliamentary support had been stated more clearly than ever before.

Victor Emmanuel II to Pope Pius IX, February 9, 1855

THE WORDS of sweetness and charity that You, Most Blessed Father, were so good as to send me, bring a supreme balm to my saddened heart in the immense sorrow I am feeling and which is destroying my whole being. If I did not write to Your Holiness in the past, I would like you to know that this was not due to indifference on my part regarding the affairs of the Church, but rather because I thought on my side that all means for reaching our goal, whether public or private, had been exhausted. It is with the deepest and most heartfelt regret that I see things going as they are; but if only the Church's ministers had shown some of the charity for Piedmont that they showed for other kingdoms, and if we had received a little more good will from their side, then this government, by means of a wise and respectful understanding with Your Holiness, would have called a halt in matters that displeased Your Holiness, even though these were demanded by the emergencies of the times and even though they are recognized as accomplished facts by Your Blessedness in other countries.

Your Holiness will remember how not so long ago, when the senate of my kingdom did not approve the marriage law, you were informed of it; and though this law was desired by the nation, my government did not bring it up again. Now I am speaking to Your Holiness from the depths of my heart when I say that a similar outcome was expected for the law on religious orders when news arrived of the words addressed to Piedmont on the matter by You, Most Blessed Father. They served only to embitter people's minds so that we may well reach the opposite goal. Excuse me, Holy Father, if I tell you the truth.

I beg Your Holiness not to give ear to certain base people who hide under the mantle of the Church, who go from here to Rome where they spread the gall of calumny against this kingdom and its ruler.

This clerical party which, here, is despised by everyone with any judgment, thinks itself more Catholic than the Pope; it has only lies on its lips, and ignorance and pride in its head.

If Your Holiness could only see with your own eyes what religion is like in Piedmont, what respect there is for the Church, and how the churches are overflowing with people, perhaps you might not be so discontented.

Most Blessed Father, with your charity as representative of Christ, do what you can for this kingdom; and when new negotiations begin, which I hope will be soon, console me finally, and with me reward those two holy souls [the King's wife and his mother] who longed so much to see this done while on earth and who will surely rejoice at it in heaven.

I kiss your foot with deep respect.

P.S. Your Holiness should know that it was I who did not allow the senate to pass the marriage law, and that it is I who will now do all in my power not to allow the law regarding religious orders to go through. Perhaps in a short time this Cavour ministry will fall; I shall then nominate a right-wing ministry and make it a *sine qua non* condition that it carries out for me a total adjustment with Rome. Have the charity to help me. I for my part have always done what I could. Your recent words addressed to Piedmont were not well timed, and I am afraid you may ruin everything for me. I shall see to it that the law is not passed, but please help me, Holy Father.

Please burn this piece of paper.

> [P. Pietro Pirri S.J.: *Pio IX e Vittorio Emanuele II dal loro carteggio privato* (Rome, 1944), vol. I, pp. 155–7]

Victor Emmanuel II to Pius IX, March 22, 1855

I MUST begin by thanking Your Holiness for what you had the kindness to write to me, which amid the hard trials to which my conscience is exposed gives me a pledge of Your Holiness's imperishable paternal love.

Now in this completely confidential letter, by a respectful and devoted son to the father of the Church, I am going to lay at your feet a prayer which I warmly beg Your Holiness to look on with a paternal eye. By this time Your Holiness will have received the equally confidential and humble appeal of some Piedmontese bishops who represent the entire episcopate and who, moved by an ardent longing for the well-being of our holy religion and by true love for my royal person, beg Your Holiness to permit them to help the government with Church revenues amounting to the 900,000 lire we need. In return it is understood that I will succeed one way or another in preventing any more talk of the law regarding religious orders—unless in the future there be some reduction that needs to be made, and that would always be in perfect agreement with Your Holiness.

Most Blessed Father, I have suffered in mind for years at constantly causing new wounds to the heart of Your Holiness. Of your charity as father of the faithful, remove me from the embarrassment in which I find myself, and I promise Your Holiness that I will so act as to cause you no more difficulties in future, but at the first possible moment will reopen negotiations for a Concordat that will console all hearts and bring peace to consciences.

I kiss your foot with the deepest respect and ask for your Holy Blessing.

[Pirri, *Pio IX e Vittorio Emanuele II dal loro carteggio privato*, vol. I, pp. 166–7]

A very different policy from Cavour's was that of a former chief minister, Solaro della Margarita, who abhorred liberalism of any kind and thought that Piedmont ought never to become too exclusively Italian. Piedmont's possession of Savoy placed her in a position which straddled the Alps, and Solaro thought that this gave her the role of a buffer state guarding the mountain passes. If she moved into Italy, on the other hand, she would be involved in a policy of aggression and warmongering, and would run a risk of losing her independence. Solaro as a devout Catholic was above all worried that in Italy she would become anti-papal and anti-clerical. He was therefore moderately pro-Austrian, especially as Austria was the safest bulwark against revolutionary change.

These ideas could be called out of date by 1854, but they were not without support. In 1857 the right-wing clerical opposition was going to obtain nearly a third of the seats in the Piedmontese parliament, and one can assume that on a really wide suffrage they would have won a huge majority. But Solaro and his colleagues had no aptitude for parliamentary politics. Occasionally they were able to score points in exposing some of the speciousness and contradictions in Cavour's brand of liberal theory, but there was never any serious possibility of their providing an alternative government. A majority of the narrow electorate was to a greater or lesser degree anti-clerical, and Cavour was shortly to ensure that they became anti-Austrian too.

One Piedmontese politician prefers friendship toward Austria

IT IS not for me to teach Austria what her conduct should be in our regard: if the statesmen who, under a wise monarch, watch over that Empire's destiny share my views, then their way is plain, and my advice would be uncalled for. Austria's interests must be better known in Vienna than in Turin, and I would never be so rash as to lay down the principles of law and justice outside my own motherland. All I can do is to state what my convictions and long experience have taught me would best serve my own loved country.

First, our policy toward Austria should aim at winning her confidence. To this purpose we must make quite clear that we have given up our idea of expanding at the expense of the Italian provinces- which belong to the Austrian Emperor—at least, unless such expansion should be effected by political combinations that at present are unforseeable by any of us. I do not exclude the possibility of lawful expansion, but I do exclude the use of unjust methods. In order to legitimize such expansion, Austria's consent would be required; nor should that Power take umbrage if anyone, myself included, should ask for her consent. But I believe that it is a vain hope, and any politician who builds on wishes and not facts will misread the present and fail to exploit the future . . .

I never found myself agreeing with any political idea professed by Cesare Balbo, but I particularly distrust the utopia on which he based his hopes for Italy and the airy schemes of his memorandum to King Charles Albert in 1844. The fixed idea of this writer is to divert Austria eastward, and with this in mind he suggested that we should promote a quadruple alliance between France, England, Austria and Piedmont. I cannot understand how a man of such talent, who had had some experience in government affairs and was a student of politics, could have dreamt up such a scheme; given our position then and now, it could not possibly succeed. It was a real example of adding up the bill without the landlord. Either such a quadruple alliance is wanted by the Powers, in which case they do not need suggestion from us; or it is not, and we would be tactless to propose it. We hardly would attract the glory of having put forward a lofty concept, as Balbo seems to think, but rather the shame of being told to mind our own business. The project is all the stranger in that its concealed aim was to remove Austrian influence away from Italy to the mouth of the Danube. But Austria's plans have never included abandoning Italy for the Danubian provinces. At the time of writing, the [Crimean] war rightly forecast by Balbo is being waged. This was the object of his wishes and the pivot of his hopes. While it is extremely difficult to foresee the consequences of this struggle and the territorial changes which it will bring, I do not see it resulting in any eventual expansion for us into Lombardy. Let our statesmen have no illusions: in our actual condition today this is not practical politics, and no other Power would help us . . .

We ought rather to condemn any underhand plan to change the government of Lombardy-Venetia, or for uniting it with Piedmont. Before 1848 we all agreed that it was blameworthy to kindle such hopes in Lombardy, so let me not suggest it now. After what we have suffered, such a dishonorable act would be a renewed imprudence and would deprive us of all right to the confidence not only of Vienna but of Paris, Berlin and even London—all the Powers, that is to say, who insist on our keeping Italy as it was established by the Congress of Vienna. It is not enough to refrain from the treacherous fomentation of insurrection in Lombardy; it behoves the press, despite its legal freedom, to respect the rights of foreign rulers; and, if it fails to do so, this is an abuse that a wise government must proceed against by law; if the law is inadequate, another should be proposed; and if that fails to get through, then the ministers should resign rather than carry on with a policy which would rob the state of credit and confidence.

To profess friendship for a Power—and such a profession is

explicit in existing treaties—while undermining that Power's authority and rights, is an iniquity too repugnant to be entertained. I
prefer to presuppose in others those feelings of honor which
inform our governors and all who love this country. Only one road
seems to me honorable and fitting for the crown and the country.
Where warlike feelings are aroused by unreasonable passion rather
than by a desire to safeguard sacred rights, they are as unfortunate
as they are ungenerous. We were very behindhand in proving our
valor in arms, but talk of a third war against Austria is generally
found repugnant.

Once we have put aside any idea of illegal expansion at Austrian
expense, we have removed the principal motive preventing frank
relations between the two Courts, and we can look on Austria just
like any other Power. Yet there will always remain a big difference
in strength between Austria and ourselves, and this should warn us
against the jealousy which a formidable neighbor may inspire in a
second-class state like our own. We must realize that the dignity
and esteem in which a state is held do not depend on the size of
its dominions, but rather on its independence and the way it defends
that independence. The Republic of Venice was never a first-class
Power, yet it has left a great name; beaten at Giara d'Adda, threatened with ruin by the League of Cambrai, the Republic of Venice
still maintained its position among the Powers, and many centuries
went by before it ceased to exist. Nations, like men, come to their
appointed time. For man the hour comes soon and cannot be stayed;
for nations it can be considerably delayed by wisdom.

I have said that jealousy must be set aside because it is an evil
counsellor, because it inclines to deceit, undermines friendship,
and indeed is friendship's enemy. If only we could content ourselves with all that Divine Providence has bestowed on us! Alexander aimed at the Empire of the world, but died young in Baby-
lonia, and his kingdom was divided. The Macedonians would have
done better if their name had not brought havoc to the kingdoms
of Asia. Through ambition, through jealousy of those more powerful, through the mad wish to achieve a parity of power, some states
have become stronger; but very many have come to ruin, especially
at the hands of other even stronger countries. So dangerous is
jealousy, that we should never feel it for Austria. We have glories
of our own. Let us be satisfied with them. In such political moderation there is a special kind of greatness which will shed luster on a

government which adopts it. If prompted by cowardice, moderation can be base; but it is a generous virtue if prompted by respect for justice.

What matters for Piedmont is to preserve herself in absolute independence from Austria. In this way she will serve as an example to the other Italian states; for the rest of Italy will gain in esteem and strength from an attitude on our part which is not peevish or arrogant, but rather dignified and noble.

[Count Clemente Solaro della Margarita: *Questioni di stato* (Turin, 1854), pp. 112–21]

A diplomatic question of some intricacy and considerable fascination was presented by the Crimean War in which Russia faced France, Britain, and Turkey. Austria remained neutral but benevolent toward the western allies, and even signed an alliance with them. Cavour eventually decided in 1855 to join the war against Russia, and it used to be thought that he did so as part of a well-prepared and far-sighted plan of foreign policy.

One factor involved was that the British wanted to recruit more soldiers, and for this purpose were negotiating with Portugal and Spain as well as Piedmont: the volunteer system of recruitment was not working well in England, and Palmerston could not stand "seeing our brave fellows killed off by a lot of Russians, ten of whom killed are not an equivalent for one Englishman." As well as wanting more troops, Britain and France were anxious to reassure their ally Austria that the Piedmontese were fully committed in Russia and so could not use the war as an excuse to renew fighting in Lombardy. In the middle of negotiations, the best-informed British observer of Italian affairs described the situation as he saw it at Turin.

Sir James Hudson, British minister at Turin, to Lord Clarendon, October 24, 1854

I HAVE not failed to pay attention to Your Lordship's orders to inform myself generally upon the Italian question, and having had the advantage of seeing several of the leading men of Lombardy, Venice, the Papal States, Tuscany and Naples, I believe I can repeat with confidence what I have already had the honor of stating to you, namely that there is a very considerable party in those states whose object is to see the extension to them of the constitutional system of Piedmont: not by revolution, by plot, and by intrigue; not by an underhand expulsion of the Austrians; but by the natural process of events springing out of the war with Russia. These men, however, see little hope of anything of the sort occurring without the guarantee, or the countenance, of England and France. They will wait patiently to the end of the war—which, if it brings no such solution of their affairs, will probably lead to another Italian revolution with the additional element of despair . . .

I perceived from your letter of the thirteenth [which also offered English support against Austria if the latter "interfered" with Piedmont] that Your Lordship considers Austria will eventually enter entirely into the views and policy of England and France—that is to say will join in the war against Russia. In that case you would naturally desire to have exact information as to the part which Italy could take when Austria is engaged with Russia. Will Italy rise in revolution against Austria, the Pope and the King of Naples? If so how is that revolution to be mastered and suppressed?

So far as Piedmont is concerned I am convinced that she will act with good faith in any case. But she would be placed in a dilemma. She would feel that she could not draw the sword for Austria and against Italians. She would do nothing. She would be neutral and neutralized; and of no use either to herself or to the Western Powers; and a source of constant anxiety to Austria. An Italian revolution would tend to the advantage of Russia and in great measure palsy the action of Austria in your cause.

To set this point at rest I considered it advisable to speak to Count de Cavour, the President of the King's government, and who has ever met me in the largest and frankest manner. I believe I can confidently state his opinion to be as follows.

The time has come when the public interest of Europe renders it necessary for all states who hold the opinions of England and France to forget their quarrels and feuds and make common cause with the Western Powers. If Austria marches with England and France, Piedmont will march by the side of the Austrians, to Moscow if necessary, and this is no idle boast: there are many Piedmontese yet living, and even serving, who marched to Moscow in 1812. The Piedmontese of 1854 will, in a given case, march there again in your cause.

This war with Russia will probably oblige the Western Powers to recolor a part of the map of Europe. The frontiers of some states will be altered. Can Piedmont take part in this war, and on what conditions?

If the Western Powers, with Austria, call upon Piedmont to take part in this war, there can be no doubt as to its termination, and probably in one campaign—for the reason that the circle round Russia would be gradually narrowed [and] that the presence of Piedmont would be a guarantee against revolution in Italy in a Russian, a Mazzinian, or in any other revolutionary sense.

Piedmontese statesmen hold that the proper position of Austria is that of a barrier to Russia on the Danube and in the Black Sea. They say:— give Austria Bessarabia, the provinces of the Danube and the Crimea; make her the eastern bulwark of Europe. In exchange for the Danube and the Crimea, give Sardinia Lombardy and Venice. This places 70,000 good and picked bayonets at the service of the common cause. Italy is tranquilized. The questions of Tuscany, Rome and Naples would insensibly, gradually, but surely, be solved. Those states would find their safety lie in granting such reforms as would disarm the revolutionary spirits; and, if not, Piedmont with the additional five millions of Italians would be strong enough to crush any and every attempt at revolution: for her dynasty, her independence and her organization are of old date, and her citizen, like her army, is accustomed to discipline and to obey.

Austria, commercially speaking, will not in the long run be a loser. The freedom of the Danube and the Black Sea will compensate for the Lombardo-Veneto. That portion of her army now occupied in watching for revolution would meet the common enemy; and her political influence would be increased both at Constantinople and at Rome; for how can Italians respect a Pope who is propped up principally by Austrian bayonets?

That eternal source of discord, the "Italian question," would gradually dry up, and a strong state in Northern Italy would be the guarantee of England against France's preponderance in Europe after the war; would compensate for the disturbance of the Balance of Power and loss of the Russian element as a counterpoise; and, by giving Piedmont a voice in the Congress for the general peace, England would have at all events one constitutional state, which she would have mainly created, on her side in the settlement.

It is not to be supposed for a moment that Piedmont would be inclined to thrust "liberal opinion,"commonly so called, upon the mass of the Italians. Piedmontese statesmen know that the people of Italy require a just but a strong government, good laws impartially administered; and that Italian states must receive their liberties as they become fitted to use them.

It is too much to expect of Piedmont that she could follow

England and France without hope of extension to territory: for altho' I believe that the principles of the King's government would lead them to adopt and to follow the Western Powers, yet the majority of Piedmontese and of Italians could not be expected to share the same opinions to the same extent.

Perhaps the main difficulty of this Italian question would be found in France, unless means were found (at Naples) to overcome it: but the jealousy entertained by France of a strong Northern Italy is as old as French history.

Neither would the erection of Lombardy into a separate King-dom solve the Italian difficulty. The first effect would be an intrigue at Milan to retake Novara and the Lomellina [from Piedmont], and even Genoa; and then a foreign power called in to the aid either of Lombardy or Piedmont; then foreign interference; and then a repetition of disturbance.

But the fate of Europe and the dynasty of Louis Napoleon, in the crisis which may occur during another prolonged campaign, ought to point out the necessity for strengthening Northern Italy by the establishment there of a liberal conservative government.

If the question were a Piedmontese question, namely of raising her to ten millions of subjects or reducing her to three, it would scarcely merit Your Lordship's notice: it might be put off or forgotten. But it is my firm belief that by strengthening Piedmont you commence the solution of all the Italian questions, even of the religious question which is the most difficult of all, and which must follow in the wake of Piedmont when strengthened: — I mean the questions of Lombardy, Venice, Tuscany, Rome and Naples.

A conservative diplomacy in Italy appears to me to have before it the task of resisting the old Italian municipal spirit, i.e., the war of one state upon its neighbor, the preference by each state of its own petty interests to the general weal: such, for instance, as would follow the rule of Daniel Manin at Venice, of Mazzini at Genoa, of Cattaneo at Milan, of the war between priests and assassins at Rome, of the asinine contest between Sicilians and Neapolitans. And such a diplomacy should check revolution—which, with a semblance of unity (the "Revoluzione Unitaria" of Mazzini), is in fact the local squabbles and the personal quarrels and passions of such men as those I have mentioned.

> [*Mss. Clarendon, dep. c. 21*, Bodleian Library, Ox-
> ford, pp. 563–74]

Cavour was uncertain throughout 1854. His instinct was to join the war, not because he had any animus toward Russia, but simply to open a credit with France and Britain. Piedmont might possibly emerge with territorial gains, and at least she might lay claim to sit at an international congress, so establishing her position as a spokesman for all Italy. But Cavour also saw the arguments on the other side, since this was likely to be an unpopular war at home, and his cabinet was strongly against being seen on virtually the same side as Austria. Piedmont could hardly afford to spend money on a remote campaign in which her interests were marginal or nonexistent; if she had the money, she should probably be spending it preparing for the third war of liberation in Lombardy. One of Cavour's closest confidants was therefore able to conclude that no one except the Prime Minister and the king truly wanted to fight.

Victor Emmanuel was intoxicated by the thought of personally leading his troops into battle, and his own instincts were to forget about any possible war of liberation in Italy. He also espied an occasion for getting rid of Cavour. The monarch may have been a "constitutional" king, but he was never a truly "parliamentary" one, and he did not like the way the Prime Minister was using parliament to upset the royalist bias of the *Statuto*. Nor did he like the way that the cabinet was trying to prevent him joining the war. Victor Emmanuel had already promised the Pope that he would overrule Cavour's religious policy, and now he secretly arranged with the parliamentary Right that they should return to power. Once war was declared, he, as commander-in-chief, would be entirely his own master again. The king even informed the French ambassador of what he was doing, and the latter cleverly used the monarch to ensure that Piedmont would have to enter the war. The Ambassador later described these events to a close friend of Cavour, Giuseppe Massari.

Victor Emmanuel wants to join the Crimean War, June 1854

KING VICTOR EMMANUEL thought very highly of Sir James Hudson and the Duc de Gramont [the ambassadors of Britain and France], and was very grateful to them for the kindness they had shown his government at the time of the controversy with Austria over the sequestrations [sequestrations by Austria of property belonging to Lombard refugees living in Piedmont]. One day, seeing the Duc de Gramont at Court, he said to him, "Why don't you ever come to see me? Do come some time about five o'clock, informally, in ordinary dress. I'll tell my *aide-de-camp* to let me know, and if I can't see you I'll say so, without ceremony. You'll simply come back another time."

A few days after receiving the note from General Dabormida

[the Foreign Minister, who was against Piedmont fighting in the Crimea], the Duc de Gramont thought the time had come to take advantage of this courteous invitation, and on June 6 or 7, toward five in the afternoon, he went to the Royal Palace, and asked, as he entered the antechamber, whether the King would receive him. "Certainly!" exclaimed a sonorous voice from the next room. The King was standing in a window recess, in hunting dress, beside a tall table on which he was writing. Turning kindly toward the French diplomat, he said:—

The King: "Ah! Ah! you've done well to come. I'm very glad to see you. Well, now, things are not going well, are they? We must have a talk. Come, sit there. Will you have a cigar?" And extracting some *trabucos* cigars from the capacious side pockets of his overcoat, he offered one to the Duke. When the cigars had been lighted, he went on: "No, things are not going well. What do you think? Come, speak frankly."

The Duke: "Well, Sire, I think the same as you. They're not going well. I was expecting something different, especially after what Cavour told us six weeks ago. I confess I think Dabormida's note somewhat too diplomatic."

The King: "Oh, yes, it's a fine letter, that one. Let's talk about it. To my mind, it's really stupid. It took seven or eight of them to write it. I've told them what I think of it. I'd have done something quite different myself."

The Duke: "Perhaps Your Majesty would have replied along the lines of M. de Cavour's overtures."

The King: "What do you mean by M. de Cavour's overtures? Really, my good man, you must call things by their right name: it was myself speaking. I told him to offer you fifteen thousand men. It's all we can give you now, otherwise I should have said thirty."

The Duke: "Then, Sire, if the proposal came from you, why did it all end by going up in smoke?"

The King: "First of all, it hasn't all ended. And then Cavour, with whom I was in complete agreement, came in for such abuse from his colleagues in the cabinet that he refused to go on. They have persuaded him that it would be unpopular to enter into an alliance on the same side as Austria, unless Austria pledges herself to lift the sequestrations on the property of the Lombard *émigrés*. But I can tell you one thing, and you can write it to the Emperor: Austria is not included in your alliance, and never will be, and if you're counting on her, you're making a mistake. I'm very well informed, and I know a lot about it."

The Duke: "I think, Sire, that events are already beginning to prove you right. But in that case nothing should now stop your ministers."

The King: "Of course nothing should stop them. But they're still stopping. Did you see them a fortnight ago, at the festival of the Constitution? Did you see them lined up on the left, one behind another? Well, it's obvious that if you want to get those fellows moving, you've got to give them a shove. Lamarmora would be all right, except that he does not really want to let the army fight. Dabormida is honest, but he listens to nothing and never gives way. There's only Cavour and myself. But wait a bit and you'll see."

The Duke: "Am I to understand that your Majesty wishes to join France in our alliance with England and contribute your contingent of troops?"

The King: "Yes, that is my wish, and it will be done. It was on my orders that Cavour spoke of it, and if the ministers have to be changed, I shall change them. But don't say anything about it; leave me to act. You know now what is at the back of my mind. Oh, they make me laugh with their fears! But it's really the only sensible thing to do. Once our soldiers are aligned alongside yours, I shan't care a fig for Austria. Besides, one must do something. If we don't send our soldiers to Russia, we shall be led instead by all these noisy revolutionaries into committing a blunder of some sort in Italy. One must be blind not to see it. Cavour is too much taken up with his Lombard friends. Their turn will come later. I want to help them too, but that mustn't hold us up."

The Duke: "Sire, I can only say that I entirely agree with you, and hope you will do what you have just said."

The King: "What do you mean by that? Do you perhaps doubt it?" And with these words he raised his head proudly and stared at his interlocutor with eyes that flashed scorn, almost menacingly.

The Duke: "No Sire, no Sire, I don't doubt it at all, and I'm very glad of it!"

The King: "Well, good evening. That's enough for today, isn't it? I'm depending on you, you know; don't compromise me either here or in your own country. But don't forget. *Au revoir.*"

> [G. Massari: *La vita ed il regno di Vittorio Eman-*
> *uele II di Savoia* (Milan, 1878), vol. I, pp.
> 249–53].

A threatened coup d'état, *January 1855, as recounted by the Comte de Salmour*

THE DUC DE GRAMONT (then Duc de Guiche) had been appointed French minister in Turin; and as he was my cousin on my wife's side and I saw him very often, I naturally became the semi-official intermediary between him and Cavour. As they were both of very lively temperament, I was sometimes even the "peacemaker" between them.

It was in this way that I intervened to make up Cavour's mind to force his colleagues to join in the Crimean War—the difficulty was to overcome the cabinet's wish for a prior condition that England and France should intervene to get Austria to cancel the sequestration of the property of the Lombard *émigrés.*

One morning Gramont sent me a message to drop in on him, and he told me *under seal of secrecy* that, as the present Piedmontese government refused to send troops to the Crimea, Cavour was unfortunately going to be displaced in favor of the Comte de Revel who would agree to send them. I told Gramont that I did not believe a word of it, for parliament was not hostile to Cavour, and other governments had no power to overthrow him.

Gramont then informed me that he had a promise from King Victor Emmanuel, and that the French were insisting on this promise being kept. The King had already spoken to Revel. When Gramont backed up his words by incontestable documentation, I begged him to release me from the seal of secrecy and let me tell Cavour; otherwise I would betray this secret rather than betray the interests of a friend so dear to me as Cavour. I added that I had good hope that, once informed of these facts, Cavour would be able to win his colleagues over to what England and France wanted. I therefore asked him for two hours' grace, at the end of which I would bring back a positive reply from Cavour. Being a deputy, I entered the Chamber immediately, and told Cavour on the Ministers' bench that I had very important and urgent news for him.

Cavour said that he must first speak in reply to Valerio, and told me to go and wait in the Prime Minister's office, where he soon joined me. After listening to what I had to say, he repeated what he had already told me, namely that when the Crimean War broke out he had put forward the idea of despatching a brigade to Russia, but he was not supported by the Foreign Minister Dabormida. The War Minister, Lamarmora, was also opposed to the idea, saying that he did not have two full brigades on a war footing. Cavour admitted that, since public opinion was with his colleagues and against our joining the Crimean War, he had no means of persuading the cabinet to share his view. I suggested to him that, rather than let Revel do what he (Cavour) had long wanted, he should dismiss those of his colleagues who would not change their opinion.

In short, I was told to inform Gramont that on the very same evening, at a ministerial meeting which the British and French ministers were to attend, Cavour would announce his unequivocal intention of despatching an expeditionary force to the Crimea; if need be he was ready to break with those of his colleagues who failed to share his view.

My noble friend did as he said, and that very evening it was decided to send troops to the Crimea—a decision which led to the resignation of Dabormida, the Foreign Minister.

> [*Carteggio Cavour-Salmour* (Bologna, 1936), pp. 82–3]

Far from being a well-considered and far-sighted plan, Cavour's decision to enter the Crimean War was to some extent just an expedient to· avoid being dismissed. By this means he saved Piedmont from a royal coup, but only by high-handedly overriding the rest of his cabinet. In a masterful speech asking parliament to sanction the war he naturally concealed these facts, as he also had to conceal that the king, in commiting himself to the French ambassador, lost Piedmont her main bargaining counter with the allies. Piedmont in the end had to join the war without a single guarantee that her interests would be considered in the peace settlement.

Cavour in parliament, February 6, 1855

THE EXPERIENCE of recent years and previous centuries has proved (at least in my opinion) how little Italy has benefited by conspiracies, revolutions and disorderly uprisings. Far from helping her, they have been a tremendous calamity for this beautiful part of Europe. And not only, gentlemen, because individual people so often suffered from them, not only because revolutions became the cause or pretext for repression, but above all because continual conspiracies, repeated revolutions and disorderly uprisings damaged the esteem and, up to a certain point, the sympathy that other European peoples cherished for Italy.

Now, gentlemen, I believe that the principal condition for the improvement of Italy's fate, the condition that stands out above all others, is to lift up her reputation once more, so to act that all the peoples of the world, those governing and those governed, may do justice to her qualities. And for this two things are necessary: first, to prove to Europe that Italy has sufficient civic sense to govern herself freely and according to law, and that she is in a condition to adopt the very best forms of government; second, to prove that her military valor is as great as that of her ancestors.

You have done Italy one service by your conduct over the last seven years. You have shown Europe in the most luminous way that Italians are capable of governing themselves with wisdom, prudence and trustworthiness. But it still remains for you to do Italy an equal, if not a greater, service; it is our country's task to prove that Italy's sons can fight valiantly on battlefields where glory is to be won. And I am sure, gentlemen, that the laurels that our soldiers will win in Eastern Europe will help the future state of Italy more than all that has been done by those people who hoped to regenerate her by rhetorical speeches and writings.

I am confident, gentlemen, that I have shown you overwhelming reasons for accepting the treaty [with France and Britain]. I am convinced that it cannot produce serious economic and financial disadvantages. Nor on the military side does it offer those dangers with which some would like to scare us. Its political consequences should be not adverse but positively happy.

[C. Benso di Cavour: *Discorsi parlamentari*, ed. A. Saitta (Florence, 1957), vol. XI, pp. 268–9]

11. A Bid for British Support, 1856

Cavour was greatly disappointed when Austria intervened in December 1855 and brought the war to a close, for this intervention would allow an enemy power to dominate the peace congress as a mediator. He had hoped that his 18,000 troops would so distinguish themselves in battle that his claims to territorial compensation would be recognized; but, though nearly 2,000 had died of cholera, they had had time to be present at only one military engagement—in which they had lost a mere 14 dead and 170 wounded.

Cavour to Emanuele d'Azeglio, Piedmontese minister in London, January 1, 1856

I MUST beg you to emphasize [to the British], though without acting the Jeremiah, the inevitable consequence of the proposed peace terms on Piedmont and the constitutional party in Italy.

If, after subjecting the country to enormous sacrifices, we withdraw and have to watch Austrian influence grow as our own declines, obviously we will lose the trust of the constitutional party and its leaders. The misfortune would be small if such a reversal of public opinion merely led to a change of government; but it would also produce a change of political system. Obviously men who have opposed our alliance with England and criticized our pro-English tendencies will get the upper hand, and this will lead us back toward Austria and absolutism. Piedmont, after acting the fool's part in this great struggle, would lose all power of action in Italy. Part óf the peninsula will go over to the revolutionaries, while the rest will desperately give way to Austrian influence.

If our allies abandon us, the triumph of Austria and the Pope will be complete. Within ten years we shall see the Jesuits and the Inquisition established from the Alps to Calabria. England cannot want such an outcome: her spirit of justice, but also her international prestige, as well as her political and religious principles, all these would be hurt by it.

If you could get these subjects discussed in the London newspapers you would advance our interests, for the present ministers, and especially Clarendon [the Foreign Minister], need jolting.

Lord Shaftesbury [the leading evangelical Protestant] could help you here. Put before his eyes the specter of Popery extending its domination over half the European continent where Austria commands. In this way you might raise a cry of alarm which would trouble the ministers' repose and echo through the vaults of Exeter Hall [where the extreme Protestants used to meet in London].

The time for action has come. So far we have left our allies undisturbed; now we must spur them on and leave them no more rest.

[*Cavour e l'Inghilterra, Carteggio con V. E. d'Azeglio* (Bologna, 1933), vol. I, pp. 154-7]

Cavour to General Lamarmora, commanding the expeditionary force in the Crimea, January 21, 1856

THIS CESSATION of war is deplorable from our of point of view. I regret it bitterly. But we must accept the inevitable and make all we can of the unfortunate position in which that artful old woman Austria has placed us.

In England, where the war was popular, we can make our discontent public and let our opinion about Austria be unreservedly voiced. In France we need to handle things more tactfully, so as not to shock the Emperor who sees this peace as the triumph of his policy.

As peace talks could open at any moment now, I thought it urgent to formulate our views as the Emperor requested of me. Azeglio [Massimo d'Azeglio, the former Prime Minister] has drawn up a memorandum, a magnificent piece of work but far too long, and it also has the disadvantage of failing to reach clear and precise conclusions. Had I sent it off to Walewski [the French Foreign Minister], probably he would not have read it, or at least not attentively. So I thought I had better put my ideas in a letter of a few pages, asking Walewski to bring it to the Emperor's attention. I have sent copies to Villamarina and Azeglio who will communicate the contents to you. As you will see, our demands are modest; but, confronted with the position adopted by Austria, we needed to show ourselves moderate and disinterested, above all in the eyes of the French.

However, if we should succeed in getting our allies to admit the necessity of forcing Austria to withdraw her troops from the Romagna [where they claimed to defend papal territory], we shall have achieved a good deal, for the destruction of the temporal power of the papacy will have been admitted in principle. Judging by impressions during my visit to England, this idea is pretty favorably viewed by their government, especially by Lord Palmerston. He spoke about giving to Tuscany the papal legations in the Romagna. At first I rejected this proposal, as I still would if the war had continued, but now we must clutch it as a straw. If the Pope's states were to be divided between Tuscany and Modena, Piedmont would inevitably have to be compensated. I personally would be satisfied with the Duchies of Piacenza, Massa and Carrara. You can say all this quite openly. It will come much better from you than from a professional diplomat.

[*Lettere edite ed inedite di Camillo Cavour*, ed. L. Chiala (Turin, 1883), vol. II, pp. 175–6]

The Congress of Paris gave Cavour his chance to stand up for Italy. He did not so much as consult his cabinet before leaving Turin, because he wanted his hands quite free. It was just possible that the Congress might allow him to annex Parma. He even thought up a wildcat scheme to obtain English help for an invasion of Sicily. But at Paris he found friendliness and not much more. Austria was too strongly entrenched there, and the other combatants were all trying to color their disinterestedness by insisting on no territorial acquisitions.

Nevertheless, a week after the peace had been signed, the delegates met to discuss if any dangers to peace existed in Italy. Cavour spoke with great moderation, realizing that the main points would be put more effectively by Lord Clarendon, the British representative. The Austrians tried to make light of it all. Their representative, however, did point out *en passant* that Cavour could hardly criticize the Austrian occupation of Lombardy when Piedmontese troops were occupying Monaco with as much or as little reason.

Cavour was disappointed with this one meager result of the war. He was also worried what public opinion would now say back home. Suddenly he became extremely excited and bellicose. Somehow he persuaded himself that Britain was ready to fight against Austria. Whether or not it was that he and Clarendon misunderstood each other's French, the fact was that British policy never envisaged the possibility of war, especially against their ally Austria. Never again was Cavour entirely trusted by the British after this; and one possible source of support was thus alienated.

*Cavour, from Paris, to U. Rattazzi, Minister of the Interior
at Turin, April 9, 1856*

I HAVE sent off a long despatch to Cibrario [Piedmontese Foreign Minister] about yesterday's session of the Congress in which
the Italian question came up, and there is little I can add. Walewski was obviously embarrassed at having to speak about the Pope's
government, and he made a very weak reply to the energetic protests of Buol [representing Austria]. But about Naples he was much
more explicit, even bitterly censorious; and he may even have gone
too far, for it prevented the Russian delegate supporting him.

Clarendon made a really energetic statement about both the
Pope and Naples. The papal regime he called the worst that had
ever existed; that of Naples he criticized as strongly as Massari
would have done. I think he thought that, as there would be no
practical result of this session, he could use a specially *extra-parlia-
mentary* kind of language. We have one more session still to come
for approving our *communiqué*, when Clarendon said he would
speak again.

As we went out I told him: "My Lord, you see we have nothing
to hope from mere diplomacy; we shall have to resort to other
means, at least over Naples." He replied: "We must deal with
Naples, and soon." As we parted I added that I would like another
word with him about it; and I think I can then put to him that we
should place a bomb under King Bomba [Ferdinand II of Naples].

What would you think, in that case, of sending Prince Carignano of Savoy to rule Naples? Or, if it is decided to let a Murat
rule there, perhaps he could go to Sicily? Something we must do.
Italy cannot be left as it is. Napoleon is quite sure about this; and,
as diplomacy is useless, we shall have to adopt extra-legal means.
Though moderate in my general views, I incline to favor extreme and audacious methods. In the nineteenth century, audacity
is often the best policy. It helped Napoleon; perhaps it will help us.

[*Cavour e l'Inghilterra*, vol. I, p. 442]

Cavour, from Paris, to E. d'Azeglio, April 11, 1856

I HAVE just seen Clarendon. Here is a résumé of our talk.
I said: "You see, My Lord, that two things now follow:
1) Austria has decided to make no concessions at all.

2) Italy has nothing left to hope for from diplomacy.
As a result, Piedmont's position is very difficult. Either we must
make a rapprochement with Austria and the Pope, in which case
I must resign in favor of the reactionaries; or else we must, pru-
dently of course, prepare to fight Austria, in which case I must
know if this would go against the views of our best ally, England."

Clarendon stroked his chin furiously, but did not seem astonished. After a moment's silence he replied: "You are quite right.
There is nothing else you can do. Only one must not say so
openly."

I then added: "You have been able to see here that I am prudent
and can keep my own counsel. I know that we will have to await
an opportune moment, but in the meantime we must know what
we are aiming at. War does not frighten me. We are determined
to fight *à l'outrance, to the knife*. But, for the short time that the
war lasted, you would have to help us."

Here Clarendon left off playing with his chin and cried: "*Certainly, certainly*, and you could count on enthusiastic, energetic
help." My last word was, "With Lamarmora we will give the
Austrians something to think about." "Yes, indeed," he replied, "I
am sure of it."

We then spoke of tomorrow's session, and he assured me that
if Buol opened his mouth he would reply even more firmly than
the other day. He encouraged me to go and see Queen Victoria. In
sum, he seemed to look very favorably on our *third war of liberation*. You can say a few words of all this to Palmerston [the British Prime Minister], but taking care to keep it *a long way below*
what I have said.

[*Cavour e l'Inghilterra*, vol. I, pp. 452–3]

Cavour, from Paris, to Rattazzi, April 12, 1856

ENGLAND, GRIEVED at peace, would with pleasure see an opportunity for a new war, which would be popular because it would
be a war for the liberation of Italy. Why should we not profit
from this fact to make a supreme effort to fulfill the destinies of
the House of Savoy and of our country?

It would be a life or death matter, so we must proceed cau-
tiously. I ought to go to London and see Palmerston and other
leading politicians. If they share Clarendon's views, we must make

secret preparations, contract a loan for thirty million francs, and upon Lamarmora's return send Austria an unacceptable ultimatum and open hostilities. The Emperor could not oppose such a war. In his heart he wants it, and he would surely help us if England enters the lists on our behalf.

Before leaving Paris I will sound out the Emperor just as I did Clarendon. The last conversations I had with him and his ministers were such as might prepare the way for a declaration of war. The Pope is the only obstacle so far as I can see. What could we do with him in the event of an Italian war?

I hope this letter does not make you think I have a touch of cerebral fever or am in a state of mental intoxication. My mental health is perfect, and I have never felt calmer . . .

I have had a long talk with Manin here. He is still somewhat utopian. He still speaks about a purely popular war, and believes in the usefulness of the press in such stormy times. He talks of unifying Italy and other such nonsense. But when it comes to the push we should be able to make use of him.

> [*Cavour e l'Inghilterra*, vol. I, pp. 461–3. The last paragraph was omitted from the version of this letter published by Chiala in 1883, vol II, p. 372.]

Lord Clarendon's later recollection of Cavour in April 1856

[CAVOUR] DID not conceal his irritation from me. He constantly told me that he could not present himself before the parliament of Turin unless he proved that he had produced some effect by his presence at the Congress. I was in the habit of seeing him daily, and I willingly listened to him upon the only subject upon which he would converse, and on which he was always earnest and eloquent. But those conversations never appeared to me to be of a character sufficiently practical to make it necessary to report them to Her Majesty's Government. Consequently there is no record of them, though I have searched, nor of those repeated assurances which I gave him that our invariable principle was to maintain our treaty engagements, and to be guided by the principles of international law. At the same time, I did not disguise from him, what he knew and what everybody else knew, that our object at that time was to free Italy from foreign occupation, and to reform the

Papal and Neapolitan governments, and that toward that end the moral support of England would be always forthcoming.

Out of the numerous conversations that I had with Count Cavour, the only one I can remember which could—I will not say justify—but give rise to his assertion that I said "If you are in a strait, we shall come to your assistance," had reference, not to a war by Piedmont against Austria, but to an invasion of Piedmont *by* Austria, which was a fixed idea in Count Cavour's mind. He always thought that the free institutions of Piedmont—her freedom of the press and freedom of debate—even her very prosperity under such a system, would always make her an intolerable neighbor to Austria. I assured Count Cavour that my conversations with Count Buol, though certainly not very satisfactory in general with respect to Italy, entirely confirmed my impression that no such apprehension need be entertained by him; and, upon Count Cavour asking me what course we should take in such an eventuality, I remember saying, "If you ask my opinion, I should say that if Austria invaded Piedmont for the purpose of suppressing free institutions there, you would have a practical proof of the feeling of the parliament and people of England on the subject."

Of course I cannot pledge myself to the exact words, but I do feel quite sure about the spirit and scope of my answer. It was a personal opinion given upon an hypothetical case, to which I did not then attach any importance, nor did I know that Count Cavour attached any importance to it until I read these [recently published] letters, in which he says—

> England, grieved at peace, would with pleasure see an opportunity for a new war, which would be popular because it would be a war for the liberation of Italy.

He then goes on to say—

> If they (Lord Palmerston and his government) share Clarendon's views, we must make secret preparations, contract the loan for 30,000,000 francs, and, upon Lamarmora's return, offer to Austria an *ultimatum* which it will be impossible for her to accept, and open hostilities.

In another letter Count Cavour says—

> Talking with him (Lord Clarendon) as to the means of acting morally and even materially upon Austria, I said to him, "Send your troops upon men-of-war to La Spezia, and leave your fleet there." And his answer was, "The idea is excellent."

Now, my Lords, upon my honor I have not the slightest recollection of any such conversation, and, therefore, I cannot deny it; but I think so wild a notion cannot have been seriously entertained even by Count Cavour himself. Bearing in mind the enthusiasm of Count Cavour in favor of his own views, and his ardent desire to make known his activity in the Congress of Paris, and to keep up the spirits of his friends at Turin, I for one—though I have the most reason to complain—can make allowances for these imaginative reports of private conversations contained in letters to his friends and colleagues, but which were evidently not intended for publication. But that I, as one of Her Majesty's Secretaries of State, without any communication from my colleagues, and contrary to the dictates of common sense, knowing that the French Emperor at that time had not the slightest thought or intention of making war against Austria, that he did not then even require her to withdraw her troops from the Legations until he had withdrawn his own troops from Rome—that I, under such circumstances, should, even in the most indirect manner, have recommended a country to which we heartily wished well to commit such a suicidal act as going to war with Austria, with her large army under Radetzky, and having the support of Tuscany, Parma, Modena, and Naples—and that, without the shadow of authority for doing so, I should have given any pledge for the support of England in such a policy as would have imbroiled us in war with half Europe—is an absurdity so palpable that I hope your Lordships will think it carries with it its own refutation, without my laying claim to that character for extreme reserve and discretion for which Count Cavour rather paradoxically on that occasion informed his correspondent I was notorious.

[*Hansard's Parliamentary Debates*, House of Lords,
London (February 17, 1862), pp. 349–51]

On his return from Paris, Cavour quickly recovered his poise and began preparing for the next European crisis which might give him another chance to insert the Italian Question into the delicate balance of international power. One immediate problem was raised by some Neapolitan exiles, who thought of obtaining French help against the Bourbons by suggesting Joachim Murat's second son, Lucien, as possible heir to his father's former throne of Naples. Cavour did not want French influence set up in southern Italy, but gradually he saw that Murat's candidature might be used to involve France against Austria.

Although a French sovereign in Naples would destroy Mazzini's hope of Italian unity, Cavour aimed less at unity than at what he called "the independence of Italy and the aggrandizement of Piedmont." As Britain could now be relied on only for friendly advice, French help would be indispensable in any future war, and for this there would be a price. For example, nationalism was much more acceptable to France than liberalism; the Papal States, guarded by a French garrison, must be untouched; and perhaps some border territory between Piedmont and France would have to be sacrificed.

Cavour, from Turin, to E. d'Azeglio, May 9, 1856

I AM taking this opportunity to write to you without reservation. I am very much annoyed that Clarendon took offense at my approach to Lyndhurst [an opposition leader in the British parliament]. Since Shaftesbury advised me to see Lyndhurst, I could not have foreseen that the government would so object, especially as I thought I had won Clarendon's heart by singing his praises at the top of my voice!! Try to calm him and restore his better feelings about me. I had this in mind when I praised him in the Chamber of Deputies, and when his name was mentioned it was drowned in applause. Unless he has a heart of bronze that must have touched him. It is of the utmost importance that he should not give the lie to what I then said . . .

I do not think revolutionary movements need be feared anywhere save perhaps in Naples and Sicily. There is a good deal of unrest in both those countries. For some time now there has been great activity from the emissaries of Murat [French pretender to Naples]. They have told their supporters to prepare for action in the near future.

This puts us in a very awkward situation. We have no wish at all to support Murat in Naples. On the other hand we can hardly oppose him actively. Not only does the wretched condition of Naples make us hold back, but so does our wish not to go against the Emperor's views. I would be very glad to obtain advice from England on this, so if the opportunity arises please ask Lord Palmerston quite frankly. Ask him what he thinks we ought to do about the Murat movement. There is no need to go into great detail, for Hudson is far better informed than I am about what is happening in South Italy and he must have given his government precise information. Should you find out that he has not done so, do not compromise him. Hudson himself does not seem particularly hostile to Murat; only he thinks that if Murat becomes King of Naples, Sicily must be separated off. It is important that we should know Palmerston's opinion of this. The Neapolitan question could blow up at any moment; warn the British government, and try to discover what they are doing in London about it. Probably some of the leading Sicilian *émigrés* will be going to London. Do not lose sight of them if you can help it.

[*Cavour e l'Inghilterra* (Bologna, 1933), vol. II, pp. 11–13]

Cavour to the Marquis Sauli, Piedmontese minister at Florence, June 26, 1856

OUR FRIENDS now think that a little legal agitation in Tuscany would be a great help to the Italian cause. Up to a point I agree; though I think that agitation, if it is to be helpful, must be spontaneous and not provoked by us. It should also have as its aim, not the resurrection of the constitution adopted in Tuscany during the revolution of 1848, but to free Tuscany absolutely from foreign and priestly influence. The Italian movement must put nationalism before liberalism if we are not to meet outright opposition from France. Napoleon III has always shown me that he is a friend of the national principle, and especially of Italian nationality. He would therefore not be displeased by any movement directed against Austria.

[*Nuove lettere inedite del Conte Camillo di Cavour*, ed. E. Mayor (Turin, 1895), pp. 371–2]

Cavour to Rattazzi, Minister of the Interior, August 1, 1856

FOR HEAVEN's sake keep in close touch with the King about this affair of the Pope. Tell him that if he enters into direct relations with Rome he will completely demolish the political edifice that we have been working to build up for eight years. It will be impossible to maintain our influence in Italy if we come to an agreement with the Pontiff. We do not need to intensify our feud with Rome, but we must not take even a half step backwards. As you know, I am not anti-clerical; indeed I am disposed to conciliation, and would like to give the Church greater freedom that it now enjoys. For instance I would agree to abandon the royal *exequatur* and the state monopoly over the universities, etc., etc.; but in present circumstances I am convinced that any attempt to come to an actual agreement would redound to our harm. Tell the King that we cannot settle the religious question before we have reformed our law on marriage. We can postpone dealing with the question, but we must never give it up.

[*Lettere edite ed inedite di Camillo Cavour*, ed. Chiala, vol. II, p. 243]

Cavour to Count Gropello, Piedmontese chargé d'affaires at Naples, October 5, 1856

IF BY chance you are questioned by the Neapolitan government, you must confine yourself to admitting a strong desire to see the King of Naples averting danger by granting wide and wise reforms. You will say that the Sardinian government views the intervention of foreign Powers in Italian affairs with regret; but that Austria's persistent determination to interfere with all the central Italian states provides England with a plausible motive for interfering in Naples. You will explain that, so long as absolutist governments maintain that an outside Power may aid a sovereign in keeping peoples under an intolerable yoke, it is hardly surprising that liberal governments consider that they, too, can intervene in favor of peoples when oppression goes beyond certain limits.

Regarding the various local parties, you must be very reserved, yet without ever dissimulating the lively interest Sardinia feels for Naples and our ardent desire to see her political situation improve. If you hear of disturbances when foreign fleets call at Naples, you must not encourage them. At the same time you must not condemn them unless there should take place a movement for Italian unity (even in a sense favorable to King Victor Emmanuel). You will tell any supporters of such a project that, at this moment, an uprising for Italian unity would meet with opposition from all the Powers, not excluding England; and that it would therefore have no chance of success.

You must not oppose any project favoring Murat, though you yourself must not favor such a movement. Murat is a bad solution, but as it is the only one with any chance of success, we must endure it with good grace. To my mind the success of that claim-

ant will depend on how much support he gets from France. If the
French back him, you must help him too.

[*Lettere edite ed inedite di Camillo Cavour*, ed.
L. Chiala (Turin, 1887), vol. VI, pp. 41–2]

Cavour had a delicate balance to preserve in foreign affairs, especially
as he had to convince both France and England that he was their
devoted friend. Over the Eastern Question, and in particular over a
difference of opinion about the frontier between Russia and the
Danubian Principalities, France first insisted that Cavour should support one view, but then unexpectedly told him to change sides and
vote the other way. Cavour had to try and do what France requested,
preferably without annoying Britain, and if possible establishing a
friendship with his late enemy, Russia, at the same time.

Sir James Hudson, from Turin, to Lord Clarendon, November 17, 1856

I PASSED two days with Cavour in the country a short time ago,
and met there Farini the historian. During my visit Cavour and
Farini spoke openly and without the least reserve upon the critical
position of political affairs in Europe. They both looked upon the
rupture of the Anglo-French alliance as the greatest misfortune.
Farini said, if it happened, that the constitutional system in Piedmont would be at an end in six months time; that England could
do no less than seek the support of Austria in holding the Principalities [Moldavia and Wallachia]; that it is a great error to suppose that Italian politicians of the constitutional school desired
the downfall of Austria, for her strength and independence are
necessary to prevent the existence of overpowering French influence in Italy; that if England could induce Austria to govern
her Italian possessions with more humanity and less of the bayonet
and could strengthen the position of Piedmont, the two together
might easily repress all republican, socialist, and Mazzinian tendencies in Italy. And he said to Cavour, "If you separate from England we are all lost, root and branch."

Cavour said he knew it, but what could he do; he could not
for the life of him make out what were the views and intentions of
the French government; that the Emperor only looked at his
boots when persons spoke to him of the conduct of his government; that he (Cavour) could not risk offending the Emperor, for

he did not know what might be the effect of Sardinia's declaring that without reference to him [Napoleon] he meant to vote unreservedly with England upon the Bolgrad business; that it was his duty to Sardinia to find out the Emperor's opinions, to see where French policy was likely to lead him, what it was driving at, before he finally made up his mind; that the English view of the question was the true one, the legal one, but that he must wait till he found out what was passing at Paris. Both he and Farini treated the stories about the Russo-Sardinian alliance with the most utter contempt. What is Russia to offer us, said they? A revolution in Croatia? Mazzini in Italy? The nationalities with popular leaders? We had enough of them in 1848-9. See what they have left us! They have brought even a legal, constitutional government in Sardinia almost into disrepute. What solidity, what chance of lasting does revolution offer us? Mazzini or some other fool like him as a political leader and Garibaldi as his commander-in-chief! —with much more of the same sort.

I cannot believe one word of the *alliance* between Russia and Sardinia. I believe that Russia would coquet with anything or anybody to feed her grudge against Austria; and that she has endeavored and will endeavor to seduce Sardinia and France and England, and any and every other Power to her views against Austria; but I do not find that anybody *seriously* inclines to her, certainly not the Italians who see her bolstering up King Bomba.

Cavour says that perhaps he is too civil to Russia. But remember, said he, we, a little state, about as big as one of the Russian provinces, had the unparalleled audacity to take that monster by the beard and make him acknowledge our constitutional government which in the bottom of his heart he abhors like poison. Let Austria remove the sequestrations and I will send a minister to Vienna immediately. Let her do us justice and be more ready to listen to our advice than to that of [Cardinal] Antonelli and Bomba and Landucci and Pallavicini, and I promise you that we shall get on very well without giving cause of complaint to her or to anybody else. But we have embarked on the stream of reform and she has not. Let her embark too and we shall make very good company. But we cannot sail in company with the concordat, and the stick, and the state of siege, and exclusion political and commercial.

This was his language, and I am inclined to believe him.

I allowed matters to rest till I learned that Persigny [French ambassador in London] had gone to Compiègne. Then Cavour sent
for me and with great glee said he believed he saw daylight; the
Emperor was alarmed at the prospect of the separation of France
from England in the Eastern Question, and doubtless would now
enquire the opinion of Sardinia on the Bolgrad question; that he
[Cavour] would give the same opinion to him that he had given to
Your Lordship, namely that England was legally in the right and
consequently (unless politics took some new and surprising turn)
that he should vote with you.

Villamarina [Piedmontese ambassador at Paris] arrived on the
12th at Turin; and returned on the 13th to Paris instructed to
report as above to the Emperor, and carrying an identical instruction to Azeglio [ambassador at London].

Had Cavour displayed more courage he would greatly have im-
proved his position in Your Lordship's estimation doubtless. The
only excuse I can find for him is the extraordinary mode in which
Louis Nap[n]. does his business. Sending the Sardinian minister to
Turin with instructions to keep their object a secret from the
French Secretary of State and the French plenipotentiary at Turin!
"La grande Nation" disappears altogether.

[*Mss. Clarendon, dep. c. 55*, Bodleian Library, Oxford, pp. 351–6]

12. Mazzini and the National Society

One of a long series of insurrections had been instigated by Mazzini at Milan in February 1853, though it did not succeed except in
provoking Austrian reprisals. Cavour was, of course, rigidly opposed
to such revolutionary movements, and indeed he tried to give Austria
advance warning on this occasion of Mazzini's plans. There is some
evidence that in later years he also warned the governments of Naples,
Tuscany, and Modena when he learned of other patriotic but republican plots. It was important for him that the revolutionaries should
not win, and it was equally important to exploit and discredit their
insurrections in order to make the rest of Europe prefer his own
more conservative solution to the Italian problem.

The failure of the 1853 rising led to a falling away among the republicans, just as it also pushed some of the Lombard aristocracy toward reconciliation with Austria. In desperation, some among the exiles came to accept Murat as a possible solution in Naples just because this would at least get rid of Ferdinand; on the other hand Manin, one of the most respected of contemporary Italians, spent his last years combating such an extension of French power into Italy. Manin's chief lieutenant was the Marquis Giorgio Pallavicino, a Lombard who had once been a prisoner in the Spielberg, and who now provided the finance and some of the ideas for a movement which later developed into the *National Society*. Republicanism for awhile remained the theoretical ideal of this important group, but gradually they came to accept the primary necessity of winning Piedmontese (and hence monarchical) support for their ideal of Italian nationalism.

Daniele Manin from Paris, to Lorenzo Valerio, September 19, 1855

I AM sending you herewith the original and a translation of my declaration which has already been published in the *Times* and is coming out tomorrow in the *Siècle*.

Our republican party, so bitterly criticized, thus makes one more act of abnegation and sacrifice in the national cause.

"Convinced that above all Italy must be made, that this is the first and most important question, we say to the Monarchy of Savoy: 'Make Italy and we are with you.—If not, not.'

"And to the constitutionalists we say: 'Think about making Italy and not of enlarging Piedmont; be Italians and not municipalists, and we are with you.—If not, not.'

"I think it is time to give up existing party divisions based on purely secondary differences; the principal, vital matter is whether we are of the unifying nationalist school of thought, or whether we belong to the separatist, municipalist school.

"I, a republican, raise the banner of unity. If all those who want Italy gather round and defend it, then *Italy will be*."

Please see if you can put these few lines into the *Diritto* [the paper of the Center Left at Turin]. Of course it will not commit the paper in any way.

[*Daniele Manin e Giorgio Pallavicino*, ed. B. E. Maineri (Milan, 1878), p. 333]

E. F. Foresti, from Genoa, to G. Pallavicino, August 7, 1856

THIS IS a summary of a short talk I had with Garibaldi yesterday.

G: Do you write regularly to Marquis Pallavicino?

Me: Occasionally.

G: Well, do please write to him, my good Foresti, because I am continually being pressed by many young activists who want me to start up a national movement. . . . We must obviously depend largely on the regular Piedmontese army and the Piedmontese volunteers, and hence any decision to act should lie, at least *indirectly*, with the government. But I simply cannot understand this apparent inertia and indifference. What is Pallavicino's National Party up to?

Me: I'm honestly not quite sure; though I guess that they are doing something for the Italian cause.

G: But is the King behind them?

Me: I don't know.

G: But for heaven's sake, we just must know. Here am I, offering my life for Italy and hence for the King; it would surely help us if we saw some preparations, or heard some indication of support or positive action.

Me: I feel the same, but I know nothing of any action.

G: Giorgio Pallavicino, and others who have the ear of the King and the government, they should be at work and making preparations so that I don't get left in the lurch.

[*Daniele Manin e Giorgio Pallavicino*, ed. Maineri, pp. 163–4]

G. Pallavicino, from Aix-les-Bains, to D. Manin, August 24, 1856

FORESTI WRITES again to me as follows:

"Our Garibaldi went to Turin on the thirteenth and I went with him. Cavour welcomed him with courtesy and friendliness and hinted that he could rely on considerable official help. Cavour even authorized Garibaldi to pass on these hints to others. It seems that he is seriously thinking about the great political redemption of our peninsula. Garibaldi took his leave of the minister on very friendly terms and with these encouraging promises of help for the cause."

It was all an act! What Cavour wants, *and I am sure of it*, is just for Piedmont to be enlarged by a few square miles of Italian soil.

[*Daniele Manin e Giorgio Pallavicino*, ed. Maineri, pp. 172–3]

G. Pallavicino, from Aix-les-Bains, to D. Manin, September 4, 1856

THIS IS my reply to Mazzini . . .

"Our view is that the 100,000 men in the Piedmontese army are indispensable for any war of independence. We want to entice, or if need be force, the King to act alongside us. We will entice him by offering him the crown of Italy; or we could force him by the threat of a republican revolution which would deprive him of the crown of Piedmont-Sardinia.

"You on the other hand propose not committing ourselves on the monarchy but remaining neutral on this issue. We absolutely disagree with you here—not out of love for the King, but because we distrust him. We do not want him to abandon us halfway through; we do not want the dynasty to exploit the revolution in order to fight Austria, and then use diplomacy to fight against the revolution. We want to *compromise the King* by dragging him into a revolutionary war; and we shall do this by proving to him that the war will help the dynasty and that it is necessary, indeed *inevitable* . . .

"Dear friend, show yourself a real hero. Sacrifice your cherished republican views on the altar of the fatherland. Another great republican, Daniele Manin, has shown you the way.

"It is not enough to say '*unification!*' The idea is too vague. If 'unification' is to be understood by the masses, it must be translated into something more solid and more personal. Our formula, '*Vittorio Emanuele King of Italy*,' is therefore a necessity. Either we adopt it, or there will be no rising; though of course we can change our program if tomorrow the conditions of Europe change.

"You say that you have *men*. But how many? You say that you have *money*. But how much? If we had between us a million men and a hundred million lire to arm them, then we could do something. But a few coins and a few hundred carbines are useless against the millions and the cannon of our enemies. The Duke of Modena by himself is stronger than we are."

[*Daniele Manin e Giorgio Pallavicino*, ed. Maineri, pp. 186–8]

D. Manin, from Paris, to G. Pallavicino, September 27, 1856

CAVOUR IS extremely able and is well known abroad. It would be a grave loss not to have him our ally, as it would be a grave danger to have him our enemy. I think we must not overturn him but urge him on. We must work incessantly to form public opinion, because as soon as opinion is clear and forceful, Cavour I am sure will follow it. Let us avoid every suspicion that we might be just aiming at ministerial office ourselves, for it would do us immense harm and our influence would be lost for ever. Only if public opinion is strong for Italy and if Cavour refuses, then we can think again. But I think Cavour to be too intelligent and too ambitious to refuse the Italian enterprise if public opinion demands it strongly enough.

. . . To start with there were only two of us. Then came a third, the excellent La Farina. But this is still not sufficient. We must find others, and we must find pulpits. Not a single newspaper in Italy can we really count on. I have to use the English press for publishing my views, and you have to resort to pamphleteering.

> [*Daniele Manin e Giorgio Pallavicino*, ed. Maineri,
> pp. 206–7]

G. Pallavicino, from Aix-les-Bains, to D. Manin, October 1, 1856

PIEDMONTISM IS for us an extremely dangerous opponent, an implacable enemy. Everyone in Piedmont—from Count Solaro della Margarita to Angelo Brofferio—is tarred with this same brush. Instead of a single Italian nation with its center in Rome, they would prefer a Kingdom of northern Italy with two capitals, Turin and Milan. Camillo Cavour is one of the most *Piedmontese* of all; and we shall harness him to our chariot only when we have a knife at his throat.

> [*Daniele Manin e Giorgio Pallavicino*, ed. Maineri,
> p. 212]

In his distant London exile, Mazzini no longer had the influence over events he had possessed in 1849, yet his name was still one to conjure with. Though under sentence of death in Piedmont, he could visit Genoa and even Turin without being given away to the police. At Genoa, said a police report, the workers all kept flowers in front of his picture. Mazzini condemned Cavour as a "pale ghost of Machiavelli," as someone who followed "a paltry, hateful program of expediency" and placed Piedmontese interests a long way before those of an Italian nation. Once or twice Mazzini seems to have been in very indirect touch with Cavour's government, but they needed each other's opposition too much to be collaborators. In one sense it was a fruit-ful opposition: "had not our own party been constantly at work," remarked Mazzini, "could Cavour have said at the Paris Conference: 'Mind! If you do not reform, you will have revolutions in Italy'?"

By 1857, Mazzini was dismayed to find that people's readiness for action seemed to be becoming less and less. Some of the doubters fought shy of political revolution for fear that it might also bring social revolution as in 1848. Others trusted that a French or Pied-montese army would one day solve the Italian Question without Italians themselves having to be much bothered. When he found that Cavour was half supporting Murat at Naples, Mazzini urgently planned that Pisacane should lead an expedition to Naples to show the strength of Italian feeling there, while at the same time the republicans would also instigate a rising at Genoa. The result was another failure. Pisacane was killed, and Mazzini and five others were condemned to death at Genoa in their absence.

Cavour had every reason to be angry, especially as he had been warned of what was afoot by Louis Napoleon and had simply been too confident to take the necessary precautions. Garibaldi thought it madness for Mazzini to rebel in Piedmontese territory. Other former disciples, Bertani, Medici, and Cosenz, all of whom had an important future in the patriotic movement, wrote to spell out their growing disagreement with Mazzini's tactics.

Cavour to the Marquis Villamarina, Piedmontese minister at Paris, July 8, 1857

I IMMEDIATELY replied to your telegram of yesterday evening with instructions that you should engage the French government to send us without delay an agent who they think could catch Maz-zini [Mazzini was in hiding at Genoa after the failure of his revolu-tionary coup]. If successful he would receive a fine reward, for, make no mistake, we ardently desire to free Piedmont, Italy and Europe from this infamous conspirator who has now become a major murderer. If we catch Mazzini, I hope he will be condemned to death and hanged in Acquasola Square.

French suspicions of us are most unfair. True enough the police at Genoa is badly organized and we spend too little on it; but even at Milan, where they spend a fortune, the Austrians have no more success against Mazzini than we do. Good old Octave de Lamar-mora is unsuitable as Intendant General at Genoa. Like all the Lamarmoras, he is brave and resolute at any moment of action, but once the danger is over he is indolent and overconfident. Though I tried hard to persuade him that a conspiracy was on foot at Genoa, he was too certain of his forces for repression and did not bother enough about the intrigues of the Mazzinian groups.

My fear now is that Mazzini has got away back to his lair in London. In that case could we not ask the British government for his extradition? If only we could establish at law that he tried to assassinate Napoleon, that could not be considered a merely political crime. [Two weeks later Cavour did ask Lord Clarendon to expel Mazzini, but the latter was still in Genoa! And in any case the British government would not expel political refugees] The Genoa movement was deplorable. But it did show up the nullity of the Mazzinian party in Piedmont and even in Genoa.

[*Nuove lettere inedite del Conte Camillo di Cavour*, ed. Edmondo Mayor, pp. 535–6]

Mazzini to Joseph Cowen, November 1857

PUBLIC OPINION is, in England, sadly mistaken about ourselves and the Italian question: and the persistence of the mistake, spite of all we have been repeatedly uttering directly or through the "Friends of Italy," is not, I must candidly say, revealing much of the practical good sense, or love of fair play, which one generally meets with in England.

The question of Italy is not one of more or less personal security or administrative improvement in one or another corner of our country; it is a question of *Nationality;* a question of independence, liberty, and unity for the *whole* of Italy; a question of a common bond, of a common flag, of a common life and law for twenty-five millions of men belonging between the Alps and the sea—to the same race, tradition, and aspiration. Everybody is free to approve or blame this *one* aim of ours; nobody ought to sift and judge our acts from a different point of view.

And for the question of means, the practical question, it is not one between republic and royalty; it is one between *action* and *inertness.* I am a republican, and such are almost all those who support me in a struggle now lasting since twenty-five years, and which will be carried on until crowned by victory. But although we deem it to be our right and duty to *spread* our creed by *words* and *writings*, we never meant or mean to *establish* it by *deeds.* Our flag of Action is a National one. We maintain that no one has a right to substitute his own will, or that of his own section, to the

National will. We ask all the fractions of opinion to bow, as we do, in reverence to this sacred principle. People may choose to wish us to act in a spirit of monarchical exclusivism; but no one has a right to tax us with being exclusive.

Lastly, as to Piedmont, we are not adverse to it; how could we be so? Is not Piedmont an Italian province? Nor are we refusing the help of its government in the struggle. We do only say that a *National* revolution is never achieved without an appeal to arms; that neither the Austrians, nor the King of Naples, nor the Pope, can ever be driven away from Italy by protocols or *memoranda;* that an open struggle cannot be *initiated* by the Piedmontese government; and that only a popular insurrection can offer an opportunity for action to Piedmont.

> [*Scritti editi ed inediti di Giuseppe Mazzini*, ed. M.
> Menghini (Imola, 1931), vol. LX, pp. 112–15;
> original text is in English]

Mazzini judged by a Garibaldian

I HAD never seen Mazzini; but for a long time we had corresponded, because I had been secretary of the Florence committee of *Young Italy*, among whom were Giuseppe Dolfi, Luigi Romei, Annibale Lapini, Carlo Bosi, Emilio Bacci and others I do not recall.

I had a tremendous desire to see him in the flesh. Alone, unarmed, and a fugitive, he had succeeded in making all the tyrants of Europe tremble on their thrones. I yearned to hear the voice which for so long had made my heart beat faster and had brought tears of sadness and tenderness to my eyes. This was the man who had given us hope. At a time when everyone was in despair, when most people were resigned to live and die as cowardly slaves, he had kept alive in us a confidence that our cause was holy and would soon triumph.

Often when watching Garibaldi, I had thought how wonderful it would have been if he and Mazzini were a single man or if anyone could have combined the virtues of each! Unfortunately they were not the same but were almost always at loggerheads. I am not even sure that they liked each other as much as many people think. Subsequently I often heard them criticize each other, and their feelings seemed like those of two women equally beautiful and admired. Neither of them was ignoble enough to be envious; but unfortunately, whenever Italy needed them to be in harmony, they looked at each other with distrust and resentment, almost as rivals. Each was anxious not to sacrifice to the other any particle of his own renown and not to appear as number two. Garibaldi, one must admit, did not mind coming second to Victor Emmanuel; but Mazzini would not come second to anyone.

[G. Bandi: *I mille, da Genova a Capua*, ed. E. di Nolfo (Milan, 1960), pp. 323–4]

Letter to Mazzini by A. Bertani, G. Medici, and E. Cosenz, January 1858

WE ARE still as patriotic as ever. We too share the anguish of our brothers, the desire for revenge, the shame of being deceived. As always we believe in liberty and in Italian unification, *nor do we believe in any initiative coming from Piedmont*. We are not asleep, nor are we opportunists, but neither are we so credulous and blind in our faith as to have the slightest confidence in the utility of the schemes you have pushed from 1852 until the insurrection of last June 29.

We must tell you, privately but clearly, that your sources of information about public opinion are wrong. Honest they may be, but they have deceived you into thinking the whole of Italy a volcano ready to erupt, as though the courage of the revolutionaries would be enough to galvanize the country, as though a handful of unarmed men could destroy a foreign domination which has lasted for centuries. You are too credulous; you think the people are behind you, whereas unfortunately they are not nearly so restless and are certainly not permanently waiting to start a revolution. The ordinary people are neither educated enough, nor have they the strength to move or to support a revolution once it has begun; they require the immediate support of that other large social class on whom they depend for guidance, for encouragement, and even for their daily bread.

These are your mistakes, the fatal delusions which have led you from error into error, and so have caused you to forfeit the allegiance of most of our republicans who still retain the ability to think for themselves. Many of your old adherents have become so discouraged that they have turned to other parties and policies; and some of them have become bitter critics and enemies of your cause. As for ourselves, we still share your political views and retain our former affection for you, but we must now be absolutely open and tell you that, henceforward, with all our strength, we shall act to stop what we think is wrong. We may even have to speak out in public and if necessary follow a different policy of our own. . . .

Your mistakes, and they are serious, are these:

to impose action at a moment chosen by yourself, even without preparation and with too few people;

to think that a simple insurrection can be converted quickly into an extensive revolution;

to impose action from outside, instead of preparing it from within. . . ;

to think that action is the main thing, and success merely secondary.

In these errors can be found the explanation of why you lose prestige and followers among us, your friends. Until they are remedied, you will bring new delusions and still more disasters on your country.

We do not ask you to remain idle and waste the brave and generous strength which you contribute to the cause; only that you will for the moment stop agitating for action, until we have plans and money and men; until we can confront a fierce and organized enemy with a substantial force of all those who believe in Italy.

[Jessie White Mario: *Agostino Bertani e i suoi tempi* (Florence, 1888), vol. I, pp. 272–4]

In 1857, largely owing to La Farina, the National Society was formed in Piedmont to support the idea that Italian liberation must now wait on Cavour and clearly renounce all dealings with republicanism or federalism. La Farina, though he was not entirely reliable on the subject, claimed that the society's newspaper reached the unusually large circulation of 10,000 copies by 1860, and that the *Credo Politico* which he wrote (and imposed not very democratically on the society) sold 100,000 copies. The society's membership, according to Professor Raymond Grew who has studied it in detail, may have been somewhere between 4,000 and 8,000. It was strongest in Piedmont and central Italy, but weak in Lombardy, Venice, and the South.

La Farina's subsequent story that he was one of Cavour's most important collaborators and used to see the Prime Minister almost every day before dawn was obviously untrue. La Farina was a hard worker and a good organizer. Though many people disliked him and his somewhat illiberal tactics and policy, his society did attract the support of Garibaldi and other patriots on the Left, and in 1859 it was to prove a useful weapon in Cavour's hands. There was a real need in such an individualistic world for an *organized* party "gathered into one bundle [*fascio*]"; and La Farina was especially helpful to Cavour in harnessing (or sometimes muzzling) certain dangerous elements on the Left. Certainly the National Society had an educative influence in purveying patriotic propaganda of a controllable, law-abiding kind, and in stirring people against Mazzini as well as against Austria.

The "Political Creed" of the National Society, February 1858

ITALIAN INDEPENDENCE should be the aim of every man of spirit and intelligence. Neither our educational system in Italy, nor our commerce and industry, can ever be flourishing or properly modernized while Austria keeps one foot on our neck. What use is intelligence to us if, over four fifths of the country, intelligence is considered a misfortune or a crime? What good is it to be born in the most fertile and beautiful country in the world, to lie midway between East and West with magnificent ports in both the Adriatic and Mediterranean, to be descended from the Genoese, the Pisans, the men of Amalfi, Sicily and Venice? What use is it to have invented the compass, to have discovered the New World and been the progenitor of two civilizations? For Austria makes us barbarians. Does it help us to have given birth to Caesar and Bonaparte if a foreign ruler can order Neapolitans to fight Romans and can enlist Tuscans, Lombards and Venetians to fight alongside the Croats in his own army?

To obtain political liberty we must expel the Austrians who keep us enslaved. To win freedom of conscience we must expel the Austrians who keep us slaves of the Pope. To create a national literature we must chase away the Austrians who keep us uneducated . . .

To recover the prosperity and glory she knew in the Middle Ages, Italy must become not only independent but politically united. Political unity alone can reconcile various interests and laws, can mobilize credit and put our collective energies to speeding up communications. Only thus will we find sufficient capital for large-scale industry. Only thus will we create new markets, suppress internal obstacles to the free flow of commerce, and find the strength and reputation needed for traffic in distant lands. Moreover if this should coincide with the cutting of a canal at Suez, our country would obviously benefit more than any other. Venice,

Ancona, Messina, Leghorn and Genoa would then become the richest ports in Europe.

Everything points irresistibly to political unification. Science, industry, commerce, and the arts all need it. No great enterprise is possible any longer if we do not first put together the skill, knowledge, capital and labor of the whole of our great nation. The spirit of the age is moving toward concentration, and woe betide any nation that holds back!

At the moment, for example, our roads are cut by customs barriers every few miles. We have many different systems of laws, weights, measures and coinages. How can you expect someone from Turin or Genoa to invest in some Lombard industry, when if the latter went bankrupt its Lombard creditors would by Austrian law take over its stores and property and obtain the whole proceeds of the sale of sequestered goods? A creditor who arrived one hour late from over the Ticino River would not receive even the cost of his fare.

No longer do our women weave at home the splendid brocades such as Kings of France and England were once proud to wear. For machines and the division of labor are putting an end to the kind of domestic industry which was the glory of Florence, Pisa and Milan. Large factories produce better, more quickly and cheaply, with the result that every day one of our industries goes out of business. Glass and mirrors are now ordered from Bohemia rather than Venice, and Venetian goldsmiths are now outdone by those of Paris. Florence has lost her production of damasks, and is losing that of straw hats. The velvet of Lyons is killing that of Genoa. The silks of Naples and Catania are more expensive and less good than those of France. Once we taught agriculture to the world, but new tools and machines have allowed England, Belgium and France to outstrip us.

Fruit costs a great deal in northern Italy, at the same time as it is being fed to pigs in Sicily. But Sicily is not allowed by our masters to be part of Italy; and it might as well be Chile or Tahiti. The difficulty of sending letters there and getting an answer, the difficulty of finding transport, and the cost and slowness of freight, all this makes it easier for Sicily to export its citrus to Liverpool and New York than to Genoa, Milan or Turin . . .

We Italians want to be master in our own house. We want a strong enough army to defend our independence against any foreign enemy. We want a large fleet to guard our commerce even in distant seas. We want our agriculture and industry to be able to withstand competition from France and England. We want uniform laws. We need to break down barriers so that every Italian province can freely buy, sell, and build up its industries. We do not want our cities to be at a disadvantage commercially with Marseilles, Bordeaux, Manchester or Liverpool. We do not want our scientific institutes to be less good than those of France, Germany or England; and we would like our writers and artists to command the same money as those of other countries. Our provincial capital cities have little to lose and much to gain from a reorganization of our nation; and we want Rome as our national capital—Rome that peerless town with its glorious history.

All this can be done if we desire it with enough force and constancy. With 25 million people we are large enough. We do not lack the necessary intelligence, courage or self-sacrifice. Ancient history will prove this, and what we are now capable of was shown in 1848-9 at Palermo, Milan, Venice, Brescia, Messina, Bologna and Rome. We do not lack glorious traditions, nor do we lack hope. All of us know that Italy will sooner or later be a single nation, and our enemies know it too. Austria herself is sure of it, and that is why she despoils Lombardy and Venice like someone who is certain that she will soon be turned out. The newspapers of other countries show that we possess the esteem and affection of all free peoples. All we lack is internal union: in this one fact is the explanation of our poverty and subjection.

This, then, is the noble and holy aim of the *Italian National Society*. We want to unify Italy so that all her vigorous efforts can be concentrated on liberation. We want to reconcile and harmonize the ideas of her intellectuals, as we want to secure a common program of action; we want concord between provinces, between her cities and classes. We will not repudiate the aristocracy if they recognize our present needs, as we also embrace the common people so long as their pretensions do not go beyond justice or equity. We want concord and tolerance between all sincerely held religions. On the one hand we support the Piedmontese government, for it has a warlike army, money, credit, reputation, and an organized administration; but Piedmont must be ready to work with the Italian people, who have the numbers, the force, the revolutionary zeal, and the inalienable, imprescriptible right to override any treaty and become free and independent. Hence we want concord between the dynasty of Savoy and Italy, so long as the former wholeheartedly supports the cause of Italian independence. We accept support from anyone so long as they put Italian independence and unity first, and otherwise our members have complete freedom of liberty and action.

> [*Scritti politici di Giuseppe La Farina*, ed. A. Franchi (Milan, 1870), vol. II, pp. 83-98]

13. The Press Laws and Orsini, 1857-1858

The government was caught completely by surprise when the elections of November 1857 showed a strong shift to the Right. Solaro della Margarita was returned by a large margin, but not a single minister except Cavour was elected by an outright majority of votes. This was a real emergency. Cavour cleverly brought up a novel technical point by which he managed to exclude a number of clergy who had been elected. Then for the next few months he set parliament to work examining in detail the conduct of the elections, and used his liberal majority to declare a dozen other seats held by his opponents vacant because of electoral improprieties. Some liberals were not too happy at this way of outlawing an elected opposition, especially as the corrupt electoral practices had almost certainly not been only on one side, yet it was an issue on which the extreme Left supported Cavour's moderately anticlerical Center. A leading Catholic editor, Don Margotti, who was one of those unseated, retaliated with a plan to make good Catholics boycott parliamentary politics, and this made Cavour's job easier, even though it vitiated the representative system in Piedmont. The Prime Minister now trimmed his coalition more to the Right and dropped Rattazzi from the government, for the elections made it important to win over the moderate conservatives and stop them joining the more extreme Right in a solid opposition. France also wanted Rattazzi's dismissal.

Another anti-liberal influence on Cavour was that, already before the end of 1857, the French were insisting that he should introduce a more severe press law. Louis Napoleon particularly disliked the fact that Mazzini's *Italia e Popolo* and the quasi-socialist but anti-Mazzinian *La Ragione* were acquitted by juries at Genoa and Turin when they published articles disrespectful toward himself.

Prince La Tour d'Auvergne, French ambassador at Turin, to Count Walewski, French Foreign Minister, December 4, 1857

I RECEIVED Your Excellency's despatch with its approval of my views on what Cavour said about the inconvenience of taking legal action against that article from *L'Italia e Popolo*. Naturally I had used the occasion to call his attention to the need for modifying the Piedmontese press laws so as to end these incessant attacks on the Emperor's person. I thought it would help if, at the beginning of a new parliamentary session and before Cavour had made any undertakings toward the various political parties, he was clear about our views.

This was an especially delicate topic to raise just now, but I was careful to say that we did not mean to create the least embarrassment for him. On the contrary, we hoped it would strengthen constitutional institutions if we pointed out the danger from the provocations and gross insults which certain Piedmontese journals contain every day. I added that we would leave him entirely free to choose the best moment for legislating in the sense that we suggest. But we think some measure absolutely necessary, and we hope that the Turin cabinet will follow our friendly advice as soon as circumstances permit.

Count Cavour was visibly embarrassed at having to talk on this subject. He said that he was well aware of the complaints at Paris against the Piedmontese press, and the Emperor had done him the honor of mentioning the matter personally. But he hoped people had now realized that newspapers in Piedmont had no influence at all and were not worth all this trouble. He said that present political circumstances made any new press law impossible. The question was highly difficult, and he had gone into it in detail without finding any solution, Mere warnings, or a stamp tax, these would not be sufficient: they would reduce the number of papers, but those that survived would become more important and more dangerous than ever; and things would remain the same underneath.

I replied that I could not understand how the French government could be expected to accept this argument when every one of the evils complained of continued to exist. I was ready to admit that Piedmontese newspapers, because of people's good sense, had not the influence here which people supposed; but abroad they had a deplorable effect. For instance they conveyed a dreadful, if inexact, sense of the situation in Piedmont and of Cavour's policy. While newspapers had no helpful function inside this country, abroad they could create continual difficulties. Nor did I see why the government was so soft toward them when everyone knew that they were all edited by refugees whose one aim was to stir up agitation and anxiety. Even if domestic politics did not yet allow a complete modification of the press laws, at least some way could and should be found of protecting foreign rulers.

Count Cavour did not formally contest the strength of my arguments, even though he carefully avoided saying anything that could be construed as agreement with them.

In short, my impression after this interview was that M. de Cavour has no wish to limit the freedom of the press. His own political past, his lifelong principles, his engagements toward a certain party [Rattazzi], all help to explain this attitude; and so above all does his fear of lowering his own popularity in the rest of Italy. Nevertheless I have hopes that circumstances, together with deference to our views, will ultimately make him follow our advice. I know for certain that the King will support us here.

Cavour now finds his position seriously weakened as a result of the elections. For this reason we perhaps ought not to risk adding to his difficulties by pushing him too hard, because that might provoke a crisis which would deprive us of the hearty support which he has given and will go on giving our foreign policy. He now knows our opinion. Would it not be better to wait until his position is stronger and he is more master of the parliamentary situation than he is today?

[Archives of French Foreign Office, *Sardinia*, 342/ 283]

Felice Orsini, who attempted to kill Louis Napoleon on January 14, 1858, was one of those republicans who by now had broken with Mazzini. His attempt failed, but 150 bystanders were wounded, of whom eight died and others were blinded. Orsini's letter to the emperor from prison was virtually a set piece by arrangement with the man who was about to have him executed, and it was at once published by the emperor's wishes. Whether Louis Napoleon was frightened of any further attempt on his life, or whether it was simply that he was becoming obsessed with the Italian problem and mindful of his early days as a conspirator in the Romagna, this was the moment that Napoleon's favor really began to be extended toward helping Cavour.

In return, the latter agreed to be more severe with the radical extremists. He was now ready to suppress opposition newspapers and to harry many of the *émigrés* who had taken refuge in Piedmont. A proposal to limit the competence of juries was at first turned down by the relevant parliamentary commission as being too obviously a surrender to French pressure. The deputies could not know that Cavour in private was complaining against French bullying, for in public he had to declare that there was no French pressure of any kind. His own sincere conviction, he said, was that the jury system just did not work well in Piedmont. To persuade parliament on this vital matter he brought up the improbable story that an attempt had also been made on the life of King Victor Emmanuel. At the same time he used other fictional propaganda to discredit Mazzini, inaccurately asserting that the republican leader was now a socialist, behind Orsini, and in the pay of Austria.

Felice Orsini, from the prison of S. Mazas, to Napoleon III, February 11, 1858

My confession in the trial which followed the attempted assassination of January 14 is enough to send me to my death, and I submit without asking for mercy. Never shall I humble myself before a man who has destroyed the hopes of liberty in my unhappy country. So long as Italy is enslaved, death is a blessing.

Though my end is near, however, I must make one more effort to help Italy, for whose independence I have always faced every danger and sacrifice, and which was the constant object of my love. Hence these last words addressed to Your Imperial Majesty.

The present state of Europe makes you the arbiter of whether Italy is free or the slave of Austria and other foreigners. I would not ask that French blood should be shed for Italians. We ask simply that France should not intervene against us, and should not allow other nations to intervene in the struggle against Austria which cannot now be far off. Your Majesty could do this if you wanted to. The happiness or unhappiness of my country depends on you, and so does the life or death of a nation to which Europe owes so much of its civilization.

As a simple individual, I dare to raise my feeble voice from prison, to beg you to give Italy again the independence that Frenchmen helped her to lose in 1849. Let me remind Your Majesty that Italians, including my own father, cheerfully shed their blood for Napoleon the Great, wherever he chose to lead them; and they were loyal to the end. Let me also remind you that neither Europe nor Your Majesty himself can expect tranquility until Italy is free.

Do not scorn the words of a patriot on the eve of his execution.

Deliver my country, and the blessings of 25 million people will go with you for ever.

> [*Textuel procès Orsini, contenant par entier les débats judiciares*, ed. C.-A. Dandraut (Turin, 1858), p. 101]

Cavour to Angelo Conte, the Intendant at Genoa, January 20, 1858

SINCE THE repeated attempts on the life of the Emperor, the French government has been keeping a constant and uneasy eye on Genoa. They complain of the toleration afforded to the Mazzinians and their press. If we are not to lose French friendship, which is all we can really count upon in the present European situation, we absolutely must do something about this. Best of all would be to silence Mazzini's *Italia e Popolo*, and for this I am ready to use all available means. I beg you to lose no time before doing something, getting in touch if necessary with the government's legal department.

Should the Advocate General think it possible to strike at that newspaper by means of frequent, even daily, confiscations, I would not hesitate to defend this not altogether legal procedure in parliament. I would say openly that we mean to destroy a journal which not only discredits us in the eyes of civilized Europe, but could place the government in grave difficulties.

Should there be refugees from other Italian states among its contributors, they must be expelled from the country forthwith, whatever the articles they write. Even the theater critic should be driven out. The mere fact of contributing to such a criminal paper makes any *émigré* unworthy of our hospitality. We must wage war to the death against that assassin's gazette. It is a disgrace and a danger to society, and its destruction would be an eminently patriotic act. Should you be able to carry this out you will earn a high claim on my personal gratitude.

I know that you have also given your attention to the workers' organizations which, under the pretext of philanthropy, are aiming at preparing a revolutionary army. You should take resolute action over these, though it will need some circumspection so as to avoid friction with the poorest classes.

> [*Lettere edite ed inedite di Camillo Cavour*, ed. Chiala, vol. VI, p. 130–1]

Cavour to Conte, February 5, 1858

IT IS impossible to achieve our purpose by legal means, because of the pretense of moderation which Mazzini's paper puts up. So other means must be found. The first and most obvious would be the refusal of the printer to go on printing, perhaps in return for a suitable bribe. Or we could terrify him into giving up his help for such a wicked and hostile journal. Love of lucre and fear are potent motives in many minds. See to it that you set one or other or both of them in motion so as to achieve the aim I have indicated; and you will have done the country an inestimable service.

> [This piece, cut out of Chiala's edition, was pub-
> lished by A. Luzio: *Rivista Storica Italiana*
> (Turin, 1930), vol. XLVIII, p. 16]

Marchese Villamarina, from Paris, to Cavour, February 6, 1858

ALLOW ME, my dear Count, to give you word for word what the Emperor said to me:—

"I can assure you, my dear Marquis, that I speak to Piedmont just as I speak to any other Power, England included. So you must not suppose that I am bringing the smallest pressure to bear on your government; far from it. My strange life has shown me better than most other sovereigns how one must admire and appreciate the dignity of small states in circumstances of such difficulty. What I am asking for is the easiest thing that an ally who is loyal, just and in good faith could agree to give me.

"Thus I can tell you frankly that, if England should refuse to accept my rightful demands, our relations with her will gradually weaken until we are on the brink of hostilities. If this happened, how would Piedmont be placed? There are two possibilities: to be with me or against me. You must not delude yourselves. Your real support lies in France; and in order to be with me it is essential you should do what I ask; otherwise you will be against me. What real advantage can an English alliance offer you? No material support, that goes without saying; for England has no army, and furthermore for a long time to come she is going to be embroiled in India and China. All she could do to help you would be to send a few warships to Genoa and La Spezia, and this would not be much use if she goes on persisting in her desire to keep the 1814–15 treaties intact. A further point is that, in this last hypothesis, I would feel obliged against my will to seek Austria's support, and once I had gone into that orbit I would inevitably be compelled to give up what I had dreamed of with such fervor. Even I, who have always wanted Italy's happiness and independence, would then be forced to ally with a government which has always aroused and still arouses my deepest disgust."

[*Il carteggio Cavour-Nigra, dal 1858 al 1861* (Bologna, 1926), vol. I, pp. 61–2]

Diary of Count Hübner, Austrian ambassador in Paris

April 1858, Friday the 9th. There is no doubt that in these agitated days Napoleon's ideas waver from one extreme to another, and the most contradictory decisions, or rather wishes to take decisions, follow each other in his mind. It is my duty to keep Count Buol [now Austrian Foreign Minister] in touch with these oscillations. I fulfill this duty conscientiously, though I try not to discourage the timid nor to encourage the bold too far. My despatch today runs as follows: "In my last talk with M. le comte Walewski, I found his language in general conciliatory, but it showed a certain reserve, not to say distrust and annoyance, with Austria. . . . This is how I explain his bad mood. There can be two causes: either the firm and independent policy of Vienna in eastern Europe; or else it may be something more indirect. It may be the trial of Orsini, and the letters of that assassin which seemed to show up Napoleon as the arbiter of Italy's fate. Moreover the continuous activity which the Italian national party pursues here, with the idea of dragging Napoleon to the point where he will intervene in the affairs of the peninsula, this too has upset his thinking, for it has flattered the Emperor's ego and reminded him of another period in his life which he can never entirely forget." [This refers to his early life as a conspirator in central Italy]

[Comte de Hübner: *Neuf ans de souvenirs d'un Ambassadeur d'Autriche à Paris sous le second Empire, 1851–9*, ed. Alexandre de Hübner (Paris, 1904), vol. II, pp. 135–6]

Cavour's ascendancy after 1857, by an intimate friend

SACRIFICED TO the exigencies of a position of affairs which seemed too much for him, Rattazzi left a blank in the cabinet which it would have been difficult to fill up, had not the time been fast approaching when it was essential that all the powers of the state should be centered in one person, and all measures guided by one mind. Cavour, President of the Council, Minister of Foreign Affairs, and Minister of Finance, now took upon himself the duties of the Home Office.

After the resignation of Rattazzi, toward the end of 1857, a marked change took place in Cavour's policy. Without ceasing to be liberal and constitutional, and to be supported by the majority, his policy became more exclusively Italian; it emanated more especially from himself, and it was more imperiously imposed upon parliament, who obeyed him as a master rather than followed him as a leader. The majority increased in numbers every day; and faith in Cavour spread far and wide. Such faith on the part of a nation which looks to a single man for the accomplishment of its destinies, so thoroughly changes the nature of the parties which it sways, as apparently to put an end to them. Accordingly, in Italy, at that time, there was but one policy—I had almost said one religion—namely, the will of Cavour. To refute the most eloquent harangue, one word, one gesture, one smile from him upon whom all eyes were turned, was sufficient. The Constitution was reduced to a mere machine.

> [William de la Rive: *Reminiscences of the Life and Character of Count Cavour*, trans. E. Romilly (London, 1862), pp. 245–6]

14. Plombières and Negotiations with France, 1858

The experience of 1848–9 had taught Cavour the invaluable lesson that the general interest of Europe would save Piedmont from losing territory even if she were militarily defeated. This knowledge gave him an exceptionally favorable position from which to plan another war against Austria, with everything to gain and little to lose. Another lesson learned at the Congress of Paris had been the extent of Louis Napoleon's overmastering desire to reverse the settlement of 1815 and restore French authority in Europe and the Mediterranean as it had been under his uncle, Napoleon the Great. France and Piedmont were both revisionist powers whose future lay in a joint alliance directed against Austria, the guardian of the *status quo*.

Even in 1852, before Cavour became Prime Minister, the emperor had told Lamarmora that he meant to do something for Italy, "his second fatherland"; and what he intended was to follow his uncle's example and create an enlarged northern Italian state which would be a satellite of France. In the process he also intended to acquire Savoy and Nice from Piedmont. Villamarina's letter of February 6, 1858, showed that the time for a more formal recognition of these arrangements had now arrived. Through the emperor's cousin, Prince Jérôme Napoleon, and Dr. Conneau, a half-Italian who was Louis Napoleon's private physician, a secret meeting with Cavour was planned. On both sides the official diplomatic channels were by-passed. Louis Napoleon and Cavour were natural conspirators who liked holding the cards close to their chest, and there were things that both of them wished to conceal from each other and from their respective ministers.

Cavour to Dr. Conneau, physician to Napoleon III, May 6, 1858

A FEW days ago I received notice of matters of extreme importance for our country's future through Prince Napoleon. I was told that the Emperor was cognizant of them. They were such as could not be discussed either in writing or through diplomatic agents however trustworthy.

If things were more advanced and basic principles had been agreed, perhaps it would have been best for me to go to Paris and talk personally with the Emperor. But, in the present European situation, a step of that kind would make everyone suspicious and would provide a pretext for tendentious comment; it might even harm the very object of our negotiations; so I feel it should only be tried if a definite agreement seemed probable, if not certain.

On the other hand, if the Emperor were to agree that you, under cover of one of your usual visits to Italy, should come to Turin, matters could be discussed with maximum secrecy.

[*Il carteggio Cavour-Nigra*, vol. I, p. 85]

Cipher telegram from C. Nigra, Cavour's personal representative in Paris, to Cavour, May 9, 1858

THIS MORNING I presented letter to Doctor [Conneau] and as he knew nothing of the project I held back explanation. I asked him to read letter to Emperor at three o'clock. Doctor communicated Emperor's answer which said that this proposal is of maximum importance. Emperor confirms its three points, that is to say the marriage [between Prince Napoleon and Victor Emmanuel's daughter Clotilde], war against Austria, and Kingdom of North Italy. But he added the war must be justified in the eyes of the people and so it is indispensable that plausible motive be found. Emperor went into no details, he will send Doctor to Turin at end of month to treat with Your Excellency. Absolute secrecy essential. My presence here arouses no suspicion.

[*Il carteggio Cavour-Nigra*, vol. I, p. 87]

Cavour to Marquis Villamarina, his ambassador at Paris, May 27, 1858

THE OUTLOOK is clouding over, the storm is approaching. We must put ourselves in the clear. Hence I beg you to send me from time to time some official despatches so that the ministry files will contain some trace of events in which our embassy has played a part.

[*Lettere edite ed inedite di Camillo Cavour*, ed. Chiala, vol. VI, p. 236]

V. Salvagnoli, from Florence, to Cavour, July 8, 1858

LAST MONTH Signor Conneau, the Emperor's doctor, came to Florence, and through a common friend expressed a desire to see me. It then became clear that the Emperor knew my writings. During the subsequent discussion, Conneau made it quite explicit that the Emperor still intended to liberate Italy just as he had in 1831; that I, who had known his brother, had *intuited* his views correctly; and that on the first *favorable* opportunity the Emperor would put his ideas into practice. Conneau went on to say that he had spoken with you in the same sense when passing through Turin. I began expounding my favourite *thesis*, that the liberation of Italy was an *urgent necessity* for the Emperor; in this way he will help to establish himself firmly in France and in Europe; and it will also help him to become the arbiter of the Eastern Question and control the Mediterranean. Conneau told me that His Majesty thought the same way and even used the same formulas as I did, especially about uniting the Latin race against the Germanic race and about forming *three states in Italy*.

[*Il carteggio Cavour-Nigra*, vol. I, pp. 94–5]

Diary of Count Hübner

July 1858, Friday 30th. The meeting which took place at Plombières haunts me day and night. What did those two conspirators agree to do? No 'one knows, not even Walewski [the French Foreign Minister]. I write to Buol: —

"The Marquis di Villamarina, about two weeks ago, without giving any reasons, asked that a meeting of our conference be put off. Later we learned that he had secretly been to Culoz near Geneva, to meet Cavour. At the same time, the Belgian newspapers, which are less discreet than Villamarina, announced Cavour's visit to Plombières. Before the last session, on Friday the twenty-second, the matter was spoken of in Villamarina's presence. But he denied it all, and swore by everything he held most sacred that there had never been any idea of such a visit. In his view, nothing was worse than the wanton inventions by the press, and nothing was more untrue than this statement about a visit by the Piedmontese Prime Minister to the Emperor of the French. But in fact, three days earlier, on the evening of Monday the nineteenth, Cavour had arrived at Plombières. He saw the Emperor on the Tuesday, and left on Wednesday. Count Walewski told me all about it without my even asking. But the meeting took place without going through the Foreign Minister and not at Walewski's request.

"What was Cavour doing at Plombières? Walewski does not even know, for his letters from the Emperor made no reference at all to it. But he will find out when his Master returns to Paris. . . . Walewski told me that Cavour has vast plans in mind, and now wants action. Cavour's political position is compromised and can hardly be maintained much longer. He cannot go further toward the Left without annoying France. He cannot accept the offers of the Right without breaking with his more radical friends, in which case he would lose his parliamentary majority. To save the situation he needs some hard fact which he can exploit in an Italian sense."

[Hübner: *Neuf ans de souvenirs d'un Ambassadeur d'Autriche à Paris*, ed. Hübner, vol. II, pp. 199–202]

Cavour, from Baden-Baden, to Victor Emmanuel, July 24, 1858

THE CIPHERED letter which I sent Your Majesty from Plombières could give only a very incomplete idea of the long conversations I had with the Emperor. I believe you will be impatient to receive an exact and detailed narration. That is what I hasten to do having just left France, and I send it in a letter via M. Tosi, attaché at our legation in Berne.

As soon as I entered the Emperor's study, he raised the question which was the purpose of my journey. He began by saying that he had decided to support Piedmont with all his power in a war against Austria, provided that the war was undertaken for a nonrevolutionary end which could be justified in the eyes of diplomatic circles— and still more in the eyes of French and European public opinion.

Since the search for a plausible excuse presented our main problem before we could agree, I felt obliged to treat that question before any others. First I suggested that we could use the grievances occasioned by Austria's bad faith in not carrying out her commercial treaty. To this the Emperor answered that a petty commercial question could not be made the occasion for a great war designed to change the map of Europe. Then I proposed to revive the objections we had made at the Congress of Paris against the illegitimate extension of Austrian power in Italy: for instance, the treaty of 1847 between Austria and the Dukes of Parma and Modena; the prolonged Austrian occupation of the Romagna and the Legations; the new fortifications at Piacenza.

The Emperor did not like these pretexts. He observed that the grievances we put forward in 1856 had not been sufficient to make France and England intervene in our favor, and they would still not appear to justify an appeal to arms. "Besides," he added, "inasmuch as French troops are in Rome, I can hardly demand that Austria withdraw hers from Ancona and Bologna." This was a reasonable objection, and I therefore had to give up my second proposition; this was a pity, for it had a frankness and boldness which went perfectly with the noble and generous character of Your Majesty and the people you govern.

My position now became embarrassing because I had no other precise proposal to make. The Emperor came to my aid, and together we set ourselves to discussing each state in Italy, seeking grounds for war. It was very hard to find any. After we had gone over the whole peninsula without success, we arrived at Massa and Carrara, and there we discovered what we had been so ardently seeking. After I had given the Emperor a description of that unhappy country, of which he already had a clear enough idea anyway, we agreed on instigating the inhabitants to petition Your Majesty, asking protection and even demanding the annexation of the Duchies to Piedmont. This Your Majesty would decline, but you would take note of the Duke of Modena's oppressive policy and would address him a haughty and menacing note. The Duke, confident of Austrian support, would reply impertinently. Thereupon Your Majesty would occupy Massa, and the war could begin.

As it would be the Duke of Modena who would look responsible, the Emperor believes the war would be popular not only in France, but in England and the rest of Europe, because the Duke is considered, rightly or wrongly, the scapegoat of despotism. Besides, since he has not recognized any sovereign who has ruled in France since 1830, the Emperor need have less regard toward him than any other ruler.

Once we had settled this first question, the Emperor said: "Before going further we must consider two grave difficulties in Italy: the Pope and the King of Naples. I must treat both of them with some circumspection: the first, so as not to stir up French Catholics against me, the second so as to keep the sympathies of Russia, who makes it a point of honor to protect King Ferdinand."

I answered that, as for the Pope, it would be easy to keep him in possession of Rome by means of the French garrison there, while letting the provinces of the Romagna revolt. Since the Pope had been unwilling to follow advice over the Romagna, he could not complain if these provinces took the first occasion to free themselves from a detestable form of government which the Pope had stubbornly refused to reform. As for the King of Naples, there was no need to worry about him unless he took up the cause of Austria; but his subjects would be free to get rid of his paternal rule if the occasion offered.

This reply satisfied the Emperor, and we went on to the main question: what would be the objective of the war?

The Emperor readily agreed that it was necessary to drive the Austrians out of Italy once and for all, and to leave them without an inch of territory south of the Alps or west of the Isonzo. But how was Italy to be organized after that? After a long discussion, which I spare Your Majesty, we agreed more or less to the following principles, recognizing that they were subject to modification as the course of the war might determine. The valley of the Po, the Romagna, and the Legations would form a kingdom of Upper Italy under the House of Savoy. Rome and its immediate surroundings would be left to the Pope. The rest of the Papal States, together with Tuscany, would form a kingdom of central Italy. The Neapolitan frontier would be left unchanged. These four Italian states would form a confederation on the pattern of the German Bund, the presidency of which would be given to the Pope to console him for losing the best part of his estates.

This arrangement seemed to me fully acceptable. Your Majesty would be legal sovereign of the richest and most powerful half of Italy, and hence would in practice dominate the whole peninsula.

The question of what rulers would be bestowed on Florence and Naples was left open, assuming that the present incumbents, Your Majesty's uncle and cousin, would be wise enough to retire to Austria. Nevertheless the Emperor did not disguise the fact that he would like to see Murat return to the throne of his father; and, for my part, I suggested that the Duchess of Parma, at least for the time being, might take Florence. This last idea pleased the Emperor immensely. He appeared very anxious not to be accused of persecuting the Duchess of Parma just because she is a Bourbon princess.

After we had settled the fate of Italy, the Emperor asked me what France would get, and whether Your Majesty would cede Savoy and the County of Nice. I answered that Your Majesty believed in the principle of nationalities and realized accordingly that Savoy ought to be reunited with France; and that consequently you were ready to make this sacrifice, even though it would be extremely painful to renounce the country which had been the cradle of your family and whose people had given your ancestors so many proofs of affection and devotion. The question of Nice was different, because the people of Nice, by origin, language, and customs, were closer to Piedmont than France, and consequently their incorporation into the Empire would be contrary to that very principle for which we were taking up arms. The Emperor stroked his mustache several times, and merely remarked that these were for him quite secondary questions which we could discuss later.

Then we proceeded to examine how the war could be won, and

the Emperor observed that we would have to isolate Austria so that she would be our sole opponent. That was why he deemed it so important that the grounds for war be such as would not alarm the other continental powers. Better still if they were also popular in England. He seemed convinced that what we had decided would fulfill this double purpose. The Emperor counts positively on England's neutrality; he advised me to make every effort to influence opinion in that country to compel the government (which is a slave to public opinion) not to side with Austria. He counts, too, on the antipathy of the Prince of Prussia toward the Austrians to keep Prussia from deciding against us. As for Russia, Alexander has repeatedly promised not to oppose Napoleon's Italian projects. Unless the Emperor is deluding himself, which I am not inclined to believe after all he told me, it would simply be a matter of a war between France and ourselves on one side and Austria on the other.

The Emperor nevertheless believes that, even reduced to these proportions, there remain formidable difficulties. There is no denying that Austria is very strong. The wars of the first Empire were proof of that. Napoleon Bonaparte had to fight her for fifteen years in Italy and Germany; he had to destroy many of her armies, take away provinces and subject her to crushing indemnities. But always he found her back on the battlefield ready to take up the fight. And one is bound to recognize that, in the last of the wars of the Empire, at the terrible battle of Leipzig, it was the Austrian battalions which contributed most to the defeat of the French army. It will therefore take more than two or three victorious battles in the valleys of the Po or Tagliamento before Austria will evacuate Italy. We will have to penetrate to the heart of the Empire and threaten Vienna itself before Austria will make peace on our terms.

Success will thus require very considerable forces. The Emperor's estimate is at least 300,000 men, and I think he is right. With 100,000 men we could surround the fortified places on the Mincio and Adige and close the Tyrolean passes; 200,000 more will be needed to march on Vienna by way of Carinthia and Styria. France would provide 200,000 men, Piedmont and the other Italian provinces 100,000. The Italian contingent may seem little, but you must remember that 100,000 effective front-line soldiers will mean 150,000 under arms.

The Emperor seemed to me to have well-considered ideas on how to make war, and on the role of each country. He recognized that

France must have its chief base at La Spezia and must concentrate on the right bank of the Po, until we command the whole of the river and can force the Austrians into their fortresses. There would be two grand armies, one commanded by Your Majesty, the other by the Emperor.

Once agreed on military matters, we equally agreed on the financial question, and I must inform Your Majesty that this is what chiefly preoccupies the Emperor. Nevertheless he is ready to provide us with whatever munitions we need, and to help us negotiate a loan in Paris. As for contributions from other Italian provinces in money and material, the Emperor believes we should insist on something, but use great caution. All these questions which I here relate to you as briefly as possible were discussed with the Emperor from eleven o'clock in the morning to three o'clock in the afternoon. At three the Emperor dismissed me but gave me another appointment at four o'clock to take a drive with him.

At the agreed hour we got into an elegant phaeton drawn by American horses. The Emperor personally took the reins, and we were followed by a single servant. For three hours he took me through the valleys and forests which make the Vosges one of the most picturesque parts of France.

Hardly had we left the streets of Plombières when the Emperor broached the subject of the marriage of Prince Napoleon and asked what Your Majesty might think of it. I answered that you had been placed in a most embarrassing position when I communicated to Your Majesty the overtures made me by Bixio, because of doubts regarding the importance that he, the Emperor, attached to this matter. I reminded him of a conversation between Your Majesty and him in Paris in 1855 on the subject of Prince Napoleon and his project of marriage to the Duchess of Genoa, so that the whole issue was somewhat perplexing. I added that this uncertainty had increased as a consequence of Your Majesty's interview with Dr. Conneau, who, when pressed by Your Majesty and myself, had declared not only that he had no instructions, but did not even know what the Emperor thought. I further added that, while wanting to do everything possible, you had a considerable repugnance to giving your daughter in marriage, because she was young and you could not impose an unwelcome choice upon her. If the Emperor strongly desired it, I added, you would not have irremovable objections to the marriage, but still wished to leave your daughter entirely free to choose.

The Emperor answered that he was very eager for the marriage of his cousin with Princess Clotilde, since an alliance with the House of Savoy was what he wanted more than anything else. If he had not instructed Conneau to discuss it, that was because he wanted first to know if such a proposal would be agreeable. As for the conversation with Your Majesty which I had cited, the Emperor first seemed not to remember it, and then after a while he said to me: "I remember quite clearly having said to the King that my cousin had been wrong to ask the hand of the Duchess of Genoa; it seemed wrong that he should speak to her of marriage only a few months after her husband's death."

The Emperor came back several times to the question of the marriage. Laughingly he said that he might sometimes have spoken ill of his cousin to you, for often he had been angry with him; but that at bottom he loved him tenderly since he possessed excellent qualities and for some time had been behaving in such a way as to earn the esteem and affection of France. "Prince Napoleon," he added, "is much better than his reputation; he is a *frondeur*, he loves to be contrary, but he is witty as well as sensible, and he is warmhearted." All this is true. That the Prince has intelligence you can judge for yourself, and I can confirm after many conversations I have had with him. That he has judgment is proved by his management of the Great Exhibition. Finally, that his heart is good is irrefutably proved by his constancy toward both friends and mistresses. A man without heart would not have left Paris amid the pleasures of carnival time to make a last visit to Rachel who was dying at Cannes, especially when they had separated four years earlier.

When answering the Emperor I tried not to offend him, yet I took pains to make no commitment. At the day's end when we separated, the Emperor said to me: "I understand the King's repugnance at marrying his daughter so young; nor need the marriage be immediate; I am quite willing to wait a year or more if necessary. All I want is to have some kind of an answer. So please ask the King if he will consult his daughter, and let me know his intentions in a positive manner. If he consents to the marriage, let him fix the date. I ask no undertaking except our word, given and received." With that we parted. Shaking my hand the Emperor dismissed me, saying: "Have the same confidence in me that I have in you."

Your Majesty will see that I have faithfully followed your instructions. As the Emperor did not make Princess Clotilde's marriage a *sine qua non* of the alliance, I did not assume the least engagement or obligation. But I beg you to let me express my frank opinion on a question upon which may depend the success of the most glorious enterprise which anyone has attempted for many years.

The Emperor did not make the marriage of Princess Clotilde with his cousin a *sine qua non* condition, but he showed clearly that it was of the greatest importance to him. If the marriage does not take place, if you reject the Emperor's proposal without good reason, what will happen? Will the alliance be broken? That is possible, but I do not believe it. The alliance will be made. But the Emperor will bring to it a quite different spirit from the one which he would have brought if, in exchange for the crown of Italy which he offers Your Majesty, you had granted him your daughter's hand for his nearest relative. If there is one quality which characterizes the Emperor, it is the permanence of his likes and his dislikes. He never forgets a service, just as he never forgives an injury. The rejection to which he has now laid himself open would be a blood insult, let there be no mistake about it. Refusal would have another disadvantage. We should then have an implacable enemy in the inner counsels of the Emperor. Prince Napoleon, even more Corsican than his cousin, would mortally hate us; the position he occupies, to say nothing of that to which he may aspire, as well as the affection and I would almost say the weakness the Emperor has for him, all this would give him many ways of satisfying his hatred.

Let us not deceive ourselves: in accepting the proposed alliance, Your Majesty and your kingdom bind themselves indissolubly to the Emperor and to France. If the war which follows is successful, the Napoleonic dynasty will be consolidated for one or two generations; if it fails, Your Majesty and your family run the same grave dangers as their powerful neighbor. But what is certain is that the success of the war and its glorious consequences for Your Majesty and your subjects depend in large part on the good will and friendship of the Emperor. If he is embittered against us, the most deplorable consequences could follow. I do not hesitate to declare my most profound conviction that to accept the alliance but refuse the marriage would be an immense political error which could bring grave misfortunes upon Your Majesty and our country.

But I know well that Your Majesty is a father as well as a King; and that it is as a father that you may hesitate to consent to a marriage which does not seem right and which is not of a kind to assure the happiness of your daughter.

Will Your Majesty let me consider this question not with the impassiveness of the diplomat but with the profound affection and absolute devotion in which I hold you?

I do not think people can say that the marriage of Princess Clotilde to Prince Napoleon is unsuitable. He is not a King, to be sure, but he is the first prince of the blood of the first Empire of the world. He is separated from the throne only by a two-year-old child. Your Majesty may well have to content yourself with a mere Prince for your daughter anyway, because there are not enough available Kings and hereditary princes in Europe. Prince Napoleon does not belong to an ancient sovereign family, but his father endowed him with the most glorious name of modern times; and through his mother, the Princess of Würtemberg, he is connected with the most illustrious princely houses of Europe. The nephew of the doyen of Kings, the cousin of the Emperor of Russia, is by no means a parvenu with whom it is shameful to be connected.

But the chief objections which can be made to this marriage lie perhaps in the personal character of the Prince and the reputation which he generally carries. On that subject I repeat with complete conviction what the Emperor said: he is better than his reputation. Thrown very young into the whirlpool of revolutions, the Prince was allowed to develop some very advanced opinions, and this fact, about which there is nothing extraordinary, has made him many enemies. The Prince has since then become quite moderate; but what does him great honor is that he remains faithful to the liberal principles of his youth while renouncing the application of them in any unreasonable or dangerous fashion, and that he has kept his old friends even when they were in disgrace. Sire, a man who when he attains the pinnacle of honor and fortune does not disavow those who were his companions in misfortune, and does not forswear the friendships he had among the defeated, such a man is not heartless. The Prince has braved the anger of his cousin to keep his old loves. He has never given in on this point, nor does he give in now. His generous words at the distribution of prizes at the Poitiers Exhibition are the proof of it. His conduct in the Crimea was regrettable. But if he could not stand the boredom and privations of a long siege, still he showed courage and coolness at the battle of Alma. Besides, he will make good on the battlefields of Italy the harm he did himself under the ramparts of Sebastopol.

The private life of the Prince may have sometimes been unsteady, but it has never given occasion for serious reproach. He was always a good son, and though he has angered his cousin more than once, still in serious matters he has always remained faithful and close.

Despite all this, I realize that Your Majesty may still hesitate and fear to compromise the future of your beloved daughter. But would she be more tranquil tied to an ancient princely family? History shows that princesses may be condemned to a sad life when they marry in accordance with propriety and ancient custom. To prove this I need not look far for an example, as I could instance what has happened recently in your own family.

Your Majesty's predecessor, Victor Emmanuel I, had four daughters, models of grace and virtue. What became of their marriages? The first, the luckiest, married the Duke of Modena, a Prince who is universally detested. Surely you would not consent to a similar marriage for your daughter. The second married the Duke of Lucca. I need not remind you of the result of that marriage. The Duchess of Lucca was and is as unhappy as it is possible to be in this world. The third daughter, it is true, mounted the imperial throne, but that was for a husband who was impotent and imbecile, and who was obliged ignominiously to abdicate after a few years. Finally the fourth, the charming and perfect Princess Christine, married the King of Naples. Your Majesty certainly knows the gross treatment which she experienced, and the griefs which brought her to the tomb with the reputation of being a saint and martyr. In the reign of your father, another Princess of Savoy was married, your cousin Philiberte. Is she happier than the others, and would you wish the same fate for your daughter?

These examples show that in consenting to the marriage of your daughter to Prince Napoleon you would have a better chance of making her happy than if, like your cousin or your father, you married her to a prince of Lorraine or Bourbon.

But permit me a last reflection. If you do not agree to this marriage to Prince Napoleon, whom do you want her to marry? The Almanach de Gotha will show, as one might have expected, that there are no suitable princes. Religious differences prevent any alliance with most families who reign in countries with similar institutions to our own. Our struggle against Austria, our sympathy for France, makes impossible any marriage with families connected with the House of Lorraine or Bourbon. This reduces the choice to Portugal and a few more or less mediatized petty German principalities.

If Your Majesty will deign to meditate on these considerations, I dare flatter myself that you will recognize that as a father you can consent to this particular marriage, and that the supreme interest of the state, the future of your dynasty, of Piedmont, and of all Italy advise its acceptance.

I beg your pardon for the liberty and the length of this report. In so important a question I could not be more reserved or more brief. The sentiments which inspire me and my motives will be enough to excuse my conduct.

Having had to write this endless epistle on a table at an inn without any time to copy it, nor even to reread it, I beg Your Majesty to be indulgent and forgive what disorder there may be in its ideas and the incoherence of its style. Despite these shortcomings, and because this letter contains a faithful and exact description of the communications which the Emperor made to me, I beg you to preserve it so that on return to Turin I can take notes from it which may serve in subsequent negotiations.

In the hope of being able, at the end of next week, to place at Your Majesty's feet the homage of my profound and respectful devotion, I have the honor to be Your Majesty's very humble and obedient servant and subject.

[*Il carteggio Cavour-Nigra*, vol. I, pp. 103–10]

Almost nothing is known from the French side about the meeting at Plombières, and Cavour's letter to the king is therefore the most direct evidence we have—not even Cavour's cabinet knew where he had been going or why. By his account, the emperor offered Piedmont not only Lombardy, but Venice and part of the Papal States. Together they would plan an aggressive war. Cavour's special task was to provoke "spontaneous" risings and so prove that the war was a respectable war of national liberation. At the same time it was part of the bargain that he should go on provoking Austria until she or her dependencies were forced to take action and so seem the real aggressor.

By now Cavour had had to overcome his horror at popular insurrections on Mazzini's pattern, but in accordance with French wishes he gave orders that any insurrection should not be too liberal in color. He still could not accept Mazzini's idea of a united Italy. So long as he obtained Lombardy and Venice he would dominate the peninsula, and that was enough. Southern Italy must not be carved up while he needed to remain friendly with Russia, but Ferdinand might be replaced by Lucien Murat. Central Italy was still more problematic. Florence and the "Etruscan race" should not be allowed to become too politically active as a rival Italian power. On the other hand, France might insist on Tuscany becoming an appanage for Prince Napoleon, in which case such a solution would have to be accepted even though it would make French influence in Italy much too strong. The best solution, so Cavour thought (in December 1858), was to bring in a Hohenzollern prince to rule an independent central Italy!

Diary of Giuseppe Massari, a Neapolitan in exile at Turin

August 2, 1858. This morning Count Cavour showed me a criminal and fatuous proclamation by Mazzini appealing to the most bloodthirsty passions. We then spoke of Naples. The Count said: "In politics, as in war, you have to concentrate your forces. Our quarrel is with Austria alone, and if we want Russia's support we must keep clear of Naples. As the Emperor of the French said to me recently at Plombières, 'that's the way it is—Russia stands by the King of Naples.' Once Austria has been driven out of Italy the Bourbons of Naples will be finished. We are now moving toward war with Austria. Napoleon III won't want to face new elections to the legislative body until he's made war." [p. 2]

August 17. Count Cavour summoned me to the Ministry of the Interior at eleven. [Massari was editor of the official gazette, and was Cavour's unofficial and badly paid Public Relations Officer] I wrote out for him my conversation with West [the British *chargé*], and he was very grateful. Then he said: "I am resigned to the fact that there are three powers in Europe who want to undo the *status quo* (France, Russia, Prussia), and two who would like it preserved (Austria and England). It's distressing to think that the first three are not the most liberal—but what can I do? I can't align with the other two." [pp. 11–12]

August 25. I went to pay my respects to Count Cavour shortly before midday. He inquired about Tanari, and this led the conversation round to the *National Society* [of La Farina]. He said, "I don't know the people behind it, but as I see things it is against' the Mazzinians and hence that much advantageous. Moreover I am convinced that all this talk about 'unification' or 'union' will go up in smoke with the first cannonshot." I told him that everyone asks me how far the Piedmontese government is behind the society. He said: "All you need tell them is that Count Cavour prefers this Association to Mazzini's." [p. 16]

September 11. On my way out of Casa San Giorgio I met Professor Francesco Ferrara [a Sicilian *émigré* economist]. He asked me about the Naples amnesty which he views as likely. I told him that Italy needs a conqueror, and that therefore I am totally devoted to the House of Savoy as the nation's conquering sword. My interlocutor does not share my opinions about Piedmont. He still thinks that "enlightened despotism" has some use in the South, and quotes General Filangieri's administration in Sicily [after 1849] as an example. Ferrara is able, but his sour and passionate nature makes him unwilling to allow Piedmont the magnificent role that is hers. As for me, it is my only hope: if there is to be an Italy, it will be thanks to the sword of Piedmont; otherwise we will never become a nation. [p. 31]

September 20. Santarosa remarked that revolution is brewing in England. Count Cavour does not believe this, at least not in our lifetime. "I think," he said, "that what is really brewing for tomorrow is the question of the relations between capital and labor.

If I weren't a minister I would take up this subject because I am absolutely sure that it is the problem of the future. Eventually it will arise in Italy, too, but our children will deal with it: we can think only of the national question." I added: "If the present state of affairs lasts too long, there is a danger that the social question may crop up before its time and complicate the national question." The Count agreed with me. [p. 41]

October 11. The Count said . . ."National feeling is stronger than liberal opinion in Italy: if tomorrow a despot, for instance the King of Naples, were to hoist the national flag and make war on the Austrians, that despot would be even more popular than constitutional Piedmont. England should get this into her head: in Italy today we have Piedmont facing Austria; if tomorrow Piedmont fell, her place would be taken by the revolution." [p. 47]

October 28. This evening I dined at Mauri's with Oldofredi and Ruffini. We talked a lot about the wretched state of the press in Turin. We also agreed that if Piedmont does not expand she is finished. The very breadth of her representative institutions calls insistently for territorial expansion. [p. 54]

November 3. I pointed out to Cavour all the jumble of nonsense in Bright's pacifist speech at Birmingham, and drew the conclusion that even from a non-Tory ministry, like the present one in England, we have little to hope for: the Tories might even be better. The Count answered: "You're right. But if we get France and Russia moving we needn't care a damn about England. What harm can the English do us? Take the island of Sardinia? They would be caught in a fine booby trap!" This spirited sally convulsed me with laughter. Count Cavour's talk is always on a high level, at once witty and pungent. [p. 57]

November 25. Mazade [a Frenchman who later wrote Cavour's biography] told me that yesterday Senator Gallina was saying that he is against the government only because not enough is being done to consolidate constitutional government. According to the right honorable senator, Piedmont today is not a constitutional state but a dictatorship; though he added that he would not know what to put in its place. I would like Mazade to be persuaded that everyone here thinks Count Cavour a necessary man . . .

At half past two Count Cavour summoned me to the Ministry of Foreign Affairs. He wants me to issue a *démenti* of the words the French and Belgian press have attributed to the King about war being arranged for next spring. At a sale of horses the King said to some officers: *buy, because perhaps you'll soon be needing them.* Then the Count told me: "Today I've invited Massimo d'Azeglio for a chat, so that when he goes to Tuscany he won't harm us by criticizing the government as he's been doing up till now." I then told him about the conversation between Gallina and Mazade. The Count remarked: "If I am a dictator, where are the lictors?" "We are the lictors," I answered. There is a good deal of truth in what Gallina said. It is the glory of Piedmont, but also a danger. [p. 72]

[G. Massari: *Diario dalle cento voci, 1858–1860*, ed. E. Morelli (Bologna, 1959)]

Cavour to Count Villamarina, official of the royal household, August 23, 1858

I FOUND your letter of the day before yesterday very disturbing, and perhaps you may have exaggerated the importance of what the King wrote to his daughter. He is not angry with you, and the idea of going against our plans has not crossed his mind. Only, as he has an extraordinarily weak character, he does not dare to be really firm with her; he wants to appear in her eyes as one obliged to yield to a political necessity. In a word, he wants me to play the part of a tyrant, while he keeps for himself the part of a noble and affectionate father. Perhaps such conduct may be called neither noble nor affectionate. But no matter; if the King is weak, I am as strong as a rock. To attain the sacred goal we have set ourselves, I would be prepared to face far worse dangers than the hatred of a girl and the wrath of courtiers.

[*Il carteggio Cavour-Nigra*, vol. I, pp. 132–3]

Cavour to Napoleon III, September 17, 1858

YOUR MAJESTY now considers that we should delay the date fixed for the outbreak of war, and that if possible we should postpone it until the spring of 1860, or at earliest until July or August 1859. On this point the King has charged me to put certain considerations before you. He thinks that postponing the war to a distant date would have grave disadvantages, both political and military; whereas Your Majesty's ability and wisdom have now placed Europe in a very suitable state for carrying out our plans . . .

Mazzini may retain a few followers among the dregs of society, thanks to the socialist ideas he has finally adopted; but he has lost all prestige with the enlightened and middle classes. These elements have almost all rallied gradually to the principles of order and moderation by which alone the emancipation of the fatherland can be achieved. After the Congress of Paris we were able to persuade the great national party to put its hopes increasingly in Piedmont, upheld and encouraged by France. These hopes have survived for three years and have made even the fiercest hotheads contain their ardor. But can they be maintained at full strength for yet another year? Surely there is a danger that the southern temperament of my compatriots will wilt. Once wearied by fruitless waiting, they may fall into discouragement or, even worse, be carried away by the senseless but seductive agitation of the so-called [Mazzinian] Party of Action. If in the interval between now and the outbreak of hostilities any sort of revolutionary manifestation occurred in Italy, the plan so admirably built up by Your Majesty would risk being ruined.

There is another danger in any increased delay before breaking with Austria. There seems no longer any doubt that, with or without Vienna's agreement, the Archduke Maximilian [Governor of Lombardy] has decided to try out on a broad front a policy which will at least in appearance be very liberal. He is making the greatest efforts to win popularity and gather the different classes of society around him. He is attempting to appeal to the masses with his pomp and ceremony, with largesse, brilliant shows and free festivities. He is trying to win over the educated classes by according favors even to the most compromised patriots if they show any signs of abandoning the national cause; and he uses a semi-liberal jargon to deceive those who are unable to see what lies behind the veil. So as to carry on the fight against us more effectively he hopes to found a big newspaper with the attractive title of *Italia*, whose aim will be to show that the peninsula can expect far more as regards freedom and nationhood from Austria than from Piedmont and France. The Archduke's efforts have so far been ineffectual. The aristocracy, the wealthy, the lower middle classes and the common people have stood against the blandishments of this essentially anti-national power. But how long can their resistance hold out against his perseverance? Far from losing courage, he is starting up new projects every day to attain his goal. Of course the chosen few will resist him. But I am very doubtful about the masses. Hence it seems in our highest interest that the struggle against Austria should begin before the Archduke has had time to gain some popularity . . .

The King begs Your Majesty to weigh up with your great wisdom these political and military considerations, and he hopes that we can agree to start hostilities if not in April at least by July 1859.

[*Il carteggio Cavour-Nigra*, vol. I, pp. 149–51]

Cavour's draft proposal for a casus belli *at Massa and Carrara,*
October 1858

IN THE course of next May, the inhabitants of Massa and Carrara will draw up an address to King Victor Emmanuel setting out in a suitable and forceful way the deplorable condition of their country, and will invoke his aid to obtain an improvement of their lot. The address might well contain five hundred signatures, including those of the most outstanding people of the country. It will be presented to the King by a deputation which will come to Turin . . .

If the Modena government replies evasively and asks to consult the Great Powers, then we could not occupy Massa and Carrara without inviting serious and justified criticism. Hence, as an alternative plan, we must arrange that, as soon as the answer of Modena becomes known, an insurrection will break out in Massa and Carrara under Garibaldi's leadership.

As soon as Garibaldi departs from Massa and Carrara, leaving a provisional government behind him, the King will order the country to be occupied and will take up a military position on the heights of the Apennines. France will send two frigates to La

Spezia. Garibaldi's insurrection and the occupation of M. and C. will inevitably bring about Austrian intervention, thereby providing the opportunity for declaring war.

[*Il carteggio Cavour-Nigra*, vol. I, pp. 182–4]

V. Salvagnoli to the Emperor Louis Napoleon, November 28, 1858

ANY SETTLEMENT of Italy must offer solid and durable advantages both to the Napoleonic dynasty and that of Savoy. This could be obtained by dividing Italy into four.

The Pope would keep Rome and its neighborhood, with a strip to his port at Civitavecchia, and financial support from the other Italian states.

Upper Italy, ruled by the Savoy dynasty, would include Piedmont (but less Nice, Savoy and Sardinia); and also Lombardy, Venetia, and the Italian parts of Friuli and the Dalmatian coast. But it will not take in the south side of the Po except at Piacenza.

The third part, i.e., Parma (without Piacenza), Modena, the papal Legations and the Marches, Tuscany, Corsica and Sardinia, all this will be given to a French prince, for example Prince Napoleon, son of the ex-King Jérôme Bonaparte.

The fourth part will be the existing Kingdom of the Two Sicilies. This would go to a ruler suggested by England, on condition that all Austrian or Bourbon princes were excluded.

Such a division would ensure Italian independence, because her states would be strong enough to defend themselves by sea and land. France would also gain the solid advantage of having three Italian allies; she would win a barrier against Germany, and a route by which if need be she could enter the Danube basin against Russia . . .

Best of all for France, this solution would close for ever the prospect of war and revolution. France would be insulated from nearby unrest by a settled Italy. Nor would any other Power attack France if her Italian alliances let her dominate the whole Mediterranean basin. At last Napoleon's phrase about the Mediterranean being a French lake could come true.

Losing Corsica would be a secondary matter in comparison, especially as France would gain a better frontier by incorporating Savoy and Nice . . .

This method of securing Italian independence would be of the greatest benefit to Napoleon, without in any way offending the national sentiment of Italians, and it would create an indissoluble alliance between France and Italy.

> [*Storia documentata della diplomazia europea in Italia dall'anno 1814 all'anno 1861*, ed. N. Bianchi (Turin, 1872), vol. VIII, pp. 15–16]

Cavour to Marquis Villamarina, ambassador at Paris, November 25, 1858

I MUST make clear, even if you accuse me of indiscretion, that I cannot agree to Salvagnoli's plan for dividing Italy. I have no more idea of losing the island of Sardinia than of asking France for Corsica. I am similarly sure that it would be a serious mistake to separate the Po Valley into two parts, especially as the local population would never agree to it. Piedmont must be given everything up to and including Ancona. It is a lot, but not too much, even if we have to throw in our last man and our last penny.

If anyone talks to you either seriously or jokingly about the reconstitution of Italy, you must be bold and maintain that this can be solidly established only if Piedmont rests her head on the Alps and her feet on Ancona. That is what I told Salvagnoli; and yet that scoundrel prefers to enlarge his own Tuscany, even though the Tuscans would never know how to govern a population with ten times more energy than their own. If Florence is united with Bologna, Bologna will be the dominant partner and take the rank of capital. The cis-Apennine race and the Etruscan race could never possibly be welded together, and any treaties in that sense would soon be torn up by the force of events.

> [*Il carteggio Cavour-Nigra*, vol. I, p. 214]

15. How Cavour Brought About War in 1859

With January 1859 began the two most dramatic and eventful years in the risorgimento. First of all, in the spring of 1859, came the long-sought third war of liberation against Austria. But the weeks of waiting between January and April brought many surprises as Louis Napoleon blew hot and cold.

Diary of Count Hübner, Paris

January 1859, Saturday the 1st. In the Tuileries at one o'clock, reception of the *corps diplomatique.* Napoleon says to the Papal Nuncio: "I hope that this new year will see our alliances being used for the good of peoples and the peace of Europe." Then to me, in a genial tone, he said: "I am sorry our relations with Austria are not as good as I would like, but please tell Vienna that my personal feelings toward your Emperor are the same as ever." My colleagues who heard these words put several different interpretations on them. Cowley thought they showed bad temper; Kisseleff and Hatzfeld thought they followed naturally from the remark about peace he had made to the Nuncio, and hence that they were intended to be pleasant. Lord Chelsea, first secretary at the British Embassy, had nothing better to do than to go to the *Union club* and spread an inexact account of the incident. Hence followed a general panic. By evening, Paris was in a state of consternation.

Sunday the 2nd. Everyone is talking of war between France and Austria. Mme de Labédoyère, lady in waiting to the Empress, who is well informed about events at the Tuileries, tells me that war is regrettable but certain. This is what happens when sovereigns play at politics in public. At nine this evening there is a reception at the Tuileries. The Emperor calls me over, shakes hands with real affection, and asks about my trip to Spain "after we parted at Biarritz," and all in the most friendly tone. Everyone was looking at us, and the *corps diplomatique* breathed again. So there will not be war, everyone was saying. *O vanitas vanitatum!* What deceivers we all are!

[Hübner: *Neuf ans de souvenirs d'un Ambassadeur
d'Autriche à Paris*, ed. Hübner, vol. II, pp. 244–5]

Massari's diary, Turin

January 3, 1859. The Count told us . . . "Eastern Europe may burst into flames at any moment. If that happens it'll be a good opportunity for us, but alas, we shall have to resign ourselves to the opposition of England." General Lamarmora [the Minister of War] said, "Then it'll be a matter of a few naval battles." The Count answered with spirit: "But England won't be able to stop us from going to burn down Vienna. Moreover, even if the Italian cause is unpopular in the *City* of London, it isn't unpopular with the English people and the army—English soldiers could never understand fighting against the Piedmontese. And Emanuele d'Azeglio [Piedmontese minister in London] has written saying that recently Lord Palmerston has been more affable and told him: 'If you go to war, try to win and win quickly.' " [p. 106]

January 17. I saw Count Cavour at eleven. He was indignant with England for opposing our plans for war in every possible way, and noted that yesterday evening Sir James [Hudson, the British ambassador] had not been present at the theater. I told him that Sir James is always saying to me: "Take care: Napoleon III is pushing you on, but he will leave you in the lurch." [p. 118]

January 18. I saw Count Cavour again at two-thirty. I showed him letters from Milan, Parma and Florence all indicating the very favorable condition of public opinion. He said: "I think the Austrians now understand their false position. As for the Duchess of Parma, I'm nervous—she's behaving too well. Why don't we transfer her to the throne of Naples? But for the moment Naples must not be touched." We then began talking about the marriage [between the King's fifteen-year-old daughter Clotilde and the forty-six-year-old Prince Jérôme]. I told the Count that the aristocracy is extremely hostile. At first the general public were hostile too, but now have been persuaded that the marriage is in the interests of the country. As a result, the French Prince, despite all the antipathy and repugnance he inspires, will be given a warm welcome. [p. 119]

January 19. At midday I called on Sir James; the much-heralded note from London had arrived this morning at last, and he has made its contents known to Count Cavour. It is dated January 13 and signed by Lord Malmesbury. It reproves Victor Emmanuel's Speech from the Throne for its belligerent tone, and reminds Count Cavour of the responsibility he is assuming before man and God— God is specifically invoked. It refers to the evils and horrors of war, to the unleashing of anarchy, to the appearance of pretenders to various thrones, etc. Lord Malmesbury has also written to Lord Loftus [the British ambassador] in Vienna—a despatch dated January 12. He has told him quite clearly that in case of war England will preserve her neutrality and will not support Austria. The despatch calls on Count Buol to preserve the peace and to add his efforts to those of France to better conditions in Rome and Naples. It praises the Archduke Maximilian [Austrian Governor-General of Lombardo-Venetia]; it speaks of Austria as an *Italian Power* (what blasphemy!). [p. 120]

January 20. I called on Hudson. He handed me the despatch because Lord Malmesbury wants the King to see it. Poor fellow, he thinks it will make a big impact! Then Sir James embarked on his favorite theme, that of not trusting N. III, and he insisted that the latter does not want war. This is what Lord Cowley has written, telling him that Piedmont would not get Verona nor Peschiera nor Mantua [the main Lombard fortresses], and would be risking her freedom; and Italy would merely change masters. Sir James believes that Cavour should now do no more than urge N. III to force the Pope to make reforms. Obviously Sir James is very agitated and upset because he feels the falsity of his position. This makes me unhappy, for he is a real gentleman. I told him outright that Cavour would be finished if he did not go to war, and the honest liberal party in Italy would be at an end. He replied that Lord Malmesbury's despatch to Lord Loftus is confidential, and that Lord Malmesbury instructed him yesterday by telegram to tell Count Cavour that England has urged Austria to observe her treaties, because there was some fear that Austria might invade Piedmont. Hudson added that this was why he omitted reading to Count Cavour the phrase in the despatch to Lord Loftus concerning England's absolute neutrality, because it would have made Count Cavour feel safer and so bolder. He ended up by telling me outright what I had already supposed for some time, that should complications arise in eastern Europe, *England would then support Austria*. [pp. 121–2]

[Massari: *Diario dalle cento voci*, ed. Morelli]

Sir James Hudson was a fairly consistent Italophile, and telling Massari privately that British official threats were partly bluff was a useful service to Cavour. Another very helpful fact for the Prime Minister was that the king finally overcame his sense of outrage at Clotilde marrying that middle-aged *roué*, Jérôme Napoleon—it was to be an unhappy marriage, for the couple soon separated, and Jérôme was disinherited by the Napoleon family. The emperor's insistence on this dynastic alliance had been quite obsessive, and Cavour, in return for his complaisance on this point, now obtained a formal treaty with France. In order to obscure the connection between marriage and alliance, the treaty was backdated to 1858. It was also marked "Secret and always to remain secret."

As Louis Napoleon had eventually been obliged to inform the French Foreign Office of his secret negotiations with Cavour, officialdom was able to intervene and make the treaty less generous than what was suggested at Plombières. No mention was now made of what territory would be annexed to Piedmont after the war, except that the papal Legations were by implication excluded. Nothing was said about the rest of Italy. The sacrifice to France of Nice as well as Savoy was specifically mentioned. And all French expenses on the war were to be refunded by Piedmont. Financial and military conventions were also concluded in which a good deal more was promised by Cavour than his country could conceivably have been able to pay.

Treaty between France and Piedmont, January 1859 (but antedated to December 12, 1858)

Article 1. If aggression by Austria leads to war between the Piedmontese King and the Emperor of Austria, an offensive and defensive alliance will come into force between the Emperor of the French and the King of Piedmont-Sardinia.

Article 2. The aims of the alliance will be to liberate Italy from Austrian occupation, to satisfy the wishes of the people, and to end the complications which threaten war and keep Europe unsettled. The object would be, if the issue of the war so permit, to create a Kingdom of Upper Italy with about eleven million inhabitants.

Article 3. The Duchy of Savoy and the Province of Nice will, by the same principle, be reunited to France.

Article 4. Whatever happens in the war, it is expressly stipulated that the interests of the Catholic Religion and the sovreignty of the Pope shall be maintained.

Article 5. The cost of the war will be born by the Kingdom of Upper Italy.

Article 6. The High Contracting Parties will accept no overtures for peace without previous agreement . . .

Military convention, Article 1. The allied forces in Italy shall rise to about 300,000 men, of which 200,000 will be French and 100,000 Piedmontese . . .

Financial convention, Article 1. All the expenses of the war will be reimbursed to France by annual payments of one tenth of all the revenues of the Kingdom of Upper Italy.

[*Il carteggio Cavour-Nigra*, vol. I, pp. 312–14]

Cavour's telegram to General Durando, Piedmontese ambassador in Constantinople, January 20, 1859

MARRIAGE PRINCE NAPOLEON, together with offensive and defensive treaty of alliance. War probable in May. Have decided to favor revolution in Hungary. But in agreement with General Klapka. He counts on support of new government in Serbia, especially on Garatchin. While maintaining absolute secrecy about our plans, show yourself very favorable to Serbs, and get in touch with some of Hungarian officers now in Turkey.

[C. Bollea: *Una silloge di lettere del risorgimento* (Turin, 1919), p. 138]

Cavour to G. La Farina of the National Society, February 1859

SIGNOR LA FARINA's opinion is requested on the following plan:—

The moment for action in Tuscany has come. But for the time being we must avoid both revolution and all friction between the liberals and the army.

The agitation must be organized in such a way that future prospects are not compromised or committed. It must be based on ideas of nationality and national independence more than on those of individual freedom; it should be such that all liberals, of whatever kind, can participate; and such that the army can accept without betraying military honor.

Hence the insurgents should:—

1) Demand the abrogation of every treaty between Tuscany and Austria.

2) Demand the union of the Tuscan and Piedmontese governments—with the object of promoting, whether by diplomacy or if necessary by arms, the independence of Italy and the reform of her present condition.

3) Proceed first by means of petitions, subsequently by demonstrations.

> [*Lettere edite ed inedite di Camillo Cavour*, ed. L.
> Chiala (Turin, 1884), vol. III, pp. 22–3]

Garibaldi, now a Piedmontese general, gives his orders for the future war, March 1, 1859

1) WHEN WAR breaks out between Piedmont and Austria, you will rise to the cry of "*Viva* Italia and Victor Emmanuel! Out with the barbarians!"

2) If a rising is impossible, able-bodied young men should go to the nearest city where insurrection is succeeding or looks like succeeding, if possible choosing the nearest town to Piedmont itself, and there all Italian forces will concentrate.

3) You will try hard to beat or disorganize the Austrian army, cutting communications, breaking bridges and telegraph communications, burning stores of clothes, food and fodder, and holding courteously as hostages any senior officials of the enemy and their families.

4) You will never be the first to fire on Italians in the enemy army, or on the Hungarians; but will try hard to win them over and welcome any of them as brothers.

5) Any of the regular Austrian troops who desert must be sent at once to Piedmont.

6) Where the insurrection wins, the person who enjoys most local confidence and esteem will take over military and civil command as Provisional Commissioner of King Victor Emmanuel; and he will remain until the Piedmontese government sends a replacement.

7) The Provisional Commissioner will abolish the food taxes, the poll tax and family tax, and all imposts which do not exist in Piedmont.

8) Ten youths in every thousand between the ages of 18 and 25 will be conscripted. Volunteers will be accepted between the ages of 26 and 35. All conscripts and volunteers will be sent at once to Piedmont.

9) A Council of War will be at once chosen to judge and punish within twenty-four hours any offense against the national cause or against the lives and property of peaceful citizens. Every class and rank must be treated the same way. No one shall be judged for political offenses which preceded the insurrection.

10) No clubs or political journals will be allowed, but an official bulletin must be published with what news you think the public should know.

11) Suspend all officials and magistrates who oppose the new order, but proceed with caution, and only on a provisional basis.

12) You must keep the most severe and relentless discipline, applying military law as it applies in time of war, and being inexorable with deserters.

[G. Garibaldi: *Scritti politici e militari*, ed. D. Ciàmpoli (Rome, 1907), vol. I, pp. 86–8]

Mazzini astonished Louis Napoleon by the speed at which he managed to obtain top secret material: his mysterious sources of information were one reason why this poor, lonely exile was so feared in high places. Rumors of the alliance brought out Mazzini's best pamphleteering style, for it was urgently necessary to warn the world and Italy that it was a Machiavellian scheme by Cavour to change Italian patriotism from a revolutionary and democratic movement into something purely governmental and conservative. Alliance with despotism and reliance on a foreign army were both major sins in Mazzini's book, and hence immoral as well as inexpedient. He claimed to have over 140 signatures to this protest, including the higher command of Italian republicanism —Saffi, Mario, Crispi, Pilo, De Boni, and Campanella. As a good pamphleteer, Mazzini did not wait to obtain all these signatures before printing them, but simply assumed that his friends and disciples would sign if they could.

Mazzini's public declaration, London, February 28, 1859

THE UNDERSIGNED, all of them, independently of any special association to which they may belong, republicans by conviction, believe it to be their duty toward their Italian brothers and themselves, publicly to declare in their own name, and in that of their friends to whom publicity is forbidden, the course which it is their solemn purpose to pursue in the crisis now impending over Italy. They believe this duty to be all the more sacred because they have seen, with deep grief, that a fraction of Italians holding the same faith has been led away by illusions—honorable in themselves, but approved fatal—from the straight path, and the true flag; they believe it all the more urgent, because, through misrepresentations and calumnies unworthy the Italian cause, the republicans are in danger of seeing their intentions mistaken and their requirements exaggerated.

In the supposition, more than probable, that a war is approaching in Italy, between Austria on the one side and the Piedmontese Monarchy and Imperial France on the other, the undersigned:

Convinced:—

That peoples cannot redeem themselves or make of themselves nations through a lie, but only through principles, an earnest adoration of truth, and testimony bravely borne to conscious right;

That the unity and liberty of an oppressed and dismembered people cannot be attained by the concessions or gifts of others, but must be conquered by the energetic efforts and sacrifices of the believers in that unity and liberty;

That no nationality can be founded by foreign arms, but only by the battles of those who are called to compose and represent that nationality . . . ;

Convinced:—

That without unity there is no country;

That without national sovereignty there is no nation;

That without liberty, true liberty for all, there is no independence;

That the country of the Italians embraces the whole extent of territory between the frontier of the Alps and the farthest shores of Sicily;

That national sovereignty consists in the free choice by the vote of the people of the institutions which give form to the internal life of the nation . . . ;

That any war wherein Italians should combat in the name of independence, disjoined from that of liberty, would lead to tremendous delusions, and the mere substitution of new masters for old;

That any war in which the Italians should delude themselves with the idea of conquering liberty and independence under the auspices of, or through the alliance of, Louis Napoleon Bonaparte, would be alike a folly and a crime; a folly, because Louis Napoleon Bonaparte cannot, without self-destruction, establish by force of arms in Italy the liberty he has drowned in blood in France; a crime, because to make alliance with despotism is to deny those principles which justify and render sacred the Italian cause, to break those bonds of brotherhood with the peoples which have made of the Italian a European cause, and lower the banner of the nation from the elevation of a *right*, to drag it through the mud of a local *egotism;* and a crime because Louis Napoleon Bonaparte, seeking to gain over that public opinion in France which is daily becoming more adverse to him, and to withdraw the thoughts of his subjects from liberty by the fascination of conquest and territorial aggrandizement, has no other object in entering Italy but the acquirement of an increase of territory as the price of his aid, the establishment in Italy of a branch of his dynasty, and the realization of the Napoleonic idea that the Mediterranean must become a *French lake;*

That between the combatants for an Italian country and Louis Napoleon Bonaparte stands the indelible eternal protest of the blood of Rome [shed by French soldiers in 1849];

That, unless for the cry of *Out with the Austrians!* be substituted the cry of *Out with the Foreigner!*, the war neither is, nor can become, national;

That a war yoked to the alliance and designs of Louis Napoleon Bonaparte can never have for its purpose or result the unity of Italy, which is repugnant to his ambitious projects, and declared by him impossible;

That to rise in insurrection and battle for the sake of a single fraction of Italy, leaving the rest a prey to tyranny, misrule, and dismemberment, would be to betray alike our country, our honor, our oaths, and our future;

That an alliance between the Piedmontese Monarchy and Louis Napoleon Bonaparte would render inevitable a European coalition against the cause patronized with views of conquest by him, and that the mere probability of that alliance has already deprived Italy of much of the favor with which she was regarded by all Europe;

They declare:—

That if the Italian war be initiated under the direction or patronage of Louis Napoleon Bonaparte, or even in alliance with him, they will sorrowfully abstain from taking part therein;

That in as far as the Piedmontese Monarchy is concerned, the present question is not, in their eyes, a question of republicanism, but of unity and national sovereignty;

That reserving their right of vote, and of peaceful propagandism, they, now as ever ready to sacrifice the immediate triumph of their individual belief to the welfare or opinion of the majority, would follow the Piedmontese Monarchy to the field, and use their every endeavor to promote the fortunate issue of the war, *provided that its explicit aim was National Italian Unity;*

That having all of them taken part in past times, in counsel and on the field, in the Italian war against the dominion usurped by Austria over their country, they are ready now to fight to free their country from that usurpation; but having been betrayed in '48 upon the very grounds (then solemnly accepted) which they now again propose, they have the right of holding themselves independent in their actions, and of assuming no obligations save toward their country, until they have some explicit guarantee as to the intention of the Piedmontese government.

[*Scritti edite ed inedite di Giuseppe Mazzini*, ed. M. Menghini (Imola, 1933), vol. LXIII, p. 186]

Cavour had what looked an impossible task. He had to tell such people as Garibaldi and La Farina that war was decided; yet, if the existence of the treaty once became public knowledge, Austria would not be the aggressor and hence France would no longer be bound to fight. Louis Napoleon simply could not afford a war which French and European public opinion thought that he had deliberately manufactured for selfish reasons.

Another difficulty was that Cavour had to keep the allegiance of Garibaldi and the militants on the Left at the same time as he had secretly promised Napoleon that the war would not be too "popular" or revolutionary; in other words, he had to make revolutionary forces enthusiastic over what he privately knew would not be allowed to become a revolutionary war.

At the same time he tried to organize apparently spontaneous demonstrations in various parts of Italy in order to prove that liberation by Piedmont was ardently desired. Indeed, when the demonstrations did not happen he was mortified; and yet their failure was largely his own fault, for he had had to give specific instructions that the movements should on no account be too popular.

Yet another problem was that he would have to increase taxes and obtain a huge loan without being able to explain why he needed them. Hence there was a fair amount of opposition and some untoward scenes in parliament. The Minister of War, moreover, knew all the time that the army was quite unready to fight, and unfortunately he told the French General Staff that he could not truly support the Prime Minister's wild, purely intuitive policy.

Then the suspicious British needed very careful treatment. First Cavour went on doing his best to tell them of his dedicated and unqualified labors on behalf of peace, but in fact they knew perfectly well that he was bent on provoking a major war from which most of Europe—and British interests in particular—might suffer. Once or twice Cavour became almost deranged with anxiety over this. He spoke of fighting against England, and even of fighting single-handed against Austria and England combined. Then he thought that Russia might come into the war on his side, and America too, and some of the Swiss cantons. There was to be a vast movement in the Balkans and a sea of blood.

Fortunately for Cavour, Sir James Hudson at Turin was friendly and on the whole reported only the right things to London. But, in mid-February, Hudson was instructed to ask an embarrassing question about Piedmont's grievances against Austria. This question Cavour could not truthfully answer without ruining all his hopes. What he wanted was not liberal reforms in Lombardy-Venetia—on the contrary, Maximilian's reforms in Lombardy were one of his main grievances. What Cavour wanted, quite simply, was war; and yet it was also vital to make it seem that peace-loving Piedmont was being bullied by an aggressive Austria.

The Prime Minister was thus in a false position, and this was partially exposed when the British Foreign Secretary, Malmesbury, replied to his protestations of innocence by insisting that it was obviously Piedmont and not Austria who was being provocative. If this could be said publicly, the treaty was void. So Costantino Nigra was again sent urgently to Paris. Nigra, young and handsome, had lately become Cavour's closest friend and was also a great favorite of both Louis Napoleon and the empress.

Massari's diary, Turin

February 4, 1859. I called on Hudson who once more emphasized the Roman question and told me that if Piedmont increased her territory she would lose her freedom. To this I replied that in our present position we were concerned with national independence and not with individual liberties. [p. 130]

February 17. Lord Cowley [British ambassador at Paris] has written to Sir James informing him that N. III had told him how pained he was that all his [Napoleon's] entourage were opposed to war. Napoleon had said that Victor Emmanuel and Cavour had lately been urging him to mobilize an observation corps on the Alps in view of the imminent threat from Austria; and that General Niel [French field marshal who had just been to Turin for military talks] had reported: "No one in Piedmont wants war except Count Cavour, Rattazzi and a few radicals: even Lamarmora, the Minister for War, is against it." Hudson concluded that, for the time being, peace is certain and therefore Piedmont should call a halt. I answered him that we can now no longer turn back. The reading of these documents and my conversation with Sir James distressed me greatly: I hope I am mistaken, but I fear England is abandoning us.

At half past one I went to give this disagreeable news to Count Cavour at the Ministry of Foreign Affairs. He was irritated but did not lose his composure. He said: "Tell Hudson that I shall expect him tomorrow. I am not put out: I shall be sorry if England manages to influence N. III, but my resolution is unchanged. We shall make war on Austria, even if we have to fight England too. As I told Sir James several years ago, I'm quite resigned to seeing Genoa bombarded by the English" . . .

I rounded off the evening at the *Fiorio* with F. Perrone: he is leaving for Florence tomorrow; this morning Count Cavour told him in no uncertain terms that it was necessary to stir up agitation in Tuscany [Perrone was an official in the Piedmontese embassy at Florence]. [pp. 140–1]

February 18. Cavour told me . . . "I now view it as certain that England will be against us: but what can we do? We can't turn back or become friends with Austria so as to please England. In any case Austria will be torn to shreds (the Count uttered these last words with an unusual and electrifying vigor). Even England had better look out. She risks having *Brother Jonathan* against her at sea, and losing Jamaica, Canada and the West Indies, all for the wonderful advantage of gaining the Ile de Bourbon and the shame of helping Austria." How can one fail to admire a man who talks and acts like this! [p. 142]

February 25. The Count said: "If Russia is with us we can laugh at England. We once conquered the whole world; and we shall do so again. My reply to England is ready, but before handing it to Hudson I must show it to the King." Then he ordered an usher to summon the Minister for War. The Minister came immediately: the Count hurried forward to meet him and said in an excited voice: "No one is indispensable here. General Niel looks on you as one of the partisans of peace. N. III himself said so to Cowley." The general was deeply upset, and answered, "That's too much. When Niel was here we simply had not begun to prepare for war and I was afraid of Austrian aggression. I was worried. I was less enthusiastic than you, certainly, but I never said what Niel attributes to me. I'm ready to write as much to him, ask for an explanation, or do anything." The Count said: "We must be careful about writing, for neither Hudson nor Massari must be compromised. Anyway Niel has also said to Astengo [a Piedmontese diplomat] 'that the honor of France was not involved and war would be wrong.'" Lamarmora replied: "I'm amazed that N. III should take Lord Cowley into his confidence like that." The Count said, "N. III does it to throw dust into the eyes of the English." I find the Emperor's politics curiously enigmatic. I have unlimited confidence in Count Cavour, but I can neither understand nor approve this tortuous kind of policy. This interchange between the two ministers was deeply upsetting . . .

I read Cavour a letter in which E. N. Browne [correspondent at Paris for the *Morning Post* of London] tells Hudson that the Italians should not count on the English. "We are a falling nation," says that good gentleman, "and Russia, by supporting nationalism, will take England's place in Europe." What a melancholy forecast! But if things go on as they are, it will turn out true. He advises Piedmont to lie low. "That's all very well," the Count said sharply, "but we are going to set fire to Europe. Today Italy is behaving in a way that couldn't have been hoped for a year ago. But I can't treat her peoples like extras in a theater and give them entries and exits according to whim, telling them one day to *get on with it* and the next day to *stay put*." [pp. 147–8]

February 28. I saw the Count and General Lamarmora at the Ministry, and they told me today they were still issuing orders to mobilize our troops at the frontier so as to forestall Austrian aggression. [p. 154]

March 2. We were speaking of the chances of Austrian invasion. The Count said: "Let the Austrians come: we shall beat them." Lamarmora added: "That won't be so easy." The Count replied with an excited and vigorous expression: "The conviction that we can beat them is half the battle."

After twelve I met Count de Saint-Simon [the Prussian ambassador]. I asked him about the chances of Austrian aggression; he answered: "None at all. Austria would never do you such a service. If she attacked you she'd immediately lose all her allies. In Austria, as in France, only the Emperor wants war." [pp. 155–6]

March 6. Went to the Count and found him in a bad mood. I asked him what impression the *Moniteur* article had made on him; he answered with feeling, "Not very good. It is one of N. III's usual tricks. But tell the Milanese they must trust me. So long as my government is in office we shall set fire to the four corners of the world rather than back down. We will be like Samson." [p. 161]

[Massari: *Diario dalle cento voci*, ed. Morelli]

Nigra, from Paris, to Cavour, March 4, 1859

THIS MORNING, without my asking for an audience, the Emperor summoned me to the Tuileries for a talk. He began by confessing that he was in the most difficult and dangerous position conceivable. Certain indiscretions had been committed, some of them unavoidable, so that Europe now guessed our plans; with the result that public opinion, especially in England and Germany, has become scared of French ambition and suddenly turned bitterly against him. He concludes that we must temporarily suspend our plans; as he said, we need a moment's rest before remounting our horse. That rest would give us more time for preparations, because it will take time to reassure public opinion in Europe and complete the *diplomatic campaign* we had already spoken about. When I asked him to be specific, so that I could report him accurately, the Emperor said that it would now be impossible to start the war until the spring of 1860. He told me to let you know this, with an injunction to keep the date absolutely secret, even from Prince Napoleon, and shared only between Count Cavour and himself.

I answered the Emperor that I would faithfully report him. But in my view, as I told him, things have reached such a point in Italy that I would think it a vain hope to calm people and restrain them until next spring, especially if the date must be kept secret . . .

Public opinion here in France, as in Germany and England, is against the war. In Paris, the middle classes, the Stock Exchange, the Orleanists, officialdom, all are against it.

> [*Il carteggio Cavour-Nigra* (Bologna, 1926), vol. II,
> pp. 51–3]

Massari's diary, Turin

March 11, 1859. I spoke to the Count about the suitability of sending Massimo d'Azeglio to London. He answered: "But I shall need him in Rome; particularly if the French garrison there is withdrawn." [p. 167]

March 14. As I was leaving the Ministry I met Rustem Bey [the Turkish minister] who spoke of the war. He told me that, if only Piedmont stood alone, everyone would sympathize with her, but that N. III arouses suspicion on all sides. Unfortunately there is some truth in this; but what can we do? Piedmont was not free in the choice of her allies. Alone she could do nothing. [p. 170]

March 15. General Lamarmora asked me to be seated, and talked about the situation. He is extremely worried. He said. "Cavour is pleased because Nigra writes that N. III is angry with Germany. Cavour is rushing things and is altogether too optimistic. But I see all Europe against N. III, and it's my opinion that French interests will come first and he won't be able to help us. How could he? Yet we cannot attack alone. Another problem is that N. III, like Charles Albert, has the absurd foible of wanting to lead his army in person. England's behavior is contemptible; when she needed N. III she fawned on him; now she's turning her back. However, Napoleon's policy of concealment and expediency is equally unpleasant. French public opinion is mounting against the war. And as for Russia, she will be happy if Austria loses face, but no more." This conversation is very worrying. The general is not a great political brain, but he has feeling and talks frankly. He left me with the very clear impression that he thinks the policy of his distinguished colleague impetuous. [pp. 170–1]

March 28. Hudson took the opportunity, rather unsuitably, to tell me that we are wrong to put the accent on making ourselves a strong state, and we ought to go back to the safer policy of reforms. To this I answered that the whole mind of Italy leant toward forming a strong state. So much the worse for the English if they see no more in this than a "Piedmontese speculation"–the ignorable term is Lord Brougham's. I said that the idea of reforms while Austria was still in Italy is laughable. "If we don't have a strong state," I concluded, "we'll have anarchy." [pp. 183–4]

[Massari: *Diario dalle cento voci*, ed. Morelli]

March and April 1859 were a nightmare for Cavour, and all seemed lost when Louis Napoleon at last agreed to back down and settle matters in congress. The Prime Minister was in despair. Victor Emmanuel hopefully thought that a congress might at least lead to the cession by Austria of Lombardy, but Cavour had set his heart on war. In public he tried to smile so that people would think all was well, but in his heart he sometimes thought of suicide. He once threatened that he might emigrate to America to write a book which would reveal the emperor's part in inciting Piedmont to bring about war.

Cavour to Napoleon III, March 19, 1859

YOUR MAJESTY knows the difficulty of our position. We concerted a plan with Your Majesty by which we would group around us all the live forces of Italy, but without allowing our cause to be contaminated by any revolutionary element. For this we need the help of a great moral force, such for instance as largely came to us from the support of Your Majesty and the weight which this gave us in Europe. But if we now are made to wait outside the door while others discuss the fate of Italy, in a Congress moreover where Your Majesty plays the chief role, the rest of Italy will see us as feeble and powerless. Even in Piedmont, opposition will grow, and it will be hard to go on governing without exceptional measures and the use of force.

I beg Your Majesty to take into account what I here frankly put before you. I am not moved by any puerile vanity or by exaggerated notion of our importance; it is just that our exclusion from a Congress would deprive us of the strength and prestige which we need for that grand enterprise which is our duty and our right and which would for ever be the glory of your reign. Incidentally I think that if you support us by formally asking Piedmont's admission to the Congress, Austria will have to refuse, and we will then escape from this great danger.

If, on the other hand, Austria does agree to debate the Italian Question with us, I think we ought to have the agenda quite clear first. Vienna does not intend to make serious concessions; for instance she will not give up her protectorate over the *Duchies*, nor over Tuscany and the papal Legations; so that she will probably refuse to agree to this preliminary request, in which case it will be her responsibility if the Congress does not take place.

I flatter myself that Your Majesty will know how to frustrate all the attempts of your enemies to prevent you accomplishing the noblest of all tasks. Your wisdom, your prudence, your moderation, and the loftiness of your ideas, will together recover the support of public opinion which may have momentarily wavered. Austria has misjudged you and adopted a menacing or even provocative tone. She is playing the role of aggressor. And this makes me hope that before long she will commit one of those *aggressive acts* which will justify your armed intervention. I hope so with all my heart.

[*Il carteggio Cavour-Nigra*, vol. II, pp. 118–19]

Cavour to Nigra, March 19, 1859

FOLLOWING THE advice of Prince Napoleon, sent to me yesterday by telegraph, I have written to the Emperor to dissuade him from this Congress idea, or at least to ask that Piedmont be allowed to attend. I avoided threats and declamation, but I tried to be as positive as possible. The King rightly observed that, if he wrote too, it would look as though he had lost hope. So he is holding himself in reserve should my letter fail.

I hope that we avoid the Congress, for I cannot see where it would lead us. How the devil could we then start a war? England would never let us raise a real *casus belli* against Austria, and would oppose us if we defied her by being belligerent at the conference table. It would be our ruin unless France were first to agree with Russia what concessions to demand from Austria; only then could we accept it.

It seems to me that the Emperor's position in France is improving. Buol's ugly tone, together with the unbelievable insolence of the official press in Austria, must surely arouse public opinion in France and make it impossible for the Emperor to back down. If he withdraws in front of these insults from Vienna, he will fall lower than Louis Philippe [Orleanist king of France, 1830–48] ever fell. If only he would give up his fears and begin fighting! I promise that Italians would do marvels. In six months we will have 150,000 men under arms, and even if he could spare only 50,000 French troops it would be no purely defensive war. You can count on it! Just wait another four or six weeks and we could explode the mine . . .

Mon cher, I miss you cruelly. You were the only person here on whom I could truly rely.

[*Il carteggio Cavour-Nigra*, vol. II, pp. 116–17]

Cavour, from Paris, to General Lamarmora, Minister of War, March 29, 1859

THE ITALIAN Question has been thoroughly messed up because of unfortunate mistakes and circumstances which I will explain when I get to Turin. Meanwhile, my impression is as follows:

War is inevitable.

It will be delayed for at least two months.

It will be waged on the Rhine as well as on the Po.

If the war is to have a fortunate outcome for Piedmont and Italy, we must be prepared to make the very greatest efforts. The French, who are being dragged into it against their will, will never forgive us if the weight of the enterprise falls mainly on their shoulders. Woe to us if we triumph solely through French help. We will save our country only if we fight better than them and put into the field a larger army than theirs in the event of a general war. [A postscript, in Nigra's hand, adds: "Cavour was not at all satisfied by his conference today with the Emperor and Walewski."]

[*Lettere edite ed inedite di Camillo Cavour*, ed. Chiala, vol. III, pp. 53–4]

The war party in Piedmont were finally saved by the bungling policy of the Austrian emperor, aided by the lack of coordination between Austrian General Staff and diplomats, and above all by Hübner's inability at Paris to gauge the motives and ambitions of Louis Napoleon. Cavour, whose analysis of the French emperor was far more studied and subtle, was at last fully rewarded for his courage, foresight, and tenacity.

Massari's diary, Turin

April 16, 1859. This morning Major Corte brought me a letter from Hudson expounding the views of the British government and requesting disarmament. I was very worried by this letter and took it round to Count Cavour immediately. It made a grievous impression on him; but he was intransigent about rejecting such a demand. . . . He exclaimed emphatically: "I'm not frightened: I'm ready to turn the world upside down. Apart from which, N. III himself has secretly told me to refuse the British request outright." [p. 206]

April 19. At my office I found despatches announcing that France too is proposing disarmament and admission of Piedmont to a general Congress together with all the other Italian states. It is very grave news. Farini and Cusani, who spent about an hour with the Count at the Ministry of the Interior, are worried. There's a real crisis. The meetings of the ministers last night and this morning were stormy; all Count Cavour's colleagues blame him for having put too much faith in N. III. At half past one this morning d'Auvergne sent Aymé d'Aquin to the Count with this disastrous proposal. The Count leapt out of bed and told Aymé very excitedly: "The only

thing left for me now is to blow out my brains." He immediately
sent off a long telegram to Massimo d'Azeglio saying that as France
asks for disarmament, he must submit. He spoke of resignation. He
was annoyed, deeply upset, and alone. But if he resigned—as I said
to Farini and Cusani, who agreed with me—it would be complete
catastrophe. We need to stop that at any price. On my way to
lunch I ran into Count Cavour. Farini was there too. The Count
looked very worried; he said to me in an excited voice and with
impulsive gestures: "English policy has won. All is lost. N. III has
abandoned us." I was completely overwhelmed by his tone and
look; I couldn't think what to say. [p. 212]

April 21. I received a note from West asking me to call on him
immediately. I rushed to the legation, but met West with Saurin
in via Bogino opposite the building where the national debt is
administered. He took a piece of paper from his pocket: it was
a telegram from Lord Malmesbury dated 2 p.m. from London
today. It said to tell Cavour that the Austrian ultimatum was sent
from Vienna on Tuesday evening, in other words that Austria has
entirely rejected the British propositions. The ultimatum has a
three-day limit. The telegram added that the cabinet was meeting
at Lord Derby's house at four. West gave me his usual serious look
and asked: "Are you ready?" "Yes," I answered, controlling with
difficulty my deep agitation; "Yes, we expected this." I accompanied West to the Ministry of the Interior where we found Cavour
and Lamarmora. I entered in quite a frenzy to tell them about the
despatch. The Count leapt up rubbing his hands more energetically
than usual, and told me to bring West in at once. What a moment!
It was a quarter to five. We all remained standing. West read the
despatch in a calm, slow voice; the Count asked him to read it over
again, and when that had been done he said with great dignity: "I
hope you will agree that we have done everything in our power to
avoid a conflagration." [p. 216]

[Massari: *Diario dalle cento voci*, ed. Morelli]

*The Austrian ministers and the Emperor Francis Joseph decide
to send an ultimatum, April 19, 1859*

HIS IMPERIAL MAJESTY referred to the decision taken on April 6
about the possibility of requesting Piedmont to reduce her army to

a peace footing and disband her volunteers corps—with a peremptory demand for an answer within three days. He then asked the Foreign Minister whether this communication had been drafted, whether the moment for presenting it to the Turin cabinet had now come, whether the procedure then laid down should be adhered to, and whether in the case of an unsatisfactory reply the army commander, General Count Gyulai, should put military considerations first and take the offensive immediately.

The Minister, Count Buol, said the note was ready and it should be presented without a moment's delay, otherwise Austria might find her freedom of action restricted as regards Piedmont. The diplomatic situation was such that France—evidently surprised by the support gradually building up in favor of Austria—was already trying to find a way out and withdraw from her former policy. It was therefore possible that Piedmont might accept the advice she would probably get from France, namely to bow to Austria's requirements. Such an act in face of a Great Power would not represent humiliation.

Our note to Turin ought to be presented not by a military functionary but a civil servant of high rank representing the army commander.

As regards the timing of our military offensive, Count Buol thought that the army commander could already begin preparations and concentrate his forces in advanced positions. This would be opportune not only for military reasons but also because it would add force to our diplomatic note. As soon as the reply from Turin was received, Count Gyulai should communicate its contents telegraphically, or say if there was no reply within the fixed time limit. If the three days went by, we should assume that there was an understanding between Piedmont and France. One way or the other we would know whether Piedmont's resistance to our request had found French support, or whether France had yielded to European pressure and persuaded Piedmont to submit. Count Buol considered that this second result was the more likely, so he thought that we should leave the Emperor quite free to decide the best moment for any possible opening of hostilities.

[F. Engel von Janosi: *L'ultimatum austriaco del 1859* (Rome, 1938), pp. 117–18]

16. The Acquisition of Lombardy

Cavour had glibly spoken of putting 150,000 men under arms; but he himself was no military expert and did not believe in discussing detailed policy or its implications with the generals. In practice, with some difficulty, he was able to mobilize 60,000 front-line men, and this of course was in flagrant violation of the treaty with France. When, in January 1859, he was advised that he would need to make more active preparations, he had had to refuse, as he was relying on the French army and did not want Piedmont to seem too obviously bellicose. He also did not want too many potentially dangerous volunteers and reservists. Though he talked of fighting Austria single-handed, in practice he had not done much to persuade the army to make serious strategic plans. Their only plan in fact was to wait for the Austrians to attack—even though, according to General Cialdini, an immediate advance by Gyulai would have found Turin defenseless. An even more serious weakness was that the king again insisted on his constitutional right to act as commander-in-chief and could hardly endure listening to expert advice from Lamarmora and the generals.

Fortunately the French army had a sound professional competence, and its victory at Magenta on June 4 made possible the occupation of Lombardy. At the subsequent and equally victorious battle of Solferino, on June 24, the 110,000 French soldiers were effectively supported by 35,000 Piedmontese.

When the war began, Cavour not only had to act as Prime Minister, but also ran the Foreign Office, the Home Office, and the Ministries of War and of the Navy. The burden was too great. To the annoyance of the king and the generals, he also tried to interfere in strategy and sharply criticized their slowness and inactivity. The king never allowed a mere civilian any say in military matters, and his reply was simply to cut off all communication. When the public at Turin asked Cavour for news of the war, he knew no more than did the newspapers. In normal circumstances he would have resigned, but in wartime there was no effective protest he could make. Subsequently their relations slightly improved.

Cavour to Victor Emmanuel, May 18, 1859

YOUR MAJESTY rightly complains that you have had no letter from me for days and no news of the political situation. My silence was due to my misunderstanding Your Majesty's intentions. Some days ago you wrote, a little angrily, that you wanted no further discussion with me; and then General Della Rocca told me that I would receive no more news from military headquarters. I concluded that you did not want any further correspondence, since discussion and news were both banned. But as I now see I was in error, I gratefully take up my pen to tell you about political developments and about my efforts as Minister of War to carry out Your Majesty's just desires.

Here, briefly, is what has happened in Tuscany. Once the Grand Duke had been chased out, there were two possibilities, either immediate union with Piedmont, or a provisional government. Against a proper union there was a very strong party in Tuscany, which includes some of the most illustrious and respected names in Europe; and even stronger was the opposition of diplomacy, even of *friendly* Russia. But the only alternative would have been a separate Tuscan government, and this might have prejudiced future political developments at the same time as hindering the decisive action needed in time of war. So we decided on a third solution, to leave these questions still open, and to appoint a temporary commissioner who would exercise full powers in your name. For this we chose Boncompagni, who had the confidence of all parties.

[Il carteggio Cavour-Nigra, vol. II, p. 197]

The Piedmontese had at first hoped that Leopold of Tuscany would grant a constitution and side with them against Austria. Cavour had been prepared, as an alternative, to have Boncompagni, his diplomatic representative in Tuscany, overturn the Grand Duke and proclaim fusion with Piedmont. Neither at Plombières nor in the treaty of January 1859 had Napoleon envisaged Piedmontese annexation of Tuscany, but Cavour was now playing his own game, and many new horizons were opening.

On April 27 Leopold fled, but the existence of a strong autonomist movement made immediate annexation by Piedmont impossible. Several times Boncompagni was told to make it quite clear that Turin would respect local autonomy. But Salvagnoli and other autonomists, perhaps fearing social unrest as much as Piedmontese expansionism, requested the help of French troops, and this gave Louis Napoleon an excuse to intervene. Prince Napoleon was sent there with the 5th French army corps, and this was the same man who Salvagnoli had recently been wanting as ruler of an independent Tuscany.

Cavour therefore urgently tried to carry out fusion with Piedmont before Prince Napoleon had time to forestall him. This annoyed the autonomists as much as it annoyed the French. Baron Ricasoli thought that words such as "fusion" and "annexation" betrayed Cavour's Piedmontese loyalties and his unwillingness to fight for a completely unified Italy. Prince Napoleon, on the other hand, chiefly resented that so little assistance for his army was forthcoming in Tuscany. The soldiers of the former Tuscan army often deserted when they found they were expected to fight against Austria, while the new troops raised there for Cavour by General Ulloa were not in fact ready to fight until the war was over.

Cavour to Count Boncompagni, Royal Commissioner in Tuscany, May 20, 1859

IF WE had proclaimed the annexation of Tuscany to Piedmont three weeks ago, it would perhaps have aroused suspicions in Europe. But, now that French troops have arrived there with Prince Napoleon, our annexation will be accepted as a guarantee against possible French ambition in central Italy. At least it will be thought preferable to republicanism or to being given a ruler from Napoleon's family. Neither in Europe as a whole nor in Tuscany itself should we encounter any serious obstacles. Most of the local inhabitants will admit that any other solution is impracticable, and that uncertainty and delay (which might go on for years) would be dangerous . . .

I do not mean that you should provoke annexation straight away. But you should arrange with the local authorities to prepare and direct public opinion toward fusion with us. There are some measures you could take at once. You should declare the Pitti Palace a *national palace*, and open it along with the Boboli Gardens to the public. You should dismiss any officials who oppose what we are doing. Nor should you pay too much regard to any opposition parties . . .

Meanwhile you should carefully study with the aforesaid authorities what would be the best method in course of time for testing the national will. Please let me know if and how we can avoid having recourse to the dangerous expedient of universal suffrage or to the equally dangerous expedient of an elected assembly. Without giving you any precise orders, I suggest as one possible idea that each municipality should individually declare its support for annexation.

[*Il carteggio Cavour-Nigra*, vol. II, pp. 202–3]

Prince Napoleon, from Leghorn in Tuscany, to Cavour,
May 27, 1859

NEITHER CENTRAL Italy itself, nor the officials you have sent here, are all they should be; and indeed a heavy responsibility will be placed on them by history. I have personally met Boncompagni, General Ulloa, the Governor of Leghorn, General Mezzacapo, the Mayor and many others: all seem like sentries without orders, and they possess little if any individual initiative.

I everywhere receive an enthusiastic welcome, with plenty of shouting, flowers and cheers, but when I try to get down to action and concrete facts I find absolutely nothing. In 1848, Italy succumbed to the cry of *Let us go it alone.* Today these particular regions seem to say: *Let French and Piedmontese military power do everything while we sit and watch.* It is a sad and discouraging spectacle. In 1848 people shouted a lot in a disorganized way, but at least they did something; today there is no disorganization, no agitation, and no action whatsoever. I am sure that at Pekin they are doing more for this war of independence than here! History will judge these people severely, and even more severely their rulers. What has been done in a whole month since the revolution? Nothing! I cannot think why the Grand Duke left. Those who gave him the pretext to go are now acting like schoolboys who know they have done wrong. It is not in this way that a great cause will succeed.

One explanation may be that you do not want to arouse too many liberal feelings because you need to avoid dissension and concentrate the country's forces on fighting. Fine, so long as some real energy is shown in organizing defense! But there is not a single liberty here now which did not exist under the Grand Duke, and perhaps there are even fewer. The same officials are everywhere; the same abuses, even more of them; not even the state lottery has been abolished as a token of morality; there are no munitions, no National Guard; the same small army is still the same and as bad as ever. A few schemes have been outlined on paper. But the volunteers are a joke, and they are commanded by friends of the Grand Duke and of Austria; they are badly armed, badly clothed and badly drilled. People call themselves volunteers, but they spend their time just in cafés and theaters. There are still 30,000 guns not distributed. No preparations have been taken for defense. Not the least effort has been made to arouse any noble sentiments of patriotism.

[*Il carteggio Cavour-Nigra*, vol. II, p. 209]

Massari's diary, Turin

May 26, 1859. After saying good-bye to our friends, I left the station with Minghetti. We spoke of the situation; it is serious. Germany is showing signs of ill-will, and that makes a general war likely, which would be a calamity for us. . . . If Italy comes into being, clearly it will be only because God willed it; men will have done little to deserve it. [p. 256]

May 28. Cipriani, who has come from Tuscany, is a partisan for fusion with Piedmont, but he says that this word "fusion" has turned everything in Florence upside down. There is a chaos of political views. Ridolfi would like a separate ruler chosen from the House of Savoy; Ricasoli wants fusion; Salvagnoli would prefer Prince Napoleon. There are plenty of partisans for Tuscan autonomy, and I think that in last analysis this is the majority view there. [p. 258]

June 16. This morning d'Auvergne [the French minister] told me: "You can rest assured that the Emperor will not give Piedmont an inch more land than he promised her" (in other words his uncle's old Kingdom of Italy). Germany's attitude, the chaos in Tuscany, and the complication of the Roman question make the political situation very grave. It is more necessary than ever to defeat Austria, and soon. [p. 273]

[Massari: *Diario dalle cento voci*, ed. Morelli]

Nigra, from Milan, to Cavour, June 11, 1859

YESTERDAY AND today I have been gleaning information from various sources about how people at Milan look on what has happened, and I am glad to say that without exception people support the King's government as personified in yourself. Your name and that of the King are very popular and everywhere greeted with respect and gratitude. Fusion with Piedmont is not only accepted but positively wanted. No one has any doubt at all about this, and no opposition of any sort is thought possible. On the day that the *Te Deum* was sung, one person was heard advocating that people should cry *Long live Italy* instead of *Long live the King;* but he was beaten until he changed his tune. At the Scala Theater last night the Emperor and the King were greeted by immense and continuous applause. The first decisions by the government were favorably received. The appointment of Vigliani as Governor of Milan was also welcomed. Everyone recognized the need for a strong, resolute government, and any really firm measure is applauded. You might even say that this liking for strong government is being taken too far. But we must take advantage of local support in order to carry out many changes, and do it quickly. . . . In the countryside the peasants are against us, or at least not favorable.

[*Il carteggio Cavour-Nigra,* vol. II, pp. 218–19]

Kept out of military affairs by the king, Cavour applied his enormous energy to schemes for winning still other parts of Italy. The war gave him a splendid opportunity to appeal to patriotic enthusiasm, and the emperor's attention was momentarily distracted. The French victory at Magenta was the signal for the rulers of Parma and Modena to flee, and the Austrians quickly evacuated their garrison posts inside the Papal States. After the Austrians had left, there were also patriotic risings at Bologna, Perugia, and elsewhere.

Cavour was greatly displeased that the local population allowed these enemy troops to retire in peace, and that, even after the Austrians had gone away, many towns made no attempt at all to declare for the national cause. Perhaps his lieutenants had deceived him about the extent of patriotic feeling in the Papal States. Perhaps, as Mazzini did not hesitate to point out, their inactivity followed naturally from Cavour's hostility toward volunteer action, since people had been positively encouraged to await deliverance by the French and Piedmontese armies. Cavour was in familiar difficulties here: even though he wanted the political credit which local insurrection would bring, he could not countenance what he referred to as *émeutes.* The trouble was that popular risings tended to be led by extreme radicals and hence would play into the hands of his political enemies. The mere hint of social revolution was enough to antagonize the solid conservative elements on whom he hoped to rely.

Massari's diary

June 24, 1859. Early this morning on my way to the office I met Pancerasi, a young doctor from Bologna. He told me that if the Pope remains their ruler they will have recourse to the dagger (sic!). These words, uttered so calmly by this young man, shocked and saddened me. There you have Italian national feeling! They talk in general of patriotism and of driving out the Austrians, but then the people of the Romagna don't want the Pope, the Neapolitans raise a purely dynastic question, the Tuscans dispute about autonomy or unification. Holy God, what confusion and what pettiness. I am dismayed by it . . .

Cavour was called to field headquarters by a brusque despatch. He set out at half past seven. He says that if they prevent him taking the provinces of the Romagna he will resign. May God preserve us from this danger. The situation is grave in the extreme. [pp. 279–80]

June 29. Albicini [leader of the deputation from Bologna who had rebelled against the Pope and were in Turin to offer a dictatorship to Victor Emmanuel] was shocked yesterday, because, having told Cavour that the Romagna was falling into the hands of Mazzini, Cavour rejoined: "So much the better; we shall intervene and shoot him." Whereupon Rasponi said, "Then you'll have to shoot an awful lot of other people too." He and his colleagues will hardly go home very edified with what they found here, nor very satisfied with the result of their mission. So, through sheer thoughtlessness and lack of foresight, more seeds of dissent are being sown among Italians! [p. 284]

[Massari: *Diario dalle cento voci*, ed. Morelli]

Cavour to L. C. Farini, de facto *Governor of Modena (supplanting Duke Francis V of Este), July 3, 1859*

I AM sending a letter to you via La Farina who is going to attempt the Venetian enterprise. It would be a great help to our cause if some people in Italy showed themselves ready to make real sacrifices for independence. It must be confessed that *patriotism* has so far given very poor results. Only the regular soldiers and the volunteers have come out well; but that is not enough. The *masses* must do something. I beg you to back up La Farina with all means at your disposal. I have put Ribotti and the volunteer *Cacciatori degli Apennini* at his disposal, and they could replace the *Bersaglieri* if Azeglio withdraws these regular troops from Modena.

The people of the Romagna in their behavior toward the pontifical troops have made me depressed and despairing. You yourself, like Beltrani and Minghetti, used to repeat every time the subject came up that there was no need to worry, since an insurrection would at once break out when the right opportunity presented itself. But now the Austrians have gone, leaving only three thousand f. . . . . . Swiss soldiers, and these are enough to terrorize three million individuals. This gives the direct lie to our statements about the condition of the Romagna. It puts both the Emperor and ourselves in a completely false position.

I have said enough, and recriminations are useless; we must somehow overcome our present difficulties; and for that reason our friends in Bologna must exercise the greatest possible energy and not be so frightened of the common people. Push ahead with the levy and find more money!

> [*La liberazione del mezzogiorno e la formazione del regno d'Italia: carteggi di Camillo Cavour* (Bologna, 1954), vol. V, pp. 434–5]

La Tour d'Auvergne, French ambassador in Turin, to Walewski, French Foreign Minister, July 3, 1859

I BROUGHT Cavour's attention to the grave and inevitable consequences if Piedmont persists in the line of conduct which she seems to have adopted in Tuscany and the papal Legations. To this he replied in a way which, as my colleagues at Rome and Florence know well, is as regular with him as it is *mal à propos*, by assuring me that his policy had been, if not in detail, at least *in general* approved by the Emperor himself. He added that the Emperor recently congratulated him on the tact and loyalty of Piedmontese policy in Tuscany. According to Cavour, His Majesty also approved what had happened in the Legations. The Piedmontese government therefore cannot understand how our ambassador at Rome, who must know the Emperor's mind, should be so surprised.

I then told Count Cavour that I was instructed to mention certain underhand, disloyal maneuvers. I hoped that this would be enough to make him judge them as severely as we did, for there could be no two opinions about it. Then I quoted some of the details given by our representatives at Rome and Florence.

M. de Cavour was visibly embarrassed and nettled. He seems to realize that his unrestrained and ill-considered policy might embarrass the French government and even prove fatal to his own country. This he certainly does not want. But the devouring activity of his mind, together with ambition, and the adventurousness of his spirit if I can put it that way, almost always overcome the counsels of reason in swaying his judgment. Despite appearances, it would be far too much to hope that he will genuinely give up the not entirely loyal and regular behavior which has sometimes brought him success. On this point I have no illusions. I have often been aware that I have little influence over him, and the only real control over his impatience and wilfulness is the firmly and unambiguously expressed wishes of the Emperor . . .

If Cavour has shown little inclination to help us in Tuscany, he is even less trustworthy in the Legations. This area has long been coveted by Piedmont and is now the main preoccupation of her statesmen. England, for obvious reasons, does not discourage this. It cost Cavour a great deal to have to renounce the policy of annexation and dictatorship by Piedmont which he had stated and promised in advance. But in the last resort he is sure that the Emperor will give him these provinces when the time comes for a final settlement; and meanwhile he continues to keep up the expectations of the local population.

[Archives of French Foreign Office, *Sardinia*, 346/ 353]

Cavour's surreptitious activity in the Papal States was one motive in making Louis Napoleon back out of the war, because France was especially vulnerable to Catholic pressure. Cavour had made the unhappy choice of that notorious anti-clerical Massimo d'Azeglio to act as Royal Commissioner, and the Pope could soon provide Napoleon with detailed facts about Piedmontese designs on papal territory here and in the Marches. Papal troops managed to reoccupy Perugia, but a number of atrocities were committed in the process. The leading Catholic newspaper in Turin dared to compare these to what happened during the

Piedmontese bombardment of Genoa in 1849: for this it was suspended and its editor imprisoned.

Louis Napoleon had many other reasons for backing down than just this appeal by the Pope. Not enough Piedmontese troops had been forthcoming to capture the Quadrilateral, and by the beginning of July the king reluctantly admitted to the French that he could not carry out the next stage in the military plan assigned to him. The emperor had also been grumbling about the little help he had received from the Lombards and the fact that they could not even keep supplies moving on the railways. On top of all this, there were signs that Prussia might intervene on the Austrian side in order to preserve Venice, Trieste, and Trent as outposts of greater Germany.

Mazzini had been quite sure all along that Louis Napoleon did not want a strong Kingdom of Italy, only a satellite which he could dominate. The truce which the Emperor suddenly made at Villafranca—without even consulting Cavour—arranged that Austria should give up all of Lombardy except the garrison towns of Mantua and Peschiera which her army was still holding. As the war had been won by France, Lombardy would be given to her, and she could then dispose of it to Piedmont. The Austrian emperor insisted on keeping Venice, and on the Habsburg rulers being returned to Tuscany and Modena. He did not mention Parma, since the duchess was a Bourbon and so presumably not indispensable.

Cavour arrived at army headquarters after all was over, and he at once resigned. Only Nigra was present at his terrible interview with the king, and Nigra never said what happened; but it seems as though Cavour was overcome by another of his momentary aberrations of judgment, just as at the Congress of Paris. A correspondent of the London *Daily News* reported that he had quite lost his usual control. General Della Rocca, who signed the armistice, heard the king's side of the story. So did the British military attaché, Colonel Cadogan of the Grenadier Guards. Cavour evidently wanted to go on fighting, even without France and even if it meant losing Lombardy. For some reason it crossed his mind that England might enter the war on Piedmont's side. He told the king that the armistice would dishonor the monarchy forever. He even started to spread the absurd rumor that the king had deliberately accepted the armistice as a means of replacing him by Rattazzi.

As for Victor Emmanuel, it used to be thought that he, too, was indignant at Napoleon's defection, but Cadogan's report suggests that this was not so. French help alone had won Lombardy for Piedmont, and the king was grateful for it. He told Hudson that Cavour had acted very improperly in antagonizing the French by trying to subvert the Papal States—"vanity and pride had turned his head." Victor Emmanuel also criticized Cavour for taking the easy course of resignation rather than accepting responsibility for the consequences of his own policy.

The settlement agreed by Napoleon and Francis Joseph at Villafranca, July 11, 1859

THE TWO sovereigns support the creation of an Italian confederation under the presidency of the Pope.

The Emperor of Austria cedes to the Emperor of the French his rights over Lombardy except for the fortresses of Mantua and Peschiera. . . . The Emperor of the French will then hand over these territories to King Victor Emmanuel.

Venetia will become part of the Italian confederation, though still belonging to the Austrian crown.

The Grand Duke of Tuscany and the Duke of Modena will return to their states, and will proclaim a general amnesty.

The two Emperors will ask the Holy Father to make certain indispensable reforms in his states.

[*Lettere edite ed inedite di Camillo Cavour*, ed. Chiala, vol. III, p. ccxiv]

Report by the chief of staff, an intimate of the king

JUST AS Cavour was declaiming against the King and everyone else, the door opened and Prince Jérôme Napoleon entered. He took part in the discussion, which was embittered by his abrupt roughness. Cavour declined to entertain the idea of a prolonged armistice, or of treating for peace, save under the condition of the liberation of northern Italy—from the Alps to the Adriatic—as announced by Napoleon III. The Prince replied that we ought to be only too glad to get Lombardy and the Duchies. I remember he wound up by exclaiming, "Do you expect us to sacrifice France and our dynasty for you?" Cavour doggedly replied that promises were promises, and ought to be kept. He threatened to promote and head a revolution rather than leave the work half done, and complained bitterly of the Emperor, of the King, of Lamarmora, of me. I could not blame him. For years he had worked to form an independent Kingdom of Italy, and now he saw his labor stultified, his enterprise diminished and again reduced to anxious expectation. He could not be expected to resign himself and bow to dire necessity as we had done, who, day by day, had watched all the phases of the Emperor's enforced withdrawal. Cavour, as a last resource, wished to carry on the war alone; but 1848 was too fresh in our memories, and, as military men, we declined the responsibility. It would have been folly, or worse, to pit 50,000 or 60,000 men against over 200,000, who, although beaten, had shown such discipline and courage at Palestro and St. Martino. Victor Emmanuel absolutely refused to stake the certain against the uncertain. The annexation of Lombardy and the Duchies doubled his army and increased the chances of ultimately liberating Venice and uniting Tuscany and the Legations, which had repeatedly invoked his aid, to the Kingdom of northern Italy. For my part, I trusted in the great political sagacity of Napoleon III. The ability with which he had prepared the Franco-Sardinian alliance, and gained his end, convinced me that necessity, not caprice, induced him to abandon us.

But Cavour would not listen to argument, and finding the King, the Emperor, and Prince Jérôme Napoleon inexorable, resigned, and left for Turin.

> [E. della Rocca: *The Autobiography of a Veteran,
> 1807–93,* trans. Janet Ross (London, 1899),
> pp. 165–6]

George Cadogan, from Milan, to Lord John Russell, British Foreign Minister, July 14, 1859

It is a difficult task to remember and class in any positive form the information derived from a very discursive interview of upwards of an hour's duration. I will do so however to the best of my ability.

His Majesty was aware that I had been at Villafranca during the conference between the Emperors, and after hearing from me a description of the out-of-doors part of the ceremony, began to fill in the picture with certain details which His Majesty held from the Emperor Napoleon, commencing, however, with the origin of the armistice which, I then heard for the first time, was asked for by His Majesty [Napoleon?]—very much however against his own inclination. "Not," His Majesty added, "that I did not think it a good thing in a strategic point of view, for had hostilities gone on we should perhaps have had to fight another battle with our diminished forces; we would most certainly in the present temper of the troops have been victorious, but at another great loss, perhaps 20,000 men, with nothing gained but the possession of certain positions in front of Verona and all the work yet to do; whilst a month's or six weeks' delay would enable [me] to put my army on a footing of 100,000 men by the arrival of the new levies now organizing; and if the

French produced from 150,000 to 180,000 men, we were more than a match for the 250,000 men the Austrians are still said to have intact. The advantage in an armistice therefore was all on our side, but I objected to being the first to ask for such a thing."

With relation to the interview between the Emperors [Napoleon and Francis Joseph], H.M. said that the Emperor Napoleon had to a certain extent yielded to a spirit of chivalry which prevented him from pressing too hard on a young sovereign who appeared almost to place himself at his mercy. Thus the question of the fortresses on the Mincio, which was mooted at the interview and evasively answered, was not insisted on at the time, and—time being thus gained probably to consult Marshal Hess—was ultimately refused. The King expressed himself much annoyed at this, as he said the first thing he should have to do would be to spend millions in making others to counteract them. His Majesty was no less displeased at the refusal of the Emperor of Austria to treat with him personally and at the expressions used on the occasion, which the King held from the Emperor Napoleon himself—it will be quite sufficient to say the word *"canaille"* was brought in to describe the feeling of animosity entertained by the young Emperor Francis Joseph to all that is Piedmontese. For the rest the Emperor of Austria's tone during the interview is described as being more that of a broken-down man than anything else, and that he implored the Emperor Napoleon not to be hard upon his family—"I beg you to look after them," etc. It is also said that the tears were in his eyes the whole time, "that he was very emotional but very proper," and had produced a very good impression upon his hearer. I was further informed that the Emperor Francis Joseph had been no less affected when he signed the preliminaries of peace brought to him by Prince Napoleon, and that he said in doing so, "I am losing my finest province."

As regards these preliminaries, the King informed me that he at first refused to sign them, but as the Emperor Napoleon insisted, and he was therefore in a great measure helpless, he consented at last, but adding a prefix "so far as I personally am concerned," by which H.M. explained to me that he meant his consent to the annexation of Lombardy, etc., but not to clauses such as that regarding the fortresses which affects the safety and integrity of the provinces in question—at least so I understood H.M.'s explanation of this point. His Majesty seemed to own that a great deal had been done, but [was] doubtful as to whether in its present shape the treaty would be a guarantee against another war. This was however more said with the tone of misgiving and real anxiety that it should be otherwise than with any appearance of menace or satisfaction. In point of fact His Majesty seemed to me personally quite contented with what had been done, urging the nature of his life and tastes in support of his disclaimer as to being moved by ambition in the part he had played. H.M. said that, if left to his own choice, his life would be spent hunting, traveling or soldiering, that he hated "his life as a King" and only followed it because it was his duty to do so—"I am an upright person and I will do my best to carry out the task which God imposed on me. I try to tell my subjects what they must do for their happiness, but I don't go out of my way to correct them when they are wrong. As for this war, my poor father died leaving me only debts: I have paid off the monetary ones, and now I am paying the rest."

After this His Majesty talked of Count Cavour who had that day tendered his resignation. I think H.M. was much disturbed at it, although professing that it was of no importance now: "He is a muddle-head who is always pushing me into some wasps' nest or other. Cavour is mad. I have often told him he was off his head. He goes off playing with follies like this rising in the Romagna, and heaven knows what else. But he is finished now. He did a good job, but he is finished." His Majesty also gave an amusing description of his having put Count Cavour under arrest before the outbreak of the war for crying out at the top of his voice every species of accusation against France and the Emperor: luckily, His Majesty added, "that lucky ultimatum" came and Cavour reappeared rubbing his hands and quite contented. To my professed incredulity as to Count Cavour's being out of office long, the King gave an apparently very serious denial, but I must say nevertheless that general opinion goes the other way here.

His Majesty enter'd also into his differences with the Pope who, he said, had threatened to excommunicate him, a proceeding which on any merely temporal question was out of all reason and at which he would snap his fingers (using a much more forcible phrase); however, it appear'd His Holiness had thought better of it. Finally His Majesty expressed himself as quite taken aback by Napoleon's sudden peacemaking with all its attendant circumstances, but explains it by the only fact in this narration which may be considered important if true, *viz.*, that Napoleon is unable to continue the war for which he was in reality anything but prepared.

[*Le relazioni diplomatiche fra la Gran Bretagna e il regno di Sardegna*, ed. G. Giarrizzo (Rome, 1962), vol. VII, pp. 385–7]

17. Tuscany, the Romagna, and the Duchies

After Villafranca, a new government was formed by Lamarmora and Rattazzi. This government proceeded to annex Lombardy, even though French garrisons remained there. Care was taken not to push Piedmontese claims in central Italy, for it was important not to offend the French. Parma, Modena, Tuscany, and the Romagna had all set up provisional regimes during the war, and these provisional governments did not need to be so cautious. Each of them now supervised the election of an assembly; and each assembly then defied the arrangements made at Villafranca by declaring the former dynasties deposed and demanding annexation to Piedmont. There was no time to waste in political niceties. Montanelli in Tuscany was almost alone among the liberals in protesting at the dictatorial methods adopted by the provisional governments. Most of the other delegates were perfectly happy to accept annexation even without debate.

The British tried to lend some help to this development, but Louis Napoleon was vexed, for it was in breach of his formal undertaking to Austria and of his obligations to the Pope. Nevertheless, though France renounced her claim to Savoy and Nice, and asked the Piedmontese for only a small part of the expenses of the war (which Cavour had undertaken to pay in full), the emperor found that the armistice had left him with much less authority in Italy than before. He first tried to persuade Piedmont to be content just with Parma. Then he produced various schemes for an Italian confederation which would have allowed the former dynasties to return. But when Farini, Ricasoli, and the provisional governments in central Italy refused to yield, he had no means of coercing them save by main force, and that was unthinkable. By December 1859 he, too, was therefore trying to persuade the Pope to give up the Romagna.

Diplomatic circular by L. C. Farini, dictator of Modena,
August 25, 1859

THE PRELIMINARIES of Villafranca left Modena once again to create her own government. I agreed to become Dictator as I was unable to refuse the pressing invitations made to me by the various town councils. But I promised to convoke a National Assembly to set up a legitimate authority and give voice to the political wishes of the people. Speedily putting this into practice, I published an edict giving the vote to all literate citizens, for this would show a genuine popular will while at the same time paying regard to the political and social condition of the country . . .

We even took scrupulousness to the point of forbidding any public manifestation of support for any group or candidate. No pressure at all was exercised, not even the pressure afforded by popular passions. Keeping order was the best guarantee of electoral freedom. No violence was committed, no threat pronounced. If liberal candidates everywhere obtained a shattering majority, if the voting was almost unanimous, that just shows the rigorously disciplined spirit among the electors. At Modena, as in the other central Italian states, it is highly significant that the partisans of the deposed Duke, in other words those most devoted to authority and conservatism, were realistic enough not to think of a restoration which might prevent a lasting social peace and tranquil political development. While not actually helping the revolution, they accepted the *fait accompli*, since they preferred law and order to any more conspiracies and revolts.

Calm, however, did not signify indifference. Almost all who were allowed to vote responded by inscribing their names on the roll and turned up to place their votes in the urn. And I insist on this fact, because our only justification in the eyes of Europe must be that conferred by popular opinion manifested in a legitimate way . . .

By now you will have heard of the unanimous decisions of the National Assembly of the Modenese Provinces. One decree pronounced the deposition of Duke Francis V and the perpetual expulsion of any prince of the House of Habsburg-Lorraine. A second decree then proclaimed annexation of the Modenese Provinces to the Kingdom of Piedmont-Sardinia under the constitutional scepter of our valiant and loyal King Victor Emmanuel.

Finally the Assembly prorogued itself having confirmed me in those powers which at the first meeting I had placed in its hands . . .

Duke Francis V, you will know, was the most unpopular of all the rulers in Italy. The people of Modena, keenly alive to the principle of nationality, knew that by turning him out they were turning out Austrian influence. One could have no illusions over a prince who sided with Austria against France and Piedmont, a prince who, in a treaty of December 24, 1854, declared that his states belonged to the league by which Austria defended her position in Italy. Nor was his method of government merely the result of weakness or bad advice; he was personally identified with it, by character and by reactionary convictions.

A special Commission is now publishing documents to show how useless it would be to hope for any reform from a ruler who publicly rejoiced that the number of pupils in his schools was being reduced, who with his own hand put flogging into the civil code, who wrote letters to his Foreign Minister which would make any honest man indignant, who addressed violent and brutal reprimands to the courts if their judgments displeased him, who constantly interfered with the course of justice and made a confusion between his own wishes and the law which would have better suited a tribal chief. An Austrian by birth and feeling, he belonged to a dynasty foisted secretly on Modena by a treaty of May 11, 1753, between the Empress Maria Theresa and Francis III of Este. Then, after a happy and flourishing interval as part of Napoleon's Kingdom of Italy, the dynasty was again imposed on Modena by the Congress of Vienna. Francis V had no other roots in the country than the bitter memories of his father's tyranny. His House has been chased away by four revolutions and as often brought back by foreign arms.

This is why it would be impossible to restore that reciprocal confidence between ruler and subjects without which constitutional and representative government would merely set up an impossible antagonism in the institutions of the state . . .

A defensive alliance has now been signed between Modena and Tuscany. The government of the Romagna has asked to join it, and this has been agreed. The alliance will be completed by the accession of the Duchy of Parma and Piacenza. This League has, as its first aim, to unite Tuscany, the Modenese Provinces, Parma and Piacenza in resisting the restoration of their deposed dynasties, and to defend the papal Legations against any attack by the mercenaries of the pontifical government.

[*Epistolario di Luigi Carlo Farini*, ed. L. Rava (Bologna, 1935), vol. IV, pp. 291–301]

Massari's diary

October 10, 1859. At half past four I called on Cavour at home. I showed him Sir James's letter [Hudson, the British ambassador in Turin] advising a rapid proclamation of a Regency [i.e., by a prince of the Savoy House over central Italy]. While reading the letter he became very agitated and nearly tore it up: "They've ruined everything; Minghetti involving Prince Carignano directly! It seems incredible. I'm becoming more and more convinced that what one needs in politics isn't cleverness but common sense. Now there's nothing more to be done. Victor Emmanuel has consulted Napoleon III, who has said No: so there it will stop. They should have proclaimed their Regency at once after the deputations from central Italy had been received. I told Farini as much through that wretch Cavallini, but the government didn't agree . . ."

Cavour then spoke of the King. "He's a gentleman, and he lets one go one's own way. If I'd consulted him we wouldn't have entered the Crimean War or made the French alliance. With him you have to act first and speak afterwards; but you must always uphold the King's prestige at all costs. We need him. He gave me *carte blanche* in politics. He's annoyed with me now because I interfered in his private affairs. But if you act first and tell him afterwards, in the end he approves." [pp. 388–9]

[Massari: *Diario dalle cento voci*, ed. Morelli]

Walewski, from Paris, to La Tour d'Auvergne, October 12, 1859

THE RECENT despatch by the Turin cabinet [of September 28, sent to its diplomatic representatives abroad] will, if published, result only in raising unrealizable hopes and so delaying the pacification of central Italy. Such pacification ought to be the wish of everybody and especially of the Piedmontese government.

Piedmont is setting herself up as the representative and protector of the Assemblies which now exist in central Italy. But she cannot conceal that these Assemblies have been elected and summoned in exceptional circumstances which hardly guarantee a free and reliable vote. Apart from the question of universal suffrage, assertive minorities in such moments of trouble and agitation can often impose their opinion on a country; so one cannot be sure that the votes lately brought to Turin reflect majority opinion.

The French government sets a high value on the expression of popular will, for it bases its own strength on this very thing. But equally one must take other facts into account, for instance questions of expediency, promises made, or rights previously acquired. The treaty of Villafranca, by giving Lombardy to Piedmont, opened what was in fact a new era for Italy, and future developments could safely be left to time and the wisdom of the various Italian governments. But it will endanger the other results of that settlement if Piedmont tries to precipitate events and extend its terms unduly.

Every contract, by its very nature as a contract, implies give as well as take, and it is wrong to repudiate contractual obligations once you have gained from them. The preliminaries agreed at Villafranca, and the treaty negotiations at Zurich, at the same time as they give Lombardy to Piedmont, allow the sovereigns of the central Italian states to return to their thrones with their old rights intact. The two things are connected. If Piedmont opposes the return of these sovereigns (or if she so much as countenances the possibility of annexing central Italy), that would nullify the cession of Lombardy.

I consider that we are giving one more proof to the Piedmontese government of our friendly attitude if we draw their serious attention to the gravity of the situation and show them what must follow from engagements already made. We shall be quite firm about this. We have carried out the task we undertook. But if we are to enforce those clauses which favor Italy, it is essential to preserve those which favor Austria. Otherwise Austria may maintain her own right by force of arms, and France would not and could not then support Piedmont in repudiating or violating the original armistice terms.

Please see that General Dabormida [the Foreign Minister] is quite clear on this matter, and I authorize you to let him read this despatch.

[French Foreign Office Archives, *Sardinia*, 347/236]

It took some time before the king realized how much he still needed Cavour. Lamarmora was a mere stopgap Prime Minister: he dreaded responsibility and was so near-sighted that he could scarcely read official documents. Having no head for policy, he remained subservient to Cavour, and without his mentor could now only mark time. The idea of supervising new elections and facing parliament was out of the question as far as he was concerned. So for six months the king was allowed to pursue his own hobbyhorses. Victor Emmanuel thought that he might persuade either Austria or the Pope to sell some of their Italian territory. Where the money was to come from did not greatly concern him.

Note by Archbishop Charvaz of Genoa, on a conversation with King Victor Emmanuel, October 15, 1859

"Events in the Romagna," said the King, "have nothing to do with me. Cavour and Napoleon planned all that, with no reference to me, by exploiting the inexperience and weakness of the Regent." The King used a coarse word against Cavour, and said he never wanted to see him again. "It was not I who sent Azeglio to Bologna. I wanted to have nothing to do with the Papal States, but they intervened there despite me. I agree I received a deputation from the Romagna, but that was only on Napoleon's advice, who told me to receive them as I had met those from Tuscany and the Duchies."

"But, Sire, Napoleon was playing an unworthy game, and you should not have followed him."

"Don't be so surprised. Napoleon loves that kind of confusion. Cavour was Napoleon's man. But he won't have the chance to be it again."

"Sire, you must stop what is happening. It is neither just nor honorable for you. It will have the gravest consequences. And where will it all end?" The King then said that the central Italian states were voting by universal suffrage. To which I said that this was a dangerous means which he would never allow in Piedmont itself; and I asked if the vote would be free of all pressure.

"It will be free," said he, "and I think it will go against the Pope. If it supports the Pope, so much the better, and I will be free of a tiresome difficulty. But if the election goes against him, I shall not know what to do."

After a moment's thought he asked whether the Pope might cede the Romagna to him for a sum of money. I said this was impossible, for the Pope had sworn to keep for his successors the patrimony of St. Peter. At which the King mentioned that St. Peter never had any patrimony, and the Pope at least did not need such a large one. He added that Piedmont could guarantee the rest of the Papal States as well as paying handsomely for the Romagna.

I replied: "Sire, the Pope can never give up any part of his domain for money. He would be blamed by everyone. He must keep it as he found it, and it is not too large for the maintenance of his dignity and his responsibilities. Humbert II of Savoy used to have far less land than Your Majesty now has, but would you have approved of it being wrested from him by force or for money? You speak of guaranteeing an ample revenue to the Pope, but what would happen to this if you had a war or a quarrel with the papacy? Does Naples go on paying the white palfrey to the Pope, or do you pay him the ten thousand crowns and chalice which your predecessors guaranteed to the Pope in return for his investing your dynasty with the lands you now possess?"

The King saw the force of these arguments, and after repeating that he saw no way out, said in dismissing me that we would talk again later. Incidentally, another point he made was that he had feared civil war might break out in the Romagna, or a massacre of the clergy like another Sicilian Vespers: and this had led him to intervene there to keep order and avoid bloodshed.

Another talk took place at dinner on the sixteenth. I was sitting on the King's left (with the Russian ambassador's wife on his right). The Romagna came up, and the King in an undertone mentioned a priest whom he thought to be excommunicated but who still celebrated Mass; and he then asked me if it was easy to get absolution after being excommunicated. I told him that absolution could only follow repentance and reparation for any wrong. I then added that, if he went further and assumed the regency of the Romagna, he might be excommunicated by name and that would be a bitter stain on his family history.

[In *Rivista Storica Italiana* (Naples, 1952), ed. W. Maturi and P. Guichonnet, vol. LXIV, pp. 233–5]

Lord Loftus, British ambassador in Vienna, to Lord John Russell,
December 22, 1859

WITH REGARD to the possible cession of Venetia by the Imperial government for a pecuniary indemnity, I venture to express my opinion that, however this project might find favor with a very large party here, yet there are considerations connected with it which appear to me to render the achievement of so desirable a step almost hopeless, unless it should be brought about by forcible means.

These considerations are the following:—

1. The utter hopelessness of being able to induce the Emperor to consent to any voluntary renunciation of territory, and the certainty that no Austrian minister would dare to make the proposal to His Majesty.

2. That the Southern Tyrol is, equally with Venetia, discontented with its present subjection to Austria, and anxious to be united to Italy; consequently, any cession of Venetia must embrace or eventually lead to a similar renunciation of the Southern Tyrol.

3. The demoralizing effect which a measure of this kind would have at the present moment on the other provinces, more especially in Hungary.

4. The military honor and national pride would be considered as deeply wounded if, in an Empire composed of heterogeneous parts like that of Austria, a precedent should be once established of voluntarily giving up a province for a pecuniary indemnity.

I would further remark to your Lordship that this question, in my opinion, is intimately connected with, and dependent on, the restoration of the Austrian Archdukes to their respective Italian sovereignties. So long as Austria looks, as she now confidently does, to the restoration of the Grand Duke of Tuscany and the Duke of Modena, the possession of Venetia is of immense political and strategical value to Austria: and no means, short of physical force, will ever induce her to renounce it.

But if, at the approaching Congress, a solution of the Italian question should be arrived at on other terms, by which the Austrian Archdukes should not be restored, it is evident that the possession of Venetia will no longer be of the same vital importance to Austria, and it might then be possible perhaps to induce the Emperor and his cabinet to take into consideration the benefit to Austria of renouncing a province which must ever be a continual source of embarrassment and expense to her; and for which at the present time, she may, if voluntarily given up, receive a large indemnity; whilst, at some future period, it may be wrested from her, after a costly defense, without any compensation.

It appears to me that fears have been entertained in Paris, and elsewhere, that Austria might be disposed to renew the war in Italy and that she entertains a secret disposition to regain Lombardy.

Whatever may be the ultimate aspirations of Austria, I am confident that the Imperial cabinet have no present intentions of a warlike character, and that they will remain purely on the defensive, provided that Sardinia should pursue a similar course; nor is it a question to them of choice, but of necessity. The present state of the Austrian finances renders it physically impossible for them to renew the war, or to undertake any military projects.

The public opinion of the country would likewise oppose any further intervention in Italy, which would impose on the nation great sacrifices of money and of life, for the welfare of an Italian sovereign, and the interests of an Italian province.

If any such course were to be taken by the Emperor and his cabinet it would, I am convinced, lead to a general bankruptcy, and finally to internal convulsions.

The great object of this cabinet, as far as I can learn, is to conciliate the Emperor Napoleon and to obtain his support in behalf of their interests in Italy. They feel their total inability to oppose him; and their policy must consequently be to act with him.

The final solution of the question regarding central Italy will, in my humble opinion, entirely depend on the understanding which may exist between Her Majesty's Government and that of the Emperor Napoleon, and Austria will, from necessity, be compelled to accept any terms of arrangement which may result from that understanding.

[Public Record Office, London, F.O. 7/578/846]

When Cavour returned to power in January 1860, he had had leisure to review the whole situation, and had seen that Villafranca, by weakening the French hold over Piedmont, provided possibilities of development which at the time he had not foreseen. His first concern was how to annex the Romagna and the central Duchies. Here he advised Farini and Ricasoli to confirm the decision of the various assemblies by holding plebiscites, for this would make it hard for the rest of Europe to maintain that annexation was unpopular. Cavour had formerly been strongly opposed to plebiscites, especially those with a wide suffrage or where voting was public and hence unfree; but Louis Napoleon had shown in France how they could be very effectively manipulated, and the French could scarcely disapprove of a result achieved by their own methods. A humble letter was sent to the Pope to explain that justice as well as *raison d'état* forced Victor Emmanuel to occupy part of the Papal States; and the reply to this was another excommunication.

In Tuscany the plebiscite was arranged by Baron Ricasoli, the man who had led the Tuscan revolution. Cavour had to offer him the governorship of the annexed province, but hoped he would refuse: for the Prime Minister was greatly affronted to find that Ricasoli had views of his own and the courage to stand up for them.

Massari's diary

December 29, 1859. Cavour said . . . "We must leave Naples out of it. United Italy will be our children's achievement; I'm satisfied with what we've got, so long as we can reach Ancona." [p. 451]

March 14, 1860. Received a letter from Ricasoli accepting the post of governor. At half past eleven I went to read it to the Count at the Ministry of Foreign Affairs. There followed an indescribable scene: he paced up and down the room; he put his hand on his head; he shouted, "It's impossible. Either him or me. I'd sooner resign. Let him become Prime Minister. I can't get on with him. He isn't an administrator. He squanders millions. And then he will land me with a revolution in Umbria and the Marches. He is quite impossible. I'll tell the King to appoint him instead. He's a pedant." I tried in vain to get a word in edgewise. Then at last, after a rage lasting half an hour, he calmed down. [p. 506]

[Massari: *Diario dalle cento voci*, ed. Morelli]

The plebiscite in Tuscany, March 1860, seen through the diary of one of Ricasoli's collaborators

March 10, 1860. Great enthusiasm for tomorrow's elections, especially in the provinces. Though the people may not have realized the importance of the vote, they are proud that they have been called to exercise a new right. I heard a shoemaker say, "Tomorrow I'm worth as much as Prince Corsini," a phrase that echoes all the old Florentine democratic feeling.

It seems the clergy will vote, at any rate some of them, and even ostentatiously in some places. Adherents of the old dynasty will also vote, but for a separate Kingdom of Tuscany. Bad tactics on their part, because by abstaining they would have represented a negative opposition of noticeable size; by voting, they will reveal themselves as a minority.

Alberi has published a protest invalidating the suffrage, saying it is not free. Actually he is wrong, because though admittedly there's a farcical element in it, universal suffrage will be as free in Tuscany as elsewhere.

March 11 and 12. The polling has been going on for two days. The countryside has been *en fête*, and everybody has hastened happily to vote, though more from pleasure at being called upon than from any conviction that they will be settling the fate of their country. And a great many reactionaries voted when they saw they could do so in freedom. There was never any sign of violence, and if anybody says he was not free to give his vote he is either a brazen-faced liar or a great coward. I myself, after careful consideration of the alternative terms of the vote formulated by the decree, felt that I could not agree with either [there was just a straight choice, either "Union with the constitutional monarchy of Victor Emmanuel," or else "A separate kingdom"]; so I wrote out a third formula that will render my vote void but which seemed closer to my own view. I am told that in the countryside the people are still just as busy voting in spite of the snow covering the hilly regions. The peasantry are thought to have voted as their landlords told them to, but this will have been the only instance of coercion. Some landlords have contented themselves with making them vote, while leaving them free to vote whichever way they liked. Others, the majority, handed out to their tenants ballot papers which were marked "Union with Piedmont." In Pescia, Giorgio Magnani said to his men: "Those that don't vote won't drink." The landowners have paralyzed the influence of the priests, and this shows that the current revolution derives its strength solely from the aristocracy.

I have gathered from reports that this great operation has been carried out in orderly fashion throughout Tuscany. Only at Brolio did the peasants attack Ricasoli's land agent when he tried to lead them to the poll. The Baron [Ricasoli] was both annoyed and pleased at this, for he felt it to be the greatest possible proof of their liberty.

Thinking over my impressions of this election, I said to myself: either the Florentines don't know what they're doing, or, if they do, they're giving the greatest possible proof of self-sacrifice for Italy. The people of Lucca, Pisa and Siena see this as one more stage in their great vendetta against Florence, and their vote will be the last outburst of municipal resentment; but the Florentines are committing political suicide.

March 16.   The Baron talked to me in a strange way today. He was melancholy, with the melancholy that comes from having done one's best and come to the end of the struggle. His energetic nature makes it difficult for him to relax. I could see that in reality power has had a certain attraction for his austere temperament. At heart he is sad to be leaving the Tuscany that he has entirely rebuilt and which responds to his touch like the keys of a well-tuned piano. We talked of the difficulties of the new phase we are entering upon, and he agreed that they are no less serious than those he has so far overcome. Without flattering him, I told him that he alone could also bring this second stage to a good conclusion. He was pleased, and I saw that he would like to be in authority, without going so far as a dictatorship, but with wide powers. When I told him that Salvagnoli, to whom I had expressed the same idea, had replied that henceforth, the annexation having been established, their task was done, and new men would be wanted, he was astonished and almost displeased. Talking over all the possibilities, he did not deny that a time might come when the Tuscans would have reason to curse the union he had brought about. Strange confession! Perhaps he was thinking that the new government might make mistakes and disregard Tuscan interests. The conversation ended sadly, as it had begun. The Baron spoke of his instinctive dislike of parliamentary life and of government from Turin under an omnipotent Cavour. He ended by saying that the best thing he could do would be to return to Brolio.

March 22,   In the King's acceptance of the people's vote there is a reference to keeping administrative autonomy and existing traditions; but these are mere phrases, and fairly confused ones too.

March 23. Great excitement here today about how the government is to be constituted. Great terror and confusion among officials, masked by forced smiles. The older men are studying the Piedmontese laws on pensions, and doing sums; the young ones, like victims of a shipwreck, are looking for a plank on which to save themselves. It's really laughable in a way; it looks as though up to today none of them had thought it would come to this. Or were they blind when they voted for the annexation?

Four Councillors of the Court of Cassation want to send in their resignation so as to be paid off under Tuscan law. This evening President Giannini summoned me to tell me he wanted to do the same, and went to great lengths to prove that his only motive was not to expose himself to dismissal. How much more dignified it would have been if all these gentlemen had resigned after the revolution of last April 27! The motive would have been the same, but at least their selfish interest would have been disguised as a nobler one. It is a disgrace; everything is corrupt here in Florence!

March 24. The Baron is back [from Turin], pleased with the King, the administration, and the reception given him. The King did not conceal the seriousness of the present political situation; he said he hoped to overcome the difficulties by negotiation, but in any case he was ready for everything, and expected to have an army of 200,000 men by the spring. The cession of Savoy and Nice appears to be an inescapable necessity if we are to remain allied to Napoleon; the French are here acting with a military ruthlessness that Piedmont finds offensive. But Cavour, by giving Napoleon this bone to gnaw, against the wish of Europe, hopes to bind him indissolubly to the cause of Italy. We shall see who wins in this war of wits.

[M. Tabarrini: *Diario 1859–1860*, ed. A. Panella
(Florence, 1959), pp. 134–41]

Telegram from Piedmontese consul at Rome, to Cavour,
March 29, 1860

THIS MORNING published major excommunication, but no individual persons mentioned by name.

[*La questione romana negli anni 1860–1861* (Bologna, 1929), vol. I, p. 15]

Louis Napoleon's stated price for allowing this annexation of central
Italy was that the secret treaty of January 1859 be applied by ceding
Savoy and Nice to France. On March 12, 1860, Cavour therefore signed
another secret treaty which agreed to this request. It was one of the
saddest moments of his political life. In private he confessed that his
agreement was unconstitutional, though in parliament he stoutly maintained the opposite; just as he privately believed Nice to be Italian and
yet in public eloquently argued the contrary. He had to accept that
French policemen and soldiers should be allowed into these territories
to ensure that plebiscites confirming the cession would produce the
required near-unanimity. All he could do in mitigation was to ask that
the document conveying his agreement should then be destroyed.

Cavour had of course to meet great opposition as a result of this courageous decision. The king was realistic about it, but did not like losing
Savoy, the home of his dynasty, and he disliked losing his Alpine hunting grounds. Fanti, the Minister of War, threatened resignation: as he
told the cabinet, Piedmont's western frontier and hence Turin itself
were now rendered indefensible. More important was that Garibaldi
became Cavour's irreconcilable enemy, for Nice was his birthplace and
this made him seem a foreigner in Italy. Garibaldi, of all people, was able
to accuse Cavour in parliament of violating the constitution. He pointed
out that, having been once rescued at Villafranca, Piedmont was again
being made a vassal state of France. Rattazzi, too, once Cavour's chief
lieutenant, finally broke with his former friend. He thought the surrender of these territories to be as unnecessary as it was illegal; and by
thus sacrificing the principle of nationality, it would incidentally place
the whole risorgimento on a doubtful footing. Once France had thus
been allowed inside Italy, Austria would moreover have even stronger
reasons for not yielding Venice.

This kind of domestic opposition never worried Cavour very much.
More alarming was the reaction of England. Palmerston now saw
Cavour as someone who would not only bring about a major European
war in order to extend Piedmontese territory, but who must be regarded as a puppet of imperial France and thoroughly untrustworthy.

Cavour to Marquis Montezemolo, Governor of Nice, March 21, 1860

THE LIKELIHOOD that Garibaldi will stand for election at Nice is preoccupying France. It may be impossible to prevent him standing, but if this could be done without an obvious official intervention I would be very glad. Since the annexation of Tuscany—which we carried out despite Napoleon and which he is obliged to endure and even recognize—the Emperor is showing impatience and insistence over Nice. To carry out his intention he is proposing unconstitutional and unseemly methods which I am not inclined to accept. But I am convinced that, now we have obtained Tuscany, the sacrifice of Nice is inevitable. So I am willing to suggest to him a vote by universal suffrage—so long as we are quite sure that such a vote would decide in favor of France. Please tell me your views.

You should work on the following assumptions:—

1. The King will issue a proclamation announcing that, because of certain specified considerations, he agreed so far as he could to the French request to reunite Nice with France. But as this move must not be made without popular consent, he frees the population of Nice from any obligation toward him, and invites them to vote as they wish.
2. The Piedmontese authorities will remain entirely passive and loyally abstain from exercising any pressure on voters.

You will realize that giving you these instructions is every bit as painful for me as carrying them out will be for you. But alas the salvation of Italy imposes this sacrifice on us. Should the Emperor receive a shameful rebuff from our side, he would become a mortal enemy not only to us personally, which would be a secondary consideration, but to our fatherland; and the country is not yet in a position to defy the simultaneous fury of the two Emperors who dominate the long Alpine chain which surrounds us.

[*Il carteggio Cavour-Nigra* (Bologna, 1928), vol. III, p.208]

E. d'Azeglio, from London, to Cavour, April 14, 1860

YESTERDAY I arrived at Brockett Hall to stay several days with the Palmerstons. Panizzi [the Italian exile who was Director of the British Museum] also came down just for Sunday. From all I hear and see, I am sorry to say that English opinion now thinks very poorly indeed of France and only a little better of us. The Emperor is thought to be a lawless, untrustworthy man; and our policy is thought tied to his and thoroughly unscrupulous. This is a highly disagreeable fact. But a Prime Minister must know all the elements in a situation if he is to devise future policy, so I cannot conceal from you that, though the English consider you a very clever minister, for a long time you will remain for them a person on whose word very little trust can be placed.

English statesmen will not speak directly to me of their distrust of you, for they know I would not stand for it and that I would resign if ever I disagreed with your policy. But I know about it from good friends of yours who in general share your views, for instance Panizzi, de la Rive, etc. (I say *in general*, for Panizzi himself criticizes as quite intolerable our giving Nice to France.)

Last night after I had gone to bed, Panizzi stayed up late round the fire with Lord Palmerston and Monckton Milnes, and Palmerston repeated what for some time has been his firm conviction, that he no longer esteems or trusts the Emperor. When he then said much the same about you, Panizzi came to your defense. Palmerston retorted: "Our quarrel with Cavour is not only for *suppressio veri* but for *assertio falsi*. Cavour not only concealed the undertaking he had made over Savoy before the war of 1859, but he recently told us once again that he had not the slightest intention of ceding, exchanging or selling Savoy. All his talk of plebiscites, votes and parliamentary decisions is a farce. Cavour's surrender of these provinces is iniquitous, especially as it was unnecessary. The Emperor would never have dared face the condemnation of Europe; or, if he had, Count Cavour would have been acclaimed for honesty as much as for his courage and skill." Panizzi tried to explain that you were compelled by the need to do something for your country and were under pressure from the sheer power of the one active ally you had. But he had to deplore the fact that France and England would now soon be facing each other in enemy camps. Lord Palm. shook his head sadly and said, "You are right to have no illusions about that."

The moral effect of ceding Savoy and Nice will be as indelible in England as the partition of Poland. Only glorious successes for Italy will expunge the memory. National self-interest may explain the material and moral sacrifices we have had to make, but the same argument also scares the English cabinet into fear of further wars and territorial changes.

There is an essential distinction to be made here. The English people and government blame some of the leading politicians in Italy. But Italy itself remains, as it always has been, a favorite country for them, and they watch its progress and education with lively sympathy. They still keep up their old interest, and would ask nothing better than that Piedmont should annex the whole peninsula. So long as we can get results by internal revolutions, they are with us. But if we need to set the whole world ablaze just to be able to fish in troubled waters, if we can obtain Venice, Umbria, etc., only by plotting to give France her natural frontiers and disrupting the whole Eastern Question, then halt! For what is at issue is no longer Italy but the peace and balance of Europe.

[*Cavour e l'Inghilterra* (Bologna, 1933), vol. II, tomo II, pp. 65–6]

18. Garibaldi Conquers Naples and Sicily, 1860

The name of Garibaldi epitomizes the popular element in the Italian revolution, the idea of volunteer initiative and enthusiasm which the regular army (and the regular politicians) liked to minimize and depreciate. Garibaldi and his friends had all received their original inspiration from Mazzini; and, though they had now largely broken away from the master, they remained radical, revolutionary, and thoroughly distrustful of politicians who could sacrifice national territory at Nice and make a deal with the tyrant of France. This made Garibaldi a difficult and dangerous person for Cavour to deal with.

Garibaldi had been condemned to death by the Piedmontese for a youthful escapade in 1834, and Charles Albert had unceremoniously refused his offer of help in 1848; but Cavour shrewdly accepted the support of the National Society, and so had allowed Garibaldi to form a corps of volunteers in 1859. During the war of 1859 these volunteers distinguished themselves as they had done in 1848–9, though the regular army restricted their enrollment and their field of action. The official attitude continued to be grudging or even outright unfriendly, as though this was just a means of putting volunteer elements under discipline with a fervent hope that they would not be too successful.

By May 1860, Garibaldi and Cavour had become bitter enemies. The attitude of France, and Cavour's evident subservience to the em-

peror, had convinced the radicals that, short of pitchforking the politicians into a popular revolution, the national cause was dead. This was
why, in May 1860, Garibaldi and his "Thousand" embarked near
Genoa on a filibustering expedition to attack Bourbon Sicily. Cavour
was at this moment in a very trying situation where he was not strong
enough to impose his influence over events. Part of his trouble was that
the king, who got on quite well with the outspoken but basically loyal
Garibaldi, was once more actively looking for another and more amenable Prime Minister. Opinion in Piedmont was greatly shaken by the
renunciation of Savoy and Nice; and for the same reason Cavour could
no longer count on British support. In his view, Garibaldi's success
might undermine the French alliance upon which his foreign policy
depended, as it also threatened the hegemony of Piedmont in Italy and
the conservative direction of the risorgimento. All the more was this
so when the volunteer forces landed en route in the Papal States.

Cavour at first tried to stop the expedition, and then acted to hinder
its success. As popular feeling and the king were on Garibaldi's side,
he did not dare to proceed too openly, but the Enfield rifles which the
volunteers had in store were officially sequestrated, so that the Thousand had to set out with a few rusty, sooth-bore converted flintlocks
which mostly had no use except for bayonet charges. The Piedmontese
navy was then ordered to chase Garibaldi and arrest him. Only some
weeks later, after the expedition had astonished everyone by its success,
did official policy change; and the story was then adjusted to prove that
the government had been secretly helping Garibaldi all the time.

Garibaldi, from Genoa, to Marquis Trecchi, an aide of the king,
May 4, 1860

TELL HIS MAJESTY not to be angry with me for I am truly his
friend for life. If I had told him my plans he would have put a stop
to them; and hence, regretfully, I preferred to keep silent. I opposed
this rising in Sicily; but when those fine Italians took action on
their own I had to help them. Assure His Majesty that, whatever
happens, the honor of Italy will not suffer.

[*Il Risorgimento Italiano, rivista storica* (Turin,
1909), Vol. II, p. 139]

Cavour to Nigra, his representative at Paris, May 12, 1860

I REGRET Garibaldi's expedition as much as does Monsieur Thouvenel [the French Foreign Minister], and I am doing, and will go
on doing, everything possible to prevent it causing new complications. I did not prevent Garibaldi carrying out his project, because
that would have needed force. Moreover the government is in no

state to face up to the enormous unpopularity which we would
have incurred by arresting Garibaldi. Another consideration was
that elections are imminent, and I need the support of all shades of
the moderate liberal party if we are to foil the intrigues of the
opposition and get the French treaty passed. Therefore I could not
take vigorous action to prevent help being sent to Sicily. But I did
everything in my power to persuade Garibaldi not to go on his
mad escapade. I sent La Farina to talk to him, who came back with
an assurance that the whole idea was off.

As we had news from Palermo that the Bourbons had lifted
martial law and that the insurrection there had almost died out, I
thought Garibaldi would be obliged to stay put whether he liked
it or not. I could never have dreamt that he was mad enough to land
in Umbria where Generals Lamoricière and Goyon [in charge of
papal and French troops] had forces far superior to his own. This
is surely convincing proof that we are not conniving with Garibaldi; for I hope no one will think me so mad as to want a revolution in Umbria at the present moment. As I communicated to you
by telegraph, I had already given orders to Rear-Admiral Persano to
arrest Garibaldi in Sardinian waters. And yesterday, as soon as I
heard that some of his followers had landed at Talamone, I gave
orders for his ships to be stopped wherever they were, except in
the waters of the Kingdom of the Two Sicilies (the King of Naples
has no need of our help for his own policing). Please explain all
this to M. Thouvenel.

[*Il carteggio Cavour-Nigra*, vol. III, pp. 294–5]

Garibaldi chose Sicily because an insurrection had been fitfully alive
for over a month in the mountains and interior of this island. Once
again, as in 1848, Sicily was proving the value of Mazzini's theory of
popular initiative. Some of Mazzini's agents and Garibaldi's friends had
combined to detonate this insurrection at the beginning of April. They
then continued to give a patriotic stiffening to what was fundamentally
a social revolution by the poor and an autonomist movement to break
away from the hated rule of Naples.

When Garibaldi landed at Marsala on May 11, he faced a seemingly
impossible task. With a thousand badly armed irregulars he had to defeat
25,000 trained soldiers supported by cavalry and artillery. Yet the
Bourbon generals did not know the tactics of guerrilla warfare; they
also failed to take the invasion seriously enough until it was too late;
and they were not prepared for a situation where the local people cut
water supplies, destroyed the mills needed for grinding wheat, inter-

rupted telegraph lines, and killed any stragglers with the greatest ferocity.

A little engagement near the village of Calatafimi was one of the decisive battles of the risorgimento. The Bourbons had twice as many troops, a far better armament, and were defending a greatly superior position. Garibaldi needed a quick and striking victory to create the illusion of invincibility upon which he relied to release the pent-up popular forces in the island. Some thirty of the Garibaldians were killed on this occasion, but the Bourbons, with even fewer casualties, were forced to retire, and the fact was soon known everywhere. Garibaldi quickly moved toward Palermo, a city of some 190,000 people where the Sicilian, General Lanza, commanded perhaps 18,000 troops. How Garibaldi overcame these odds, overruning Palermo and the rest of Sicily and Naples, is a special chapter in Italian military history. But without his initial success at Calatafimi, the chances are that he would have perished like the Bandieras in 1844 and Pisacane in 1857. The peasants of southern Italy could be brave fighters, but they could also be fickle toward their would-be liberators, and the *mafioso* underworld of western Sicily would not throw any of its enormous power on the side of an obvious loser.

Sicily, 1860: the battle of Calatafimi, by one of Garibaldi's men

May 14, Salemi. The General has ridden through the city on horseback. When the populace sees him they take fire. There is a magic in his look and in his name. It is only Garibaldi they want.

The General has assumed the dictatorship of Sicily in the name of Italy and Victor Emmanuel. There is a good deal of talk about this and not everyone is satisfied. But such will be our battle cry. At the street corners one can read the proclamation issued by the new dictator. He addresses the *buoni preti*, the good priests, of Sicily. A purist among us has said that it would have been better Italian style if he'd written *preti buoni*.

The Sicilian insurgents come in from all sides by the hundred, some on horseback, some on foot. There is a tremendous confusion and they have bands which play terribly badly. I have seen mountaineers armed to the teeth, some with rascally faces and eyes that menace one like the muzzles of pistols. All these people are led by gentlemen whom they obey devotedly.

May 16, above Calatafimi. . . . "Don't fire! Don't reply to their fire!" shouted our commanders; but the bullets passed over us with such a provocative whine that we couldn't restrain ourselves. One shot after another was heard, then the General's own trumpeter sounded the call to arms, then the charge.

We got to our feet, closed up and rushed like a flash down to the plain below. There we came under a perfect hail of bullets, while from the smoke-wreathed mountain two guns began a furious cannonade against us.

The plain was quickly crossed and the first enemy line was broken, but when we came to the slopes of the opposite hill it was not pleasant to look upwards. I saw Garibaldi there on foot with his sheathed sword over his right shoulder, walking slowly forward, keeping the whole action in view. Our men were falling all round him and it seemed that those who wore the red shirt were the most numerous victims. Bixio came up at a gallop to offer some shelter with his horse, and he pulled the General behind his animal calling out, "General! Is this the way you wish to die?" "And how could I die better than for my country?" replied the General; and freeing himself from Bixio's restraining hand he went forward with a frown. Bixio followed respectfully.

Goro da Montebenichi and Ferruccio at the battle of Gavinana, I thought to myself, and I was pleased that I remembered the episode [popularised in Guerrazzi's novel *L'assedio di Firenze*]; but the mood quickly passed and I began to fear, and even to guess that the General thought it impossible that we could win this fight, and that he was therefore seeking death on the battlefield.

At that moment one of our guns thundered from the road above. A cry of joy from all greeted the shot because it seemed as though we were getting the aid of a thousand strong arms. "Forward! Forward! Forward!" was the cry heard on all sides, and the trumpet that had continuously sounded the charge now pealed out with a kind of anguish as though it were the voice of our country in danger.

The first, second, and third terraces up the hillside were attacked at the point of the bayonet and passed, but it was terrible to see the dead and wounded. Little by little, as they yielded ground, the royalist battalions retreated higher up. They concentrated and thus grew stronger. At last it seemed impossible that we could face them. They were all on the top of the hill and we were around the brow, tired, at the end of our tether, and reduced in numbers. There was a moment of pause; it was difficult to recognize the two opposing sides, they up there and we all flat on the ground. One could hear rifle fire and the royalist troops started rolling down boulders and hurling stones; and it was said that even Garibaldi was hit by one of these.

Already we had lost a great many of our men and I heard friends bewailing their comrades. Near by, among the prickly-pear bushes, I saw a fine young man fatally wounded, propped up by two of his comrades. He seemed to want to continue to charge, but I heard him ask his two friends to be merciful to the royalist soldiers because they too were Italians. Tears came into my eyes.

The whole hillside was covered with fallen, but I heard no complaints. Quite close to me was Missori, commander of the Scouts, who, with his left eye all bloody and bruised, seemed to be listening to the noises floating down to us from the hilltop. We could hear the heavy tramp of the royalist battalions up there and thousands of voices like waves of an angry sea, shouting from time to time, "Long live the King!"

Meanwhile new reinforcements came up on our side and we felt stronger. Our commanders moved about among us encouraging us. Sirtori and Bixio had come up the whole way on horseback. Sirtori, dressed in black with a little bit of red shirt showing from beneath his lapel, had many rents in his clothes made by bullets, but he was unwounded. Impassive, riding whip in hand, he seemed hardly present in all that confusion. Yet on his pale, thin face I could read something as though he felt a passionate desire to die for us all.

Bixio was to be seen on all sides as though he were one man divided into a hundred; the right hand of Garibaldi. I saw them up there for a moment together. "Take a rest lads, take another short rest," said the General, "one more effort and the job's done." And Bixio followed him through our ranks.

Lieutenant Bandi stood up to salute him, but he was on the point of falling, at the end of his tether. He could do no more. He had been wounded several times, but the last bullet had struck his left breast and blood was pouring out. He will be dead in another half-hour, I thought, but when the companies charged on a last assault at that hedge of glittering bayonets pointed so menacingly at us, I turned and saw that officer in the leading rank. Someone, who must be a friend of his, called out, "How many lives have you got?" And he smiled happily.

The supreme clash came when the Valparaiso banner, which had passed from hand to hand and finally to Schiaffino, was seen waver-

ing for some instants in a furious bloody tussle and then go down.
But Giovan Maria Damiani of the Scouts snatched it up by one of
its streamers. He and his rearing horse formed a group such as
Michelangelo might have carved in stone against a confused tumult
of fighting men, friend and foe.

As long as I live I shall never forget that scene.

At that moment the royalists fired their last salvo and a certain
Sacchi from Pavia was blown to pieces. Then there was a shout of
joy because the gun was captured. A rumor went round that the
General was dead, and Menotti, wounded in his right arm, was
running round asking for him. Elia lay wounded to death; Schiaffino, the Dante da Castiglione of this battle, was dead and I saw
his tall body lying on the bloody ground.

Almost on the hilltop, near the hut, I recognized, by his clothes
more than his face, the body of poor Sartori. Certainly he must have
been killed instantaneously because only five minutes before I had
seen him climbing up the hill and he had greeted me by name. He
lay on his left side, all huddled up with clenched fists. He had been
wounded in the chest. I fell on him, kissed him, and bade him fare-
well. Poor Sartori, in his staring eyes and drawn features, something
still remained of his longing for yet one more breath of that heroic
air. All those who knew Eugenio Sartori from Sacile will for long
speak of him. Like a hero, he had kept the promise he made at
Talamone.

The dead Neapolitans were a piteous sight. Many of them had
been killed by the bayonet. Those who lay on the brow of the hill
had nearly all been wounded in the head. Yonder I could see a little
dwarfish monster, who seemed by his clothes to be a local peasant,
ferociously stabbing one of the dead Neapolitans. "Kill the brute!"
yelled Bixio and spurred against him with raised saber, but the
savage creature slid away among the rocks and disappeared; more
brute than man.

As details of the great picture I can see those Franciscan friars
who fought on our side. One of them was cramming a muzzle-
loader with handfuls of bullets and stones, then he climbed up and
let loose a hailstorm from his ancient piece. Short, thin, filthy dirty,
as we saw him from below tearing his bare shins against the prickly
bushes which gave out a nauseating cemetery stink, he was an object
for laughter and applause. How brave those monks were! I saw one
of them, who had been wounded in his thigh, pull out the bullet

from the flesh and return to fire against the enemy. During the battle we could see crowds of peasants intently watching the fierce spectacle from the high crags around us. From time to time they uttered yells which must have terrified our commom enemy.

When the Neapolitans began to retreat under cover of their riflemen I saw the General again watching them with a look of exultation. We pursued them for some way and then they disappeared into a fold of the ground. When they emerged they were out of range on the opposite mountainside, followed by some hundreds of their cavalry, who had been under cover up to that moment and now rejoined them at full speed. From the battlefield we could see their long column climbing up to Calatafimi, which appeared as a gray mass halfway up the gray mountain, until finally they were swallowed up in the town. It seemed a miracle that we had conquered. A chill wind began to blow. We lay down on the ground. There was a melancholy silence. Night came all at once, and Airenta and Bozzani and I went to sleep in a little cornfield, caressed by the ears of corn bending over us.

> [G. C. Abba: *The Diary of One of Garibaldi's Thousand*, trans. E. R. Vincent (London, 1962), pp. 30–9]

Garibaldi claimed to rule in the name of "Italy and Victor Emmanuel," but he decided not to hand over power until he no longer needed a base for operations. His plan—and the king secretly encouraged him— was to continue his movement to eastern Sicily, up through Calabria to Naples, and then if possible into the Papal States. Cavour's problem was to guess the right moment when he could intervene and stop him.

Events in Sicily might have been expected to shake Cavour's self-confidence, for this was a type of warfare which he disliked and did not understand. He had failed to stop Garibaldi going to Sicily; then he failed to annex the island after Garibaldi proved successful, and his envoy, La Farina, was summarily expelled for trying to undermine Garibaldi's authority; then he tried and failed to prevent the volunteers conquering Naples; and all the time he knew that Victor Emmanuel was secretly in touch with Garibaldi and pursuing a private policy of his own. But Cavour's realistic acceptance of what was happening then showed him at his best, as he waited in patience until he could regain the initiative. He fairly judged Garibaldi's immense services to Italy, and acknowledged that the failure of his own conservative revolution at Naples made Garibaldi's easy success there the more astonishing.

Nevertheless, the nearer the revolution came to Rome, the more necessary it was to stop it.

Cavour to Nigra, his envoy at Paris, July 12, 1860

GARIBALDI HAS become intoxicated by success and by the praise showered on him from all over Europe. He is planning the wildest, not to say absurdest, schemes. As he remains devoted to King Victor Emmanuel, he will not help Mazzini or republicanism. But he feels it his vocation to liberate all Italy, stage by stage, before turning her over to the King. He is thus putting off the day when Sicily will demand annexation to Piedmont, for he wants to keep the dictatorial powers which will enable him to raise an army to conquer first Naples, then Rome, and in the end Venice. Some people even maintain that in private conversation he does not conceal his intention of taking Nice back from France! But I find that too hard to believe.

The government here has no influence on him. On the contrary he mistrusts everybody whom he imagines to be in touch with us. La Farina has been treated in a disgraceful way, first isolated, then expelled from Sicily without the slightest reason, and everyone has been dismissed who tried to interfere. Even Garibaldi's principal lieutenant, Medici, has fallen into disgrace for telling him that he ought not to quarrel with us. Garibaldi has a generous character and the instincts of a poet; but at the same time he has a wild nature, and certain impressions have stamped him in a way that cannot be effaced. He was deeply hurt by the cession of Nice which he views almost as a personal and unforgivable insult. His grievances have been embittered by the recollection of his conflict in central Italy with Fanti and Farini [in November 1859]. I even think his desire to overthrow the government is as strong as his desire to drive out the Austrians.

The King still retains some influence over him, but if he tried using it on this occasion he would lose it to no purpose. That would be a grave misfortune, as circumstances could arise in which the King's influence would be our only hope.

If harmony between Garibaldi and Turin could be re-established by my resignation, perhaps we might come to that. But who would replace me? For the moment I view Rattazzi as impossible. Anyway he is too sensible to accept Garibaldi's program. Garibaldi has shown deep trust in Depretis, but neither the country nor Europe would tolerate such a man [Depretis became Prime Minister in 1876].

As we cannot change either the ministry or Garibaldi, as we cannot obliterate this antagonism between the most lively forces of the country, we must devote ourselves to trying to prevent any fatal consequences. We must therefore prevent Garibaldi from conquering Naples, and we must try to annex Sicily as soon as possible.

Were Garibaldi to become master of all the Neapolitan provinces, we would not be able to stop him from compromising us with France and Europe; we could no longer resist him. Hence it follows that it is of the very greatest interest to us and the Emperor that, if the Bourbons have to fall, it should not be by Garibaldi's agency.

Our annexation of Sicily will be a means of nullifying Garibaldi, or at least of diminishing his influence so that it ceases to be dangerous.

> [*Il carteggio Cavour-Nigra* (Bologna, 1929), vol.
> IV, pp. 70–1]

Cavour to B. Ricasoli, Governor-General of Tuscany, July 8, 1860

WE AGREE about the end and almost agree about means. Any disagreement is only over the outward semblance of our policy, over its coloring.

I cannot reject out of hand the offer of an agreement [with Bourbon Naples] if it is presented to us under French auspices and with their advice. I agree with you that we are heading toward a European war, and that is why I cannot break with the Emperor, for we could not wage a European war alone. Even were we to be helped by England, we could not fight simultaneously on the two fronts of the Mincio and the Alps. To reach our goal we must therefore restrain our indignation and use a certain amount of artifice.

What I have done is as follows. When the Naples government made its first overtures for an alliance I answered that I could not hear of any such proposal until their government had allowed Sicilians to dispose of their own destiny. Now if Naples agrees, the home-rule party there (who want to keep southern autonomy) will abandon a government that out of cowardice sacrifices the finest part of their Kingdom. If she refuses, then there will be a clean and open break between Naples and ourselves . . .

We must not be in a hurry for an uprising in Umbria or the Marches [the Papal States]. The fate of Rome is sealed unless we give it new life by some imprudence. Therefore all acts of rashness on the border must be stopped, cost what it may.

[*Carteggi di Bettino Ricasoli*, ed. M. Nobili and S. Camerani (Rome, 1962), vol. XIV, pp. 27–8]

Cavour to Prince Carignano, the king's representative in Florence, July 20, 1860

IF RICASOLI reaches the point of saying that we should send France packing and do without French help, I am ready to agree provided we could be certain of the support of public opinion in Europe. For instance, if France opposes our annexing Sicily, I think we could act without her because European public opinion would be on our side. But if France should break with us because we had brought about revolution in Naples, that would be unfortunate, because Europe would think us in the wrong.

War against Austria has no terrors for me, even though there would be more than one chance of things going wrong. I would have no doubt about the result so long as our recently acquired provinces were inspired with the same spirit as Piedmont. But Your Highness knows how hard it is to find men or money in central Italy, and so you will understand that my confidence in the outcome of such a war is not unlimited.

Whoever wins at Naples [ourselves or Garibaldi], it is very important that there should be no aggression against the Roman States. I know that Your Highness is as much concerned about this as I am, so we can be perfectly at ease about it.

[*La liberazione del mezzogiorno e la formazione del regno d'Italia* (Bologna, 1949), vol. I, pp. 353–4]

The king's policy was very different from Cavour's: as quoted by Victor Emmanuel's aide-de-camp Count Trecchi, August 5, 1860

"WHEN GARIBALDI reaches Naples, he must do whatever circumstances suggest: he could himself occupy Umbria and the Marches [in the Papal States], or let volunteer units go there. Once in Naples he should proclaim union with the rest of Italy, just as he has done in Sicily. He must prevent disorder, for that would harm our cause. He should keep the Bourbon army in being and ready, for Austria may declare war on us shortly. He should let the King of Naples escape; or, if the King should be captured by the people, Garibaldi should protect him and let him get away."

These words were dictated by Victor Emmanuel for me to take to General Garibaldi.

[*Nuova Antologia di lettere, scienze ed arti* (Rome, 1910), vol. CCXXXI, p. 426]

Cavour to Nigra, August 9, 1860

YOU SUGGEST recalling parliament and having a big parliamentary battle: nothing would please me more. But even though this might succeed in saving my prestige, I think it might lose Italy. My dear Nigra, I can tell you without laboring the point that I would readily lose my popularity and reputation so long as Italy were made. But to make Italy, as things now stand, Victor Emmanuel and Garibaldi must not be set against each other.

Garibaldi has a great moral power. He commands enormous prestige in Italy, and even more in the rest of Europe. In my view you are mistaken when you say that I stand as Europe's defense against him. If tomorrow I were to fight against Garibaldi, even though most of the old diplomats might approve, European public opinion would be against me, and rightly so. Garibaldi has done Italy the greatest service that a man could do: he has given the Italians self-confidence; he has proved to Europe that Italians can fight and die in battle to reconquer a fatherland. Everybody recognizes this, from the conservative paper, *Débats*, to the radicals of the *Siècle*.

There are only two possible occasions in which we would contemplate a fight against Garibaldi:—

1. If he wanted to drag us into a war against France.
2. If he repudiated his present program and turned against the monarchy and Victor Emmanuel. As long as he remains loyal, we are forced to march at his side.

This notwithstanding, it would be highly desirable if a revolution in Naples came about without him, for that would reduce his influence to reasonable dimensions. If, in spite of all our efforts, he should liberate southern Italy as he has liberated Sicily, we would have no choice but to go along with him and wholeheartedly.

That might involve us in war against Austria, and I realize that this may cause apprehension, though I think its dangers exaggerated. On every occasion when our soldiers have really wanted to fight, they have beaten the Austrians. If we were drubbed at Novara it was because three quarters of the army did not want war.

[*Il carteggio Cavour-Nigra*, vol. IV, pp. 144–5]

Baron Talleyrand, French ambassador at Turin, to E. Thouvenel, French Foreign Minister, August 24, 1860

SEVERAL TIMES in the course of an intimate talk, Cavour raised the theoretical possibility of Italian unity, and what he said was this:—"I have always favored a federal system. You, moreover, have known me long enough to be sure that I have never recoiled from the extreme but inevitable concomitant of every federation, namely the establishment of a republic. After the armistice of Villafranca, however, federalism was no longer possible. The kind of marriage there proposed to us was quite impossible, for Italy contained too many incompatibilities of temperament. So I came to believe that the only possibility was a unitary state, pure, simple, and monarchical."

I can guarantee, M. le Ministre, the rigorous exactness of the words I have quoted here. Cavour seemed to have chosen them with great care. Everything leads me to think that it will now be useless to offer him advice if he thinks that advice wrong. He will follow the path he has chosen with all the courage and skill which so distinguish him. Cavour possesses a gift for intrigue which can reach quite heroic proportions. In the last few days he has recovered his lost self-confidence. Far from seeking the alliance of Rattazzi, as some newspapers have prophesied, he seems to disdain it. And that means that he is really sure of himself. The day that he throws off the mask to ally openly with the conqueror of the Two Sicilies, he will put himself incontestably at the head of an immense reconstituted liberal party.

[Archives of French Foreign Office, *Sardinia*, 350/162]

The last Bourbon of Naples, Francis II, fled on September 6, and Garibaldi entered the capital of southern Italy the following day. The last stages of his march had been a triumphal progress. Not much of an in-

surrection had taken place in the southern provinces to help him, but
at all events the vocal enthusiasm was enormous, and the existing administration simply abdicated as his advance guard drew near.

For six weeks Garibaldi then ruled Naples as a dictator while he planned a final battle with the Bourbons on the Volturno River, but in
the meantime he prepared for union with the rest of Italy. The followers of Mazzini, together with many who believed in regional autonomy, would have preferred to elect an assembly where they could discuss a new constitution for united Italy. Just in time, however, Cavour
and his party managed to persuade Garibaldi that this might open the
way to all the old differences of opinion which had made 1848 so disastrous.

Voters were therefore summoned simply to approve or disapprove
of a new unitary state of Italy under Victor Emmanuel. Cavour's word
"annexation" was not used in Garibaldi's plebiscite, nor was "fusion."
The vote was for a new Italy, not for joining the old state of Piedmont.
But this was hardly a serious test of opinion. Many Piedmontese laws had
already been introduced. Already General Cialdini had crossed the
Neapolitan frontier, and Cavour was issuing decrees "for those provinces not yet annexed." Nor was there much secrecy about the ballot,
but two voting urns, one marked "yes" the other "no," were on a
rostrum for all to see. In the Sicilian plebiscite only 667 negative votes
were recorded, against 432,053 affirmative, and most electoral districts
could show no negative votes at all. In Naples, a Swiss writer described the scene as he saw it, and the extraordinary fascination of
Garibaldi which made this success possible.

Garibaldi the victorious Dictator of Naples, 1860

September 10, 1860. Today I managed to get quite close and
hear him speak. He is quite admirable, like a lion, with a firm voice,
thick-set body and limbs. He must be terrible when angry, but in
repose his eyes are quiet and his smile soft. More than a genius, he
is an apostle, a man of faith, strength and fearlessness, a miracle-
worker. He would be someone who in a storm could leave his ship
and walk on the water. He proceeds straight ahead to fulfill his
mission, to follow his star like a true conqueror.

The other evening, in the fight at the Carmine, when the Bourbon
soldiers were even using cannon on the people, he did not blench,
but offered cigars to the national guardsmen and said, "Let us have
a smoke while we wait for them." If there is any real danger, however, he goes to the spot at once and cannot be held back.

He is strangely but utterly simple in character, the only great
man I have ever met who never poses. In talking, like all believers,
he is somewhat grandiloquent, but out of real conviction. Away

from society he is familiar and cordial, accepting the most unreasonable requests with a martyr's patience. No one is kept away. He puts on no sententious airs, but is simple and good . . .

There was a lot of masquerade and carnival about the recent explosion of popular excitement which has left everyone here so hoarse. But it was the exaggerated expression of a profound, universal feeling which was absolutely genuine. To the *lazzaroni*, Garibaldi was a saint sent by God to deliver them. Many even thought him to be Jesus Christ, with his generals as the apostles. Devotion to him is absolute. Even the beggars ask for alms in his name.

The Dictator felt all this with the rare good sense (like his eye for military tactics) which takes the place of political knowledge and finesse. He was shrewd enough to respect religious feelings, and his first proclamation praised the priests . . .

Neapolitans think that he is invulnerable, that he has only to shake his red shirt and bullets will fall harmless at his feet. Perhaps this superstition saved him from assassination. Don't forget, he arrived in Naples alone, when there were still apparently six thousand Bourbon soldiers here. They controlled the forts and could easily have shelled the town. The Royal Guard had still not left the palace when he was haranguing the people from the Foresteria.

October 22. I wanted to see the plebiscite, so I went to St. Francis' Square. Opposite the palace the vote was taking place in the church portico. The National Guard was on duty in the square. Astonishingly, there was perfect order . . .

Yesterday's promise that the vote would be free was honored, nevertheless the method of voting left much to be desired. The ballot box was between two baskets, one full of *yes* slips, the other full of *no* slips. An elector had to choose in clear view of the Guards and the crowd. A negative vote was difficult or even dangerous to give. In the Monte Calvario district, a man who voted *no* with some bravado was punished with a stiletto blow—assassin and victim are now at the police station. I am told that, unfortunately, things were just the same in Tuscany.

At such an agitated moment, when it is dangerous to declare opposition openly, the voting should have been secret. This intimidation is useless as well as bad. Most of the country was so obviously in favor of Victor Emmanuel that no serious opposition was to be feared. Another kind of fear is, however, undoubtedly the dominant sentiment at Naples. Almost everyone here is timid and cautious about expressing an opinion. They were like this under the Bourbon Ferdinand II, for they feared the cannon of St. Elmo castle and the Swiss soldiers. Now their fear turns them in favor of Italy, because they are afraid that the Bourbons with their Bavarian troops may come back. There is no sign of any opinion frankly and positively in favor of annexation by Piedmont. And yet annexation is the only possible solution. Cavour has triumphantly converted what was a dream into a necessity, despite Austria, despite the Pope and even France.

October 24. Annexation has been proclaimed wherever the results of the plebiscite are known. Almost everywhere it was unanimous. There were few abstentions and very few negative votes, for open and covert resistance could not muster 1 per cent in favor of the Bourbons. Moreover the Mazzinians, who as could be expected made common cause with the reactionaries, either abstained or voted *no*. So over 99 per cent are against the [papalist] blacks and the [republican] reds, and have voted for the tricolor with the cross of Savoy.

I have already described the voting in St. Francis' Square, and everywhere else things went equally according to plan. The sailors voted as a body. Foreigners who have lived here for a long time also claimed that as citizens they had a right to proclaim Victor Emmanuel. Pallavicino, Garibaldi's pro-dictator, was given the same right by acclamation, and voted to the sound of fanfares. Old men who could not walk were carried to the ballot boxes weeping with joy at exercising a privilege which they had awaited for a century. They say that one blind man groped his way and held out his hand for the *yes* he could not read. Also the popular heroine, *la Sangio-vannara*, of whom I have already spoken and who is the boss of a whole region of the town, she too was allowed to vote because they say she has been fighting against the Bourbons at Capua. This Sunday will live for long as one of Naples' finest memories.

Garibaldi arrived early to vote for his King in the town which he had himself already conquered by force. Then he went to the Hotel d'Inghilterra to dine with some colonel who was a friend.

Outside, the crowd made such a noise that the Dictator was forced to come out on the balcony and speak, finishing with the popular gesture with his index finger which means "united Italy."

[Marc Monnier: *Garibaldi: Histoire de la conquête des Deux Siciles: notes prises sur place au jour le jour* (Paris, 1861), pp. 301–3, 368–72]

19. The Unification of North and South

Such had been Garibaldi's quite unexpected success that Cavour now announced his belief in the hitherto heretical formula of Italian unity. To allow the radicals a monopoly of national sentiment would have been much too dangerous. One of Cavour's most brilliant decisions was accordingly to regain the initiative by invading the Papal States in the fall of 1860. First he sent Farini to convince Louis Napoleon that this was the only way to stop Garibaldi marching on Rome (where there was still a French garrison). Once accepted in principle, the plan was to send Piedmontese troops down through Umbria and the Marches so that they could cross the Neapolitan frontier and stop Garibaldi's progress. There would thus be the good "conservative" excuse that an invasion of papal territory was needed to stop republicanism and control anarchy. As well as Umbria and the Marches, Cavour would force Garibaldi to hand over Naples and Sicily. Probably Cavour would also inherit the large Bourbon army at Naples. It may be that Farini left the French in some confusion about future plans for the Papal States, and, sincerely or insincerely, very strong protests came from the French Foreign Office when they discovered what was afoot. But Cavour now saw this invasion as a culminating step in his policy of annexation. "The destruction of the Pope's temporal power," he could now say, "will be one of the most glorious and fruitful facts in all history."

In the greatest secrecy, on September 5 the fleet left Genoa to be ready to bombard Ancona, and notices were smuggled into the Marches that people should rise on the eighth and appeal for Piedmontese protection against the Pope. Petitions had already been prepared for their use which specifically mentioned the brutality of the foreign troops in papal employ. When all was ready, a formal ultimatum was sent to Pope Pius asking him to dismiss these soldiers, and an invasion was then timed to begin on September 11. The local rising did not amount to much, but more important was that the invading army had a three to one superiority in numbers. After a victory had been won at Castelfidardo—where the Piedmontese lost 61 killed and the papalists 88—only Lazio and the region round Rome itself remained in papal hands.

Cavour in his speech to parliament was anxious to stress the magnanimity and justice with which this war was fought. But in fact, like all civil wars, the fighting was inevitably conducted with some bitterness and cruelty on both sides. Cavour's generals called upon people to revolt against the papalist "assassins." Peasants who were captured defending themselves against the Piedmontese were executed; and priests, too, were executed; for the only legitimate fighters whom General Cialdini would recognize were the "mercenary" Belgians, Irishmen, and other uniformed soldiers. The Cardinal Legate of Pesaro, who refused to surrender, suffered no greater punishment than being kept standing all night in the rain with only his underclothes; but any papalist commanders who supported him were warned by Cialdini that they would be shot as traitors. Whether or not this was magnanimous, it was certainly inexpedient. Cialdini acted as though this was another patriotic war against the foreigner; whereas it was largely a civil war against other Italians, who did not easily forget this kind of treatment.

Cavour to Nigra, September 12, 1860

YESTERDAY, as you had warned me, I received from Baron de Talleyrand [French ambassador at Turin] the note which threatened to break off relations with us if we continue with our plan to invade the Marches and Umbria. I am deeply sorry about this French move, but I could not compromise the King's dignity by asking him to back out of a project which had already begun.

M. Talleyrand's step did not come unexpectedly. France obviously must not give the appearance of complicity with us in this expedition and she has to make our plan seem an impetuous gesture in the eyes of those who do not fully understand our difficult position. But I am sure we are taking the only step which will allow us to emerge with honor.

You realize all I have done to forestall Garibaldi in Naples. I have been as bold as I possibly could be without risking civil war; and I would not have even held back from civil war if I could have hoped that public opinion would support me. But Garibaldi, after conquering Sicily, triumphantly reached Salerno without meeting opposition; it thus became impossible for us to seize Naples by force and steal from him the fruit of victory. The whole of Europe, peoples as well as governments, would have criticized such a mean and thankless act, and the only advantage would have been reaped by Mazzini and his adherents.

That being so, I tried conciliation. By means of a naval captain who is a childhood friend of Garibaldi's, I sent him a letter and tried to persuade him to work together with me. This was only half successful, as Garibaldi went on talking about going to Rome, seizing Venice, taking Nice back, etc. So I had to bring forward my long-meditated plan which Farini had explained to the Emperor at Chambéry.

The day after Farini and Cialdini got back to Turin, I wrote to tell you that the Emperor had unreservedly approved our plan. He had talked over its chances of success, and even went so far as to prescribe the limits of our army's field of operations. He saw it as a good way of flattening the clerical and legitimist plotters, of putting an end to Lamoricière's threats (which are aimed more at Paris than Turin), and of applying the Italian policy contained in a celebrated pamphlet last year. Count Arese who saw the Emperor only two weeks ago found him in the same mood. We had every reason to think, therefore, that if we declared immediately that we would stop short of the patrimony of St. Peter, and also showed that we had no intention of attacking Austria, we would not receive the Emperor's disapprobation, even though he might scold us in public.

I have no idea why carrying out our plan can have displeased the French government. Probably M. Thouvenel, though informed of the Emperor's private views, thought it his duty to make a more public separation between French policy and the policy imposed on us by circumstances.

Whatever be the truth, I note with gratitude that the Emperor is increasing his garrison in Rome. By reassuring the Catholic world over this so-called danger to the Holy Father, France is doing us a big service. Moreover it will strengthen our position as regards Garibaldi, who I hope will now listen to reason. Once we have avoided being involved by his imprudence in a struggle simultaneously against France and Austria, we will proceed energetically against the party of hotheads, and so try to regain the confidence of Europe.

All this is for your private ear. I will send you tomorrow an official memorandum on our motives which you can show to M. Thouvenel. You must explain to him that, though our policy may have been unskillful, it is always governed by the sincere wish not to create embarrassments for France.

[*Il carteggio Cavour-Nigra*, vol. IV, pp. 202–4]

*Cavour speaks to the Senate in favor of annexing
southern and central Italy, October 16, 1860*

OUR POLICY, far from being revolutionary in the ordinary sense
of the word, must surely be recognized as highly conservative, but
conservative in the truest sense. If by revolutionary one means
that which aims to uproot society and disturb civil order, to substitute other rash and perilous principles for the ordinary rules of
family and social life, you must admit that King Victor Emmanuel's
government has fought such principles with the greatest firmness.
Gentlemen, you have only to compare the state of Italy today with
what it was in 1848 to see that those extreme and excessive principles which are generally and rightly called revolutionary have
lost all force here. In these last two years Italy has given a wonderful example of civil wisdom by her attachment to the principles of
order, morality and civilization. I think I and all of us can say with
pride that in the whole of history there is no comparable example
of another such political revolution as we have effected since last
July, none that has been accompanied with fewer crimes and
other social disorders . . .

How should we have reacted to recent events at Naples? Clearly
the Neapolitan government was unable to withstand a handful of
volunteers and so lacked the essential conditions for political
existence. No restoration of the Bourbons would be possible without foreign help; and that, gentlemen, would have been the greatest
possible disaster for Italy. As such a restoration was impossible,
and as the Bourbon government had recognized its own power-
lessness by surrendering the town of Naples without a fight,
morally it was dead. What were we to do? Should we have left
that noble part of Italy helpless before events? Should we have
allowed the germs of revolution which we had destroyed in northern Italy to multiply elsewhere? No, we could not.

By resolutely seizing the direction of political events in southern Italy, the King and his government prevented our wonderful
Italian movement from degenerating; they prevented the factions
which did us so much harm in 1848 from exploiting the emergency
conditions in Naples after its conquest by Garibaldi. We intervened not to impose a preconceived political system on southern
Italy, but to allow people there to decide freely on their fate.
This, gentlemen, was to be not revolutionary but essentially conservative.

In the Roman States, too, our presence can be equally justified. Even those most considerate of papal rights cannot surely believe that these states under the Pope could go on existing once they found themselves caught between liberal northern Italy and a revolutionary Italy in the south. In vain did the Pope appeal to the sentiments and religious prejudices of the Catholic world and enlist foreign troops to defend his territory. These brave soldiers, though captained by a great general, could not resist revolution pressing up from the south; nor could they stop the irresistible movement in the north for delivering those Italians still under papal domination. The Pope's temporal power in the Marches and Umbria was doomed from the day that the rest of Italy, from the Po River to the Gulf of Messina, had become free.

No doubt he could have gone on fighting for awhile, but the final outcome was certain, and this was a fact with which we had to reckon. We had to stop any conflict which might divert our national movement or arouse revolutionary passions. We had to carry out a great act of justice and remove that blemish in central Italy where Italian provinces were bent under an iron yoke by the force of foreign mercenaries. Perhaps the means we adopted to carry out this great act have not been entirely regular; but I do know that the cause is holy, and the end perhaps will justify any irregularities in the means. *(Signs of approval)*

Even in these provinces, gentlemen, we have not brought revolution and disorder. We are there to establish good government, legality and morality. Whatever people may say, I proclaim with certainty—and this will be confirmed by the impartial voice of enlightened, liberal Europe—that no war has ever been fought with greater generosity, magnanimity or justice.

[*Il Conte di Cavour in parlamento*, ed. I. Artom and
A. Blanc (Florence, 1868), pp. 620–6]

Telegram from General Cialdini, commanding the Piedmontese troops in the Abruzzi, to the Governor of Campobasso, October 20, 1860

MAKE IT known that I am shooting all peasants caught carrying arms. Quarter will be given only to regular soldiers. Executions have already begun today.

[L. Zini: *Storia d'Italia dal 1850 al 1866* (Milan,
1869), vol. II, pt II, p. 706]

The next problem was to take southern Italy from Garibaldi, and for this purpose the king went to Naples accompanied by Luigi Farini as civilian governor. Farini was deliberately chosen despite his personal feud with Garibaldi; and so were the army officers on the king's staff. Cavour tried from a distance to suggest the mixture of firmness and magnanimity which should be employed toward the volunteers, but the king, the governor, and the generals all disagreed with him and with each other on this critical point. Farini was soon writing home in desperation that, out of seven million people, he had found fewer than a hundred genuine believers in national unity. "The country here is not Italy but Africa, and the bedouin are the flower of civic virtue when compared to these people." Cavour encouraged him not to despair, but to ignore local advice and impose northern administrators and northern institutions. Neither Cavour nor Farini knew anything of southern laws and customs. In this emergency they thought they had no alternative but to assume that Piedmontese laws were superior; and on this assumption it would be better to introduce as many changes as possible before an Italian parliament could meet and decide otherwise.

Cavour to Farini at Ancona, October 8, 1860

GARIBALDI DOES not want to, nor could he, oppose the King, otherwise the better part of his men and the great majority of the country would turn against him. Everything depends on whether he will yield with good or bad grace, whether he will ask for reasonable or unreasonable conditions.

The King ought to be inexorable about Mazzini and the Mazzinians whether open or disguised. Crispi, Mordini, and all their followers must be swept away [Crispi was another future Prime Minister]. But we must show ourselves magnanimous to those who have actually fought. If Garibaldi's army acclaims the King, we must treat them well. Our problem here will be the demands and pedantic traditions of the regular army. Do not give way to the generals. Imperative reasons of state demand firmness. It would be disastrous if we behaved indifferently or ungratefully toward people who have shed their blood for Italy. Europe would condemn us, and in this country there would be a terrible reaction in favor of the Garibaldini.

I had an extremely lively discussion with General Fanti on this very point. When he spoke about the army's demands, I answered that we were not in Spain and this was a country where the army carried out orders.

I do not mean by this that we ought to confirm all the ranks conferred by Garibaldi or on his behalf. Good heavens no! But we must not send home all his volunteers with a mere gratification as Fanti would like.

> [*La liberazione del mezzogiorno e la formazione del regno d'Italia* (Bologna, 1952), vol. III, pp. 63–4]

The king's attitude to Mazzini, in a conversation with Cavour and Niccola Nisco in September 1860

WE WERE talking of the rumors that Mazzini was in Naples, and the King said to me: "Let him be. In making things difficult for others, he is only helping us. If we create Italy, Mazzini will be no trouble. If we fail, then it is better that he should succeed. I should be no good as a schoolmaster, but I could take up estate management. As simple *Monsieur* Savoia I would applaud his success . . ."

> [N. Nisco: *Storia civile del regno d'Italia* (Naples, 1890), vol. IV, p. 339]

Cavour to Farini, Governor of Naples, November 9, 1860

MANY THANKS for thinking of having me summoned to Naples by the King. Even though I beg to be excused, I am still grateful. But I cannot leave Turin until the diplomatic question has been resolved. Moreover my presence in Naples would serve no purpose. You yourself must have all the prestige that comes from being the sole representative of the government. My presence could only take something of this away without being of any help.

Finally, to put it frankly, both myself and the king would be embarrassed. He does not like me and is jealous; he endures me as a minister, but is glad when I am not near him. La Rosa [the king's mistress, Rosina] is in Naples. She would be annoyed by my arrival, and she would take it out on him.

As for me, it would be a lie if I pretended that I had forgotten the day when he arrived at the Palazzo Pitti [in Florence, April 1860]. Far from addressing to me a single word of thanks, he began abusing me outrageously and said things which, from the mouth of anyone else, would have led to a fight. As representative of the monarchic principle, which is the symbol of our national unity, I am ready to sacrifice my life and property for the King, in fact everything; but, as a man, I want only one favor from him, to keep as far away as possible.

[La liberazione del mezzogiorno, vol. III, p. 302]

Farini, Governor of Naples, to Minghetti, Minister of the Interior at Turin, December 12, 1860

IT IS a good thing that the Deputies who have come here from Italian Italy will have seen what a hell-pit Naples is. It will enable them to be fair to us if we fail to turn swine into heroes.

There is at least this to be said: things cannot get worse. After the fall of Gaeta [still a Bourbon fortress], I will show our strength and lay down the law. I have had all the heads of the Camorra deported from Naples to the island of Santo Stefano—during the revolution they were in charge of the police and of the customs. My action was a gross illegality, but there was no means of keeping Naples quiet without getting rid of that lot. Their followers seem to have taken fright, and so far the anti-government press has kept quiet about it.

You know how I used to think it was for Italy's well-being that we should not take Rome too soon. Now I have changed my view. By getting to know Naples I have acquired a solid conviction that we must enter Rome in 1861 and complete our national unity, for otherwise this cancer will spread everywhere else. In seven million inhabitants of Naples there are not a hundred who want a united Italy. Nor are there any liberals to speak of.

Nothing matters here except the town of Naples itself. The provinces can hardly maintain man or beast: they are just bossed by the odd baron or landowner. In the capital we have twelve thousand tricksters to contend with, that is to say attorneys, tangle-weavers, law-twisters, casuists and professional liars with the conscience of pimps. They run everything here, whether in public places, in the courts, on the stock exchange, in cafés, clubs and theaters. What can you possibly build out of stuff like this! And by God they will outnumber us in parliament unless we in the north stay closely united.

How will the election turn out here? Who knows? We have no facts to go on. Will those we rely on turn out to be reliable? I don't think so, at least not most of them. *Naturam expelles furca,* etc. They *never* tell you the truth. As a good native of Turin would say, they have a double face. But we are at the dance, and dance we must. Oh if only our *accursed* civilization didn't forbid floggings, cutting people's tongues out, and *noyades*. Then something would happen. We would have a clean slate and create a new people. The land is fertile, and the human animal is prolific here.

> [*La liberazione del mezzogiorno e la formazione del regno d'Italia* (Bologna, 1954), vol. IV, pp. 56–7]

Cavour, from Turin, to King Victor Emmanuel at Naples, December 14, 1860

FAR FROM failing to understand the difficulties with which Your Majesty has to struggle, the inclination here is to exaggerate them, and many think the situation desperate. I don't agree, for I fully trust Your Majesty's energy and good sense.

It is not an easy matter to say what should be done when one is far from the spot, but I will set down my views frankly. In my opinion the only way to emerge from this business lies in using greater firmness. Once we have captured Gaeta we must make it quite clear that discussion will stop. There must be no compromise with the various parties, whether these be followers of Mazzini or the Bourbons, revolutionaries or autonomists. We must then act in accordance with our views and at once start unifying the various administrative systems. It would be wise, for instance, to join part of the Abruzzi to the [ex-papal] province of Ascoli, and another to Rieti. Furthermore we need to publish our Piedmontese penal code at Naples, to reform the system of law courts and do a lot else to show that we mean to impose a unified system.

The Neapolitan consultative council will not like this. So much the worse for them! Garibaldi erred in appointing that council and it will be a good thing if it is dissolved. If this causes a public outcry, it will not matter; and if any riots break out, the grenadiers are there to repress unrest with severity. We must convince the country that we intend going ahead despite all obstacles. Nothing will be more fatal than hesitation and doubt. If we show unbending will, people will settle down and adapt themselves to the new regime, because our institutions are in all respects preferable to those from which they were liberated.

Our good Farini will be just the man to follow and carry out this policy—at any rate when he manages to pick up from the nervous crisis brought on by his first experiences of Naples. Encourage him to go ahead regardless. The goal is clear and is beyond discussion. We must impose national unification on the weakest and most corrupt part of Italy. As for the means, there is little doubt: moral force, and, if that is insufficient, then physical force.

[*Il carteggio Cavour-Nigra*, vol. IV, pp. 292–3]

The king did not manage to ingratiate himself with his new subjects in southern Italy. He liked to go off shooting for most of the day, and used to treat his Neapolitan visitors with some condescension. This was one contributory factor in the widespread opposition which northern government soon encountered. It is true that the king showed more common sense than Farini and Cavour in his open attitude toward Garibaldi and the radicals, but on this point it was not his policy which won: instead of trying to inherit Garibaldi's enormous popularity, officialdom misread the situation and gratuitously invited another element of antagonism.

It might have been different if Cavour had been able to come south and see things for himself, but he feared to leave Turin, and in any case his relations with the king and the king's mistress, Rosina, made accompanying Victor Emmanuel impossible. Early in 1859, the Prime Minister had put himself in a false position by trying to break this long-standing affair with Rosina. With a certain lack of finesse he directly accused her of being unfaithful to the king. The latter turned to Rattazzi, who had none of Turin's upper-class distaste for this lady, and Rattazzi investigated the matter and tactfully declared that Cavour's attack was unfounded. This strange episode played an important part in separating the two leaders of the *connubio*, and Cavour never forgave Rattazzi for it, though it is hard to see what else Rattazzi could have said. Even Cavour's friends thought that the Prime Minister's judgment on this occasion had been inexplicably at fault, and its effects on politics were serious. Part of the background was sketched in the memoirs of the secretary of the French embassy at Turin.

King Victor Emmanuel, Turin, 1861

THE CHARACTER and habits of the King reflect the uncouthness of his exterior. He hates society, show, and Court receptions; he dislikes appearing in public, but this unsociability springs from shyness rather than pride. The immense popularity he enjoys in the old provinces of Piedmont owes more to the monarchical sentiments of the people than to the personal qualities of the King.

There he is as popular and beloved as our Henri IV was among us, though far from equalling Henri in heart and mind. Events, and above all the genius of his Prime Minister, have raised him to the position he now occupies in Italy and Europe. If ever his name becomes famous in history, his only merit, his only glory will have been "to have allowed Italy to create herself."

It would be unfair, however, to represent him as a sovereign of no account. He has the acute shrewdness inherent in the Italian race, and is not wanting in mother wit. I had occasion to see several letters written by him to a celebrated woman, Madame . . . . , and was surprised to find a tenderness and delicacy of feeling in them that I was far from suspecting. His predominant quality is that of courage carried to the point of rashness. Although his father, King Charles Albert, brought him up with almost cruel severity, his education has been greatly neglected: he is lazy and ill-informed. Attending to public affairs, presiding over the cabinet, coming to decisions, are so many forms of torture to him, and the Comte de Cavour does his best to spare him these occupations. The King realizes the superiority of his Prime Minister, but has never forgiven it him; he submits while hating him with all his heart.

Like all mediocre men, Victor Emmanuel is jealous and quick to take umbrage. He will find it difficult to forget the manner of his triumphal entry into Naples, when, seated in Garibaldi's carriage—Garibaldi in a red shirt—he was presented to his new people by the most powerful of all his subjects. People are mistaken in crediting Victor Emmanuel with a lively liking for Garibaldi. As soldiers they probably have points of contact in their characters and tastes, which have allowed them at times to understand each other and join forces; but the hero's republican, often protective, familiarity is very displeasing to the descendant of the House of Savoy. After all, what sovereign, placed in the same situation, would not resent the fabulous prestige of Garibaldi's name? In any case, the frankness with which the King has spoken of him on certain occasions shows the real measure of his appreciation of the man. It was in the month of June 1860; Garibaldi had just landed in Sicily, and the result of his venturesome expedition was not yet known in Turin, when the French minister, Baron de Talleyrand, was ordered to present a note to the Turin cabinet in which the Emperor's government, while complaining bitterly of this fresh violation of the Law of Nations, referred to the fact that they were fully aware of the understanding between the Sardinian cabinet and Garibaldi. After a frank discussion with the Comte de Cavour, M. de Talleyrand asked to see the King. After his audience with the sovereign, the French minister felt convinced that His Majesty was far less pleased with the hero's attempt than people imagined. "*Mon Dieu,*" said the monarch to M. de Talleyrand, "of course it would be a great misfortune, but if the Neapolitan cruisers were to capture and hang my poor Garibaldi he would have brought this sad fate upon himself. It would simplify things a good deal. What a fine monument we should get erected to him!"

That day, certainly, the King would have been easily consoled for the death of the Captain of the Thousand. The bold attempt succeeded, thanks to the courage and prestige of Garibaldi, greatly assisted by Neapolitan treason. Naples gave itself to Garibaldi, and Garibaldi offered his conquest to the King. But to anyone in Turin who has followed events closely, it must be evident that, far from instigating and organizing the invasion of the Two Sicilies, Cavour at least at first did try to oppose it. It was not till he realized that he could not possibly put a stop to the enterprise, outflanked as he had been by the Garibaldian war party, that he kept aloof, tolerating everything, and prepared to take advantage, as he did, of a conquest he rightly considered dangerous and premature.

Without fear of contradiction, it may be said that His Sardinian Majesty is a braggart, no friend of the truth and very imprudent. He never misses an opportunity of talking of his twenty wounds, and he delights in a fabulous recital of the dangers he has experienced both in war and out hunting. Everybody knows, however, that, although he is extremely brave, the King has seldom suffered injury.

As for his amorous conquests, he describes them with a frankness and *sans-gêne* that have nothing of the gentleman about them. And what is stranger still, he often confuses the successes he has had with those he would have liked to have.

According to him, he alone directs the affairs of the State, and he is crushed every day under the burden of work.

The King makes a point of dressing simply, in complete contempt of ceremony. Abstemious, eating only one meal a day, though an abundant one, he prefers coarse, popular dishes. When he is obliged to attend an important political dinner, or a meal at Court, he will not even unfold his napkin; he refuses every dish;

with his hands on the pommel of his sword he scrutinizes his guests without attempting to conceal his impatience and boredom.

He is passionately fond of horses, hunting and physical exercise. Often, toward the end of autumn, and even in winter, he starts off alone with two *aides-de-camp* to hunt chamois in the mountains. These outings often last several days, sometime weeks...

Though love is not Victor Emmanuel's ruling passion, it must be admitted that the King has a decided taste for womanizing. "No sovereign," they say in Turin, "has been more successful in becoming the father of his subjects." He has five children by the late Queen and three by his favorite mistress.

Queen Adelaide, Archduchess of Austria, was a veritable saint. Her name and memory are revered throughout Piedmont. The King himself, selfish, hard and sharp-spoken as he is, had an unfailing respect for his wife, although admittedly the feelings inspired by the lovable character of the Queen, her mildness, her resignation, did not prevent him bestowing pledges of his affection on other women.

His relations with Rosina had already begun in the Queen's day. Rosina was the daughter of one of the Palace Guards, a body resembling the Austrian *Trabanten* and the French *cent-gardes*. She was sixteen years old and beautiful. Clever and intelligent, she succeeded in captivating Victor Emmanuel from the first. Of all his mistresses, she is the only one that has ever contrived to exert any real influence over him . . .

After the death of the Queen in 1855, the King acknowledged and legitimized Rosina's children, and their mother received the title of Countess Mirafiori, together with an endowment. Mirafiori is the name of a royal farm near Turin. Even today, and in spite of many infidelities that he does not trouble to conceal, Victor Emmanuel is still under the spell of his favorite. She is a commonplace woman, of no education; the King is afraid of her, but does not attempt to escape from the influence she exerts over him. The Comte de Cavour has tried many a time in vain to break this chain. At one time, the King having manifested a desire for a secret marriage to his mistress, a lively and very stormy altercation took place between the would-be Henri IV and his Sully, after which the minister's credit came near to being shaken.

[H. d'Ideville: *Journal d'un diplomate en Italie, 1859–1862* (Paris, 1872), vol. I, pp. 53–61]

20. Cavour's Final Problems, 1860-1861

Cavour's restless mind was never happy unless he was two stages ahead of the field and considering some possible, or even improbable, turn of events. At the same time as his troops were invading central and southern Italy, he was getting ready for another war against Austria. Until the British knew about this, they were trying to persuade the Austrians that a peaceful surrender of Venice would be in the interests of European peace. Cavour, however, said he did not want a peaceful cession, for a war would help to weld the nation together. A secret cargo of arms on its way to the Balkans then inadvertently fell into unfriendly hands, and, though Cavour disclaimed all knowledge of it, his agents had forgotten to remove the labels which showed that the crates came from the royal arsenals in Turin and Genoa. A European war was precisely what the British wanted to avoid, and they accordingly showed much less interest in helping Italy to win Venice.

A statement by Cavour, as quoted on November 30, 1860, by Férencz Pulszky, a Hungarian who was helping him to organize a conspiracy in eastern Europe

ABOUT VENICE, I can say nothing [remarked Cavour]. No proposition has been made to me, even indirectly. You know as much as I do. Only from the newspapers have I learned that the English ministers are working toward a peaceful cession of Venice in return for compensation to Austria. But no official move has been made, and for my part I don't want one. I want war with Austria for reasons of internal order. Without war it will be hard to fuse north and south Italy. Anyway I think that the cession of Venice just now is impossible. Austria does not want it. She is continually reinforcing her garrisons there, with arms, provisions and men. So you need have no fear of any peaceful cession. But I must make it clear that if, as I think unlikely, the diplomats induce Austria to give Venice up, I will not be able to refuse. No step has been taken yet, and I think none will be. In fifteen years perhaps, if there is no war, Austria might be forced by her other provinces to surrender Venice. But at the moment, since war seems inevitable, she will do nothing. Write and tell Kossuth this.

[L. Chiala: *Politica segreta di Napoleone III e di Cavour in Italia e in Ungheria, 1858–1861* (Turin, 1895), pp. 157–8]

Cavour to L. Valerio, Royal Commissioner in the Marches, December 28, 1860

I MUST warn you confidentially that, after the liveliest pressure from the French government, I have had to promise that the Order of Missionaries (Lazarists) should be exempted from the laws against religious orders which we have proclaimed in Umbria and the Marches. In Piedmont we have found the Lazarist missionaries harmless and well liked, so I think it good policy to humor the Emperor's special interest here.

I also beg you to avoid any expression which could lead people to think that the new Italian kingdom aims at conquering not only Venetia but Trieste, Istria and Dalmatia. I am fully aware that along that coast there are places where the population is Italian in race and aspiration. But in the countryside the inhabitants are of the Slav race. Moreover, if we showed any intention of barring the Mediterranean outlet of such a large part of central Europe, we would make gratuitous enemies of the Croats, the Serbs, the Magyars and all the German peoples. Any rash phrase could be a terrifying weapon in the hands of our enemies; and they might profit by it to antagonize England, who herself too would take an unfavorable view of the Adriatic becoming once more an Italian lake such as it was in the times of the Venetian republic.

[*La liberazione del mezzogiorno e la formazione del regno d'Italia*, vol. IV, pp. 144–5]

Cavour was always a skillful parliamentarian. His most reliable support against the king and the left-wing radicals was found in the men of substance and education who, under Piedmontese law, constituted the narrow electorate. It is true that he rarely let parliament help in policy-making, and the exclusion of clericals and Mazzinians made his liberalism in some respects more theoretical than applied; but royal power became weaker and that of parliament greater under his administration. Louis Napoleon advised him that it would be impossible to unify Italy by parliamentary means, and Ricasoli thought that a temporary dictatorship by the king was advisable. Garibaldi and the king himself had similar views. But Cavour refused to listen. In a sense, as his opponents made quite clear, he was a parliamentary dictator who already had all the power he needed. Any opposition to him was more verbal than substantial, and the deputies were mostly disciplined to act just as he wished.

Early in 1861, Cavour obtained an excellent result from the first general elections to be held in the newly unified kingdom. Parliament on March 14 declared that a Kingdom of Italy was officially in existence. On March 20, the king for the last time tried to get rid of him, and privately offered his job to Ricasoli "to show Europe that there is more than one man in Italy." But Ricasoli did not know the rules of this particular game, and had more sense than to accept. There did not exist the talent and experience to form an alternative government.

Cavour to the Comtesse de Circourt, December 29, 1860

I HAVE no confidence in dictatorships, above all nonmilitary dictatorships, and I think that parliament enables one to do many things which would be impossible for an absolutist ruler. Thirteen years' experience has convinced me that an honest and energetic ministry, so long as it has nothing to fear from any scandalous revelation in the Chamber and so long as it refuses to let itself be intimidated by party violence, has everything to gain from parliamentary controversy. I have never felt so weak as when parliament was shut. Quite apart from this, I could never betray my origin and my life-long principles. I am a child of liberty and owe it everything that I am. If ever it should be necessary to draw a veil over the constitution, it will not be myself who does it. If ever Italians come to think that they need a dictator, they would choose Garibaldi, and they would be right.

The parliamentary path is longer but more sure. Thus, the elections in Naples and Sicily do not frighten me. People say they will turn out badly. But I am convinced that the Mazzinians are less to be feared in parliament than in the clubs. What happened last year in Lombardy reassures me; for the electors were in a bad mood there too, and the deputies they chose were detestable. Cattaneo, Ferrari, Bertani were returned with enormous majorities, and these gentlemen came to parliament full of threats and insults. Yet what did they do? Beaten soundly on two or three occasions, they became so inoffensive that in the last big debate they voted with the majority. So don't fear. The same will happen to the southerners. The calm, heavy atmosphere of Turin will pacify them. They will go home tamed.

Big mistakes have been made at Naples. Farini did not act strongly enough at first; and then he fell ill, and the most terrible things began to happen. Farini is a man of heart and courage, but a series of disasters overtook him, and he no longer has the strength to continue with the difficult assignment which he had accepted with his usual devotion. He is urgently demanding to be allowed to resign. But the day an energetic and fresh mind takes over at Naples, all will go smoothly again.

The majority of the nation is loyal to the throne. The army is free from all Garibaldian taint. Turin is ultra-conservative. If in these circumstances we fail, we shall be imbeciles.

[*Cavour e l'Inghilterra*, vol. II, tomo II, pp. 284–5]

Sir James Hudson, from Turin, to Lord John Russell, February 8, 1861

CAVOUR TELLS me the King's speech will take the bull by the horns and will declare against attacking Austria in Venetia. This is the first result of his majority in parliament.

I don't think you sufficiently alive to the difficulties he has to contend with. Italy, thanks to Austria, the Pope and the Bourbons, is without public men, i.e., men versed in public affairs as applied broadly to internal and external politics. How could there be "men" amongst twenty millions of human beings born under Concordats and an Index Expurgatorius?

I have been with Cavour this morning. He was going patiently through a list of Lombards to find a Lombard minister. He named one after another, and looked wistfully in my face. I was constrained to imitate Lord Burleigh and shake my head all through the list. Next he turned to Neapolitans: *not one*, save Poerio (who won't accept). Next to Sicilians: here he brightened up a little; he has got two!—Torrearsa and Cordova—but the first perhaps won't accept, and the other is unknown to the public. But there is no ground for despair, the men will turn up; there are many men coming forward, but they must go through the parliamentary sieve.

To prove you what a big-hearted man Cavour is, he said—"I have brought forward Rattazzi as a proper person for the presidency of the Chamber of Deputies." If Rattazzi were stronger in opposition, Cavour would not have brought forward his name for President. But he says, "We are beginning a new life, I have sunk all personal and past differences, I hold my hand out to all save anarchists." With courage and conduct such as this we may hope to see Italy redress the balance in Europe.

The King of Sardinia did not succeed, as you truly say, in

pleasing the Neapolitans. No man ever will. But they must be made to walk in the light of the constitution, and they will be made to walk whether they like it or not. They are the most contemptible race in or out of Europe, and, I confess, I apprehend no great difficulty in their government. I am sure that Cavour does not. I told him what you say of the gold keys to be attached to their coats, and he roared.

> [In *Archivio Storico Italiano* (Florence, 1961), vol. CXIX, ed. N. Blakiston, pp. 373-4]

Of all Italian regions, Piedmont contributed the most to the risorgimento, and it was understandable that she should want to obtain most out of it. Cavour was quite insistent that, far from a Constituent Assembly being permitted to discuss a new constitution, united Italy should in practice be a continuation or projection of the sub-Alpine state which he had served so long and so well. Turin was not as large as Naples, nor as rich as Milan, nor as safe strategically as Florence, but there were other reasons why its predominance had to be protected. By preserving the king's old title, and by keeping the *Statuto* of 1848, it was made clear that Italy was not in any serious sense dependent on plebiscites or the popular will, but was rather an extension of the old monarchy of Savoy. Nor was this just a matter of form. Throughout the 1860's, the king, for example, was sometimes able to use the provisions of the 1848 constitution in order to pursue a personal policy of which his cabinet was entirely unaware. Some members of the cabinet continued to be his personal nominees and were used by him to spy on their colleagues.

Cavour to O. Vimercati, at Paris, March 13, 1861

THE CHAMBER OF DEPUTIES will tomorrow be voting the law about the title of King of Italy. Some of the Tuscan deputies want Victor Emmanuel II to become Victor Emmanuel I. But I am energetically opposing this, for it is based on sophistical claims which impugn the honor of the dynasty and threaten our principles of public law. I hope to prevent a vote on it, but I cannot stop Crispi, Brofferio, Petruccelli, etc., parading their eloquence on the subject. It is too good an occasion for the declaimers.

> [Bollea: *Una silloge di lettere del risorgimento*, pp. 434-5]

Unification had come so fast and unexpectedly that not even Cavour was prepared for it. Few Italians had clear ideas about what kind of organization to give the country. Few, indeed, possessed enough knowledge of the former states of the peninsula to have any views as to whether the disparity of social and economic conditions would be aggravated or relieved if a uniform system of laws were applied. Probably not a single person truly knew the various Italian regions well enough to be able to compare and choose between their methods of administration and codes of law.

Cavour himself hardly had time to make up his mind. In general he was no enthusiast for the French kind of centralization which in the end prevailed, but in the initial state of emergency there was a lot to be said for a quick, simple, and uniform solution, and there were powerful elements in his party which wanted a strong and centralized state. Among the intellectuals, Tommaseo and Montanelli disagreed with this, but they could be ignored. Cattaneo was another out-and-out federalist, who thought that too strong a concentration on national unity would be sure to obscure or enfeeble the individual freedoms which he placed before everything. Giuseppe Ferrari, another Lombard, strongly agreed with Cattaneo that Italian history could not be argued out of existence. The differences between neighboring regions were, as they always had been, incontrovertible, and indeed they constituted some of the greatest glories of the nation. According to Ferrari and Cattaneo, variety could still be compatible with unity if a federal constitution were adopted.

Ferrari's plea to parliament for a federal Italy

THE MOVEMENT for liberating Italy was begun by people brought up in the Piedmontese system of government; their ideas were developed with eloquence and honesty, after which those ideas were reduced to popular maxims and accepted with enthusiasm; though eventually, like all mortal things, they were condemned to die and disappear. These ideas, first enunciated by Count Balbo, were later amplified by the Abbé Gioberti. They were taken over, substantially unchanged, by others I will not name because they are still alive. The general idea was to say to the Lombards, the Venetians, the Modenese, Romans and Neapolitans, to all the peoples of Italy: "Revolt! for your grievances against the Pope, against Austria and the Dukes of central Italy, are justified; but after the insurrection there must be no discussion; you must become Piedmontese." (*Uproar*)

On this understanding, Lombardy revolted and became Piedmontese. Other states followed suit and Piedmont dominated all the cities of Upper Italy. Nothing was more natural. Gradually, too, it became clear that the Italian people were anxious to take advantage of the fact that Piedmont was a government already in being, and they decided to compel her politicians and generals to take arms against Austria and the Pope. Once it was laid down that the insurgents--disorganized, unarmed, without legitimate spokesmen, without guns or allies—had to appeal to Piedmont, it was only logical that Turin should impose herself on each state in turn, since otherwise her army and even her honor would have inevitably suffered.

Liberty was thus inaugurated by means of weapons, ministers, generals and governors selected in Turin; and how was it to be supposed that the Piedmontese, who had had to use their own money and equipment, would not then want to make Lombardy, Modena, Parma, the whole of Italy Piedmontese?

Cries of: No! No!

Ferrari: It was strange and almost incredible to see the way in which almost all the parties in this one small country managed to agree in assuming the role of Italian Liberator. I do not know anything in Italian history to equal the ingenuity displayed in diffusing this idea throughout the rest of Italy. Lacking any preconceived idea on the subject, even the rest of Europe accepted the Piedmontese leaders at their face value as leaders of Italy in the fight against Pope and Emperor. And these affirmations on my part should convince you, honorable colleagues, that I am far from slighting or calumniating the Piedmontese system. On the contrary, I believe in the great advantages that have made it popular. I myself can confirm that whenever Piedmontese troops have entered Italian territory they have been festively received and acclaimed. The Piedmontese system, just because it is clear-cut and uncompromising, was able to uproot the Italian despots and displace the Duke of Modena, the Duchess of Parma, the Grand Duke of Tuscany and the King of Naples. No Italian ruler could stand up to it. *(Movement in the Chamber)*

This system I speak of, gentlemen, is not something I have invented; it is history, pure history. I hope you are capable of understanding our own history. *(General signs of disapproval)*

President: I beg the honorable Ferrari to be as temperate in his speech as at other times, and not allow himself expressions that may offend the dignity of members sitting in parliament.

Ferrari: I confess to the honorable President that I am astonished to see that my words are considered hostile at the very moment when I am rendering the most profound homage to the past and present of Piedmont and the Piedmontese. *(Interruptions)*

Massari: Piedmont no longer exists.

Ferrari: . . . When the government said that Naples must surrender unconditionally, it was weighing its words, and you must permit me to weigh my words equally, on your scales not mine.

Unconditional surrender means that Piedmont could destroy all the Neapolitan laws and replace them by her own. *(Prolonged murmurs)*

Cries of: No! No!

Ferrari. Unconditionally, gentlemen; this was the word used. I am not censuring any idea or any intention; I am not attacking the government at the moment; I am discussing this word without reference to its author.

Whoever talks of *unconditional annexation* must mean that a country is to yield itself up in such a way that the annexing or seizing state can behave just as it likes. *(Noise)*

Cries of: We are not seizing anything!

President: I beg the Chamber to allow the speaker to develop his ideas freely. There will be plenty of other speakers to reply to him later.

Ferrari: I may be mistaken, but the word *unconditional* implies that the Neapolitan Kingdom will find itself at the mercy of a Piedmontese King and government; which comes to the same thing.

I am not talking here of a form of government; the discussion is not concerned with whether the annexing government is monarchical or constitutional, liberal or absolute; but we ought surely to consider, from the economic point of view, whether Upper Italy is on the same level as Lower Italy, and whether our government has the right to impose itself on the Kingdom of the Two Sicilies which has different laws and a centuries-old autonomy of its own.

I must stress a fact of which some are probably ignorant, but which I myself became aware of recently in Naples. I heard a thousand justified accusations against the Bourbon government, but Garibaldi was received with the greatest enthusiasm. Politically his revolution was accepted and considered above discussion. Everybody expected a new government to succeed the old one, and a new dynasty to replace the Bourbons; but no Neapolitan ever admitted to me that existing laws were bad or that people were waiting impatiently for new legal codes. The laws of the Two Sicilies are very good and compare well with those of other civilized nations; perhaps they are the very best in all Italy. The Napoleonic codes are already in force in southern Italy, yet you want Naples to submit unconditionally and immediately, with her eyes shut, to a kingdom whose laws are unsettled, whose finances are rocking, and whose administrative organization seems to be a mystery even to the members of the cabinet themselves.

Would it really be such a disaster if annexation were delayed for a month, even for a year? What misfortune would result if southerners were given time to reflect on their own future? . . .

Our very history rejects the possibility or desirability of our becoming a unitary nation; on the other hand a federal system will enable us to reach the very highest goals. In a federation every big city is transformed into a capital on its own, surrounded by its own territory. *(Protests)* In a federation every individual Italian state would continue to exist and would have an assembly of its own to perpetuate its own particular traditions. Each of these assemblies would then nominate representatives to the national parliament, in which the whole country, even those areas still under the Pope, would end by working out their own destinies. With a federation we shall still have a single army, because, as is also true in Germany and the United States, our purpose would be to unite and not disunite. We should also have a single foreign policy decided by the national parliament.

There is a widespread fallacy that federation means division, dissociation, separation. But the word *federation* comes from *foedus*, which means pact, union, a reciprocal bond; and the bond of federation is so flexible and strong that in Germany it is able to unite republics and principalities, and can raise ᵗhe President of the central Diet from being a simple citizen to rank with an Emperor or King. We may regard federation as the purest form of constitutional government, founding liberty on a written pact, on a multiplicity of assemblies, on the inviolability of all internal frontiers, and the solemnity of its central parliament. If you aspire to the Athenian or Lombardic kind of democracy, you may look to ancient Greece for your model; if you prefer the development of individual liberty, the United States offers you the best guide. Do you admire force? Then remember how the loosely organized Germans once destroyed the Empire of Rome, or how the Tartars invaded China, the most unitary nation that has ever existed.

I believe the moment has come to renovate Italy. I see the Pope reduced to the last degree of dementia *(Murmurs)*; I mean, of course, in his capacity as a temporal sovereign. *(General hilarity)* You have already engaged him in hostilities. Neither the brain of Pellegrino Rossi nor the valor of General Lamoricière succeeded in saving the government of Rome. It seems to be in its death agony, and reminds one of the fatal obstinacy of the Senate of Venice at its last hour. I know that in every federal nation there comes a crisis in which central authority triumphs, and this might help to destroy the more perverted institutions of our country. But construction will succeed destruction only when federal institutions come properly into being.

> [G. Ferrari, speech in *Atti parlamentari: Camera dei deputati* (October 8, 1860), pp. 930–6]

C. Cattaneo to Jessie White Mario, November 1860

OUR RESOURCES are very limited and uncertain. Nobody cares nowadays for scientific or literary questions, and as for politics every party read[s] exclusively what has been intended for them. Everybody is like a King and wants a flatterer. I confess I would be very happy could I hear in wide Italy one single echo of my own voice: *liberty and the truth*. Mazzini, Garibaldi, and all their friends have been expelled from Naples at the joyous cry of *Unity* (*Unity* meant *Cavour*). It would not have ended so had they begun with the pure, unequivocal cry of *liberty*.

> [Archivio Cattaneo, Museo del Risorgimento, Milan]

Cavour had not given up his early belief in decentralization, and he went on exploiting it for all it was worth as an electoral program in places where a strong autonomist feeling was known to exist. His government even made a half-hearted decision to introduce a new system of regional government with considerable devolution of power to the localities. But there were several opinions in the cabinet on this issue. Some of his party were anxious to kill off the old regional differences, or at least they wanted a system of local government which did not perpetuate the old frontiers of Tuscany, Modena, Parma and so forth. Minghetti who introduced the new measure showed such a lack of enthusiasm and conviction that the law was never passed. Not until 1946 did Italy decide to introduce a degree of regional self-government on the lines which not only Ferrari, but even Cavour and Mazzini himself, had vaguely adumbrated. The failure of Minghetti's bill, why it failed, and what consequences flowed from this, were to be much debated in subsequent years. No doubt Cavour, had he lived, would have given a much stronger lead, and one way or another would have managed to give better expression to local energies and loyalties.

Cavour to Marquis Montezemolo, Governor of Sicily, January 15, 1861

PROFESSOR EMERICO AMARI, as a distinguished and learned lawyer, will I hope admit that I am as keen on decentralization as he is, and that our political theories in no way involve the tyranny of a capital city over the provinces, nor the creation of a caste of bureaucrats who would subjugate all parts of Italy to an artificial center. Habit and tradition, to say nothing of geography, would make Italy in constant revolt against any plan of centralization. I have had occasion to express my ideas on this subject several times to the professor's brother, Count Michele Amari. Once we have settled the agitation that a few trouble-makers are trying to stir up purely from personal anger, it will be very easy to make some arrangement by which the central power would retain enough force to complete the great work of national redemption, while yet allowing the regions and provinces to have a genuine *self-government*. I will be grateful if you would remove any doubts people may have about my own ideas on this subject.

[*La liberazione del mezzogiorno*, vol. IV, p. 220]

Minghetti proposes a scheme of regional decentralization

GENTLEMEN, WE are all agreed on two points, on two negative points, if I may so express myself. For one thing, we do not want French centralism. In spite of the great advantages of centralism, in spite of the useful results it has had in France and elsewhere, in spite of the incontrovertible trend toward it in Europe today, the drawbacks it usually entails, and especially would produce in Italy, are such that I believe it to be the common opinion of this Chamber, and outside it, that this system is precisely what we must avoid.

On the other hand we do not want too much local administrative independence, as in the United States or Switzerland; though even in those countries I fancy nobody would dare to decentralize the administration to the extent of imperiling political and civil unity. There is a great distance between these two extremes, and there may be many and various compromise systems leaning more to one or the other side. Who can say which compromise would best suit the present and future situation of Italy?

This, gentlemen, must be the object of your study and your parliamentary discussions. To decide the question *a priori* would, in my opinion, be an act of great presumption and temerity.

And this feeling is not only mine but that of my cabinet colleagues, and it should influence not only the decisions of the ministry but the Chamber as a whole.

The ministry, to which I communicated my ideas at length before doing so to you, was unanimous in accepting them, while recognizing that most of the details should not be treated as a so-called ministerial question; ministerial questions are only legitimate when the political direction of the state is involved, or when agreement has to be not merely precise but immutable.

> [Session of *Camera dei deputati* (March 13, 1961),
> quoted in: *Discorsi parlamentari di Marco
> Minghetti* (Rome, 1888), vol. I, pp. 103–5]

A bitter scene in parliament on April 18 was an early indication that some fundamental disagreements were not far under the surface. The regular army, and in particular General Fanti the Minister of War, was still angry that the volunteers had been able to take so much of the limelight. Far from wanting to absorb these irregular forces as a new element of national strength, Fanti was determined that Garibaldi's officers should lose their rank if they transferred to the Italian army. A government regulation on April 11 further prescribed that only a limited number of volunteers would be allowed to transfer.

When this decision was questioned in parliament, Fanti argued that Garibaldi had appointed too many officers; but the opposition said that the proportion of officers to ordinary ranks was no higher than in the regular army; and moreover the small armies of the central duchies had been automatically incorporated even though their ratio of officers was ridiculously high. Fanti also argued that the officers of the defeated Bourbon army should have preference because they were professionals and more experienced; but the opposition replied that the volunteers were the most experienced and successful troops in Italy, and it was utterly wrong to prefer the Bourbon soldiers whom they had so soundly defeated.

Cavour agreed that many of Garibaldi's senior officers should be taken on, but he made it quite clear that volunteers and regulars could not be treated on the same footing, and his view prevailed. Much ill feeling was generated by this decision, and an important force was lost which might have been very useful in helping to pacify the south.

Garibaldi was not at ease in parliament. When he arrived there in April the deputies stood to applaud him, but his red shirt and American poncho looked absurdly incongruous among the frock coats and top hats. He took his seat on the extreme Left. He had a written speech, but put his script aside. When he accused Cavour of fighting a fratricidal war he was being unjust and tactless; yet, we now know, Cavour had given orders to "drive the Garibaldians into the sea" if they did not surrender Naples.

Garibaldi clashes in parliament with Cavour, April 1861

President of the Chamber [Urbano Rattazzi]: I call upon Deputy Garibaldi to speak. *(General stir of attention)*

Garibaldi: I shall first allow myself a brief reference to the speech by the honorable Ricasoli, and thank him for having introduced a subject of vital concern to myself, since it concerns the defense of my companions in arms. I thank him from my heart. I agree with him that Italy is now a nation. I feel certain of it because I have faith in our powerful army, and because I rely, too, on the enthusiasm and generous will of a country that has already given so many proofs of valor, even before there existed a disciplined, regular army. Yes, like Deputy Ricasoli, I repeat: Italy is made, in spite of the obstacles that intriguing persons are trying to raise.

I must also say a word about that part of the honorable Ricasoli's speech in which he touched on the subject of *dualism*.

Although he did not say so, the Chamber will permit me to state frankly that I think the person designated as the leader of one side in this dualism is alleged by the honorable Ricasoli to be myself. *(Sensation)*

And now that I have unfortunately been led into personal considerations, I must say further that I am entirely convinced that this dualism did not originate from me.

Suggestions of reconciliation have been made to me, it is true; but these suggestions were made in words, and Italy knows that I am a man of deeds; my deeds have always been diametrically opposed to the word reconciliation. Whenever any internal division was likely to injure my country's great cause I have submitted, and shall always submit. *(Applause in the Chamber and from the galleries)* However, as an ordinary man, I leave it to the conscience of the representatives of Italy to decide whether I can hold out my hand to one [a reference to Cavour's cession of Nice] who has made me a stranger in Italy. *(Loud applause from the galleries)*

President: I warn the galleries that all signs of approval or disapproval are forbidden; if order is not maintained, I shall be obliged to have them cleared. *(Hear! Hear!)*

Garibaldi: So much for dualism. It follows, therefore, that I do not agree with the honorable Ricasoli that Italy is divided in half. Italy is not divided, she is whole; because Garibaldi and his friends will always be on the side of those that champion Italy's cause, and will fight her enemies on every occasion. *(Cheers)* . . .

With regard to the Southern Army [the volunteers with whom Garibaldi had conquered Sicily and Naples in 1860], I must first remind you of its glorious deeds; the marvels it accomplished were obscured only when the cold, hostile hand of the government made its maleficent influence felt. *(Noise and disturbance)* When my hopes for concord were confronted by the horrors of a fratricidal war provoked by the government *(Lively protests from the ministers' bench interrupt him—Violent interruptions in the Chamber)*

Many shouts on the Right and Center: Order! Order!

President: I beg the honorable General Garibaldi *(Noise dorwns his voice)*

Conte di Cavour, Prime Minister (with vehemence): It is unpardonable to insult us in this way! We protest! We have never had any such intentions. *(Applause from the Deputies' benches and from the galleries)* Mr. President! See to it that the government and the representatives of the nation are respected! Call people to order! *(Interruptions and noise)*

President: I demand silence. It is the business of the President alone to maintain order and regulate discussion. Let nobody disturb it by protesting!

Crispi: I beg leave to ask for orderly discussion.

Garibaldi: I thought that, after thirty years' service rendered to my country, I had won the right to tell the truth before the representatives of the people.

President: I beg the honorable General Garibaldi to express his opinions in terms that will not offend any member of this Chamber or the ministers.

Conte di Cavour: He said we had provoked a fratricidal war! That is something very different from the expression of an opinion! *(Interruptions and various shouts from all the benches)*

Garibaldi: Yes, a fratricidal war! *(Uproar in the Chamber and the galleries)*

Cries of: Order! Order! It's a repeated insult! It's an insult to the nation! It's a deliberate provocation!

Shouts from the Left: No! No! Allow freedom of speech!

(Many deputies leave their seats. Noise on every side of the Chamber. The President buries his head in his hands. A number of deputies go up to the auditorium where a heated dispute is carried on)

(The session is suspended for a quarter of an hour)

(When the worst of the excitement has died down, the session is resumed at four o'clock in profound silence)

President: I am obliged, to my regret, to express the highest disapproval of the words that lately escaped the honorable General Garibaldi, in which he accused the government, unfairly and in unparliamentary fashion, of having wished to provoke a fratricidal war. I beg the honorable General Garibaldi to abstain from such accusations in his speech, because if he goes on in this way I shall be obliged to impose silence on him. Meanwhile he may speak.

Garibaldi (General attention): Then I will not speak of ministerial action in south Italy.

Our warlike King, a man of honor, has more than once declared that the Southern Army has deserved well of the country. The Chamber, I hope, will not suffer me to be alone in declaring that it has done its duty. *(Signs of assent)*

Cries of: That's true!

Garibaldi: Impartial history will tell the rest of the story.

But what has the Minister for War done with this body of volunteers?

He could have amalgamated it with the national army, as he did the armies of central Italy. If he considered the Southern Army of less value than the Central, he could have made it into a separate corps in the national army.

If he did not wish to keep the Southern Army in existence in any form, he should have disbanded it, but not humiliated it . . .

If it is desired to retain the Southern Army, it would be better to give every man one, two, or three months' leave, instead of offering him six months' pay as an inducement to quit. (*Applause, and a loud shout from the galleries:* That's true! That's true! *Sharp protests from the Chamber*)

President (vehemently): Again I request silence in the galleries.

Shouts from the Center and the Right: Have them cleared! Have them cleared!

President: At the slightest sign of approval or disapproval from the galleries, I shall have them cleared without mercy.

More shouts: Have them cleared at once! It's a fresh scandal!

President: I beg the Deputies to keep silence. It is the business of the President alone to maintain order in the Chamber.

I call upon Signor Bixio to speak.

Bixio (Stir of attention): I rise in the name of concord and of Italy. (*Hear! Hear!*) Those who know me, know that I am concerned above all with the interests of my own country. (*Signs of approval*)

I am of those that believe in the sanctity of the ideas that have guided General Garibaldi in Italy. (*Hear, hear!*) But I am also among those that have faith in the patriotism of Count Cavour. (*Applause*) I therefore beg that in the Holy Name of God there should be an Italy above parties. (*Prolonged, loud applause in the Chamber and the galleries*)

I have just come back from Paris, where I have met friends from all countries including our own, men from Poland, Germany, Hungary; and all of them, believe me, gentlemen, all of them are sad to see the two men who, in my opinion, represent the highest form of patriotism in Italy, sometimes in disagreement with each other. (*Stir*) I say this to General Garibaldi (*Hear! hear!*), and I say it to Count Cavour. (*Hear! Hear!*) General Garibaldi knows that when on active service he gives me orders as my superior, I carry them out without ever disputing them; but here I shall allow myself to express my opinion with frankness. As for the honorable Count Cavour, I have never paid court to him; I admire him for what he has done, while recognizing that even he may have made serious mistakes. I shall not attempt to enlarge upon these mistakes here, because I am not accustomed to using measured terms or to keeping to the strict limits of an argument, and possibly I might speak too frankly; but nevertheless I believe (forgive me if emotion prevents me from speaking with as much orderliness and coolness as I should like to), I am profoundly convinced that in reality General Garibaldi's words should not be taken too literally or be given the same weight as if they were written.

Cries of: He was reading from a script!

Bixio: We must remember that Italy needs all her military units. I am convinced that the army must be respected even in its prejudices. I am a sailor, but I am sufficiently acquainted with modern military history to know that Italy will not be able to fight another war without a thorough development of her army.

I attributed much of the bloodshed in France to the little confidence that the reactionary elements in her army used to inspire in the country, especially when France was threatened on all her frontiers. *(Signs of assent)*

If, therefore, we have had the great good fortune to succeed in war with these volunteer units, we must continue to use them.

I ask the Minister of War to join our various military bodies into one army, for we have need of them all. The war is not yet over; we have not yet reached our natural frontiers.

> [Session of *Camera dei deputati* (April 18, 1861),
> quoted in: *Il parlamento dell' unità d'Italia*
> (Rome, 1961), vol. II, pp. 610–19]

21. Italy after Cavour

Cavour's sudden and quite unexpected death on June 6, 1861, was an absolute disaster for Italy, not least because he had held so many of the strings of power in his own hand. He alone knew the answers. He had not trained any successor. For all his personal charm, he had found it impossible to work closely with anyone except subordinates: the king, Azeglio, Rattazzi, Lamarmora, Dabormida, Ricasoli, had all found him extremely difficult as a collaborator. Sometimes Cavour had held almost half the departments of state in his own hand. The only other person he truly trusted was Nigra, who was an intelligent and nice man, but useless for making policy and not a strong character. In April 1861, Hudson was writing that "altho' Cavour is admired and feared and followed, he is not loved."

Sir James Hudson to Lord John Russell, Turin, June 30, 1861

THIS MORNING I had a long talk with the King: he asked me your opinion of the cabinet which he has formed with Ricasoli as Prime Minister: I told him that you approved his maiden speech on taking office: H. M. said you may assure your government that the policy of my cabinet shall be moderate and temperate: I have to finish the Italian Question: I know that time, and temper, and perseverance, will all be necessary to enable me to do so: but I can well afford to wait: I am adverse to any violent or sudden motion in it: the Pope is ill: the conclave of Cardinals is gradually becoming conscious that the civil and ecclesiastical authority can be harmonized: I believe extensive changes in opinion are taking place in that body: I wish the changes which must take place to be the result of conviction and not of violence: I have, thro' Arese, proposed to the Emperor a mixed Italian and French garrison in Rome: Arese is not a diplomatist nor a politician but he is an honest conscientious man, and that is why I sent him to Fontainebleau.

He then went on to talk of Cavour and his early death: he rendered full justice to his many great qualities of heart and head: but he (the King) could not shut his eyes to the fact that his great statesmanship was at times most hazardous to the state: in his passion (said H.M.) he has sometimes kicked over every chair in this room. He has called me "Traitor," and worse, but I knew this was merely the effect of temper, and I used to sit quietly making my own notes of the particular matter which had driven him to this extremity of heat, and when he cooled I used to read them to him. After his bursts of temper he was cool and collected: I believe his reason forsook him in those moments, for he seemed to have no recollection of them: and hence I often doubted whether he were a safe guide, tho' I am the first to do justice to his immense courage and his great capacity for details of business.

I am not at all sure (he continued) but what we might have attained the same end with less labor and without alarming all Europe: just as I propose to conclude in peace the Union of Italy: for I am convinced whether it takes a little more or a little less time that we shall complete the unity of this peninsula.

He then passed in review the different provinces. Our chief difficulty, he said, is Naples. A country utterly demoralized: it exceeds all I have read or heard of. I have removed Durando from his command. He was too pliant. I have sent him sixty battalions and he is always asking for more men: I now send Cialdini who has temper, decision and judgment. I regret Durando's fall, for it is a *fall*, because he is an honest man and a respectable soldier: but he wants decision: San Martino will do very well, I think: he has tact and energy and great perseverance.

He spoke of all the crowned heads in Europe. He said, you English have the wisest, the best and the most meritorious of all sovereigns. The Queen of England is the wisest because she never oversteps her prerogative—the best, for she is the best example to the whole nation—the most meritorious for there is not a blot on her whole reign—and he then spoke very feelingly of the death of the Duchess of Kent.

Altogether the King shone upon this occasion I thought; I have known him for ten years and it appeared to me that those ten years have improved his character. Experience has softened him. Responsibility has moderated him. From a mere soldier and hunter he is rising into the politician.

He spoke of war as a sad necessity. He (today) had lost altogether that tone of a sabreur which five years ago was one of his characteristics, and he spoke of his children and of the Prince of Piedmont with affection and anxiety.

[*Russell Papers*, Public Record Office, London, 30/ 22/68/161]

The Kingdom of Italy was at once recognized by the British in March 1861, but by the French only in mid-June after Cavour's death, and with some reservations.

Thouvenel, from Paris, to Count Rayneval, French chargé d'affaires *at Turin, June 15, 1861*

HIS MAJESTY'S GOVERNMENT has never concealed its views about what happened last year in Italy. In now giving our official recognition to what then occurred, France is not making any guarantee about the future, just as she would not be giving retrospective approval to a policy about which she has always reserved complete freedom of action. Even less should Italy see in our recognition an encouragement for further enterprises which would endanger peace. Our point of view has not altered since the Warsaw meeting [October 1860] when we made our views clear to Europe as well as to Turin. At that time we thought that nonintervention should be the policy of all the Powers, and we added that we would not approve any aggression by Italy whatever its outcome. We still say the same, and so the Italian government cannot look to us but must bear the responsibility and take the dangerous consequences for any plans she may have.

The Turin cabinet, moreover, will realize our obligation toward the Holy See. It is superfluous to add that, by reopening official relations with the Italian government, we in no sense wish to weaken the force of papal protests against the invasion of Umbria and the Marches. King Victor Emmanuel's government could not, any more than our own, dispute the weighty considerations which inevitably dominate our attitude to the Roman Question. You must understand that, even though we may recognize the King of Italy, we must continue to occupy Rome so long as there are insufficient guarantees to maintain the interests which took us there in the first place.

> [*Lettere e documenti del Barone Bettino Ricasoli*,
> ed. M. Tabarrini and A. Gotti (Florence,
> 1891), vol. VI, pp. 18–19]

Baron Ricasoli, the new Prime Minister, was a proud and unyielding man, greatly admired for his honesty, but with little skill for the compromises, the minor deceits, and the personnel management inherent in parliamentary practice. As a Tuscan, he had not always seen eye to eye with the standardizing and centralizing procedures of the Turin bureaucracy: he had even called it "a yoke which I find more antipathetic than that of Austria, for they do not realize that we wish to be Italian and feel a new Italian spirit." Ricasoli's enthusiasm for Italy enabled him to sympathize more with Mazzini and Garibaldi than Cavour had ever done. He equalled Cavour in his capacity to override his cabinet even when it was unanimous against him on a point of real importance. His refusal to submit to French bullying on the subject of Rome was another example of the authoritarian temperament which finally persuaded the king to dismiss him.

The Prime Minister, Baron Ricasoli, to Count De Launay, Italian ambassador in Berlin, July 15, 1861

IT IS my duty to stress Italy's rights very firmly: her right to complete her unity, to assure her independence and peace. We claim Rome as our natural capital and Venetia as an integral part of our national soil. If only these rights were generally admitted, if only the Powers instead of opposing them would make them a priority in the councils of Europe, then our problems would be greatly simplified and many possible uncertainties and dangers would be removed. We are fully aware of the difficulties of other governments and of the interests which they are obliged to take into consideration, so we do not want to force events. So long as we were sure that our goal will one day be achieved, we would not want to precipitate a solution which could be otherwise achieved through the wisdom and sense of justice of the Powers.

Why are governments as enlightened, as patriotic and as just as that of Prussia unwilling to adopt an attitude that would confirm these legitimate hopes? Why will they not exert their influence in a cause that would serve to maintain general peace as well as the interests of civilization?

As you know, my dear Count, it is in no domineering spirit, nor out of timid condescension to revolutionary demands, that the King's government makes itself the interpreter and upholder of the Italian people's designs on Rome and Venice. Our conduct is guided by higher principles. By geographical position, as by her traditions, Rome is the natural center of Italy. Indeed it would be hard to think of a strongly established Kingdom of Italy without Rome as her capital. The papal government is so weak that it will always be dependent on foreign arms for protection and support. At this very moment it is under the protection of a foreign [French] flag, although a friendly one; and under that flag plots are being hatched and acts of brigandage organized which are spreading terror over our southern provinces.

Henceforward the temporal power of the Popes stands condemned alike by the spirit of the Christian religion as by the interests of civil society, for there are radical incompatibilities between the exercise of the priestly ministry and the cares of temporal government. The populations of the Papal States suffer from this and are no longer willing to support a system of government which condemns them to inertia and a material and intellectual prostration in sad contrast to the progress seen everywhere else in civilized Europe. As long as this state of affairs lasts, the Romans will be caught in a terrible vicious circle between mass insurrection and foreign occupation. Neither Italy nor Europe can accept indefinitely a situation which is such a permanent threat to peace.

> [*I documenti diplomatici italiani, prima serie*, ed. W. Maturi (Rome, 1959), vol. I, p. 251]

Cavour's financial policy had been to run a growing deficit each year as he tried to modernize the country and prepare it to meet war with Austria. Some Italians from other regions, instead of being grateful to Piedmont for her sacrifices, complained after 1861 that the rest of Italy was made to pay for old Piedmontese debts. Cavour had half-concealed this growing deficit. Indeed it took some time after 1861 before the financial situation became clear, and by that time heavy obligations had been undertaken in enlarging the armed forces. Roads and railways were another enormous undertaking, especially as so many of the railways did not pay and had to be heavily subsidized. Constant loans had to be obtained at more and more disadvantageous terms on the international capital market, until more than a third of Italian government bonds were held abroad and the Italian railways were mostly owned by foreign stockholders.

Quintino Sella in 1865 was the first Finance Minister who clearly explained what was happening. His answer, effective but extremely unpopular, was a heavy tax on flour which could not help but fall largely on the poor. As he frankly explained, poor people would be better helped by restoring a balanced budget than by Italy continuing to live in a world of financial illusion.

Francesco Ferrara was the most distinguished Italian economist of his day. His article was written soon after Sella's revelations had led to a heavy withdrawal of foreign money and a collapse of the stock market.

Financial difficulties as seen by a leading Italian economist, 1866

VERY CAREFUL consideration is needed if we are to obtain a proper idea of the present depression. Stock exchange prices in northern Europe will show us what northern countries think of Italy, for we are almost classed with bankrupt Greece; or linked with Spain, who recently made a vain effort to obtain a loan at 12 per cent in Paris; or with the Venezuelan republic which has had to repudiate a loan it raised not so long ago.

In almost any independent newspaper you will find words of warning or reproof addressed to us. Some throw in our face the stupidity of being so impatient; they remind us that England waited a good century before incorporating Scotland, and longer still before including Ireland; and they conclude that, in view of

our deplorable balance of payments, committed as we are to annex
Rome and Venice, we will surely end up losing Naples and Sicily
instead. Others want Italy to learn from Austria who, by sacrifices,
has won a far better balance in her economy than we in ours. Others
point out that the United States is preparing to bear a thousand million francs of extra taxation to serve the fifteen billions of debt
incurred by the civil war. And with these examples of how to
provide against great financial straits, people make fun of the streak
of sensitiveness which leaves us in puzzled debate about the tiniest
defects in some food tax. We are told to be less theoretical, or more
generous; we are mocked for our long hesitation in choosing between bankruptcy or a tax on flour.

In foreign eyes the very name of nation thus seems something like
a mockery when applied to our Italy which we admire so much.
She seems a beggarwoman knocking at the door of every banker
in turn, a girl at the beck and call of any strong man, a bankrupt
country which could at any moment involve in her own ruin
anyone simple enough to accept her pledges. However unjust and
maliciously exaggerated such estimates may be, the truth remains
that our country is getting a bad name; and if we ask why, if we
seek to find what mistakes we have committed, one single explanation can be heard: everyone points out that we are just not paying
our way.

Wherever we turn we can see the signs of this secret poison that
is corroding the vitals of the country. If we did not already know
that twenty-two million people had broken down the barriers that
held them apart and almost at enmity in various groups; and if we
did not know that, for some years now, they had been gathered into
a common life and government; if we did not know these facts
there would be very little in our economic situation to prove that
this great agglomeration of civilized men had now come together by
an act of will. Such fitful movement as our industry shows is no
more than an artificial and ephemeral achievement of a government
whose industrial aim can be no more than to clothe soldiers and
found cannon. The nation remains immobile and imprisoned in a
world which is now quite out of date. No spark of progress has
touched it. Our fields are cultivated in the same way as before, and
ancient skills go on being exercised; but no need is apparently felt
for large-scale enterprises, or at least no means can be found of
carrying them out, for the spirit of association is just nonexistent . . .

All our limited annual savings are thus absorbed by government stock which lures the courageous with an 8 per cent interest. This unusual fact reflects the discredit into which the country has fallen in the opinion of suspicious people. For our budget consistently shows outgoings exceeding revenue by a good third.

> [F. Ferrara: *Nuova Antologia* (Florence, January 1866), vol. I, pp. 154–6]

Advice to the Minister of Finance from the London Economist, *1865*

THERE CAN be no doubt that a better application and administration of the existing taxes would enormously increase their yield; and to this reform [the Finance Minister's] first efforts ought to be, but we regret to say are not, directed. For example, the produce of the customs is disgracefully small, especially at the port of Naples, partly owing to extensive smuggling, partly to the old leaven of corruption which used to permeate every branch of official life under the former regime, and which has not been by any means eliminated yet. The functionaries of Ferdinand the Second were systematically and notoriously robbers; their illicit gains were out of all proportion to their nominal salaries; and their venality was connived at if not actually encouraged by the Court. It takes a long time no doubt to eradicate a vice like this; but almost any steps, however harsh and peremptory, in that direction would be better and safer and more productive than raising the rate of duty or laying on fresh taxes.

Then the income tax, which is heavy and ought to yield a large revenue, has been mismanaged in more ways than one. First of all, instead of making it very light to begin with, and keeping it light till the machinery for levying it was perfected and the people accustomed to its operation, and a certain equality in its pressure obtained by experience and modification, it was deemed so good and so tempting an impost that the government, under the exigencies of the times, actually raised the assessment, or rather the rate, for the second year even before the first had been completely paid up. The consequence was that those who might have borne and cheerfully contributed a very moderate percentage, began to dodge and cheat in order to evade a severe one. Then it was made to descend too low, embracing nearly every class, except the very poorest who can obtain from the municipality a certificate of poverty; so that if a peasant or laborer is honest enough to admit that he gains two or three francs a day, he has to pay income tax on that, as well as small tradesmen whose profits scarcely reach £50 a year . . .

In the introduction of railways, again, considerable mistakes would appear to have been committed. The government were too grand in their ideas and wished to do too much at once. They were well aware of the enormous value of these fresh arteries of communication in developing resources, opening markets, spreading civilization, and promoting union. But they did not sufficiently consider that *feeders* to these arteries are essential to their use, and they spent much on railways that would have been more profitably expended in making crossroads and parish roads—*routes communales et vicinales*. Then they made railways where they were useful indeed but not necessary, and neglected them where they were the very first condition of improvement. Thus a glance at the map will show a great network in the north, in Piedmont and Lombardy, and scarcely a single line in the Neapolitan dominions. It was right and very important to make the great railway along the Adriatic coast from Milan to Lecce; but in all the rest of the south there is scarcely a single mile which did not exist or was not begun under Ferdinand; and no part of the country needs increased means of communication for the development of its resources and the satisfaction of its grievances and wants half so much as the provinces of the old Kingdom of Naples. On the other hand the line from Turin to Cuneo might have waited indefinitely; and that from Genoa to Spezia, which will be very costly, being nearly half of it tunnelling, was not wanted at all, there being quick and easy communication by sea.

But this was not all: the government, in their anxiety to have their railway system as complete and as rapidly organized as possible, made very injudicious bargains with the companies to whom they granted the concessions—guaranteeing so ample a dividend as greatly to diminish the motive for promoting the accommodation of the public. The proprietors are secured a certain return for their money, and they do not see their way to obtain a very much larger return even by extra exertions and more numerous or cheaper trains —at least not yet. The consequence is they are acting as rich and *secure* monopolists are apt to act, and take no pains to develop traffic by increased facilities.

In conclusion, we may briefly signalize one other blunder—or what seems so not only to us but to some of the most practical among the Italians themselves—the extravagant expenditure on the navy. It may be necessary to keep up a vast army: it cannot be necessary to attempt to become a great maritime Power for years to come. Italy cannot rival or approach France or England, and she need not guard against Russian attack. All that she needed in this direction is to have a marine a fraction more powerful than that of Austria—to secure which would have cost her little. Instead of this she has wasted many millions in the purchase of ironclads, in the building of experimental ships of war, and in the construction of naval arsenals and dockyards at Spezia and Taranto—from which she can scarcely hope to reap any advantage beyond that of giving employment to a certain number of laborers and artisans, many of whom are foreigners. On the whole, no one can visit Italy or see much of her public men without being convinced that a large reduction in her expenditure and a regenerated administration of her finances are at present her most urgent wants.

[*The Economist*, (London, October 28, 1865), pp. 1299–1300]

One of the saddest things about the concluding years of the risorgimento was that Mazzini, whose own contribution had been so fundamental, remained in exile and in opposition. His own joy in Italy decreased little by little after 1849 as he had to watch her formed on lines very different from those of his own prophetic dream. He had expected too much. He had wanted Italians to rise and deliver themselves without outside help, and had failed to see that patriotism in its early days was bound to be a minority creed. Living away from Italy he could not believe that so many Italians could acknowledge a loyalty to the Pope which might confuse their political allegiance. Most Italians were farm laborers who lived on pittance wages and a diet of bread, water, and vegetables: in 1861 such people could have little idea what was meant by Italy or parliament—*L'Italia*, or rather *La Talia*, was thought by some Sicilians to be Victor Emmanuel's wife.

Mazzini had genuinely expected to bring about a moral change in human beings. He could not reconcile himself to the growing fierceness of the division between various classes and nations. The advance of socialism came as a severe disillusionment to him, and so did the fact that nationality was sometimes becoming a divisive and even an illiberal force intead of being the simple emancipation of suppressed peoples. He now found that Italians were as much corrupted as other peoples by materialism and egoism, and it almost broke his spirit.

Several times Mazzini was elected to parliament, but he was still technically a rebel, and parliament did not want his brand of republicanism represented in the Chamber. Several times he made clandestine visits to Italy with false passports made out in the names of Charles Smith and John Brown. Always he remained the conspirator, and in 1870, betrayed for the last time, he was caught on a boat in Palermo harbor and spent a few weeks in an Italian prison. Only after his death, which occurred in 1872, was it thought safe for official Italy to recognize him as the first of the founding fathers.

F. D. Guerrazzi speaks during a debate which ended by nullifying the election of Mazzini to parliament

IN ONE of our most unhappy, abject periods, it was Mazzini who gave us the idea and hope that Italy singlehanded could defeat the seven or eight tyrants who ruled her and become a single, strong nation. Is there anyone with an Italian heart who would not embrace such a man and want to welcome him home and offer him every kind of hospitality?

Mazzini first had his vision in Liguria, and thence it spread into Tuscany. Some young men who shared his hopes welcomed the message, though for them it meant persecution, death or exile. Even among our friends we were thought madmen; even our mothers and our families rejected us! (*Cries on the Left:* Well said. It's true.) . . . Here is a man who is old and infirm, of whom Saffi tells us that he laments only the fact that he may die before Venice is Italian; who does not complain of his physical sufferings, nor of the filthy slanders put upon him by a vile and mercenary press (forgive me if I offend your ears and my mouth by mentioning such a degrading fact). Will you refuse such a man the permission to return to his native land, where his father's legacy has by now been reduced to a pittance of 40,000 lire? Will you refuse to let him visit his mother's grave which the common people go to kiss on his behalf every year? Will you let him die overseas in a foreign country, laid to rest by foreign hands? No, gentlemen, that you cannot and must not do. People can forgive a great deal. I myself was born a common man and have spent my life among ordinary folk: I assure you that such people can forgive offenses against property and persons where they will never tolerate an insult such as this would be to their feelings of piety.

[*Atti parlamentari: Camera dei deputati, discussioni* (March 21, 1866)]

Mazzini to Giuseppe Ferretti, August 25, 1871

THE ITALY which we represent today, like it or not, is a living lie. Not only do foreigners own Italian territory on our frontiers with France and Germany, but, even if we possessed Trieste and Nice, we should still have only the material husk, the dead corpse of Italy. The life-giving touch of God, the true soul of the nation, is lacking.

Italy was put together just as though it were a piece of lifeless mosaic, and the battles which made this mosaic were fought for reasons of calculating dynastic egoism by foreign rulers who should have been loathed as our natural enemies. Lombardy, scene of the great Five Days in 1848, allowed herself to be joined to Italy by the fiat of a French despot. The Venetians, despite their heroic defense in 1849, come to us by kind permission of a German monarch. The best of us once fought against France for possession of Rome; yet we remained the slaves of France so long as she was strong. Rome therefore had to be occupied furtively when France lay prostrate at Germany's feet [in 1870] just because we feared to raise our ancient war cry against the Vatican. Southern Italy was won by volunteers and a real movement of the people, but then it resigned its early promise and abdicated to a government which still refuses to bestow on Italy a new national constitution.

The battles fought by Italy in this process were defeats. Custoza and Lissa [in 1866] were thus lost because of the ineptitude or worse of our leaders. Italians are now a vassal people, without a new constitution that could express their will. We can therefore have no real national existence or international policy of our own. In domestic politics we are ruled by an arbitrary violation of the law; administrative corruption has been elevated into a system; a narrow franchise means that we are governed by a few rich men who are powerless for good. Our army is not popularly based, and it is used only for internal repression. Rights of the press and of free association are fettered, and a corrupt political system inevitably is bringing a slow but growing financial collapse. Abroad we waver as before between a servile attachment now to France now to Germany. The alliance with the people has been betrayed, and our relations with Europe have thrown morality overboard just as in the worst centuries of Italian decline.

Some of our party are indignant with what is happening; though many of them forget our splendid past traditions and are eager to copy the maddest and most ruinous foreign political systems based on force. Ordinary people, however, are disillusioned. They had watched with an astonished presentiment of great things to come as Italy, once ruler of the civilized world, began to rise again; but now they avert their gaze from what is happening and say to themselves: "this is just the ghost of Italy."

> [In *Roma del Popolo* (August 31, 1871); reprinted in *Scritti editi ed inediti di Giuseppe Mazzini*, ed. M. Menghini (Imola, 1941), vol. XCI, pp. 162–4]

22. The Southern Problem

The ministers who ruled Italy after 1860 were mainly northerners, and those who came from the South had mostly spent long years in exile which left them out of touch with their home provinces. Cavour never traveled further south than Florence, and never spent more than several days even in Tuscany. The problems of Naples and Sicily were still less easy for him to comprehend than those of the center.

Sicily in 1848 and 1860 had dramatically started the two most decisive nationalist revolutions in Italy, and yet Sicily was a good deal less nationally conscious than Lombardy and Piedmont. Educated Sicilians spoke of their own island as an ancient and glorious nation in its own right. One impetus to revolt in 1848 and 1860, apart from sheer poverty, was the strong dislike of Naples, in other words a revulsion from, rather than an attraction toward, the mainland. Another paradox was that, inside Sicily itself, the same landowners who opposed the revolution while its success was in doubt were the first to become out-and-out patriots when Cavour's soldiers and policemen offered the best chance of putting down social disorder; and for the same reason the peasants, who had earlier helped Garibaldi, often changed their allegiance when the social revolution was brought to an end. A third complication was that other parts of Sicily had preserved many resentments against Palermo, the island's capital. Palermo was the home of most of the aristocracy, a privileged tax haven, with a virtual monopoly of jobs, government subsidies, and the like. But in 1860–1, Messina, Catania, and other towns looked to Turin for help in breaking free from Palermo and establishing more municipal autonomy. Filippo Cordova came from this other side of the island. For years he had been an exile in Piedmont and a colleague of Cavour's. Now he was the foremost Sicilian inside the government.

F. Cordova, from Sicily, to Cavour, January 4, 1861

FIRST A short account of the situation, and then a word about the past to explain it. Outside Messina, and to some small extent Catania, Sicily had no feelings of *Italianità* until April 4, 1860. As usual, the island then followed Palermo, whose real desire has always been to maintain a separate King with a royal court and an entirely artificial life at the expense of Sicily as a whole. This was the aim of Bentivegna's attempted revolution [December 1856], and I went against the general opinion by writing as much at the time in the columns of the *Risorgimento*. Italian nationhood and annexation to Piedmont were proclaimed by Pisani in Palermo on April 4, by Pilo and his friends up in the mountains, and then were spread all over the island by the men who landed at Marsala.

Palermo accepted the annexation in a shamefaced way, but later regretted it just like a forced marriage. Palermitan opinion is always shifting; it is dissatisfied, though does not want to admit the fact. But thank God all the rest of the island has joined up with the Italian kingdom in a sincere and cordial spirit.

[*La liberazione del mezzogiorno*, vol. IV, pp. 175–6]

Northerners in general had been so ignorant of southern Italy that many expected to find a potentially rich area which needed only the benefits of an honest administration to become prosperous. They had not quite understood what it would mean to encounter 90 per cent illiteracy, a thoroughly feudal countryside, an unintelligible language, and ways of behavior associated with the Neapolitan camorra and the mafia of western and central Sicily. They brought with them sophisticated procedures such as elections and juries, though in a feudal environment these liberal practices could assume an altogether different and less liberating guise. They introduced higher taxes and lower tariffs which had been devised for a country at a much more advanced level of economic development. They introduced the Piedmontese compulsory education act, but they could not suddenly provide teachers and school buildings, let alone the wish to be educated. They dissolved the monasteries without reckoning the effect of such a revolution on the provision of charity, on unemployment, or on religious sensibilities. Almost none of these northerners liked being sent to Naples or Sicily, and few survived there without losing their reputation. An enormous and variegated opposition soon made the near unanimity of the plebiscites look very puzzling indeed.

*C. Nigra, Secretary of the Naples administration, to Cavour,
March 17, 1861*

WE ARE in no way through with the dangers here, especially as
there is an infinitude of Bourbon soldiers at a loose end, without
work or provisions. We also have brigands who will be occupying
the mountains by springtime. We have a hostile clergy; and Garibaldi's followers are discontented, angry, even starving. Five hundred of them who were demobilized with three months' pay are
now a prey to that worst of counselors, hunger—they are wandering
through the streets of Naples and stealing for their livelihood. We
have outbreaks of typhoid raging among the soldiers who have
returned from Gaeta, and this causes considerable difficulties. The
officers of the former Bourbon army and navy are cross and discontented; and they are looked down on by northern officers. The
aristocracy is hostile and in mourning for the Bourbons—Portici has
become our Faubourg Saint Germain. The arsenal workers and rail-
waymen are restless. The vast number of municipalists, desiring
local autonomy, feel their interests to have been badly damaged.
The devout have been thrown into confusion by the dissolution of
convents and monasteries.

Nothing seems to appease the official employees, the infinite
number of lawyers, or the huge mob who used to live on official
alms and robbery. The municipal authorities, together with the
mayor and corporation, were offended by General Ricotti's letters, and ordinary citizens grumble constantly against the burden
of military requisitioning. The Piedmontese officers, the Piedmontese civil servants, and everyone coming from northern Italy,
never stop complaining quite openly about the multifarious injus-
tices they find (often quite rightly). Then we have saboteurs;
others who just like fishing in troubled waters; a minority who still
cling to Murat; and also a handful of Mazzinians. This is the sort
of hell you have sent me to.

To add to the difficulties, we are short of *carabinieri* and men
for policing the provinces. The administration is corrupt from top
to bottom. The press is appalling. The people may be docile but
they are unstable, lazy and ignorant. Food is relatively dear. And
dominating the picture we have the gigantic figure of Garibaldi

growing bigger and bigger on his rock at Caprera and casting his enormous shadow even at this distance.

[*Il carteggio Cavour-Nigra*, vol. IV, p. 363]

Massimo d'Azeglio, the elder statesman of Italy, had disliked what he called the underhand deceit of some of the methods by which Cavour had created the nation. He strongly opposed the idea of making Rome into the national capital, for he feared the effect on Italy of this clerical environment. The annexation of Naples was in his view like sharing a bed with someone who had smallpox. The manifold signs of opposition in Naples were obvious proof that something had gone wrong. His confidential letter on this subject to Matteucci was soon, perhaps not unintentionally, published in a French newspaper. Azeglio was a pessimist. Maxime du Camp in the following year received a much more hopeful impression of Naples.

Massimo d'Azeglio to C. Matteucci, August 2, 1861

IN NAPLES we drove out a King in order to establish a government based on universal consent. But we need sixty battalions to hold southern Italy down, and even they seem inadequate. What with brigands and nonbrigands, it is notorious that nobody wants us there.

What about universal suffrage you may say! I know nothing about suffrage; but I know that battalions are not necessary to the north of the Tronto River, only on the south. So there must have been some mistake somewhere. Our principles and our policy must be wrong. We must get the Neapolitans to tell us once and for all whether they want us there or not. I realize that we Italians have a right to make war against those who wish to keep the Austrians in Italy; but we cannot preserve the same hostility toward Italians who, while remaining Italians, reject union with us. I think we have no right to use guns on them, unless you want to put us on the same level of expediency as Bomba [Ferdinand II] when he bombarded Palermo, Messina, etc. I know that this is not the general view, but I have no intention of abandoning my right to use my reason and to say what I think.

[M. d'Azeglio: *Scritti e discorsi politici*, ed. M. de Rubris (Florence, 1938), vol. III, pp. 399-400]

Opinion at Naples in 1862, as seen by a Frenchman

NEAPOLITANS HAVE now accepted, quite rightly, that administrative reforms must be postponed a little. Italy still has no real capital, no proper frontier to the northeast, and is still occupied in part by an enemy Power; hence national unity must come first. Progressive reforms will follow, as indeed was implied in the government's acceptance of the plebiscite in southern Italy; but first the government must be helped to make the nation.

Patriotism, which many would say was the highest ideal of all, comes absolutely new to most Neapolitans. Former governments carefully fostered a local loyalty and increased the general antagonism between north and south. It was this selfish isolation, practiced by Italian rulers who lived under Austrian protection, which largely explains how Austria managed to dissolve the common front and end the revolution of 1848–9. Only five years ago, if I asked someone if he was an Italian, he would answer: "No, I am a Neapolitan"; and, apart from Neapolitans, also Calabrians and Sicilians each thought of themselves as quite separate peoples. Even though these southern provinces belonged to a single kingdom, they contained a veritable Babel of different *patois*.

Today things have changed. You will now be answered: "I am an Italian from Naples"—or from Messina, Brindisi, or Maida. Everyone is now an Italian and feels it. In 1860, after Garibaldi's arrival at Naples, people at first saw in him just a new, easier master replacing the old; and many of the common people would cry "Long live united Italy," and then ask us "What is *Italy*, and what does *united* mean?" But during May and June of this year, 1862, I have spoken to many people—sailors, peasants, and those delightful layabouts who would now be humiliated to be called *lazzaroni*—and all of them know about Italian unity. They speak about it together, and think of Rome. About Venice they say that "it is at the other end, as it were, the Reggio of northern Italy." Anyone who knows Neapolitans, and who remembers how indifferent they used to be to everything, will recognize that a striking progress has been made.

[Maxime du Camp: *Revue des Deux Mondes* (Paris, September 1, 1862), vol. XLI, p. 8]

Azeglio's outburst was chiefly provoked by what the government politely called "brigandage," since normal kinds of banditry were now being given a strong political overtone of pro-Bourbonism. Brigandage also contained a strong element of Catholic reaction against the provocative and ungenerous treatment given to the clergy. Some of the brigands were just peasants fighting back against Cialdini's executions in the Abruzzi, or were registering the only effective protest against rising prices and the enclosure movement in the countryside. The landowners no longer had a paternalistic government to keep them in check. One result of the risorgimento was that the landholding classes became more powerful than ever: they were the electors; they controlled local government; their wishes decided the appointment to jobs, the apportionment of local taxes and public works' contracts. They could now ignore Bourbon social legislation and enclose the common lands in each village to their own exclusive advantage, with the result that peasant families were deprived of grazing lands which for centuries had been the basis of their livelihood.

Ulloa was a Neapolitan jurist who had served the old regime with loyalty and had followed Francis II into exile at Rome. There he became Prime Minister of a Bourbon government in exile, an anomalous position that he held with some dignity. In this pamphlet he pointed out that 90,000 Italian troops were tied down for years by this "brigandage," in other words more soldiers than had taken the field against Austria in 1859; and they were not nearly enough. Indeed there were probably more casualties in this submerged civil war than there had been in all the patriotic wars of liberation put together. Ulloa was strongly partisan and told only one side of the story. Much of the brutality was an almost inevitable reaction of desperate soldiers trying to exist in a hostile country against an enemy who could be as cruel as he was hard to confront and defeat.

Naples in July 1863, as reported by the Prime Minister of the Neapolitan government in exile

PIEDMONTESE TROOPS are in occupation of southern Italy, but only thanks to a rigorous and pitiless enforcement of martial law. Under the old regime, before 1860, Naples could be placed under emergency regulations after an insurrection, but just for a matter of three days, and without people being arrested, without suspending freedom of the press. The Piedmontese, on the other hand, have kept Naples under martial law for six months; and Neapolitans are treated by them not as people fighting for their independence, but as slaves who have revolted against their masters. Naturally bloodshed breeds more bloodshed. This always happens in civil strife, and Naples is now the scene of a civil war as well as a war between sovereign states.

Those who will not submit are simply exterminated. Pinelli, Neri, Galateri, Fumel and their kind, have announced a war of extermination in which "pity is a crime." Wherever an insurgent has fallen into Piedmontese hands he has ruthlessly been shot out of hand. Sometimes we have seen human sacrifices of forty or fifty prisoners at once . . . [There follow three pages of details]

The official gazette at Naples announced that a Piedmontese unit had entered Trevigno and killed "forty brigands." The truth is that these were just poor unfortunates who had fled from fear, but who then heard that supporters of the King [Francis II] had recaptured the town, and so were misguided enough to return home with a safe-conduct from the mayor. This is known by everyone, but fear makes people keep silent. Yet a Piedmontese minister now has the face to tell Europe that, if pacification is proceeding slowly in the ex-Kingdom of Naples, it is because he does not want to override constitutional freedoms!

Half a century ago, General Manhès was the terror of Calabria; but this Frenchman, Fumel, has proved himself far worse.

Everyone has heard the frightful story of how Pontelandolfo and Casalduni were destroyed. A band of insurgents had fallen on a detachment of Piedmontese and killed some soldiers. In reply, an example was made. Another detachment was rushed up, and soon all the inhabitants, men, women, the old, the young, were buried in the ruins of their burning homes! General Cialdini, who ordered this extermination, simply gave out that: "Justice has been done at Pontelandolfo and Casalduni." Subsequently, after a massacre at Castellamare in Sicily, the authorities at Palermo inserted these words in the official gazette: "At Castellamare the guilty have been rigorously punished." The magistrate here uses a soldier's language. Not even the conquest of Ireland saw such enthusiastic ferocity, even though Saxons and Celts were quite as different from each other racially as Neapolitans are from Piedmontese. Yet England which has seen many civil wars has known nothing like these horrors.

Pardon was promised to every brigand who gave himself up of his own accord. But those who surrendered at Livardi, Caserta, Nola and many other places, were at once shot; and their unhappy families, crazed with grief, were seen combing the fields for the remains of their murdered children. Only the cut-throats of 1793 were capable of such terrorism.

At the end of 1861 several dozen Neapolitans and Spaniards decided to give up the Bourbon cause and flee to the Papal States. When they were surrounded just before reaching the frontier, they surrendered without a fight in the belief that their lives would be saved (if they had thought otherwise they would have put up a desperate resistance). As once they were disarmed and shot.

Compare this with when, in 1844, the Bandiera brothers landed in southern Italy to start an insurrection; they were captured with arms in their hands, and yet were at least given a trial with lawyers to defend them. One of the accused was even found not guilty; and twelve out of the other twenty-one were not executed. Of course some then said they had been assassinated, even though they had made incendiary proclamations and started a revolt. Borjès and his companions, on the other hand, had given up the insurrection and made no resistance: yet they were ruthlessly shot on the order of a Piedmontese major. Is this kind of bloody holocaust really necessary to make Italian unity?

[P. Calà Ulloa: *Lettres Napolitaines* (Paris, 1864), pp. 87–92]

Brigandage in Sicily took special forms of its own, and some of them were discussed by General Govone in parliament when he returned after a period as commander of the Italian forces in the island. Govone, like many other Italians, found the Sicilian situation very hard to understand. It may be that his failure to put down the Sicilian rebels was due to his refusal to establish some kind of *modus vivendi* with the mafia: the Bourbons and Garibaldi, like later Italian governments, had not been so scrupulous. A vast amount of money continued for decades to be spent on repression in the southern provinces of Italy, and this protracted military campaign helped to divide the two halves of the country.

Speech to parliament by General Govone after leaving his military command in Sicily, December 3, 1863

GENTLEMEN. FOR a long time Sicily has been a prey to ferocious family hatreds. Bad government and poor administration of justice may have contributed a good deal to this; but the basic reason is the struggle for power in each village. The revolution of 1860 gave these hatreds the chance to break out into the most cruel assassinations. I could without any difficulty mention twenty villages where faction fights then took place: sometimes it was "liberals" against "reactionaries," or "Greeks" against "Latins," or the "cavaliers" against the "scribes," or other such names. But usually the names covered rival kinship groups. Whole families, men, women and children were wiped out. Houses were sacked and burnt. Sometimes distant relatives were driven to emigrate out of fear. It was really something out of the Middle Ages. And apart from major acts of slaughter, many individuals were killed as part of some vendetta.

Naturally hatreds increased after these killings, and many people especially among the common people were implicated merely because they were employed as assassins. Some 10,000 jailbirds had escaped in 1860, and had to be amnestied by Garibaldi when he could not recapture them. After that came our introduction of conscription, which created a new and dangerous class of deserters and shirkers who took to the hills in thousands to avoid the draft. As a result of these hatreds, vendettas and outlawries, we have an official list of 1,500 homicides in two years, and the real figure would be more like a thousand a year. *(Sensation)* . . . [Then follow several columns with details of arson and other crimes]

In some provinces, and especially in Girgenti, as I reported to the Minister of War, people dared not leave their villages, and sometimes not even their homes. I recall a rich proprietor who, when he traveled from the interior to Palermo, employed a bodyguard of forty armed horsemen. Even from villages very near Palermo, citizens would not go into town except in armed caravans. Ransoms were generally paid with the utmost promptitude from fear of the alternative. Public spirit was as low as could be.

The political and judicial authorities were powerless to change this, because people were too frightened to ask their help. Moreover there is an old, ineradicable prejudice by which Sicilians utterly despise the man who gives evidence against even the worst criminal. This attitude of silence has a special name among the common people–*omertà* or submission. Fear of possible vendettas is, alas, all too justified. Every day people were killed even in the center of a town for suspicion of being in touch with the police. . . . [He quotes three examples]

This is a tremendocs problem for Sicily. Since no one will go to the ordinary courts for redress, everyone seeks his own method of self-defense. Rich landowners thus employ notorious criminals as bailiffs and field-guards; which people, because they terrify others and are in touch with the underworld, can save the life and goods of their lord. If, as under emergency regulations can happen, one side of this partnership should be arrested, the other will intervene to have him set free . . .

A little improvement can now be seen. But my small experience tells me that such improvement is only temporary. So long as social circumstances do not allow the courts to arrest and condemn guilty men, crime and criminals will continue to flourish, and in a few months' time we will be back with all the old complaints unless parliament in its wisdom and authority can do something to stop it.

Nevertheless there is some comfort to be derived from this unhappy state of affairs. This comfort comes from remembering that Sicily has not yet emerged (as all nations must emerge) out of the cycle which leads from barbarism to civilization. England, France and all the other Italian states had to make this passage, and so I believe that time, helped by the right measures, will bring the desired result here too. Sicily is on the right path, and we must help her. This, at least, is my view, and I ask parliament to consider it. (*Cries of* Bravo *come from the Right and Center*)

[The next day Govone apologized for using this phrase about barbarism]

> [*Atti parlamentari: Camera dei deputati*, discussioni (December 3, 1863), pp. 2115–2122]

Two young aristocrats from Tuscany, Leopoldo Franchetti and Sidney Sonnino, were the first serious students of the "southern question." Their reports described a society which was very slow to change, where for a long time national unification brought only marginal benefits. Even in 1875, most of the rural aristocracy in Calabria and the Basilicata were avowedly nostalgic for the Bourbons; those in western and central Sicily were all involved with the mafia. Franchetti and Sonnino threw a specially revealing light on the peasants in areas where city dwellers rarely or never penetrated. In a sense these peasants were the real Italians. They formed well over half the population. They were still, almost all of them, illiterate. The political aspect of the risorgimento meant little or nothing to them, except that, by giving more power to the local bosses and men of property, it had in many places left them worse off than before.

Peasant life and local government in the Abruzzi

HERE THE peasant depends on his landlord even for food. There is nothing of commerce or industry except some shops and a few artisans in the towns, and hence the vast majority of people belong to one of two classes; they are either landlords or farm laborers. The only way to escape is by emigration. What exists here is a system of real slavery, and not just economic slavery but personal bondage. In agricultural contracts this personal subjection is maintained by various harsh or indeterminate provisions. Apart from rent, a peasant will almost everywhere pay contributions in kind, and will owe free services at the discretion of his lord. The landlord's crops are produced and carried for him by peasants who come for a longer or shorter time as they live near or far, and who will eat in his house while they do it. In his eyes this is a patriarchal relationship, and the peasants will think of it in just the same way . . .

This laboring class is not immoral but amoral. Whatever the bosses or the authorities do is right; justice does not come into it. The bosses are revered, not out of esteem, not rationally, but instinctively as a morally and materially superior force against which there can be no revolt or escape. The peasant rather looks on the *galantuomo* as his natural protector. If the police summon him, he will first consult the *galantuomo*, and according to the latter's advice turn himself in or escape. I was told by an intelligent and progressive landlord, who lives not far from where the reactionary rising was at its worst, that in an ex-fief lately inherited he had been obliged to use a cudgel to prevent the peasants kissing his hand. If they came for advice or for some favor, they would bring a gift of chickens or eggs, so much so that he now insisted on paying for whatever they brought.

These peasants have an inveterate feeling of inferiority. They can hardly believe that the landlord's son will be drafted as a simple soldier unless they actually see him in uniform. For them the *galantuomo* is omnipotent. If not their employer, he is their moneylender, their go-between with the government (officialdom speaks a language which the peasants do not begin to understand, nor are their replies usually understood). They sometimes need him to help fill in tax forms or claims, to help obtain some right, some licit or illicit favor. The peasants are still convinced that influence or a bribe will make any official yield to a *galantuomo*. These various facts combine to make them, everywhere and in all circumstances, dependent on their employer.

The new dispensation after 1860 has confirmed or increased this dependence. Local affairs have now been completely given over by law into the hands of the possessing classes. Village councils, as well as town and provincial councils, are elected by the few taxpayers from among their own number. Education, local charities and other executive functions are carried out by the same people; and though the mayor will be chosen by the government, he will be one of the elected councillors. These men are then given complete control over everything. As councillors, or as controllers of local charities and cereal deposits, they administer the local revenues. Their influence extends to personal incomes, because their control of taxes is almost absolute. The mayor himself has large administrative and judicial influence, since the authorities will look only to him for fiscal and economic information; he has to give the various certificates which are so important; on his advice the police use their terrible weapon of putting people on probation; over most of the countryside he is the sole police officer himself, and possesses some powers of arrest and criminal investigation—to say nothing of the influence which his information and his denunciations carry in the law courts . . .

Under the Bourbons the possessing classes were kept deliberately in ignorance by the government and systematically isolated from the rest of Europe. They had no chance of acquiring any public spirit, but pursued their own petty interests in agriculture and moneylending. They could have no idea about Italian unity, for they were cut off from books and commerce by an impenetrable tariff barrier. For a thousand years, under many different regimes, this area had always been insulated from the rest of the peninsula by frontiers, by different political systems, by inveterate popular customs. The town of Naples was the one political, administrative, economic and intellectual center in the whole of the Kingdom of Naples, and this kingdom was their only fatherland.

Arriving in this region with my mind full of the sublime and heroic sacrifices made by Neapolitan martyrs for liberty, and knowing the considerable and protracted sacrifices made by the Neapolitan exiles before 1860, it is sad to find that these martyrs and exiles represented little more than themselves alone. They were ready to give their lives for freedom; but behind them was lacking that essential body of people who, while not brave enough for real sacrifice, might have been sympathetic to the national movement and shrewdly able to calculate the advantages of at least conserving their liberties once gained. This fact helps to explain what Colletta wrote about the Neapolitan character and why the revolution of 1821 failed. The social and political conditions of Naples could produce heroes, but not everyday liberals. And unfortunately the heroes are everywhere in a minority. All this was due to social conditions which are still in existence . . .

One will find, to take a single example, that the corn banks—designed to lend grain at sowing time to peasants who cannot afford it—are being used by landowners to lend the grain to themselves, putting it in the name of their own peasants but naming themselves as a surety. Or again, if the government asks for a list of families who have suffered for the Italian cause and to whom an indemnity is due, the list is drawn up, the indemnity sent, but distributed between the town councillors. The same people appropriate to their own use the fines imposed for minor offenses. Such examples could be multiplied. As one defrauded peasant said to me, "What can you expect? I would have been revenged on anyone else, *but the mayor is King* and he can simply arrest anyone he wants to." To make an enemy of the mayor is to antagonize councillors, employees, and every official down to the village gamekeepers. In such circumstances, and with such people, a knife thrust is in its own way a guarantee of constitutional rights, and fear of assault takes the place of fear of justice. For this reason any reform of the administrative system in a democratic sense would be a mistake.

Many villages have, among the boss class, some who make their living as go-betweens, as interpreters between government and the plebs. They fill out forms, they intercede or pretend to do so when someone seeks justice or some simple favor, and naturally they claim payment and "expenses" or what they describe as such. This is a crime by our legal code, but here it is common. The authorities are equally the victims of it, especially as it turns ordinary people against authority; yet they cannot stop it, because the language of these officials, their habits of behavior and their ignorance of what is happening here, all mark them strangers.

What benefits, therefore, have been derived from the new Italian

government? The normal constitutional guarantees mean little to
the common people. Peasants who cannot write or read, and who
know absolutely nothing of civil and political rights, can derive
little advantage from freedom of the press or of association. Even
where they are electors [illiteracy and tax qualifications meant that
little more than 1 per cent of the population had the vote], they
cannot use this right for their own advantage. Nor does religious
liberty have any significance to a population which is without
exception superstitious. . . . Any such constitutional guarantees
could not possibly be used by the poor unless through upper-class
intermediaries who might have an interest in taking up their defense.
But it is precisely this upper class against which the poor need to
be defended, and which is by nature their enemy and tyrant . . .

Free trade has without doubt brought great advantages. Along
with new roads it has led to better agricultural prices, and this has
aided those few peasants who still have something to sell at the
end of the year. Some new things, for instance the introduction of
postal orders, are extremely useful to those peasants who want to
send money to their sons in the army, or to receive it from relatives
in America. But these few gains are far outweighed by increased
taxation. The *macinato*, or grist tax, is very hard on these people,
so much so that the government is mainly known in the countryside
through the tax collector. Efficient application of some laws certainly makes a good impression: for instance, conscription is applied
fairly and this compares well with the barefaced deceit under the
Bourbons; moreover the honest behavior of our police has nothing
at all in common with that of the Bourbon gendarmes. But these
few advantages do not greatly help to make all classes believe in
the honesty and trustworthiness of the authorities. One police
sergeant told me that at first he was regularly offered bribes until
people at last became convinced that *personally* he was an honest
man. The real fact is that hardly anyone is ever aware of the
central government, and every day they see dishonest local officials
go unpunished.

The new regime has opened a new path for the few who are
intelligent, honest and energetic; but their scarcity makes them
impotent, while their way of looking at the country, their ideas on
how to behave, are so far away from common experience that they
have little effect on others. There is little moral or intellectual link
between these progressives and the rest of the population. They

base themselves on the not always relevant practice of other parts of
Italy or Europe, which invariably is something more enlightened
and prosperous than is found here. They try to bring science into
agriculture when even the first principles of good farming are quite
unknown; they start luxury public works when basic necessities are
lacking; they construct a theater in a small town where even the
roads are not yet built; or they borrow money at high rates for mere
embellishments, when the countryside lacks roads or railways—and
their excuse is that a railway would cost too much.

> [L. Franchetti: *Condizioni economiche ed amminis-
> trative delle provincie Napoletane* (Florence,
> 1875), pp. 18–38]

The peasants in Sicily

SICILIAN FEUDALISM remained legally established until 1812. Its
legal abolition in that year produced no social revolution, because
the Sicilian fiefs, apart from some land given out in copyhold leases,
went to the barons as freehold. In other parts of the world, feudal
relations were replaced by giving the peasants new rights of property in the land; but in Sicily, though agricultural laborers found
themselves legally free from feudal ties, in fact they were more enslaved than ever, having lost rights as well as duties.

No doubt it is correct to lament that Sicily was at that time protected by the English occupation from the liberating influence of
the French revolution. But almost more to be deplored is the fact
that reforms came to Sicily under English influence just when a
reactionary, revived medievalism became dominant in Europe.
When Sicily experienced her first real wish for liberation, the
atmosphere was already corrupted, because these reforms had been
given her by the Bourbon Kings in a time of complete reaction.
The year 1860 thus found her with modern laws but thoroughly
medieval traditions, and the oppression of one class by another was
still just the same as ever.

Things have not changed even in the years since 1860. By herself, Sicily could have found a remedy, for her people are intelligent and energetic, her economic potential is immensely rich; a
social transformation would have been inevitable, either through
a prudent yielding by the rich, or by a violent revolution. But we
Italians from other provinces have prevented this. We have legal-

ized the existing system of oppression and guaranteed impunity to the oppressor.

In present-day society, any legal tyranny is normally kept in bounds by fear of rebellion. But in Sicily our institutions are based on a merely formal liberalism and have just given the oppressing class a legal means of continuing as they always have. All power has been handed over to these people, to use or misuse as they please. However harsh their conduct, we guarantee them against rebellion, at the same time as no legal opposition is possible since they control the laws and their application.

In some parts of Sicily, along with all the enthusiasm over national victory, certain things happened in 1860 which might have warned us that something was badly wrong and needed powerful remedies. At Pace, at Collesano, Bronte and many other places, the peasantry rose in fury against landowners and the rich, to the cry of "Down with the rats." Without any doubt these were social insurrections. They revealed a deep-rooted evil which should have made people think. Violence was put down with violence, and quite rightly; but, once order had been restored, remedial action should have been taken. Absolutely nothing was done. The nationalization of Church property was the only government action which might possibly have helped the peasants; but in practice it was a merely financial operation, designed to make money for the government itself, and did nothing to help the island's economy. Apart from this one thing, there was talk but no action. Hence the symptoms of the disease are still there to be seen.

[S. Sonnino: *I contadini in Sicilia* (Florence, 1877), pp. 461–4]

23. War, Defeat, and the Acquisition of Venice, 1866

It was generally accepted in Italy that, sooner or later, Austria must be made to give up Venice. It was also assumed that France must one day withdraw her garrison from Rome so that the last remaining corner of the Papal States could be annexed. The king occasionally hoped that Britain would give up Malta, and other expectations had been aroused over the German-speaking Trentino—known also as Alto Adige or the Italian Tyrol. There were also claims upon Trieste, Istria, Fiume, and the Italian-speaking settlements on the Dalmatian coast. Venice, however, was the most obvious and evidently the easiest target of attack.

Julian Fane, Secretary at the British Embassy at Vienna, to Lord John Russell, October 28, 1863

I RETURNED yesterday from what has proved a very interesting trip to Venice. I am not sorry that an attack of indisposition delayed my journey, as I saw there one or two Italians of political authority whom I should not have found earlier.

The situation of affairs remains very much what I found it to be a year and a half ago. The Austrians have not gained an inch of ground in the affections and good will of the Venetians, and the latter have not yielded an inch in their attachment to Victor Emmanuel and the national cause. Annexation to Italy appears to be the dominant idea among all classes, and its genuineness is, I think, indicated by the fact that the people are patient rather than passionate in their desire for its realization. They have no wish to jeopardize, by attempting to forestall, an event which they regard as certain to be accomplished in due time, and they manifest therefore but little sympathy with the so-called "party of action" who in their opinion love Italy well but not "wisely." They look no doubt with considerable interest at the present aspect of affairs in Europe as foreshadowing trouble in which Austria might be seriously involved, but I think that the general sentiment was accurately expressed to me by a Venetian who said, "It is not for us to judge of opportunities; *that* is Victor Emmanuel's business; but when the King makes his sign we will rise as one man." There are of course objectors to this passive policy, just as there are individual exceptions to the dominant anti-Austrian feeling. There are some who think that the recent military demonstrations in Lombardy have proved that Italy has an army fitter to cope with any that Austria could bring into the field; that Italy cannot possibly be unified while she is partially dismembered; and that valuable time is being lost, and dangers engendered, by a procrastination which will be construed into acquiescence with the actual condition of things. Again, there are a few Venetians of birth and education who are willing to accept office under the Austrians, who would probably not object to sit in the Reichsrath at Vienna, and who are advocates, in a general way, of a present which they think not bad, against a future which they think will prove delusive. But the persons composing both these categories are, so far as I can judge, numerically weak and without influence, and may be regarded therefore merely as the exponents of such erratic opinions as are sure to detach themselves from the mass of public conviction however compact it may be.

The sentiments which I have represented as prevalent in the City of Venice prevail also, as I am assured, in all the towns of the province, but there is a great doubt as to how far they are shared by the peasantry. In the country districts the ecclesiastical influence is great, and it is all exercised in one direction. Those of the parish priests who draw their opinions from Rome labor strenuously in the Austrian cause; while those (confessed a minority) who have formed independent opinions are deterred from propagating them by the fear of authority both civil and ecclesiastical. The rural population is supposed therefore to be, on the whole, not ill-affected to the present government, although it is asserted that they would do nothing to defend it. Their comparative docility is attributed in great part to the fact of their being lightly taxed, and conjectures are ripe as to the spirit in which they will receive the recent proposal of the government to raise a poll tax in Venetia as in the other provinces of the Empire.

The thoughts of the Venetians are just now occupied with the reported intention of the government to promulgate the new statutes for the province. These statutes were framed in accordance with the principles of the Constitution of February, and provide for the election of deputies to represent Venetia in the Reichsrath. It is said that Monsieur de Toggenburg is opposed, on the grounds of expediency, to the application at the present moment of these enactments, and that if the government persists in carrying them out he will resign his governorship. I found some of the Venetians disposed to resent very strongly the application of the statutes. They think the government might be able to find persons who, after a mock election, would consent to proceed in the capacity of legislators to Vienna, and that the national cause would be prejudiced and discredited by such a proceeding. But the majority of persons with whom I conversed on the subject expressed complete indifference as to whether the measure was carried out or not. If the government, they argue, should succeed in getting deputies for the Reichsrath, they will be persons without authority or consideration, whose opinions are already notorious, and whose actions will in no manner compromise the Venetians or the cause which they have at heart.

Venice certainly wears a very mournful aspect. Commerce stagnates, and the trade of the city is in a state of collapse. The great theater has been closed since 1859, and there are no public festivities. The Austrian military bands play on the great place of St. Mark's, but this is an entertainment which the Venetians sedulously eschew. Meanwhile the political police are active, and domiciliary visits frequent. In many cases, however, I am assured that the householder receives timely notice of the visit about to be paid to him, by some sympathizing official who betrays the designs of the police; from which it would appear that the Austrians in Venice are sometimes served by their agents with the same fidelity as the Russians in Warsaw. If a person belonging to the upper classes is somewhat unreserved in the expression of liberal opinions, he is requested to take his immediate departure beyond the frontiers, lest greater evil befall him. Under such a condition of things there is of course much discontent and despondency; but, as I said at the beginning, the Venetians on the whole bear present misfortune with a patience which implies confident hope in the fortune of the future.

[*Russell Papers*, Public Record Office, London, 30/22/42/598]

By 1866, when the fourth war of liberation was fought against Austria, Italy had increased her army to about 220,000 men. Some patriots had grumbled that expenditure on the armed forces was too small, while the economists sometimes called it greatly excessive. A more obvious objection would have been that the army budget was incommensurate with the foreign policy which the government decided to adopt. Worst of all, the generals and the Minister of War were directly responsible to the king and hence largely immune from public scrutiny; the higher command therefore remained totally inadequate.

The senior general, Lamarmora, was Prime Minister between 1864 and 1866. Bismarck had made it clear that Prussia would soon challenge Austria for hegemony in Germany, and this gave Lamarmora his opportunity. A treaty was signed with Bismarck in April 1866 which envisaged a joint war against Austria within three months. At this point Austria was sufficiently alarmed to offer through France that she would cede Venice if Italy would back down from her engagement. Lamarmora refused, because for the stipulated three months he thought himself morally committed; moreover the idea of Venice being ceded via France (as Lombardy had been) was much less attractive than winning Venice and perhaps Trieste and Trent by military victory.

Austria's offer was a confession of weakness, and perhaps it made Lamarmora too confident. Bismarck wanted him to concert a joint plan which, avoiding the two remaining fortresses of the Quadrilateral, would aim at the heart of Austria. The Germans were also anxious to use Garibaldi to foment insurrections in Hungary, Dalmatia, and other subject parts of the Austrian Empire. But Lamarmora refused. He was against Garibaldi, and against giving the volunteers another chance to outdistance the regulars, just as he was on principle against popular insurrection. He was also against letting Prussia know his military plans. With astonishing secretiveness he refused not only to formulate common strategy but even to exchange information with Bismarck. He intended to ignore his ally and simply concentrate the Italian military effort on occupying Trent and Venice.

The campaign of 1866 was, partly for these reasons, a disaster. The king unfortunately refused the suggestion of his ministers that he ought not to act as supreme commander. The personal vanities and jealousies of the generals were also such that Lamarmora, Cialdini, and Garibaldi had to be given what amounted to entirely separate commands. When fighting began on June 16 there was still no plan of attack, but another week passed in general discussion while the Prussians launched their brilliant campaign. Failing to obtain any cooperation from Cialdini, Lamarmora advanced on his own with only a quarter of the forces available. The second battle of Custoza (June 24) was not in itself a defeat, but it was a check from which Lamarmora's morale never recovered, and he fell back even though not pursued. There then followed another inexplicable halt to operations, while the German forces proceeded toward their decisive victory at Sadowa. Lamarmora was trying to resign; Cialdini refused to take his post; and Victor Emmanuel still refused to give up the supreme command.

When war began, Ricasoli had come back as Prime Minister. He had far more political sense than his predecessor, more sympathy for Garibaldi, more firmness with regard to the king; but it was too late to undo the damage already effected by inexpert diplomacy and worse than inexpert military planning. Garibaldi and his volunteers in the Trentino, though they were poorly equipped, scored the only memorable successes of the war on the Italian side.

Baron Ricasoli to General Lamarmora, June 26, 1866

I AM TRYING to devise with the populations of the Danube valleys and those of Dalmatia, Croatia and Hungary, etc., ways and means of carrying out an insurrection which, if successful, should bring confusion and weakness to the Austrian army. Part of these operations, indeed the main part, would consist in the diversion to that area of a body of volunteers under Garibaldi, for he enjoys a prestige there even greater perhaps than in Italy. In my opinion it would be wise to take advantage of this remarkable fact, unique in all recorded history.

The opportune moment for such a diversion by volunteers will, in my opinion, depend largely on how our main campaign develops; but, apart from that, I think it important to decide straight away whether the plan shall be adopted or ruled out, for it will take time to prepare the expeditionary force.

It is my belief that, when Garibaldi and his volunteers reach those regions, insurrection will follow as a matter of course. Failing his presence, success would be doubtful, for few people would be tempted to revolt if there were no hope of success.

It is my belief that in war one should do the greatest possible harm to the enemy; hence it would be imprudent to leave Garibaldi unused; for through him the war can be extended to other parts of the Austrian Empire which otherwise would remain outside it. Thus I recommend the proposed expedition for Your Excellency's approval, both in principle and in practice [It was rejected].

Our arms have had the worst of it in the early stages of the war. We have a saying: *he who laughs last laughs loudest*. Hence my conviction that, thanks to the experience and good sense of the generals, the initial setbacks will be remedied, and our army, having regained its confidence, will do its utmost to show both Italy and Europe that it lacks neither courage nor perseverance and can resume the march toward victory.

> [*Lettere e documenti del Barone Bettino Ricasoli*,
> ed. M. Tabarrini and A. Gotti (Florence,
> 1893), vol. VIII, pp. 24–5]

Garibaldi to Baron Ricasoli at Florence, August 14, 1866

EVERYONE IS aware that Italy is in a very dishonorable as well as a wretched condition.

The blame lies with the two ministries, those of war and the navy, or rather with those who up till now have controlled those two ministries.

As regards the navy this is obvious, because men like Ricci and La Mantica know nothing of their job. There is an absurdity about having ministers who are ignorant as well as being repugnant to honest and able men: this is why we lost the battle of Lissa with a fleet superior to the enemy's; and now I myself understand why on Lake Garda I was given six gunboats of which only one could be put into operation—and carried only one cannon at that—whereas the Austrians had eight gunboats mounting thirty-six cannon. The Ministry of the Navy has been wrong all through. The guilt lies with all the ministers in turn during the whole period since we first possessed a navy. And how could it be otherwise with people in office who knew nothing of naval affairs?

Italy possesses sailors in no way inferior to those of England and America.

With magnificent army material, we have nevertheless fought on land hardly any better than at sea, and this is obviously due to the same defect in leadership.

The worst of it is that nothing is being done to change the leadership. The men who led the way to the catastrophes of Lissa and Custoza are still at the head of affairs. And what guarantee is there that Italy will see herself restored to her dignity as a nation? This is the question I permit myself to put to you, dear Baron, and I would be grateful to have a reply.

> [*Lettere e documenti del Barone Bettino Ricasoli*,
> ed. Tabarrini and Gotti, vol. VIII, pp. 104–5]

Proclamation by Garibaldi to his volunteers at Brescia, August 20, 1866

WE HAVE still not driven the oppressors from our homeland, so we must remain ready for battle. To arms, therefore, and finish it off once and for all. You must be constant of purpose and feel an anger that the oppressed should always feel for their oppressors. You must abhor the servility and fear with which ordinary folk still look on these foreign soldiers in our midst. Instead you must regard them with horror and hatred.

In 1859 I used to see Austrian soldiers walking freely and undisturbed among the hardy citizens of Piedmont and Lombardy. Those Austrians were few in number and far from their regiments, yet they requisitioned whatever they needed, beat up those who failed to spring immediately to their service, and then laden with spoils, gorged and drunk, calmly returned to camp without molestation.

These same citizens since then have given many volunteers to the Italian army; and yet in 1859—from indifference or because ordered to do so—they allowed foreign mercenaries to ill-treat and despoil them with impunity.

What happened then in Piedmont and Lombardy has now happened again in these unfortunate provinces of Venice near our northeastern frontier. I can well understand that a village could find itself at the mercy of a foreign army, but I cannot see how half a dozen soldiers can be allowed to take what they like without a single shot being fired at them. It just proves that Italy has not so far been waging a national war or a war of liberation. Yet she would be quite capable of doing so, as we have been able to see at Milan, Brescia, Palermo, Bologna, Genoa, etc., where citizens who had a mind to it put whole armies to flight.

Let us renounce this shameful apathy. Let us prove that we are worthy of that much-vaunted independence which we have still not achieved. The regular army is strong and brave, and the volunteers will be fully worthy of them. But apathetic villagers must no longer treat foreign soldiers like fellow citizens. They must take arms, hide in the woods, behind hedges, in ravines, and be ready with their cudgels to teach others that this land is Italian, that these harvests are Italian, that these women are Italian.

The priests are on the Austrian side, you will tell me, and that explains how the foreigners can obtain so many spies. This indeed is a canker in the heart of Italy. Brigandage is being supported from Rome, and so is enabled to diminish the reputation of our national cause. Most of the peasants are learning to hate Italy. Do you want proof? Just look for a single peasant among our volunteers, and you won't find one. They join the army, but only when drafted. Among the volunteers there is not one! And what fine irregular troops that strong, industrious and frugal class would make! But the priests won't allow it. They fear that among the volunteers the peasant would learn something; he would learn to curse the instruments of obscurantism that keep him in his filthy pit of ignorance and poverty. Far from serving Italy, the peasant thus looks upon our free and regenerate nation as something which is against the priests and so against God. Meanwhile successive governments allow this curse of the human race to continue in existence. When mothers kiss a priest's hand and kneel down before him, they do not know that they are at the feet of an assassin of their sons, of an assassin of their country. Yes, victim of the priests for so many centuries, Italy still lies in the coils of that serpent which is the hope and mainstay of the foreigner.

Meanwhile, the volunteers should profit by the present truce. They should drill and practice maneuvers and above all sharp-shooting. They have seen the enemy at close quarters and learned to their cost the value of skilled marksmanship. Officers and experienced underofficers must do all they can to instruct their young companions; they must warn them about the shameful panic to which adolescents are subject, and the trivial fear of enemy cavalry. One single foot soldier is worth a platoon of cavalrymen in a country of hills and valleys like ours. In the Tyrol, which was a difficult terrain for us in many ways, and where we faced an enemy both valiant and hardened in war, that enemy never made us retreat a step. On the contrary we pushed him back so far that he was out of sight when we first heard of the armistice. Each town must therefore maintain and extend the target practice which alone can succeed in transforming a nation of slaves.

And our women, who are the finest thing in Italy and have such power over the spirit of our youth, they must urge our young men to join these courageous volunteers. They will see their beloved ones back all the sooner, and so we shall all have contributed to national liberation.

What a lucky generation! We are entrusted with the sublime mission of regenerating Italy after fifteen hundred decadent years during which she dithered and grovelled before the stupid soldiery of the oppressor! Heads up, heads up, men of destiny! Do not let yourselves be discouraged by a few cowards. Now that we have been tempered once more by adversity and danger, let those who threaten us with such arrogance hide in their fortresses; for here we stand imploring God to be able to fight them again.

[G. Garibaldi: *Scritti e discorsi politici e militari,
1862-7* (Bologna, 1935), vol. V, pp. 335-8]

The Italian navy in 1866 was stronger than the Austrian, with twelve ironclads against only seven; but the commander, Admiral Persano, held his position by nepotism and seniority. Despite several premonitory disasters in his early career, and despite the strongest hostility from the other senior officers, he was in command when the first occasion arose for the fleet to show its mettle.

The navy had been built solely for use against Austria, yet little attempt was made to have it ready when war had been decided, nor were maps prepared for an attack on the Austrian naval bases. The Austrian Admiral Tegetthoff arrived on June 27 outside Ancona harbor and challenged the Italian navy to emerge, but Persano was caught completely unawares, unable to reply with a single shot or even to get up steam. Early in July, when the Germans asked for urgent action, the government desperately sent orders that Persano was to seek out and destroy the enemy fleet. The admiral spent five days cruising around waiting to be attacked, and then returned to port.

Ordered out again by the politicians, this time under threat of dismissal, suddenly Persano improvised a scheme to capture the island of Lissa off the Adriatic coast. But he was caught by the Austrian fleet while his own ships were scattered round the island and unable to see his signals. At the last moment he made confusion worse by tranferring his flag to a different ship. This gave an excuse for what seems to have been a deliberate decision by the other admirals to ignore his orders and not to cover up his mistakes. The way that he and his colleagues later accused each other in public was among the other unfortunate episodes of his subsequent trial and condemnation.

A defense of Admiral Persano after the battle of Lissa

ITALY WAS resolved to have a navy; upwards of 12,000,000 of pounds sterling had been spent within five years, in forming a fleet far superior to that of Austria in size and in guns. She had two plated steam frigates of nearly 5,700 tons each, the *Re d'Italia* and the *Re di Portogallo*, built in America, each with two Armstrong guns of 300 lb., 10 mortars of 80 lb., and 24 rifled cannon, with conical steel balls of 90 lb. The *Formidabile* and *Terribile*, of 2,700 tons, were built in France; the monitor *Affondatore*, was a steam ram, which arrived from England the day before the battle of Lissa. The Italians were in a fever of enthusiasm, they counted on the most brilliant successes by sea and by land; perhaps they would even march to Vienna, but they would certainly take Rome; and then came the disastrous battle of Custoza, the indecisive battle of Lissa, and the Italians broke forth into howls of rage and disappointment.

The people and the troops had done all that men could do—they had given their sons, their husbands, and brothers, their money and their blood, and after all they had gained nothing. What they won was won for them by Prussia, and it was necessary for the ministry to find a victim to throw to the wolves, that they themselves might escape. Custoza would not bear inquiry—the maladministration, the absence of preparation, the peculation, the want of necessaries, of clothing, of arms for the troops, for the volunteers, for the sick, all these things, which were the real causes of their nonsuccess, must be hushed up and slurred over—and Persano was the most convenient victim.

This is the secret of the affair, but the history of it is as follows. On the 21st May, 1866, Admiral Persano reported to the Minister of Marine that "the fleet was not fit to go to war," that "it would take three months to make it tolerably ready," "that the ships on joining were short of men." . . . Up to the 7th of July he had neither got guns nor order, and was so exasperated at the delay that he threatened to resign his command, while the Minister confessed that it was impossible to send him any plan of operations. On the 9th of July he received orders to go in search of the enemy, and to attack him; to make himself master of the Adriatic, to blockade the enemy's fleet if it remained in Pola, but *not to risk* any of his own ships by attacking the forts which defend Pola; not to go too near the coast, for fear of marine torpedoes or mines. The Admiral cruised up and down in the Adriatic (endeavouring by a well-planned maneuver to draw the Austrians toward the south), and the Minister complained of the consumption of coal!

The third charge against Count Persano was for disobedience of these orders, but Lamarmora (the Prime Minister) himself ordered him to wait for the *Affondatore*, and to blockade Pola was impossible. On the 15th of July the Minister of Marine arrived at Ancona, and vehemently urged the Admiral to go and take the fortified island of Lissa. Persano replied that it was the very thing he wanted to do, but that he must have 5,000 men for disembarkation, with engineer and artillery officers. The Minister could only let him have 500 marines, which, with the sailors who could be spared, gave him a landing force of 1,500 men. While they were disputing about it a letter arrived from Lamarmora, who wrote to the Admiral in the name of the King and Ministry lamenting the inaction of the fleet, and ordering him to put to sea and attack . . .

Stung by this unreasonable letter, Persano determined to attempt a *coup de main*. Neither he nor the government had any positive knowledge about the island, not even a map of it. He sailed on the afternoon of the 16th of July, and the next day, at sunset, received information from D'Amico, the chief of his staff, who had gone to Lissa under English colors, that the three forts on the island were defended by about 2,500 men. Vice-Admiral Albini came on board to dissuade the Commander-in-Chief from attacking, declaring that Lissa was the Gibraltar of the Adriatic, but Persano was not to be turned from his purpose. He himself, with eight plated steam frigates, undertook the attack on the principal fort of San Giorgio, and ordered his Vice-Admiral, Albini, with four wooden ships, to silence a battery, and effect a landing at Porto Manego, on the southeast of the island, while Rear-Admiral Vacca, with three plated frigates, was to shell the batteries of Porto Carniso, on the northwest. The action was fixed for daybreak, but "owing to the difficulties of communicating orders at night" it did not begin till eleven a.m. After a hot engagement (during which the *Re d'Italia* fired 1,300 shot), Fort San Giorgio lowered its colors at half-past three p.m., when Vacca finding the batteries at Porto Carniso too high to attack, returned *without orders*, and at five o'clock the news came that Albini had done *nothing whatever* . . .

Persano is accused of having formed in line presenting his flank to the enemy. Tegetthoff advanced in three divisions, seven armored ships, with the flagship *Max* at their head, the wooden *Kaiser*, of 92 guns, leading the iron-plated wooden ships, and the smaller vessels bringing up the rear, all disposed chevron fashion. He gave the word, "Run down the enemy and sink him." It was a *coup d'essai* of a battle with plated ships and steam rams. Vacca's fire did no damage, and Tegetthoff passed through the enemy's line without doing him any harm, but fell upon the *Re d'Italia* with four plated ships, and he himself ran into her, then backed, and the ill-fated ship went down. Her rudder, which was exposed, is said to have been broken by a shot. The two ships were of equal horsepower (800), but the *Max* was 1,200 tons less, and had only sixteen guns to the *Italia's* thirty-six . . .

The *Ancona* and the *Varese* fell foul of each other, the *Palestro* was set on fire, being only partially plated, and finally blew up. In vain did the Commander-in-Chief, seeing his reiterated signals disobeyed, go in person toward the second division to make sure that they were perceived. In vain did he rush after the laggards among the cuirassed ships, and endeavor to bring them into action. The *Principe Umberto*, a wooden frigate (just returned from a long cruise in the Pacific, and therefore in good order), under Captain Acton, and the *Re di Portogallo*, were the only ships which obeyed his orders to close with and chase the enemy. Rear-Admiral Vacca confessed to seeing the signal, and to having disobeyed it, because *he thought* the fleet should form in line first! What could Persano do with such officers, to whom the very first principle of military obedience was unknown? The battle lasted little more than an hour. The French Admiral declares that both fleets were at that moment perfectly fit to resume the battle; but not only did most of Persano's fleet refuse to fight, but the Italian gun practice was so bad that 1,450 shots of their magnificent artillery made scarcely a mark on the Austrian fleet.

We are not upholding Admiral Persano as having made no mistakes as a naval tactician, but we consider that his character for honesty and courage remains unblemished, and that the most skillful maneuvers would have been frustrated by such disobedience as was manifested by many under his command, Vice-Admiral Albini being the foremost culprit.

After the battle Persano resigned his command, sent in charges against Albini and Vacca, and demanded a Court of Inquiry. This was certainly the act of an innocent and honorable man. The government would not publish his report of the battle of Lissa, and it was semi-officially stated by the *Nazione* that they did so on account of the accusations it brought against almost all his officers. For publishing the same narrative in a pamphlet, entitled "*I Fatti di Lissa*," the Admiral was placed under close arrest for about two months, and not allowed any communication even with his wife and son; yet the official narrative, drawn up by Rear-Admiral Brochetti, and finally published by the government, agrees with that of Persano in every respect, excepting only the omission of all notice of the fact that it was the Ministry who forced him to immediate action in the middle of July, before he had received any troops . . .

All the leading men in the Senate voted for him, but he is a Piedmontese, and the Genoese, Neapolitans, and Venetians confess that they had made up their minds beforehand to condemn him. And so he was condemned to lose his rank, to be dismissed the service, and to pay the expenses of the prosecution, while his subordinates go scot free.

> [*The Spectator* (London, June 15, 1867), pp. 660–2]

Lissa need not have been considered a major defeat. Italian dead were only 600—as they were only 750 at Custoza. Much more depressing was that no rising by Venetians took place to coincide with the attack on Austria. Worse still, just when the nation was distracted by war, a major rebellion broke out in Sicily, which had to be put down by sending an expeditionary force to recapture Palermo from the revolutionaries.

By the treaty with Austria, Venice was given to France, and then the French gave it to Italy; after which another plebiscite resulted in a huge majority for union. Trieste and the Trentino were to remain Austrian until 1918.

Pasquale Villari was a Neapolitan and a distinguished professor of history. His books on Savonarola and Machiavelli were translated into English and enjoyed considerable fame. He was also a highly respected politician of the Right, and his enlightened social views gave him a special place in public life.

"Whose fault it is?" asks Pasquale Villari, September 1866

THE WAR is over and we possess Venice. After six years of preparation, it cost us less effort than we expected. Yet no one is content. Above all the war destroyed many illusions as well as destroying our unlimited self-confidence. The traditionally slow Germans were seen to move like lightning, while the fiery Italians crept like a tortoise. In one victory after another, Prussia annihilated the Austrian forces against whom we could do so little on land or sea. Never again can we look at ourselves quite as we used to do.

Whose fault is it? Everybody will at once reply in chorus, "Lack of leadership; for while our soldiers and sailors fought like heroes, the higher command failed at the crucial moment of action, and the rank and file found themselves abandoned." It all seems so easy, until more accusations are made adducing yet other errors and more blame. Food was lacking, or munitions; an order arrived too late, another was badly executed, the volunteers were given no equipment at all; and, as for the navy, everyone has something to criticize since everyone now claims to know all about the art of war.

When trying to explain all these mistakes, blame is variously placed on the political system, on general factiousness, on the reactionaries, on Piedmontism, or on the bosses. But this is not the end of the story, for you must then explain how Italy let herself be governed for so long by such men. We have a freer government than France or Prussia, to say nothing of Austria. Our ministers had the support of parliament; the deputies were elected freely without government pressure. Perhaps, then, we are just ignorant and let troublemakers lead us by the nose. Perhaps public opinion is undirected and we simply lack enough men of ability.

The problem thus becomes more complex on a closer examination. One can easily accuse the generals, the ministers, the deputies, the civil service, and even the general public. But those who lay all the blame at the government's door must ask themselves whether *local* government is any better, whether private and public enterprise is doing all that we expect, whether industry, commerce and science have acquired from freedom and national unification the drive which might have been hoped. Weigh up all this and then say if you can blame so many errors on just a few people. Could these few men not have been criticized and removed if they were responsible? Is it right to close our eyes to those errors which were the collective responsibility of us all and which are much more dangerous and hard to remedy? . . .

Look at Prussia, which with hard work and wonderful administration has made a poor country rich and has paid for the war out of current taxation. German books are eagerly sought in France, Italy and England; our own do not cross the Alps. Our mathematicians, engineers and mechanics find it hard to keep up with the progress of science in Germany. We have to import rails, guns, ships, and sometimes even ships' engineers—all the things which win wars. The rifled cannon was invented in France and the needle gun in Prussia, for these two nations possess large-scale industry, and Prussia in particular has prodigiously developed her arms' manufactures. Armored ships come from America, and Armstrong guns to penetrate their armor come from England . . .

Like it or not, Piedmont provided the nucleus for our national army and the administrative machinery with which our government subsequently had to work. It was the toughness of the Piedmontese system which bound all the various elements of our revolution into one. But how solidly was this done? Before 1848 Piedmont was not even one of the more civilized regions of Italy and had been less permeated than other areas by the influence of the French revolution. After 1848, slowly and even pedantically, it became freer, more vigorous, and produced a new kind of person. Its hard-working and disciplined people quickly began to prosper. Commerce, industry, popular education, all leapt forward. Many fine people who were exiles from other regions contributed to this, and so did the febrile activity of Cavour. Though this small country was still not on a level with Belgium or Holland, it was a kind of model state and an example to the rest of Italy.

But the old traditions had not been broken. Despite this development, despite many favorable circumstances, the administrative machinery was largely antiquated and run by worn-out veterans. This had been hardly if at all visible in a small state, but when applied to the much larger area of Italy the knots and tears in the fabric began to appear. Defects were suddenly shown up and on a gigantic scale. As difficulties accumulated quickly in a fast-changing situation, great speed, great flexibility and tactful adjustment were needed in order to create a new country without any hiatus in administration. Instead, old traditions ensured that things remained slow, pedantic, painstaking; and something which had hardly worked in small Piedmont suddenly had to be applied to the whole of Italy.

Obviously a prison or police official in tranquil Piedmont would face completely new problems when suddenly transferred to revolutionary Italy. So did tax officials and magistrates. If it had simply been a matter of Piedmont giving us her officials, her laws and her administration, the government machine would therefore inevitably have run down and become disorganized. But there was more yet. Though the employees of the deposed governments and the various provisional regimes all had to be fused with the Piedmontese, the latter provided the main element in the bureaucracy. The laws of Italy were taken from Piedmont, and Piedmontese officials had a greater reputation than others for honesty, hard work and ability. But a sudden dilution of her existing cadres and a rapid promotion of junior staff was necessary.

In schools, for instance, the provisional governments in Sicily and Naples enacted a variation of the Piedmontese laws which made elementary education compulsory; but teachers, administrators and inspectors were all lacking and had to be improvised in a hurry. So the Piedmontese elementary teacher became a headmaster and had to recruit other teachers; sometimes he had to run a teachers' training college, or become a school inspector; and someone who at Turin had been a fine teacher, in southern Italy now became a bad headmaster or inspector. This one example was multiplied a hundred times. Army captains became colonels, colonels became generals, and divisional commanders took over army corps, so that instead of commanding 40,000 men they now had two or three hundred thousand. In the civil service, without any proof of capacity, heads of sections had to take over whole divisions, to replace their superiors who became prefects. Elementary schoolmasters likewise taught in secondary schools. So Italy was badly governed at the same time as standards fell in Piedmont itself. Good officials became mediocre or bad, for those who had been quite able to command a small ship in quiet times were incapable of piloting the ship of Italy through a stormy sea . . .

Italy must now begin to recognize that she has at home an enemy which is stronger than Austria. I refer to our colossal ignorance, our multitudes of illiterates, our machine bureaucrats, childish politicians, ignoramus professors, hopeless diplomats, incapable generals, unskilled workers, primitive farmers, and the rhetoric which gnaws our very bones. It was not the Austrian garrisons in Mantua, Verona and the rest of the "Quadrilateral" which barred our path, so much as our seventeen million illiterates, nearly a third of whom still live in truly arcadian simplicity.

Every man of good will must therefore set his hand to a new war of internal conquest. Italians are ready for any sacrifice so long as their best instincts are appealed to. Every party must examine its own failings and open a new page. Everywhere people are asking how we can reorganize the country, and this should be the dominant issue in politics. Woe to us if we and the government let this moment of truth go by without action. Woe to us if we go on trusting blindly to laws and decrees, for executed unintelligently they are depressive and not enlivening. Nothing will happen if we go on expecting manna from heaven, if the government still expects wonders from people who cannot even read, or if the country goes on thinking that they can leave everything to their rulers or that some mysterious new *system* will suddenly emerge to save us.

Humility, good will and hard work—that is the only recipe for practical results. Lack of will power, sheer inertia, a measureless self-glorification, these are the enemy. We are drowning in political rhetoric. Everyone believes they have found a magic elixir of salvation which will regenerate the country painlessly and without toil; whereas the truth is that we can be saved only by our own exertions. With application we can do miracles. By instructing the new generation we will rapidly alter our own, and supported by the lessons of our late revolution we will make Italy truly civilized once again. By sheer enthusiasm and untutored natural forces we have in a remarkably short time created Italy and won the esteem of the civilized world. No one can doubt that with education and discipline we could redouble those forces and win the position to which our past history calls us.

> [P. Villari: "*Di chi è la colpa?*" in *Il Politecnico* (Milan, September 1866), series IV, vol. II, pp. 257–88]

24. Rome

A culminating point in the history of unification was the acquisition of Rome. The neo-guelphs had tried to reconcile religion with patriotism, and Gioberti had even cast the Pope as a national leader. But the papal Allocution of April 1848 made this attitude no longer tenable. In Piedmont, the Siccardi laws and then the dissolution of the monasteries divided Church and State. Cavour's annexation of the Romagna in the spring of 1860, followed by that of Umbria and the Marches in the autumn, had encountered the obvious rejoinder of excommunication against anyone who thus dared to filch ecclesiastical territory. Pius IX firmly refused to recognize the existence of the Italian state after 1861, as he also ordered Catholics not to vote in the parliamentary elections. Cavour and his successors made several covert attempts to negotiate a settlement, but these failed when it became clear that neither side could afford to yield much ground. Cavour here overestimated the strength of his position and assumed too easily that the Pope would have to give way.

Odo Russell was the official British representative in Rome. Pius was very free in talking to him, perhaps because he was detached from this particular struggle, and not even a Catholic. The following discussion took place just after five cardinals and dozens of bishops had been arrested by Cavour's government. Those who had sworn allegiance to the temporal government of the Pope found it hard to adjust to being "annexed" as a result of Piedmontese "aggression."

Odo Russell, from Rome, to Lord John Russell, January 16, 1861

THE DIPLOMATIC BODY having been admitted some days since to the honor of congratulating the Pope on the occasion of the New Year, I was equally honored with a private audience this morning for the same purpose. With his usual benevolence and kindness the Pope spoke on many different subjects and then inquired after the

health of Her Majesty. He had read in the papers that the Prince
of Wales was about to become a freemason, a circumstance he
greatly regretted . . .

"England is ever at work against us," His Holiness continued,
"favoring and assisting revolution. Your people hate the Pope, your
parliament hates the Pope, your ministers and especially your uncle
[Lord John Russell] hate the Pope, and even the English Catholics,
who were always good, are not at present animated with a very
proper spirit."

I here explained to His Holiness, as I had done on a former occasion, that I deeply regretted to see that he misconceived the
spirit which animated the people of England and the policy of Her
Majesty's Government. Although the people were Protestant and
Her Majesty's Government liberal in their feelings, no personal
hatred to His Holiness biased the minds of our public men; but we
differed in our views on the system of administration pursued by the
late sovereigns of Italy, which had been productive of discontent
and revolution, while we thought a more liberal and national government might have given peace to the country.

The Pope then explained to me, as he had also done before, that
the petulance of the Italian people rendered self-government impossible, and that the present movement in Italy could never succeed;
we Englishmen would not understand that Italy must be ruled by
strong armies and a firm hand. It would take him several hours to
discuss the matter thoroughly with me and then he knew I would
not believe him, because he perceived that I entertained the same
ideas on matters of administration as the late Lord Minto.

I replied that those ideas were the ideas of Englishmen, and that
without much discussion we had but to look to facts to see that
Lord Minto's advice had been good. When, at the commencement
of his reign, His Holiness had pursued a national policy the people
of Italy had been at his feet. Since then, several years of foreign occupation had turned the national sympathies toward Piedmont,
which offered Italy the realization of a dream of many centuries,
Independence, Freedom and Unity.

"But Unity is impossible," the Pope interposed, "because the
Great Powers of Europe will prevent it. They dread the formation
of a sixth Great Power, and England above all dreads the future
maritime greatness which Italy would acquire."

"We do not dread a danger so remote," I replied, "nor can I take upon myself to explain the secret policy of the Great Powers of Europe, but I can answer for the sympathies of England represented by Her Majesty's advisers. They sincerely desire to see Italy free from that foreign interference which has been her greatest curse, and the Italians once more in possession of their native land, building up the edifice of their liberties and consolidating the work of their independence so that Italy may again become an element of order and of progress in the great European family."

The Pope's eyes flashed, he clenched his fist and exclaimed: "No, they do not wish it, and you do not believe what you say! The policy of England is not so generous. She is guided by commercial interests and selfish ends, she encourages revolution and disorder abroad and her ministers enjoy no independence. They have to yield to mobs to retain their places, and now they may appear to yield to a passing popular cry, but they will be the first to prevent the unity or even the pacification of Italy!"

I replied: "I have listened with painful surprise to Your Holiness's words, for they have again proved to me how thoroughly Your Holiness is misinformed as to English affairs. I hereby solemnly give Your Holiness my most sacred word of honor that I am speaking my innermost conviction when I say that Her Majesty's Government sincerely and honestly desire the welfare of Italy and that they think that end can best be attained by the cessation of foreign intervention and by the Italians being left to settle their own affairs—in one word Italy for the Italians. And is it not natural that we should desire to see Italy once more at peace, happy and improving, Italy to whom we owe all the greatest blessings we enjoy, Italy the cradle of our laws, of science, art, literature and I might almost say of religion? Did we not assist Greece in obtaining her independence, did we not favor Belgium, and why should we withhold our moral support from Italy? Are her demands and wishes not just? I appeal to Your Holiness as an Italian prince."

The old man's Italian heart warmed as he spoke and he said: "Do you know what Italian Unity means? It means a nation of five and twenty millions harboring more talent, mind and energy than any nation in the world, with an army of three hundred thousand men and a fleet of three hundred ships. History proves the eminence of Italian generals, and our admirals would soon command the seas. Italy left to herself would soon be the first of the

Great Powers of the world, and therefore the Five Powers of Europe will ever prevent her unity."

"Your Holiness," I replied, "has now spoken as you did at the commencement of your reign and then all Italy was at your feet, you were the national idol. But since Your Holiness has allowed foreign bayonets to stand between yourself and your people, they have turned to the only Italian power left, to seek the realization of their wishes. But the day that Your Holiness will extend your hand to Piedmont and say: 'Let all hostilities cease, there shall be peace in Italy,' then the people will bless the name of Pius IX and the great work will be accomplished."

"No, it will not," the Pope again exclaimed, "and you do not believe what you say!"

"And who is to prevent it," I asked, "if Your Holiness and Italy agree?"

"The Great Powers of Europe," the Pope replied.

"With the Pope's blessing and England's moral support, Italy has nothing to fear from them," I said.

"Monsieur Napoleon will prevent it," the Pope continued, "whatever England may wish. He wants Naples for his family."

"And if that really were the case," I said, "would it not be better to save Italy for the Italians than to give time for the establishment of a French Italy? The substitution of French for Austrian supremacy can be of no advantage to your country. Your Holiness commenced the work of liberation in 1846, it rests with Your Holiness to complete and crown it in 1861 without shedding one more drop of Italian or of foreign blood. If you do not, your successor will; while Your Holiness will find no other alternative than to accept for the remainder of your reign a permanent French occupation of Rome."

"But I have never been consulted," the Pope said, evidently laboring under great excitement, "I have never been consulted by the Italians for whom I then hoped to do so much. See how they have treated and abandoned me!"

"Because Your Holiness placed a hedge of foreign bayonets between them and yourself," I replied.

"But I have never been consulted either by the Great Powers," the Pope continued.

"Has not France," I inquired, "repeatedly offered Your Holiness the very best advice?"

"The Pope needs no advice, the Pope has a right to be consulted," His Holiness replied. "Everything that has been done has been done against me. My states have been torn from me, my former friends have looked on without assisting me, but a cry of indignation will be raised throughout the Catholic world and the faithful will not forget their duty, nor the Pope be abandoned."

I replied: "The time has passed, the worst of the crisis is over, and how has the Catholic world answered Your Holiness's appeal? The Peter's Pence will not suffice to support the Holy See, and to obtain foreign soldiers Your Holiness's government has been obliged to pay a higher premium than any government in the world. To the support alone of France is due what remains of Your Holiness's Temporal Power, while all around the cause of Italian freedom is gaining strength. If Your Holiness has a right to be consulted, you have also a right to speak and take a generous initiative both as an Italian prince and as head of the Roman Catholic Church. In the miraculous course of events which all seem to turn in favor of the Italian cause, does Your Holiness not see the hand of God?"

"The hand of God is everywhere," the Pope answered. "He allows all that occurs, but we do not yet know what He intends." And then His Holiness added for the third time and with great force, "But I have never been consulted on all these matters, I have been ignored and forgotten. In England you hate the Pope, but you are enthusiastic for Garibaldi, and why do you admire Garibaldi?"

I said: "In Garibaldi we have admired a disinterested patriot, who, without seeking one single personal advantage, has loved his country better than his life."

"Lord John Russell," His Holiness continued, "you say is a friend of Italy, yet he will listen to Garibaldi, but he would never consult the Pope."

I said: "Our diplomatic relations with Rome have unfortunately not been what they ought to be. I speak to Your Holiness as a private individual without official authority and I must thank Your Holiness for so patiently listening to the free expression of my personal convictions, but if Lord John Russell could consult the Pope on Italian affairs, might I know what Your Holiness would reply?"

After some hesitation, the Pope said with a smile: "I would say that Italian unity and independence is a great and a beautiful idea, but that it is impossible."

"But it would become possible," I answered, "if Your Holiness ceased to oppose it and no longer withheld your blessing from it. Thousands of the most devout and devoted Catholics in Italy pray that the Pope may acknowledge the work of God in the late events, may treat with Piedmont, give peace to Europe and bless the cause of united Italy."

"They pray, do they? And do you pray, for I think you Protestants do not know how to pray?" the Pope inquired. "I will tell you how to pray. You must say at the end of all your prayers, 'Father, not my will, but thine, be done.' For although things may appear evident to us, we cannot fathom God's ultimate ends."

I replied: "We are Christians and have all learned to pray from one Master, and I am sure Your Holiness also adds at the end of your prayers as we all do, 'not my will but thine be done.' And Your Holiness who commenced the task and who have been chosen to complete it, will not withhold your blessing from the work of God, and your memory will be blessed by your grateful country."

"Pray, my good Russell," the Pope said, "pray, it will do you good. I also will pray." And then extending his hands he wished me good-bye.

I knelt to receive the old man's blessing and said: "Holy Father, I will pray that the next time I have the honor of being admitted to your presence, Italy and the Pope may be at peace."

He waved his hand and smiled with strange emotion and I withdrew.

In writing the foregoing conversation I have taken great pains to give Your Lordship an accurate and conscientious account of all that passed between His Holiness and myself. The impression it has left on my mind is, that the Italian feelings of the Pope would again prevail if other and more truthful advisers surrounded his throne.

> [*The Roman Question, Extracts from the Despatches of Odo Russell from Rome*, ed. N. Blakiston (London, 1962), pp. 152–9]

So long as a French garrison remained in Rome, the Italian government could not afford to attack this last remaining outpost of papal territory. Instead, Rattazzi on two disastrous occasions when he was Prime Minister, in 1862 and 1867, secretly allowed Garibaldi to raise volunteers and march on Rome himself. In 1862, as soon as it became clear that

Garibaldi's movement was not succeeding, Rattazzi changed round and sent troops against him, on which occasion Garibaldi was permanently crippled by a wound he received from these Italian soldiers at Aspromonte. In 1867 the government left it to a French army to defeat the Garibaldian volunteers at Mentana.

The government and the king thus put themselves in a difficult position which did them no credit with either the patriots or the anti-patriots. Clearly they had not made up their minds quite how far they could afford to back the kind of piratical venture that had been so successful in 1860. Perhaps they thought that the Romans would make things easier by rising and appealing to Italy for deliverance from the Pope, but if so they deceived themselves; and as a result they had to put down by force a movement which they themselves had helped to instigate. The government denied that they had been conniving with the revolutionaries, but the denials were untrue.

Sir James Hudson, from Turin, to Lord John Russell, August 19, 1862

THIS MORNING the King sent to desire me to wait upon him. I have known the King so long and so intimately that a conversation between us is certain to end in a confidential manner. As soon therefore as I had delivered to him Her Majesty's letter announcing the marriage of the Princess Alice he rushed into politics.

He began by a sharp, but good-humored, attack about the aid "given by England to Garibaldi." I replied, in the same tone, that H.M. could feel no surprise at that, for the English who support Garibaldi, now in arms against His Majesty's present cabinet, conceived they were following out His Majesty's own plans—inasmuch as it was generally understood and believed that His Majesty had instructed Garibaldi to proceed to Sicily where, indeed, H.M.'s Government had previously [in 1860] prepared and established a Garibaldi government.

The King seemed somewhat "bothered" by this answer and asked me the age of H.R.H. the Princess Alice. From that H.M. entered upon a discussion of his daughter's marriage with the King of Portugal, saying she was much too young. He expressed no satisfaction at all at this union but seemed to treat it with indifference.

He was evidently preoccupied with politics for he returned to Garibaldi. I said Garibaldi is a very honest man who doubtless believes he is serving the interests of the crown in taking up arms against the King's government. The crown would appear to have given some countenance to this extraordinary posture of affairs because it is broadly stated that Garibaldi had H.M.'s orders to go to Sicily and he never ends a speech without proclaiming his solidarity with the King and using H. M.'s name as a shield, guide and monitor for all he does. Even the King's proclamation, by its reticence as to Garibaldi, does no more than hint at a condition of civil war. There must be a reason for this, and the public had come to the conclusion that Garibaldi was acting under the King's orders. Other persons had arrived at an intimate conviction of that fact.

The King changed the conversation. He spoke about a recent chasse after Ibex on the glaciers and described a fall which had nearly cost him his life, adding that after all, if he had so lost his life, it would be quite as well as to live as he lived in a state of anxiety.

As to the anxiety, I said, you sir are not to be blamed but rather your Majesty's relative and ally at Paris. If your Majesty is, politically, in trouble, the cause is Rome and the presence of the French there.

I know that, replied the King, but I have appealed to him again and again. It's only three days since that I addressed a personal representation to him to which he replied by an insolent telegram. I now send Pepoli to him with a memorandum. Rattazzi has no courage (he said this as tho' thinking aloud) but I am not alarmed, I will not put up with this atrocious conduct, I will not be his victim; if the blow falls it will smash him as well as myself. For my part I want nothing. God knows I never entered into this Italian business from motives of personal aggrandizement, ambition, or avarice. The Italians were worried to death, deceived by forsworn princes and foreigners. Because I kept my word as a prince and a soldier they elected me their King. I have nothing to lose. I fought not for myself but for Italy. But this man, this parvenu, he comes here, gets paid above his merits and then goes away leaving us all in boiling water—and then Garibaldi gets between my legs.

But Garibaldi, sir, says he acts under your inspirations.

Inspirations, forsooth, said the King. He does more than I ever told him to do. Yes—he had my orders to a certain extent, but he adds something of his own to them and makes a mess of everything.

Garibaldi, sir, is a sea captain and probably knows as much of politics as your Majesty does of navigation.

I will destroy him, growled the King.

Well, sir, and what will be the result of that measure?

Why I shall be the most unpopular man in Italy. But the Emperor [Louis Napoleon] who is the cause of all this mischief, his turn will come too, later it is true, but it will come.

Pray sir, has Garibaldi any ships with him?

Yes, five Americans, one of them armed.

Do you intend to allow him to embark on board those ships?

I cannot prevent him if he goes in American vessels.

But sir, those ships are in your ports and cannot violate your Municipal Law.

To this the King replied, I am not strong in Municipal Law. The deputy Musolino has been to see me and he has proposed as a remedy that I shall permit Garibaldi to lay down his arms and pass into Calabria or to Naples, whence he is to make a peaceable promenade to Rome accompanied by an enormous mass of Italians.

But your Majesty has not given any countenance to that scheme.

No, said the King, none whatever.

This conversation, which was still continued, did not offer other salient points, but I think it is clear:

1st, That there has always been a secret understanding between the King and Garibaldi, and between the King and, to a certain extent, the Emperor of the French.

2nd, As I wrote to you recently, these three have been playing a game of revolutionary hide-and-seek, and that Rattazzi, ever the pliant tool of the King, has consented to all the expeditions to the east, first at Sarnico and now in Sicily.

3rd, That Garibaldi who feels that he has been played upon by Rattazzi is now bent upon his destruction as Minister.

4th, That the King is the first to feel the effects of his own intrigues and imprudence and is now drifting helpless on the tide of those events which he creates, and cannot control, save by the loss of his own agent, and at the risk of his own popularity. I think that part of the King's instructions to Garibaldi was to make a "demonstration," but that he never intended Garibaldi to denounce his ministry and make civil war.

[*Russell Papers*, Public Record Office, London, 30/22/69/103]

By a convention in September 1864 with France, the Italian government obtained an undertaking that French troops would at some point
be withdrawn from Rome. In return, Italy engaged that she "would
not attack territory held by the Pope, and would resist by force any
other attack on that territory." There seems to have been a certain
amount of deceit here, for most Italian politicians continued to see the
withdrawal of French forces as a step along the road to Rome. But,
to make their promise look more plausible, it was agreed to move the
existing capital from Turin to Florence. A great amount of feeling
was aroused over this change of capital. The Left, and the extreme
patriots in all parties, saw that the convention was either a lie, or it
was a renunciation of Rome. Some Neapolitans argued strongly that
their town would make a more fitting capital than Florence. The inhabitants of Turin were outraged when the news suddenly broke that
their city was being abandoned, and serious rioting occurred which was
put down with considerable bloodshed.

Florence replaces Turin as the capital city: minutes of the cabinet, September 10, 1864

DISCUSSION WAS opened on which city should be the national
capital. General della Rovere, Minister of War [and a Piedmontese],
stressed the political reasons why it should still be Turin. The
Ministers Peruzzi [a Florentine], Visconti-Venosta [a Lombard],
Pisanelli and Manna [both Neapolitans] advanced other political
reasons why Naples should be chosen. General Cugia [from
Sardinia] and General Menabrea [from Savoy], on military and
political grounds, preferred Florence, and Amari [a Sicilian] agreed
with them. The Prime Minister, Minghetti [a Bolognese from the
Romagna], after giving his opinion in favor of Naples, then summed
up the discussion. He mentioned a conversation with the King,
whose preference on strategic grounds was for Florence. The
cabinet then, with only one negative vote, decided for Florence;
though they asked the King if he would have the matter discussed
once again by an extraordinary committee of generals under His
Royal Highness the Prince of Carignano.

> [E. Re: "*I verbali del Consiglio dei Ministri*," in
> *Notizie degli archivi di stato* (Rome, January
> 1942), vol. II, p. 8]

The Encyclical *Quanta cura* in December 1864, with its annexed list
of eighty erroneous propositions, was Pius IX's response to the gradual
advance of secularism. Basically it was a condemnation of religious

liberalism; but the Pope was still a temporal ruler, and it was some-times hard to keep religious and political ideas completely separate.

A number of commissions had been at work for years preparing this list of current errors. It was a strange collection, some of the errors being important, some seemingly quite trivial. But the cumulative effect made it look as though the Church was renouncing its normal attitude of ambiguity about these matters and instead was taking a firm line of opposition to the modern State. Lord Acton, a leading Catholic in England, thought the *Syllabus* a damnable document, for it would seem to justify intolerance, the Inquisition, and the stake, and would make the position of Catholics in liberal countries very difficult. Car-dinal Newman tried to maintain that the *Syllabus* had no dogmatic force and merely revealed a momentary error of judgment by Cardinal Antonelli, the Secretary of State. Other clergy, including some "lib-erals," came to its defense, arguing that the Pope had in mind an ideal society, and was not intending to lay down precise rules for everyday life. Subsequently it became a matter for embattled scholarly debate whether or not the Pope had been speaking infallibly in this instance.

At the time, however, nearly all the hierarchy took this pronounce-ment as official and infallible. It seemed in direct and uncompromising opposition to Cavour's idea of "a free Church in a free State." By taking Catholicism into extreme ground, the *Syllabus of Errors* made it easier for Italy to move toward the capture of Rome and the ending of the temporal power.

The Papal Syllabus of Errors, *1864*

The Syllabus of the principal errors of our time,
*   which are stigmatized in the Consistorial*
*   Allocutions, Encyclicals, and other*
*   Apostolical Letters of our Most Holy Lord,*
*   Pope Pius IX . . .*

12. The decrees of the Apostolic See and of the Roman Con-gregations fetter the free progress of science.

13. The method and principles by which the old scholastic doctors cultivated theology are no longer suitable to the demands of the age and the progress of science.

•   •   •

15. Every man is free to embrace and profess the religion he shall believe true, guided by the light of reason.

•   •   •

17. We may entertain at least a well-founded hope for the eternal salvation of all those who are in no manner in the true Church of Christ.

18. Protestantism is nothing more than another form of the same true Christian religion, in which it is possible to be equally pleasing to God as in the Catholic Church.

•   •   •

23. The Roman Pontiffs and Ecumenical Councils have exceeded the limits of their power, have usurped the rights of princes, and have even committed errors in defining matters of faith and morals.

•   •   •

55. The Church ought to be separated from the State, and the State from the Church.

76. The abolition of the temporal power, of which the Apostolic See is possessed, would contribute in the greatest degree to the liberty and prosperity of the Church.

77. In the present day, it is no longer expedient that the Catholic religion shall be held as the only religion of the State, to the exclusion of all other modes of worship.

•   •   •

80. The Roman Pontiff can and ought to reconcile himself to, and agree with, progress, liberalism, and civilization as lately introduced. [This came originally from the papel Allocution *Jamdudum cernimus*, March 18, 1861]

[Section IV of the *Syllabus* also condemned:—Socialism, Communism, Secret Societies, Biblical Societies, Clerico-Liberal Societies; and attention was especially drawn to the Encyclical *Qui pluribus*, Nov. 9, 1846; Allocution *Quibus quantisque*, April 20, 1849; Encyclical *Noscitis et Nobiscum*, Dec. 8, 1849; Allocution *Singulari quadam*, Dec. 9, 1854; Encyclical *Quanto conficiamur*, Aug. 10, 1863].

[P. Schaff: *The Creeds of the Greek and Latin Churches* (London, 1877), pp. 213–33]

In July 1870, just when France was about to begin her war against Germany, the Vatican Council established papal infallibility as a dogma of the Church. Two weeks later the last French troops were withdrawn from Rome, and the government of Giovanni Lanza had to decide: should it, despite undertakings by the Convention of September 1864, take this chance and move into the Holy City?

The king was more interested in joining the war against Germany. The Foreign Minister, Visconti-Venosta, assured the French that Italy still accepted her promises under the Convention, and he repeated in parliament that Rome was by international law inviolate. Lanza was in two minds. But when France was unexpectedly defeated early in September, it could be casuistically argued that Italy's undertakings toward Louis Napoleon lapsed. In parliament the Left threatened open rebellion, and were pacified only when some members of the cabinet privately promised to force Lanza's hand. It was also hoped that there might be some kind of rising inside Rome which would appeal to the king to intervene with the excuse that he alone could prevent anarchy; but everything remained calm. Little by little, as Castagnola, the Minister of Agriculture, noted in his diary, the government was maneuvered into a position where it would have to make up its mind; but the reluctance of ministers to decide indicates something of the conflict of loyalties, as well as the muddle and lack of premeditation involved.

The cabinet decides to take Rome, August–September 1870; diary of events by the Minister of Agriculture

THE MINISTERS Gadda and Castagnola call on the King during a performance at the Principe Umberto Theater. He does not conceal his annoyance at the vacillating conduct of the present government. Armaments must be speeded up, he says, and 150,000 men mobilized, adding that before the end of the year the Roman Question would be clarified.

In the cabinet meeting of August 31, we continue discussing the articles designed to ensure the independence of the Pope. They are much the same as those proposed by Cavour and Ricasoli. The only addition is a hybrid plan for the Leonine City [round the Vatican] over which the Pope would remain sovereign.

In the evening Castagnola is told in confidence by the deputy Malenchini (who declared himself disgusted by the ministry's lack of courage) that there were three Roman citizens in Florence, one of them a lawyer and another a railway engineer, who for 500,000 lire would get the 1,200 native troops of the Pope to revolt. Their plan was then to carry out a coup at Viterbo and other points, and to seize the Roman railway stations. The plan was for these native troops to check the Pope's foreign troops for a few hours, during which time two of our regiments must be sent at speed to their assistance.

At 9 a.m. on September 1, 1870, the ministers go to make their usual report to King Victor, and he begs them to free him from the importunity of Prince Napoleon, who was persisting in his impracticable and ruinous schemes for an Italian alliance with the declining French Empire.

The ministers continue to discuss the Roman Question, with a dilatoriness that causes no little surprise to the public.

In the evening, Castagnola is formally assured by the deputy Dini that great efforts are being made to work up popular demonstrations on papal territory.

Another deputy, Maurizio, summoned by Lanza for questioning about Rome, suggests conferring with Monsignor Cerruti, Bishop of Savona. Castagnola complains that too much time is being wasted.

Telegrams arrive from the prefects in various provinces informing the government that, on the initiative of deputies of the Left, popular meetings had been organized for Sunday, September 4, in the principal Italian towns to force the government to occupy Rome. The cabinet decides not to prohibit the meetings so long as they do not go beyond expressing an opinion, but we shall break them up if they instigate disorders or accuse the government of not intending to go to Rome.

On September 3 the news of the French capitulation at Sedan reaches Florence [the Italian capital from 1865 to 1870]. The Emperor Napoleon has surrendered his sword to the King of Prussia and is a prisoner.

Prime Minister Lanza asks Prince Napoleon to leave Florence. This decision had been agreed earlier, but this is a strange moment for communicating it, as the Prince might now be considered a political refugee.

The party of the Left presents parliament with an ultimatum requesting the immediate occupation of Rome, otherwise they will resign in a body, as they had already threatened to do over the Roman Question on August 20.

At the cabinet on September 3, there is an urgent discussion as to whether the time has come to occupy the Papal State. Some want this done at once, others prefer to be assured first that Prussia would agree.

Castagnola reminds them that Prussia has more than once agreed, as is clear from explicit declarations by the German minister, Brassier de Saint-Simon.

The only members who vote for immediate occupation at all hazards are Sella and Castagnola. Gadda is absent. The other six ministers are against.

When another vote is taken about occupation subject to Prussia's consent, seven are in favor, Visconti-Venosta opposing.

The discussion renewed on September 4, and the Prime Minister feels obliged to take a fresh vote. After a long debate the following motions are drawn up:

1. The Papal State to be occupied immediately, without awaiting further events, except diplomatic procedure:—this is carried, Castagnola, Correnti, Sèlla, Raeli and Lanza voting in favor, Govone, Acton and Visconti-Venosta against.

2. The occupation also to include the actual city of Rome:— this is defeated, only Castagnola, Sella and Raeli voting in favor, with Correnti, Govone, Acton, Visconti-Venosta and Lanza against.

3. But occupation to take place only if we have Prussian support:— carried by six votes, those against being Castagnola and Visconti-Venosta.

The Prime Minister also asks for a vote on the following points:

4. If Prussian support is assured, the city of Rome itself to be occupied as well as the rest of the Papal State:— this is defeated, only Castagnola, Sella and Raeli being in favor.

5. Given this support, the Papal State is to be occupied without Rome:— four votes are in favor (Castagnola, Correnti, Raeli and Lanza), but four against.

So what now? Upon this disastrous clash of opinions, Castagnola says that, as the cabinet could not reach any real agreement, it should resign. Otherwise it might provoke the greatest of calamities, namely inaction in a question of vital national importance. After all, the government's program had originally concerned only finance and the balance of payments; if we had incidentally become involved in the fundamental question of national unity, it is not surprising that we are at variance and unprepared.

The suggestion is immediately resisted by Correnti and Lanza, who point out that the present ministry could not resign after the vote of confidence by parliament; they could not hand over their powers to no matter whom; they must rather take immediate steps in readiness for every contingency.

The cabinet therefore decides to mobilize fifteen divisions, call up the three last classes of the draft, and fit out our eleven ironclads by calling up another class of marines.

But a fresh event puts an end to all disagreement and hesitation, the proclamation of the Republic and of a provisional government in France on September 5, 1870. President Lanza summons the entire cabinet and declares that, in face of this new event, all dissension must cease. The cabinet decides unanimously on immediate occupation of the Papal State, including the city of Rome. Count Ponza di San Martino will go to notify the Pope and assure him that he will be given the fullest guarantees for the exercise of his spiritual powers. They also decide that our envoy in Paris shall recognize the provisional government, and to accredit Baron Ricasoli to it. Finally they decide to mobilize another class of second-category soldiers.

Next day, September 6, General Govone sends in his resignation as Minister for War, which is accepted. He says that the financial policy of the cabinet, which included radical economies affecting even the army, had exposed him to attacks against which he could no longer defend himself. Besides which, his health is impaired, and indeed he shows clear signs of mental disturbance.

Victor Emmanuel reminds the cabinet that the Minister for War must be chosen in close consultation with the King himself, since the monarch is commander-in-chief of the army.

At another cabinet meeting on the same problem, the ministers decide that the commander of the expedition to the Papal States must not enter Rome or attack it by force without an explicit order from the government.

Meanwhile telegrams come in from the prefects, because provincial councils are insisting on the immediate occupation of Rome, while some popular unrest is noticeable.

After reporting to the King on September 7, Prime Minister Lanza asks him to agree to the appointment of General Ricotti as Minister for War. The King rebukes Lanza harshly for not proposing a general who was more in royal favor, for example Bertolè-Viale; the result is that the Prime Minister now resigns, though he later withdraws this out of respect for the King.

The Count of San Martino agrees to undertake the official mission to the Pope, but this rouses the anger of Visconti-Venosta, who is in the government as representing the party of the Right.

The cabinet refuse General Garibaldi's request for permission to go to fight for the provisional government in France, as they felt this would be a breach of neutrality. Besides which it was known that Cernuschi and other members of the Roman Constituent Assembly were intriguing in Paris to revive recognition of the Roman Republic of 1849, and the presence of Garibaldi in France would only add fuel to this particular fire. Moreover there are reports of serious disturbances in Nice where there was even fear of invasion by the so-called *voraces*. As there is a danger of conflict with France, the Minister for Foreign Affairs is therefore charged to warn the French.

It is also decided that our occupation of Rome shall be preceded by a letter from the King to the Pope, and one from the Prime Minister to Cardinal Antonelli, stating our reasons. The customs border between our territory and that of the Pope is to be removed, and postal and telegraph services will be taken over by us at once. It is also settled that we should at once use force to prevent the destruction by the papalists of the Tiber bridges. Lastly, the Minister for the Navy has to arrange for some fishing boats flying the Italian flag to go to [the papal port of] Civitavecchia, with the purpose of provoking a fight and introducing other complications.

The Italian people have been all too impatiently longing to occupy Rome, as continual telegrams from the prefects have shown. Lanza replied to these telegrams with his usual prudence that they must *leave it to him*.

An announcement has been made to foreign governments about an imminent occupation of Rome, accompanied by due guarantees for the Pope. This has been well received, especially in Vienna. There has, however, been no acknowledgment from Paris. Visconti-Venosta, in telling us this at the meeting of September 7, also shows us San Martino's instructions and the King's letter to the Pope. Here the rim of the bitter cup is smeared with honey. We are also shown Lanza's letter to Cardinal Antonelli, and the instructions given to the officer commanding our occupying forces. The Minister for Foreign Affairs insists on having it specifically entered in the cabinet minutes that the latter may not use force to occupy Rome, and he declares loudly that if force is used he will resign.

This entry is made, however, with the declaration that every minister reserves his freedom of action should force become necessary.

That same evening Conte Ponza di San Martino leaves for Rome.

[S. Castagnola: *Diario storico-politico del 1870–71*
(Turin, 1896), pp. 26–40]

When General Cadorna finally received orders to attack, he placed his artillery outside the Porta Pia and breached the old walls of the city. After a token resistance, in which some seventy soldiers lost their lives, Rome fell. The large majority in the plebiscite speaks for

itself. How matters looked to the defeated side was described by one
of the papal Zouaves.

The plebiscite of Rome, 1870, seen by a hostile critic

THE FARCICAL PLEBISCITE rounded off the sad drama of the annexation of Rome, and a more ridiculous comedy or a grosser imposture was never seen. October 2 was the day fixed when people
were called on to answer by a *yes* or a *no* whether they would accept the domination of Victor Emmanuel, King of Italy. We will
not now go into the question as to whether Piedmont, having won
Rome by force, had any right to legalize the outrage; at least the
Holy Father forbade Catholics in Rome to vote, so as not to give
the least recognition to such a challenge to his inalienable right.
Quite apart from this fundamental injustice, however, every kind
of illegality contributed to make the plebiscite absurd.

The first task was to draw up a list of electors. This was done
by consulting parish registers, if need be by forcibly wresting them
from the hands of the clergy. The electoral lists were then composed according to the whim of the new master, sometimes eliminat-
ing the most honorable and celebrated people, sometimes inscribing
jailbirds and malefactors despite the fact that this was illegal.

To increase the number of electors—which the general abstention
of Catholics was likely to make tiny indeed—all Romans absent
from the city were called back home. This appeal was answered by
a crowd of temporary Romans who were no more real citizens than
were the Italian patriots who had arrived on September 20. From
every quarter the railways brought them at state expense, and they
were so many that, according to the official *Gazette*, a large proportion could not find lodging in Rome and spent the night in
cafés or in the public squares. Moreover they included such desirable folk that General Cadorna had to despatch strong patrols
through the streets during the nights of October 1 and 2 to prevent
disorder and crimes.

The walls were plastered with notices proclaiming in gigantic
letters: *Yes, we want annexation.* Throughout the whole day of
October 1, voting cards were distributed marked with the annexionist *yes*; and in the Corso a French engineer attached to the
Acqua Marcia works was arrested and detained for an hour at the
police station for having dared to ask out loud for a card marked
No.

So as to frighten off decent people who would have liked to vote according to their consciences and against the annexation, the agitators and patriots were allowed to make what noise they liked. This, incidentally, is a familiar maneuver with the Italian government, and over the last three years it has been employed before every measure introduced against the Church and the monasteries, etc. Many examples could be quoted.

October 2 "dawned brilliantly; a splendid sun smiled on the national festival," said the newspaper *Roma degli Italiani*. Numbers of people had cockades in their hats made of pieces of paper with *Yes* on them. They went in excited groups to vote, marching arm-in-arm, led by bands playing, "and from time to time the fanfares were interrupted by cheers for Italy, Victor Emmanuel, Garibaldi, Bixio and Cadorna." At the head of one group was the wretched Fra Amedeo, who was not even a Roman, and another equally dishonorable canon; both were bedecked in tricolored ribbons and were voting quite illegally. Votes were also accepted from many young men who had not reached the prescribed age.

To kindle enthusiasm that morning there had been a free distribution of bread and meat; this took place in various quarters of the city, for instance in via Capo le Case. To prevent hesitant minds from believing that the annexation of Rome might bring trouble with Prussia and other powers, on October 1 and 2 thousands of copies were sold of a letter from the King of Prussia to the Holy Father—in which he said that "his government's policy prevented him intervening on the Pope's side, and that he was on the best possible terms with his *brother*, the King of Italy." The letter was apocryphal and the Prussian government issued a *démenti*; but that did not prevent thousands of copies circulating under the eyes of the Piedmontese authorities who knew how things stood and whose authorization helped to spread the lie.

The great ballot box destined for collecting the voting papers was placed on the Capitol; but other offices had been set up in the various quarters so that everyone could get to vote. To deposit a voting paper one had to show an elector's card; but besides the fact that this card was given indiscriminately to all who asked for it, even to foreigners, it was not withdrawn when voting had taken place; people voted either individually or with their friends, both at their own district office and elsewhere. As the elector's card was not withdrawn, each person could deposit his vote—better, his votes—in the ballot boxes of as many *rioni* as he fancied, or wherever his legs would carry him. This is what a large number of patriots certainly did; and foreigners too, if they wanted to see the real worth of the plebiscite, sometimes added to the affirmative votes. A number of Germans thus had a good time going from office to office and leaving an unlawful *yes* in each. Three Frenchmen deposited *eighteen* votes in the same way; and we have good authority for saying that a young Belgian sculptor singlehanded put *twenty-two* annexionist voting papers in the boxes . . .

At half past six in the evening the voting was over. When all the ballot boxes had been carried into the great hall of the Capitol to be counted, the junta took up position on an elevated platform and the business of counting began at eight. There were 40,831 votes—40,785 were annexionist and said *yes*; and *noes* amounted to forty-six. Forty-six! As a Piedmontese put it: "The Roman vote for Italian unity could not be more sublime, more imposing!" Nor, we might add, more farcical and more obviously untruthful.

On the same day the peoples of all the Papal State had been summoned to vote on their future destiny. The result, brought about by similar or even more blatant methods, was the same. At San Gallicano, near Palestrina, for instance, *all* the inhabitants had voted *no*; yet all the votes except five or six had been changed, so that an almost unanimous *yes* was proclaimed as the final result. At Monte San Giovanni, *nine hundred* affirmative votes were counted, whereas only *fifty* voters had turned up.

Given such methods, there was no difficulty about attaining the desired goal. So, on October 7, the Roman junta was able to proclaim solemnly from the Capitol balcony the following figures for the Roman states:

Registered Electors	167,548
Voters	135,291
Voted *Yes*	133,681
Voted *No*	1,507
Invalid Votes	103
Total	135,291

Surely the world had never before seen such incredible unanimity. The sheer absurdity almost makes one forget the gross imposture.

> [Le Comte de Beauffort: *Histoire de l'invasion des États Pontificaux et du Siège de Rome par l'armée Italienne en septembre 1870* (Paris, 1874), pp. 392–400]

General Bibliography

Of works available in English, Bolton King's *A History of Italian Unity* (London, 1899, 2 vols.) is still extremely useful; so is W. R. Thayer, *The Life and Times of Cavour* (Boston, 1911, 2 vols.); A. J. Whyte, *The Political Life and Letters of Cavour, 1848–1861* (London, 1930); and G. F.-H. Berkeley, *Italy in the Making, 1815–1848* (Cambridge, 1932–40, 3 vols.).

On more specialized topics, mention should be made of K. R. Greenfield, *Economics and Liberalism in the Risorgimento: A Study of Nationalism in Lombardy* (Baltimore, 1934); J. Rath, *The Fall of the Napoleonic Kingdom of Italy, 1814* (New York, 1941); Bolton King, *The Life of Mazzini* (New York, 1929); E. E. Y. Hales, *Revolution and Papacy 1769–1846* (London, 1960); R. M. Johnston, *The Roman Theocracy and the Republic, 1846–1849* (London, 1901); G. M. Trevelyan, *Garibaldi's Defence of the Roman Republic* (London, 1907); Raymond Grew, *A Sterner Plan for Italian Unity: the Italian National Society in the Risorgimento* (Princeton, N. J., 1963); W. K. Hancock, *Ricasoli and the Risorgimento in Tuscany* (London, 1926); D. Mack Smith, *Cavour and Garibaldi, 1860* (Cambridge, 1954); L. M. Case, *Franco-Italian Relations 1860–1865* (Philadelphia, 1932); Shepard B. Clough, *The Economic History of Modern Italy* (New York, 1964); Harold Acton, *The Last Bourbons of Naples* (1825–1861) (London, 1961).

Among general books in Italian, the best for the years up to 1849 is Cesare Spellanzon, *Storia del risorgimento e dell'unità d'Italia* (Milan, 1933-50, 5 vols.). For the period after 1848 there is especially Adolfo Omodeo, *L'opera politica del Conte di Cavour, 1848–57* (Florence, 1940, 2 vols.); and Giorgio Candeloro, *Storia dell'Italia moderna* (Milan, 1964, vol. IV). Candeloro's volumes have a good and up-to-date bibliography for more detailed subjects.

Index